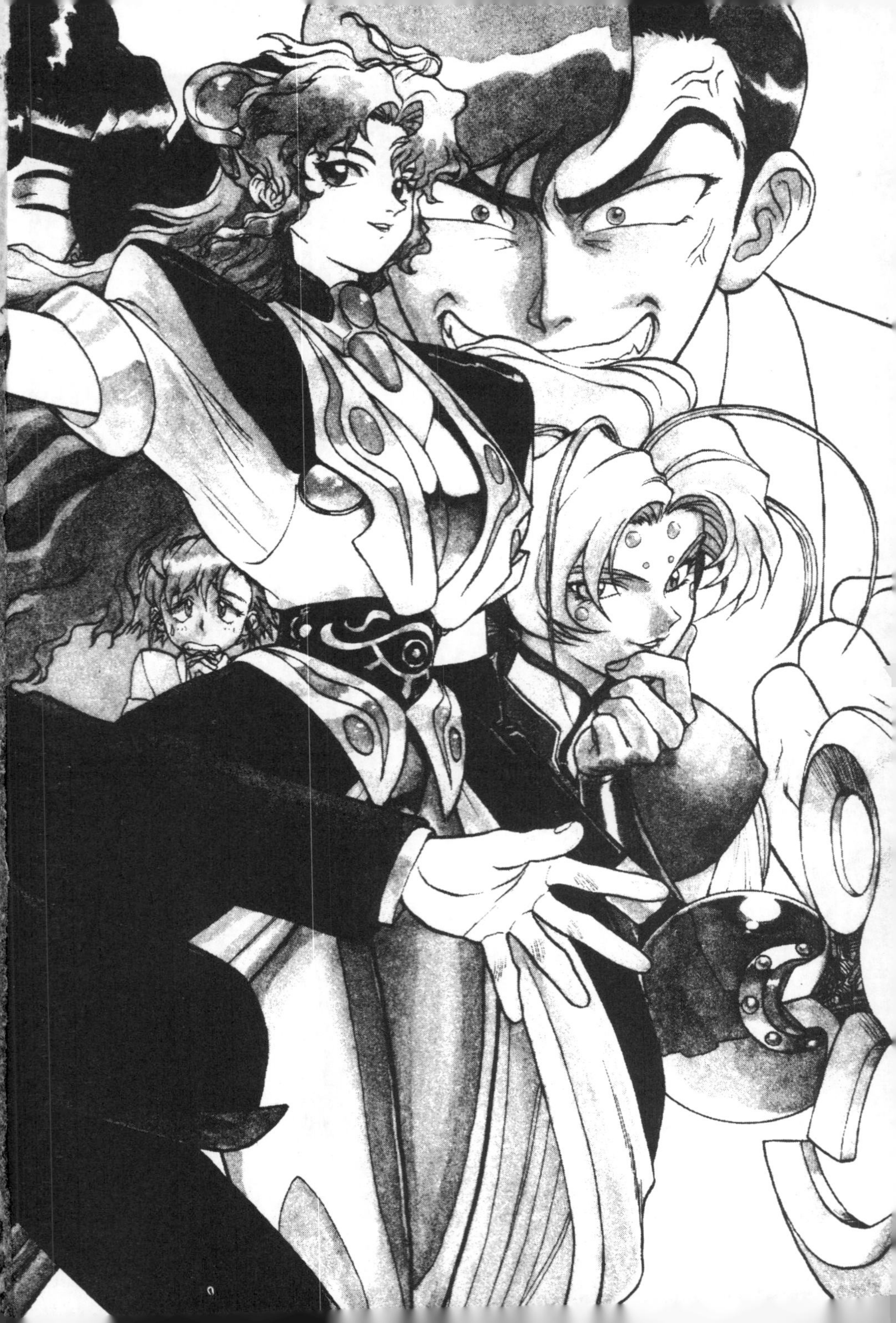

This volume contains the monthly comics *El-Hazard* Volume 1 Number 1 through Number 5 in their entirety.

Story & Art by
Hidetomo Tsubura

English Adaptation by
Gary Leach

Translation/Lillian Olsen
Touch-up & Lettering/Dan Nakrosis
Cover & Graphics Design/Sean Lee
Editor/Andy Nakatani

Managing Editor/Annette Roman
Vice President of Sales and Marketing/Rick Bauer
Editor-in-Chief/Hyoe Narita
Publisher/Seiji Horibuchi

Original Japanese edition published by TOKUMA SHOTEN CO., LTD. Tokyo.
English version in U.S.A. and CANADA published by Viz Communications, INC. under the license granted by TOKUMA SHOTEN CO., LTD.

Printed in Canada.

Published by Viz Comics
P.O. Box 77010
San Francisco, CA 94107

10 9 8 7 6 5 4 3 2 1
First Printing, May 2002

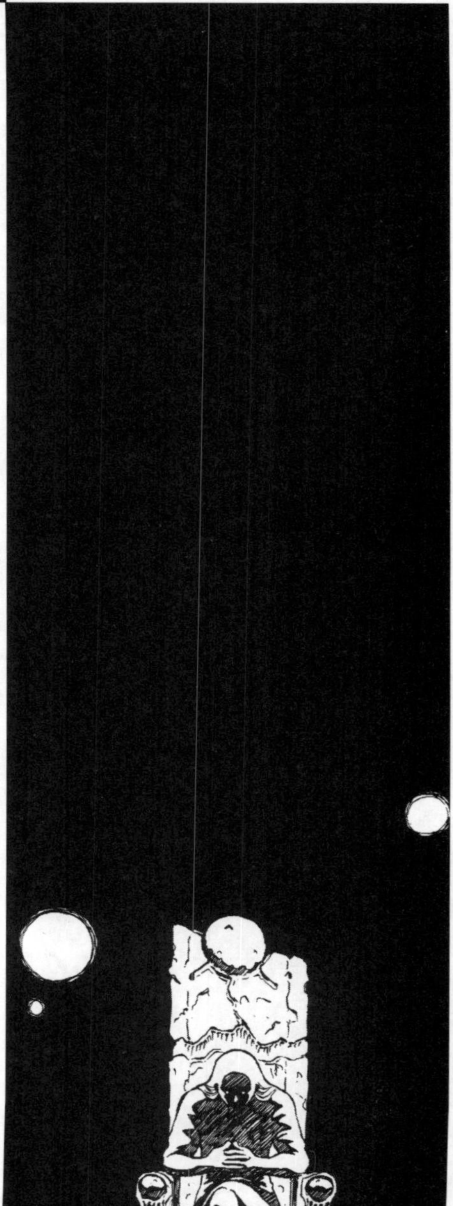

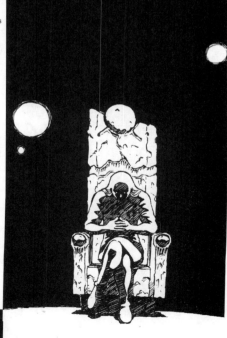

VIZ GRAPHIC NOVEL

EL-HAZARD

THE MAGNIFICENT WORLD

volume 1

Story and Art by Hidetomo Tsubura
Based on El-Hazard
Created by Hiroki Hayashi and Ryoe Tsukimura

CONTENTS

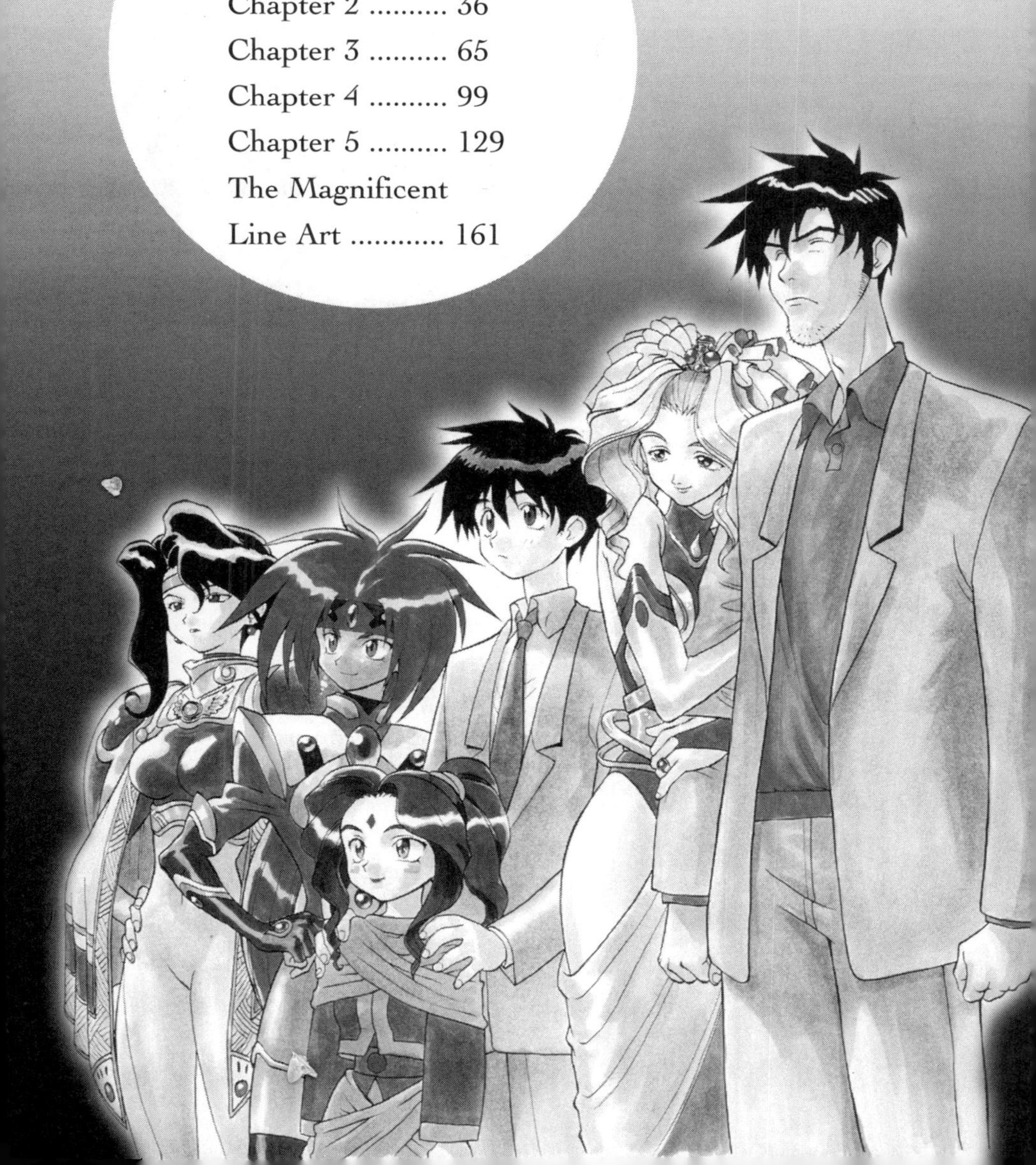

VIZ GRAPHIC NOVEL

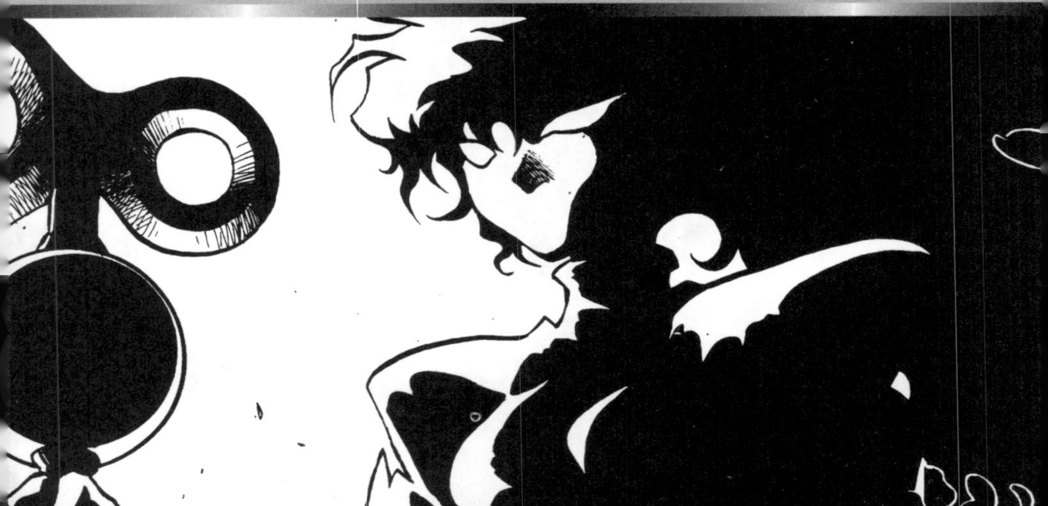

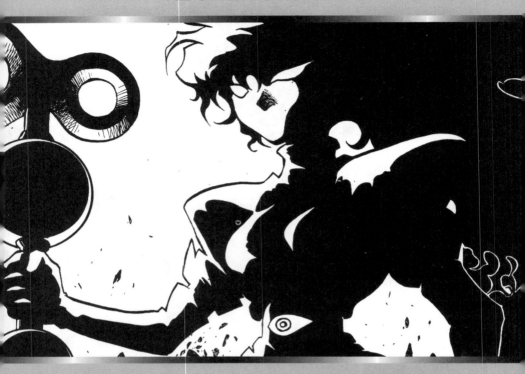

EL-HAZARD

THE MAGNIFICENT WORLD

volume 1

Story and Art by Hidetomo Tsubura

Based on El-Hazard

Created by Hiroki Hayashi and Ryoe Tsukimura

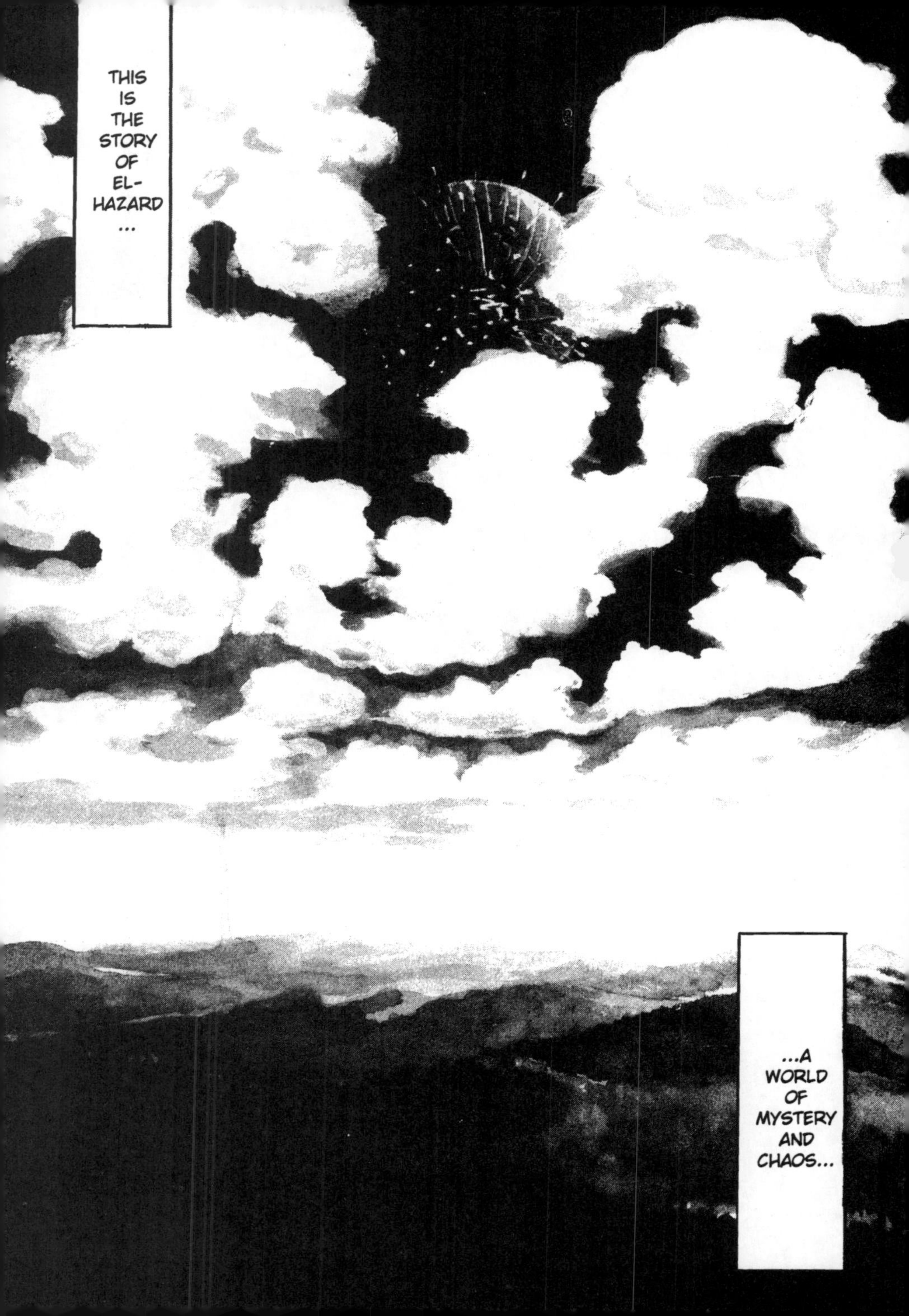
THIS IS THE STORY OF EL-HAZARD ...
...A WORLD OF MYSTERY AND CHAOS...

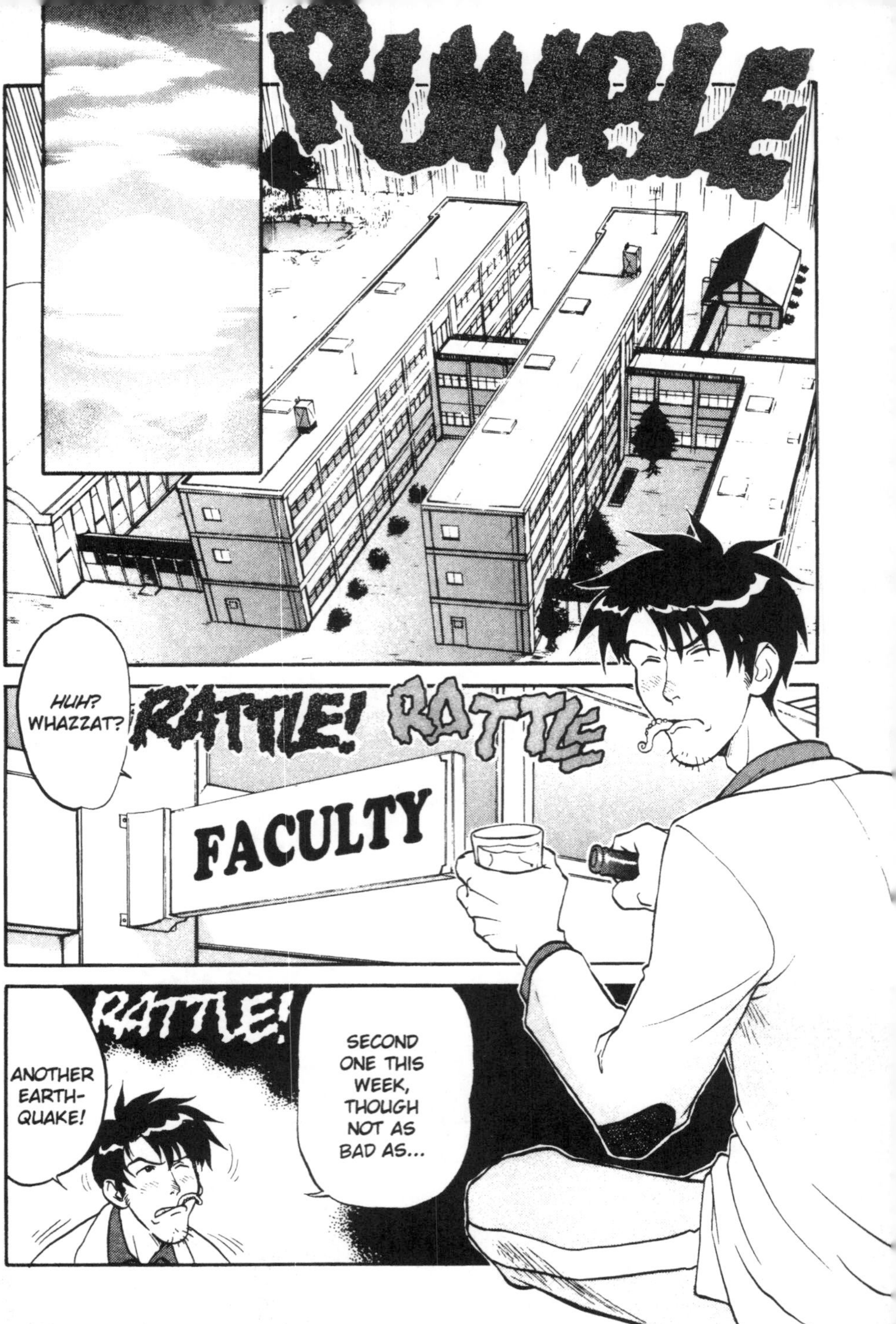
RUMBLE
HUH? WHAZZAT?
RATTLE! RATTLE
FACULTY
RATTLE!
ANOTHER EARTH-QUAKE!
SECOND ONE THIS WEEK, THOUGH NOT AS BAD AS...

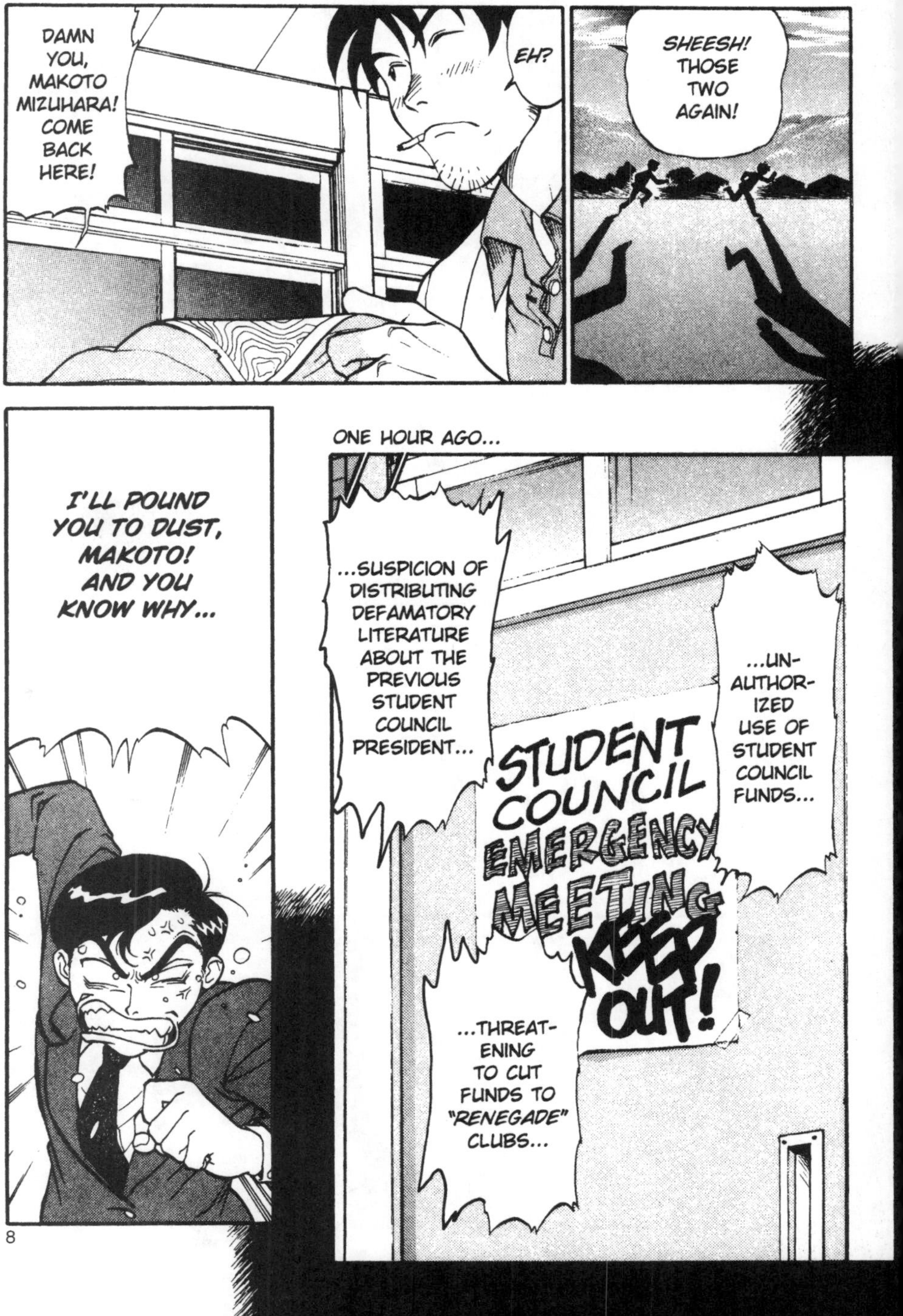
DAMN YOU, MAKOTO MIZUHARA! COME BACK HERE!
EH?
SHEESH! THOSE TWO AGAIN!
I'LL POUND YOU TO DUST, MAKOTO! AND YOU KNOW WHY...
ONE HOUR AGO...
...SUSPICION OF DISTRIBUTING DEFAMATORY LITERATURE ABOUT THE PREVIOUS STUDENT COUNCIL PRESIDENT...
STUDENT COUNCIL EMERGENCY MEETING KEEP OUT!
...UN-AUTHOR-IZED USE OF STUDENT COUNCIL FUNDS...
...THREAT-ENING TO CUT FUNDS TO "RENEGADE" CLUBS...

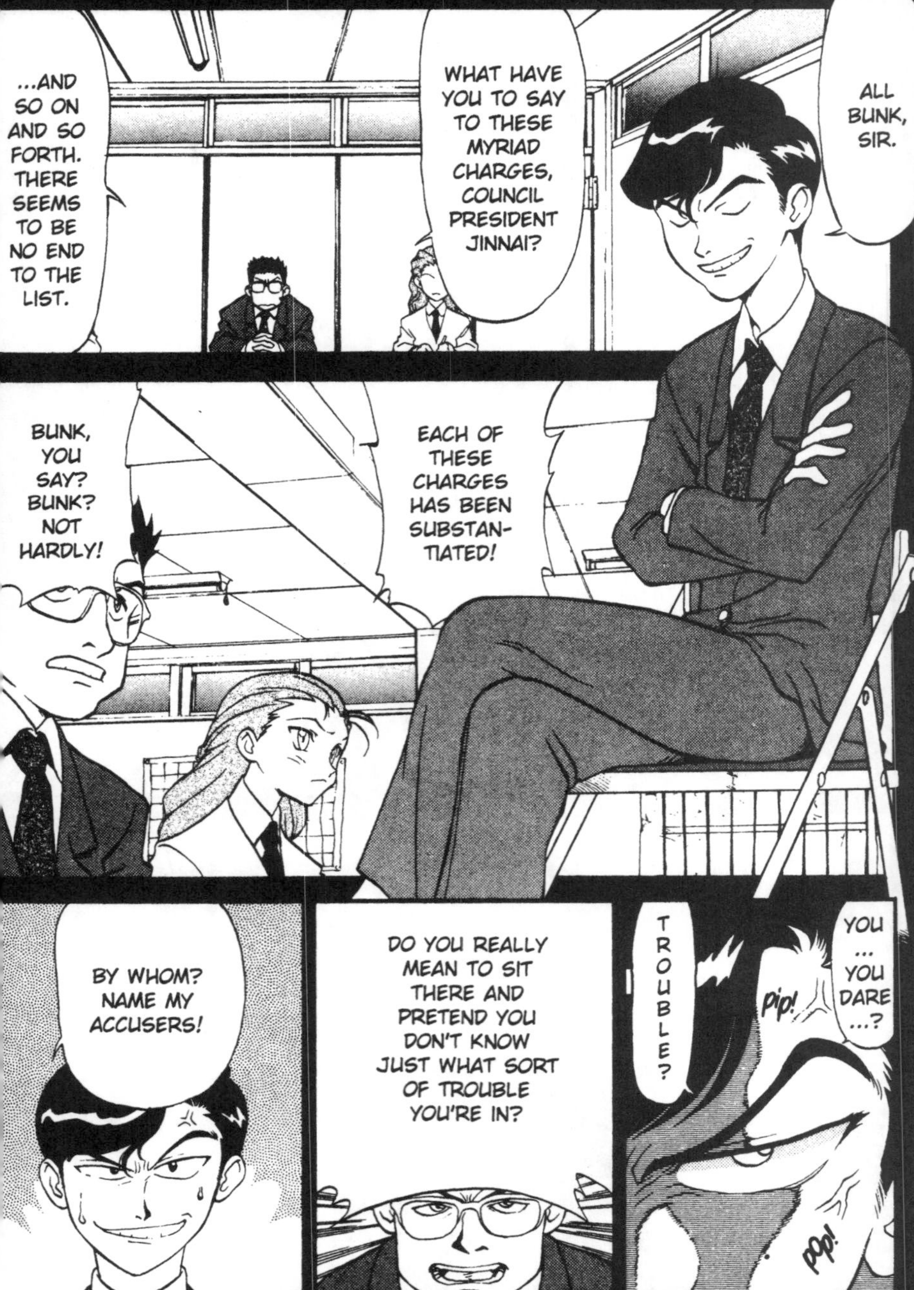
...AND SO ON AND SO FORTH. THERE SEEMS TO BE NO END TO THE LIST.
WHAT HAVE YOU TO SAY TO THESE MYRIAD CHARGES, COUNCIL PRESIDENT JINNAI?
ALL BUNK, SIR.
BUNK, YOU SAY? BUNK? NOT HARDLY!
EACH OF THESE CHARGES HAS BEEN SUBSTANTIATED!
BY WHOM? NAME MY ACCUSERS!
DO YOU REALLY MEAN TO SIT THERE AND PRETEND YOU DON'T KNOW JUST WHAT SORT OF TROUBLE YOU'RE IN?
TROUBLE?
pip!
YOU ... YOU DARE ...?
pop!

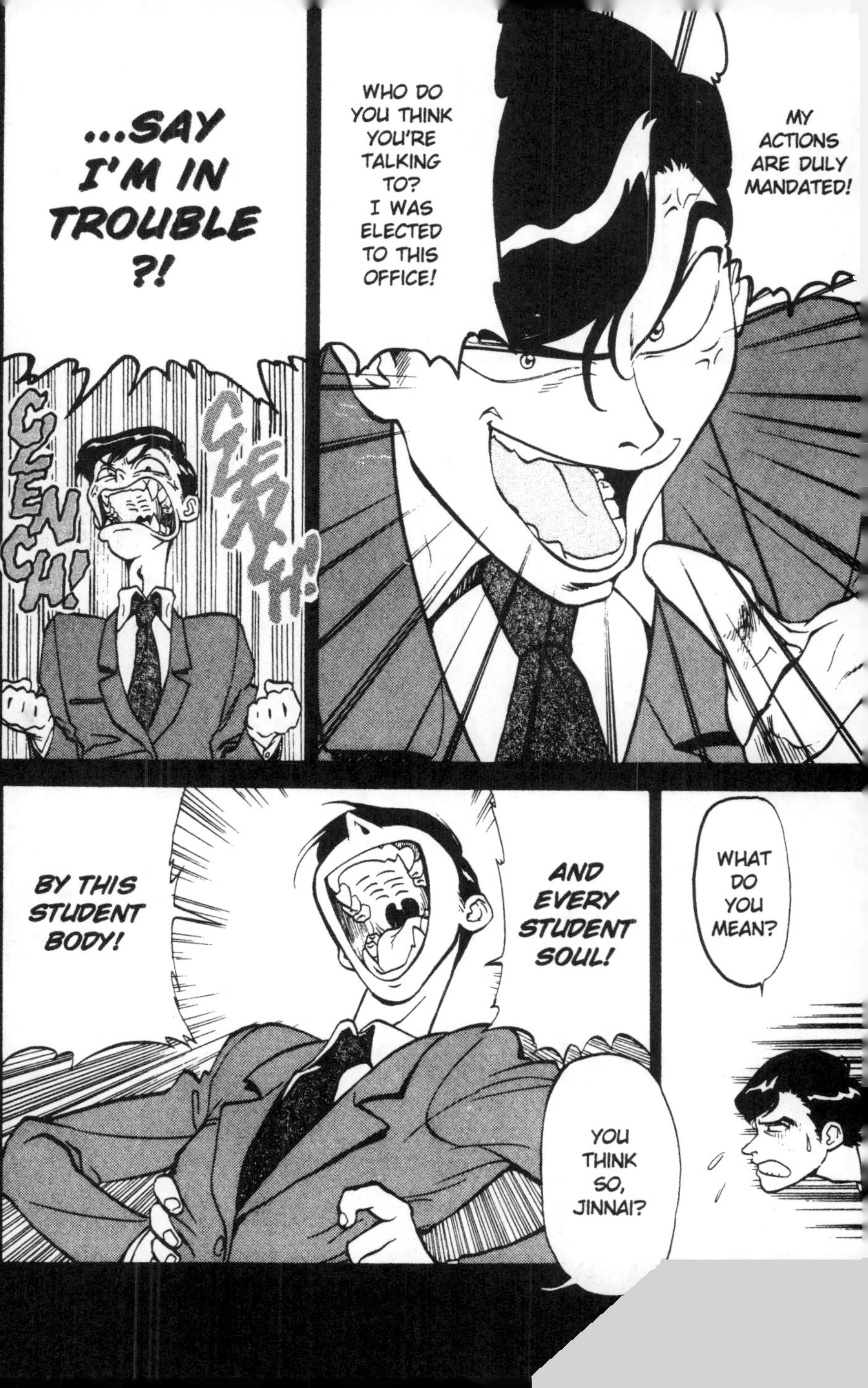
...SAY I'M IN TROUBLE ?!
CLENCH!
GFRAHH!
WHO DO YOU THINK YOU'RE TALKING TO? I WAS ELECTED TO THIS OFFICE!
MY ACTIONS ARE DULY MANDATED!
BY THIS STUDENT BODY!
AND EVERY STUDENT SOUL!
WHAT DO YOU MEAN?
YOU THINK SO, JINNAI?

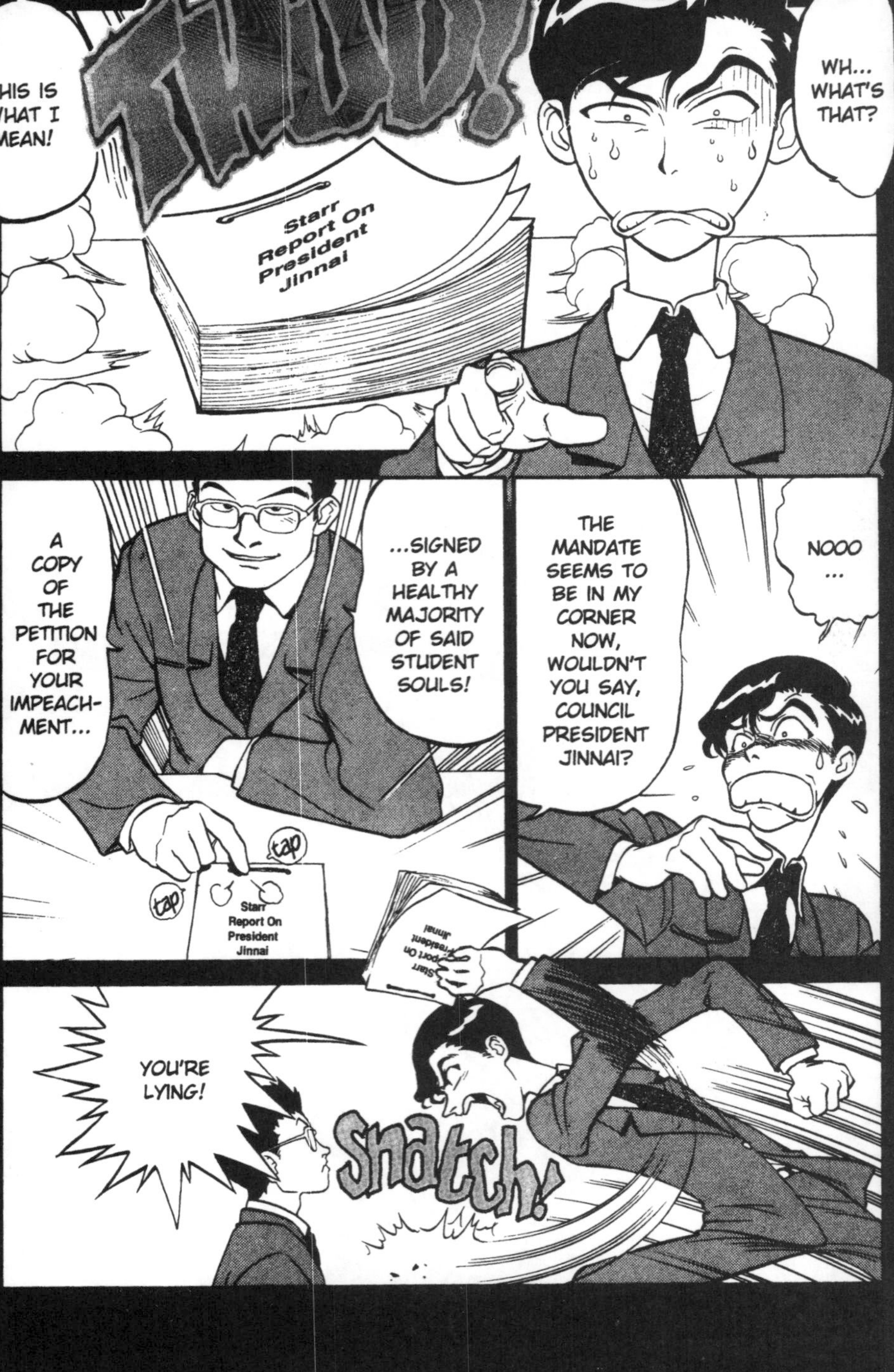
THIS IS WHAT I MEAN!
THUD!
Starr Report On President Jinnai
WH... WHAT'S THAT?
A COPY OF THE PETITION FOR YOUR IMPEACHMENT...
...SIGNED BY A HEALTHY MAJORITY OF SAID STUDENT SOULS!
tap
tap
Starr Report On President Jinnai
THE MANDATE SEEMS TO BE IN MY CORNER NOW, WOULDN'T YOU SAY, COUNCIL PRESIDENT JINNAI?
NOOO ...
YOU'RE LYING!
SNATCH!

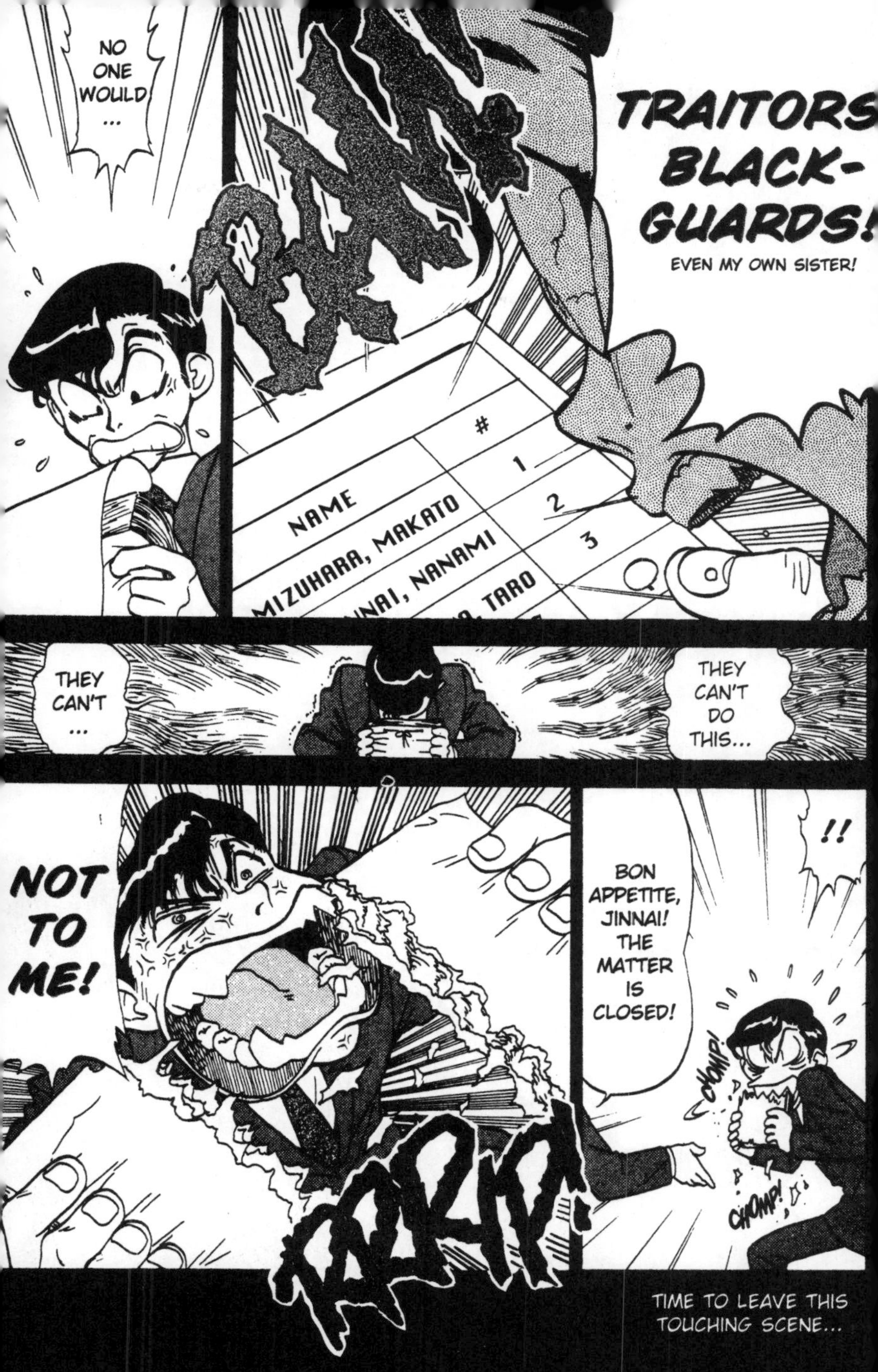
NO ONE WOULD ...
TRAITORS! BLACK-GUARDS!
EVEN MY OWN SISTER!
NAME
#
1
2
3
MIZUHARA, MAKATO
THEY CAN'T ...
THEY CAN'T DO THIS...
NOT TO ME!
!!
BON APPETITE, JINNAI! THE MATTER IS CLOSED!
CHOMP!
CHOMP!
TIME TO LEAVE THIS TOUCHING SCENE...

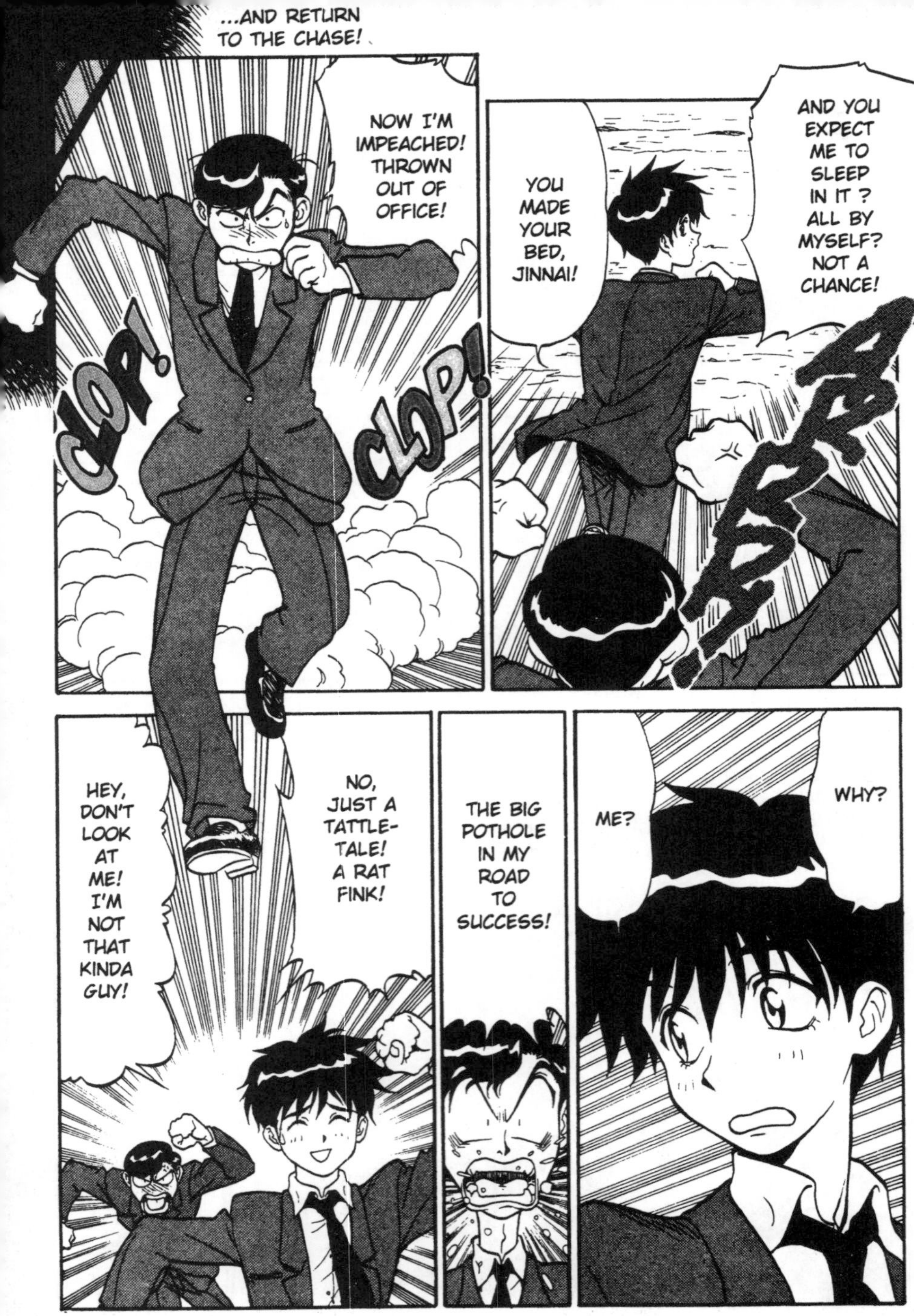
...AND RETURN TO THE CHASE!
NOW I'M IMPEACHED! THROWN OUT OF OFFICE!
CLOP!
CLOP!
YOU MADE YOUR BED, JINNAI!
AND YOU EXPECT ME TO SLEEP IN IT ? ALL BY MYSELF? NOT A CHANCE!
HEY, DON'T LOOK AT ME! I'M NOT THAT KINDA GUY!
NO, JUST A TATTLE-TALE! A RAT FINK!
THE BIG POTHOLE IN MY ROAD TO SUCCESS!
ME?
WHY?

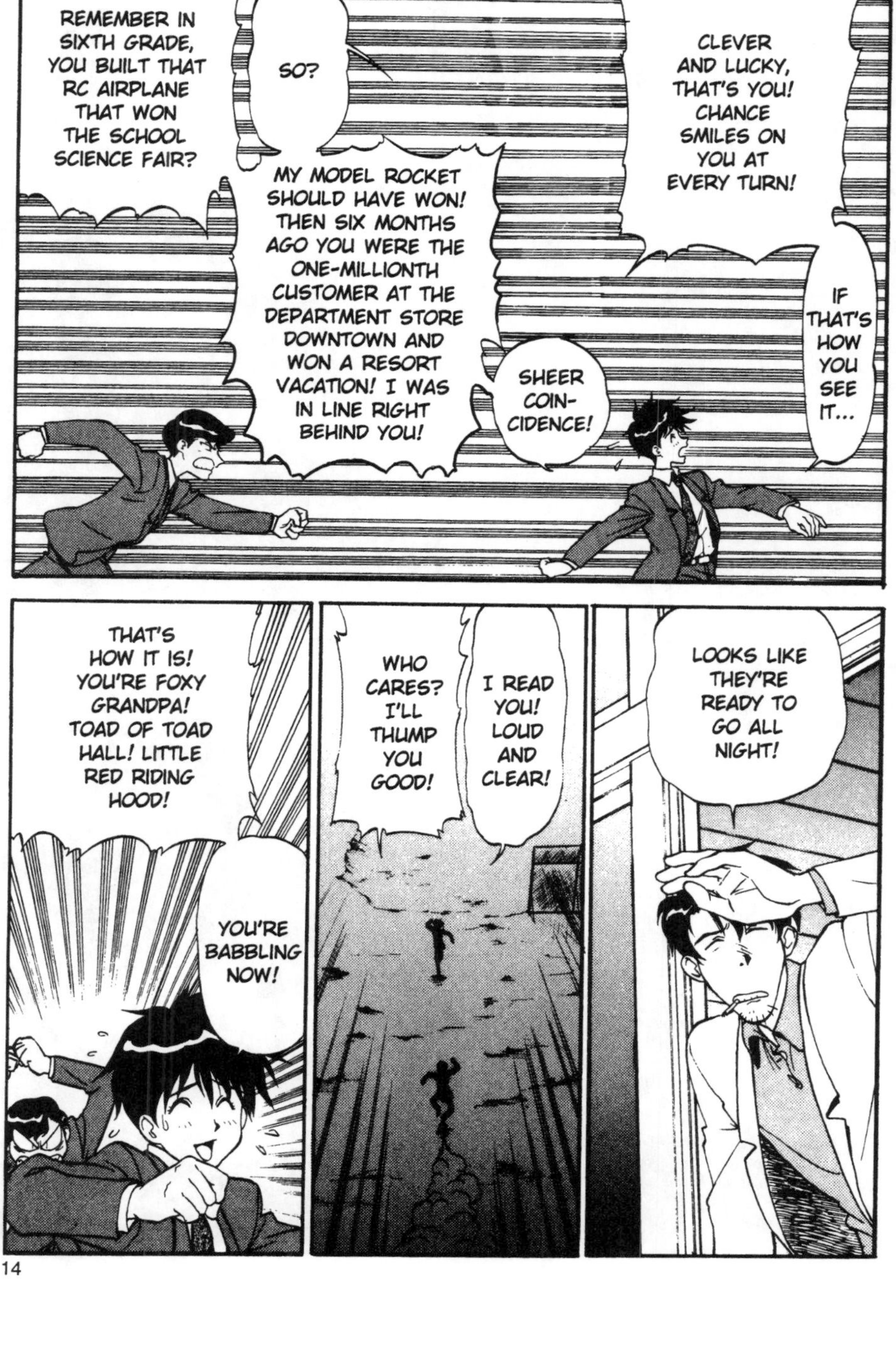
REMEMBER IN SIXTH GRADE, YOU BUILT THAT RC AIRPLANE THAT WON THE SCHOOL SCIENCE FAIR?
SO?
MY MODEL ROCKET SHOULD HAVE WON! THEN SIX MONTHS AGO YOU WERE THE ONE-MILLIONTH CUSTOMER AT THE DEPARTMENT STORE DOWNTOWN AND WON A RESORT VACATION! I WAS IN LINE RIGHT BEHIND YOU!
CLEVER AND LUCKY, THAT'S YOU! CHANCE SMILES ON YOU AT EVERY TURN!
SHEER COIN-CIDENCE!
IF THAT'S HOW YOU SEE IT...
THAT'S HOW IT IS! YOU'RE FOXY GRANDPA! TOAD OF TOAD HALL! LITTLE RED RIDING HOOD!
YOU'RE BABBLING NOW!
WHO CARES? I'LL THUMP YOU GOOD!
I READ YOU! LOUD AND CLEAR!
LOOKS LIKE THEY'RE READY TO GO ALL NIGHT!

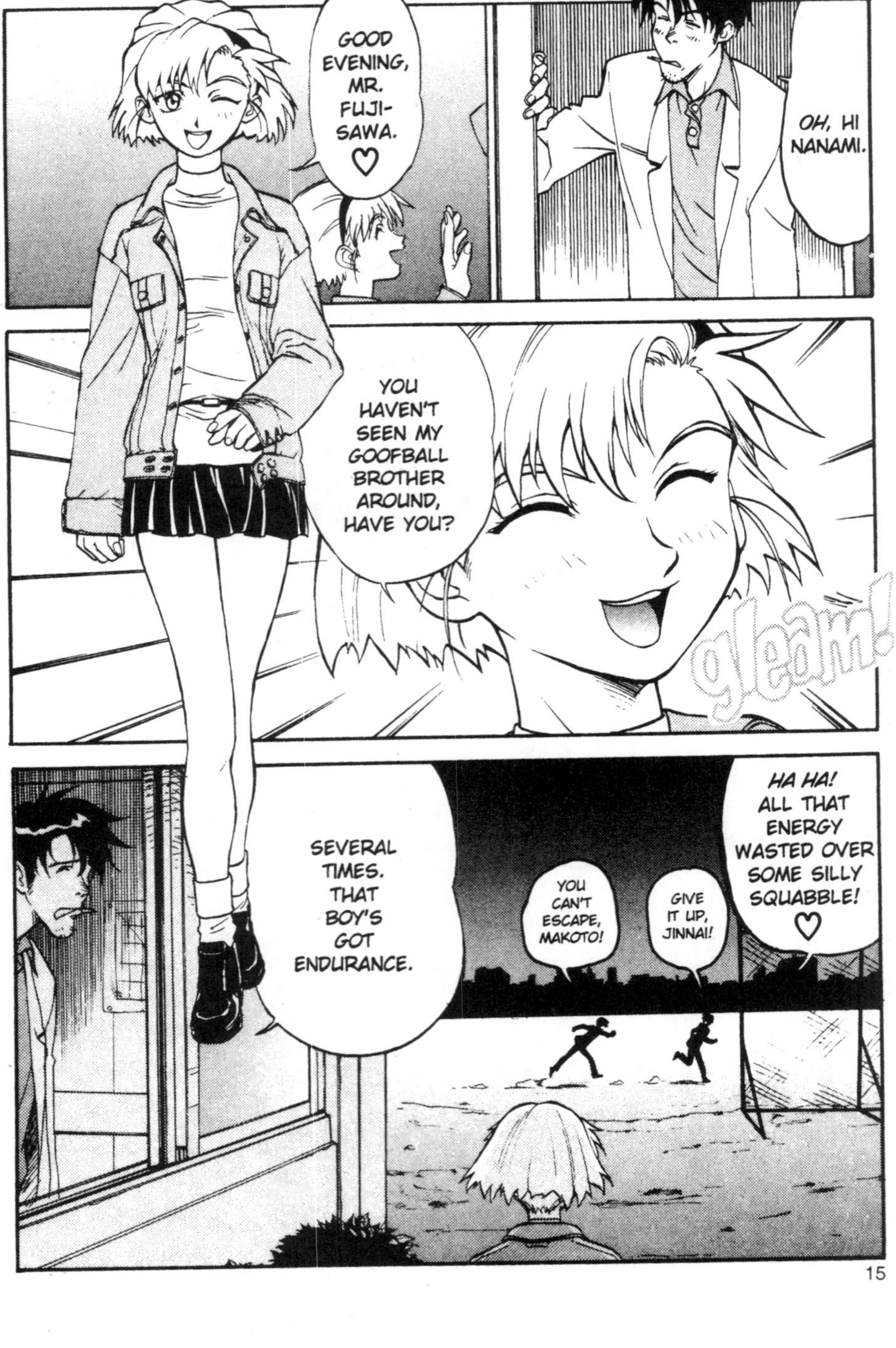
GOOD EVENING, MR. FUJI-SAWA. ♡
OH, HI NANAMI.
YOU HAVEN'T SEEN MY GOOFBALL BROTHER AROUND, HAVE YOU?
gleam!
SEVERAL TIMES. THAT BOY'S GOT ENDURANCE.
YOU CAN'T ESCAPE, MAKOTO!
GIVE IT UP, JINNAI!
HA HA! ALL THAT ENERGY WASTED OVER SOME SILLY SQUABBLE! ♡

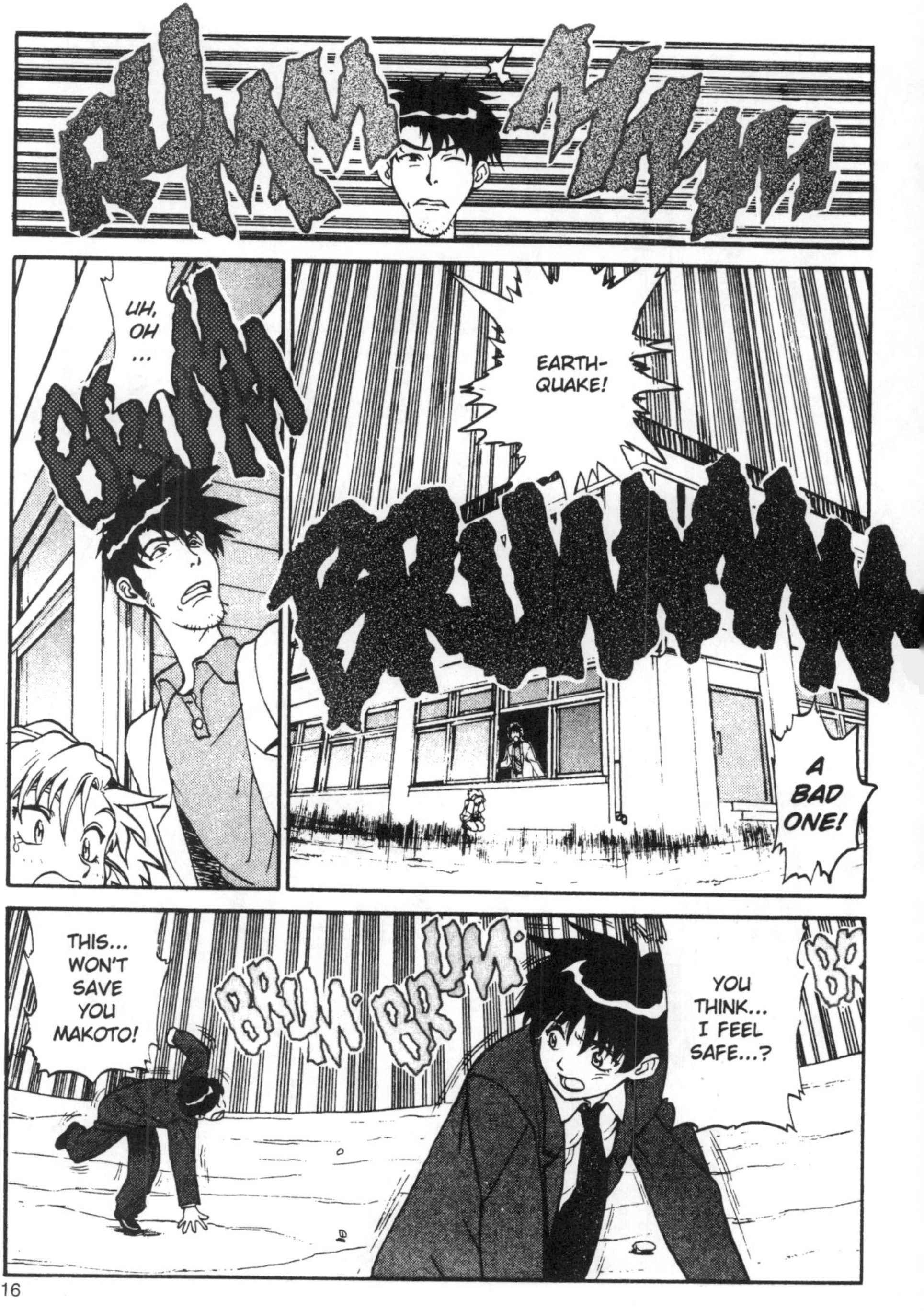
UH, OH ...
EARTH-QUAKE!
A BAD ONE!
THIS... WON'T SAVE YOU MAKOTO!
BRUM BRUM
YOU THINK... I FEEL SAFE...?

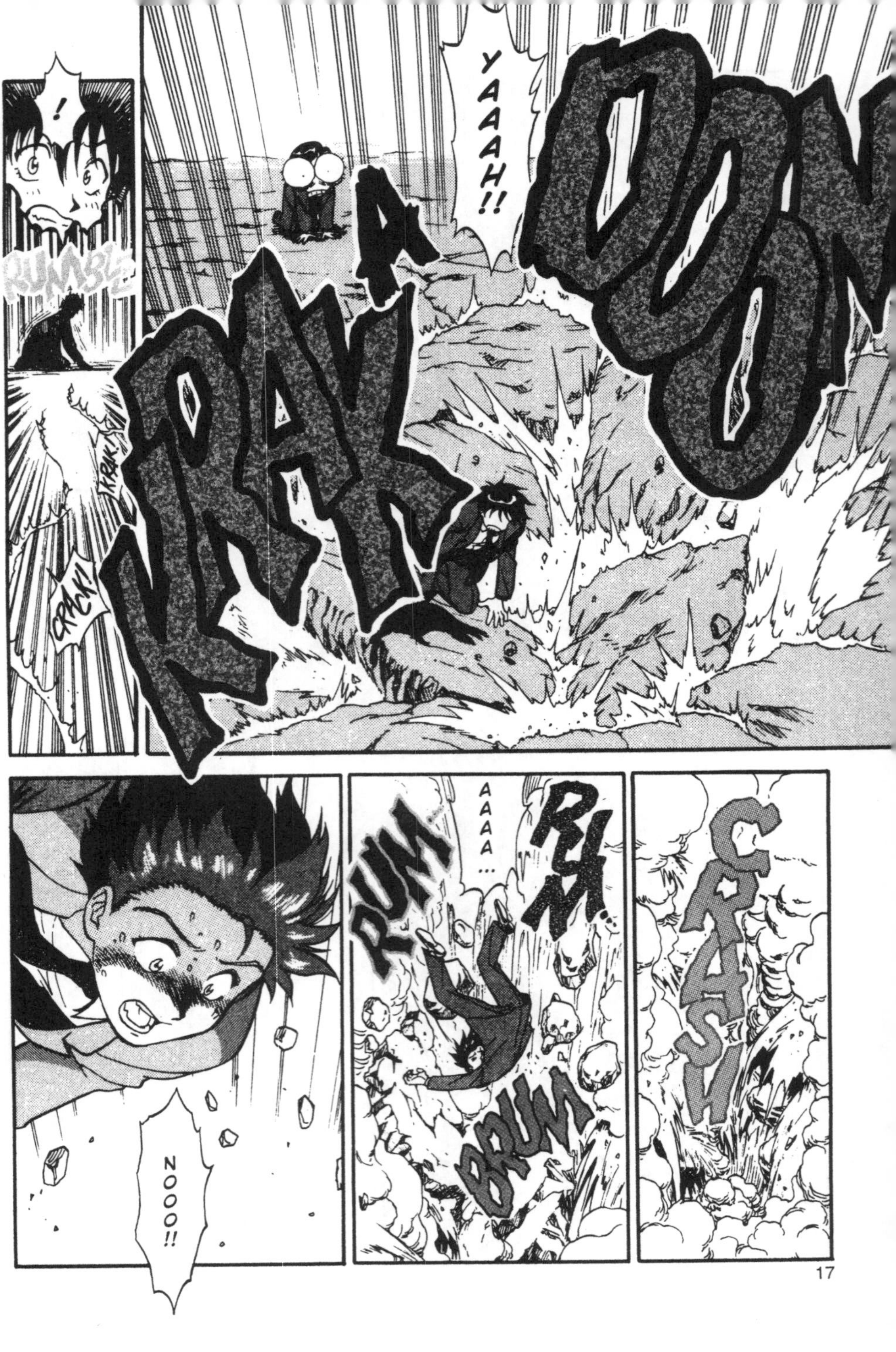
!
RUMBLE
KRAK!
CRACK!
YAAAAH!!
FRAKA
NOOOO!!
RUM...
AAAA...
RUM
BRUM
CRASH

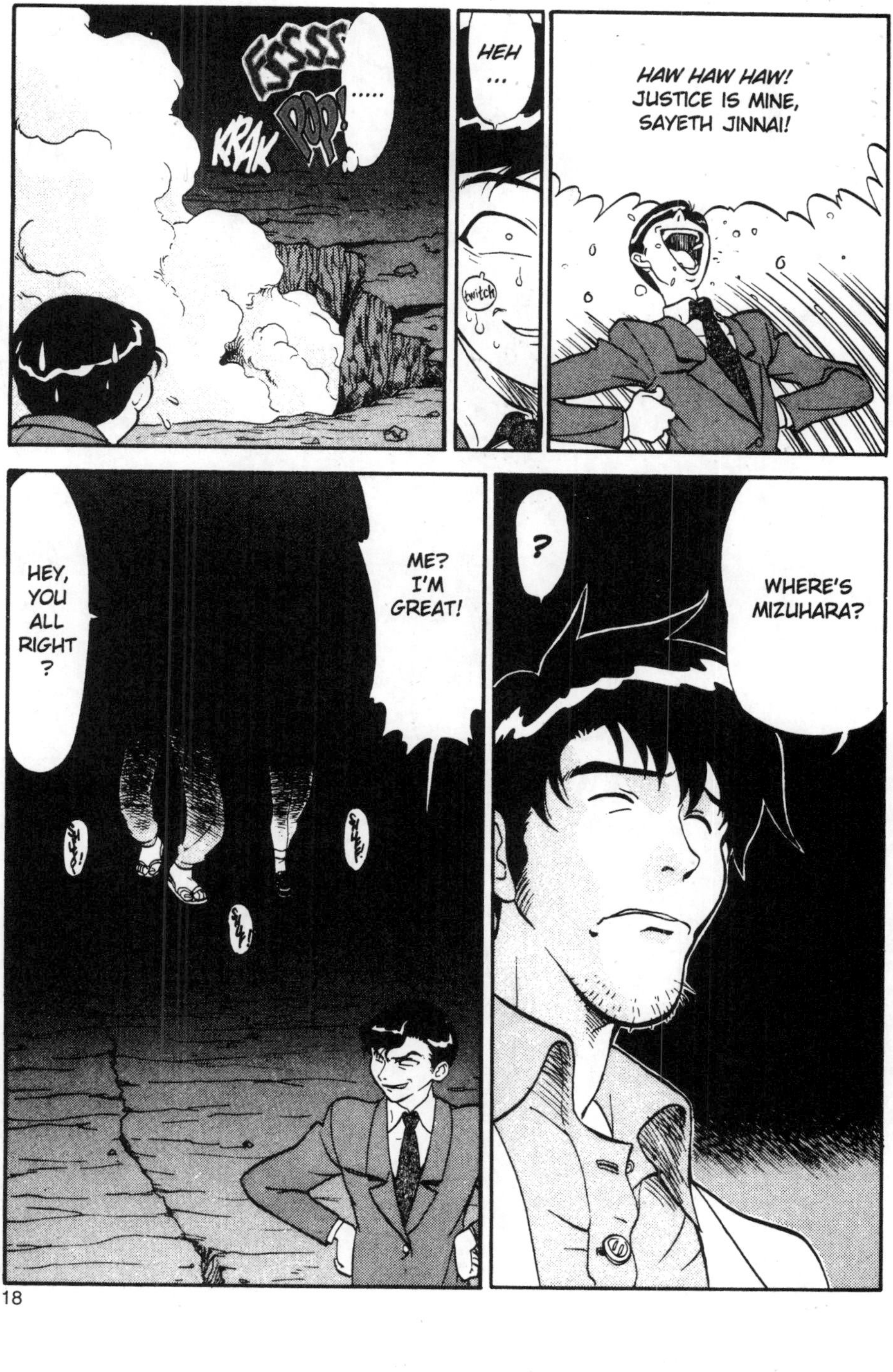
FSSSS
KRAK
POP!
......
HEH ...
twitch
HAW HAW HAW! JUSTICE IS MINE, SAYETH JINNAI!
HEY, YOU ALL RIGHT?
ME? I'M GREAT!
?
WHERE'S MIZUHARA?

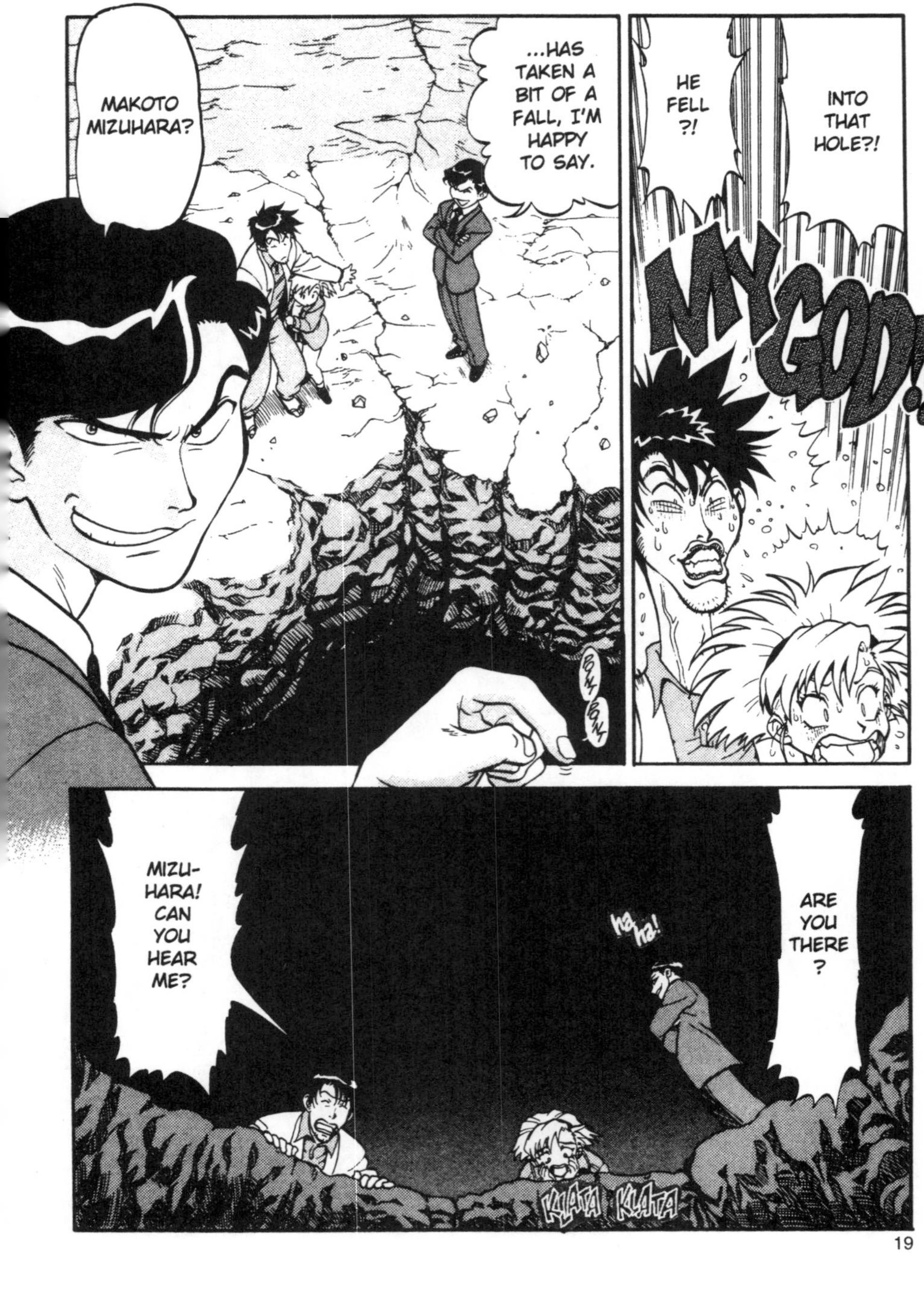
MAKOTO MIZUHARA?
...HAS TAKEN A BIT OF A FALL, I'M HAPPY TO SAY.
HE FELL ?!
INTO THAT HOLE?!
MY GOD!!
MIZU-HARA! CAN YOU HEAR ME?
ha ha!
ARE YOU THERE ?
KLATA KLATA

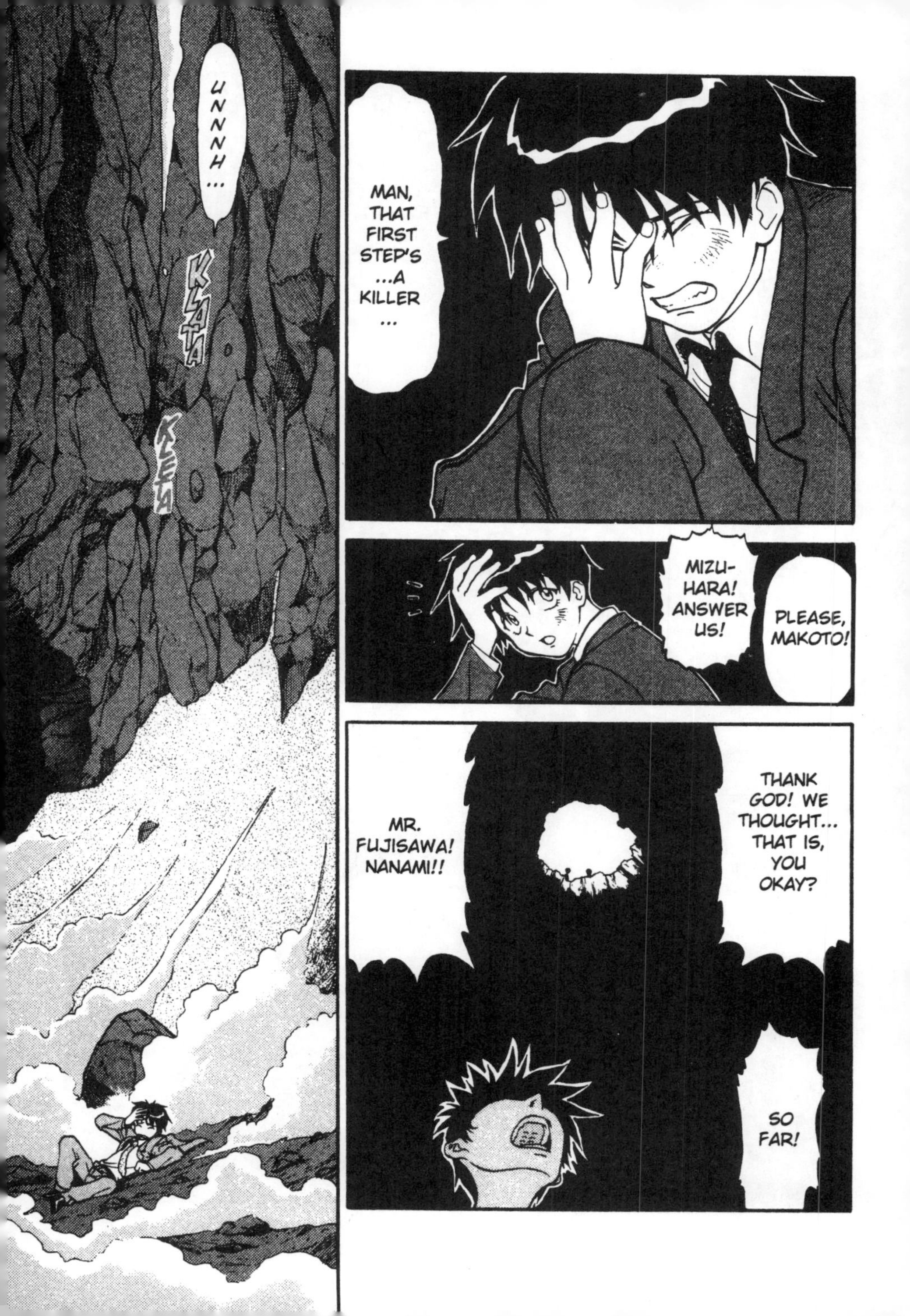
UNNNH...
KLATA
KLETA
MAN, THAT FIRST STEP'S ...A KILLER ...
MIZU-HARA! ANSWER US!
PLEASE, MAKOTO!
MR. FUJISAWA! NANAMI!!
THANK GOD! WE THOUGHT... THAT IS, YOU OKAY?
SO FAR!

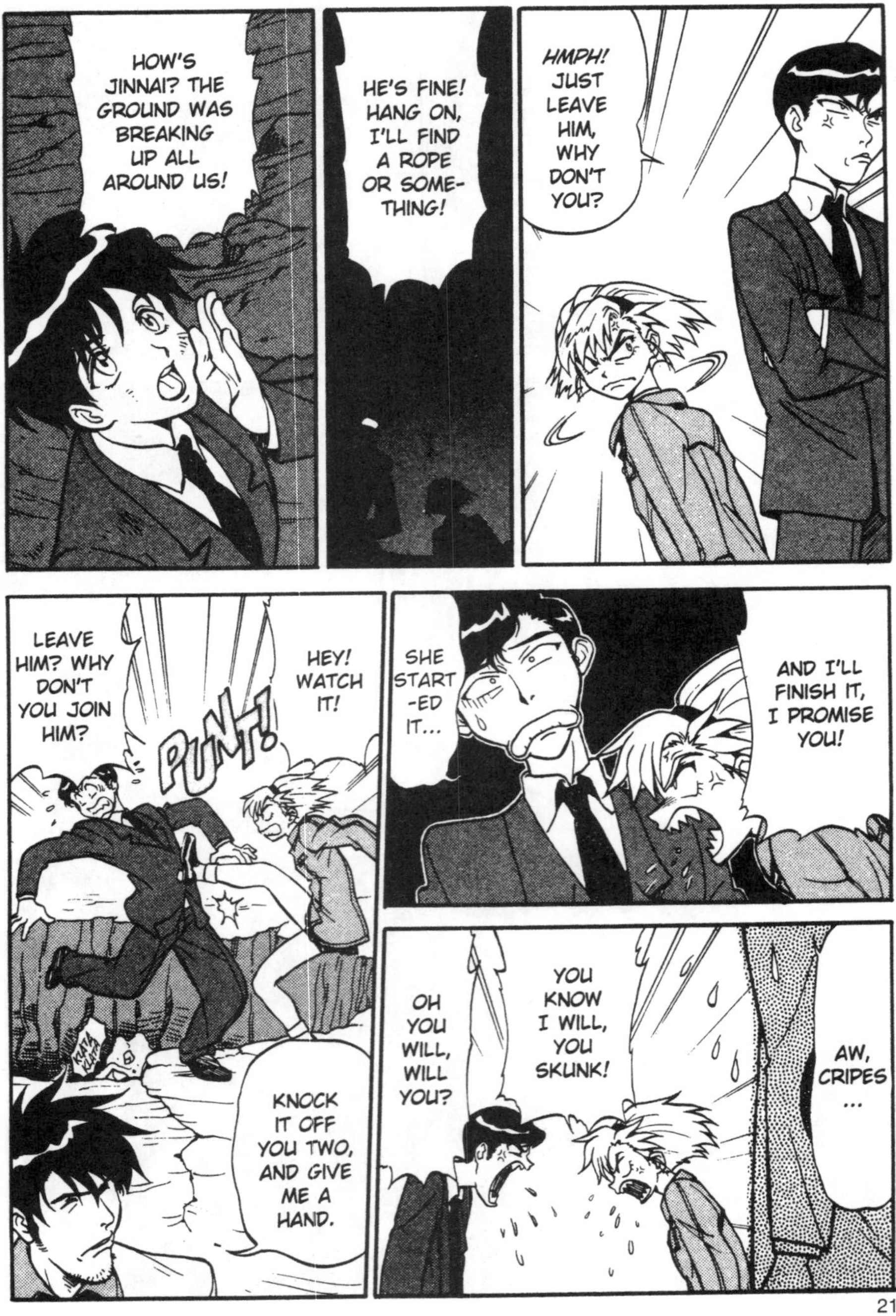
HOW'S JINNAI? THE GROUND WAS BREAKING UP ALL AROUND US!
HE'S FINE! HANG ON, I'LL FIND A ROPE OR SOME-THING!
HMPH! JUST LEAVE HIM, WHY DON'T YOU?
LEAVE HIM? WHY DON'T YOU JOIN HIM?
HEY! WATCH IT!
PUNT!
KNOCK IT OFF YOU TWO, AND GIVE ME A HAND.
SHE START-ED IT...
AND I'LL FINISH IT, I PROMISE YOU!
OH YOU WILL, WILL YOU?
YOU KNOW I WILL, YOU SKUNK!
AW, CRIPES ...

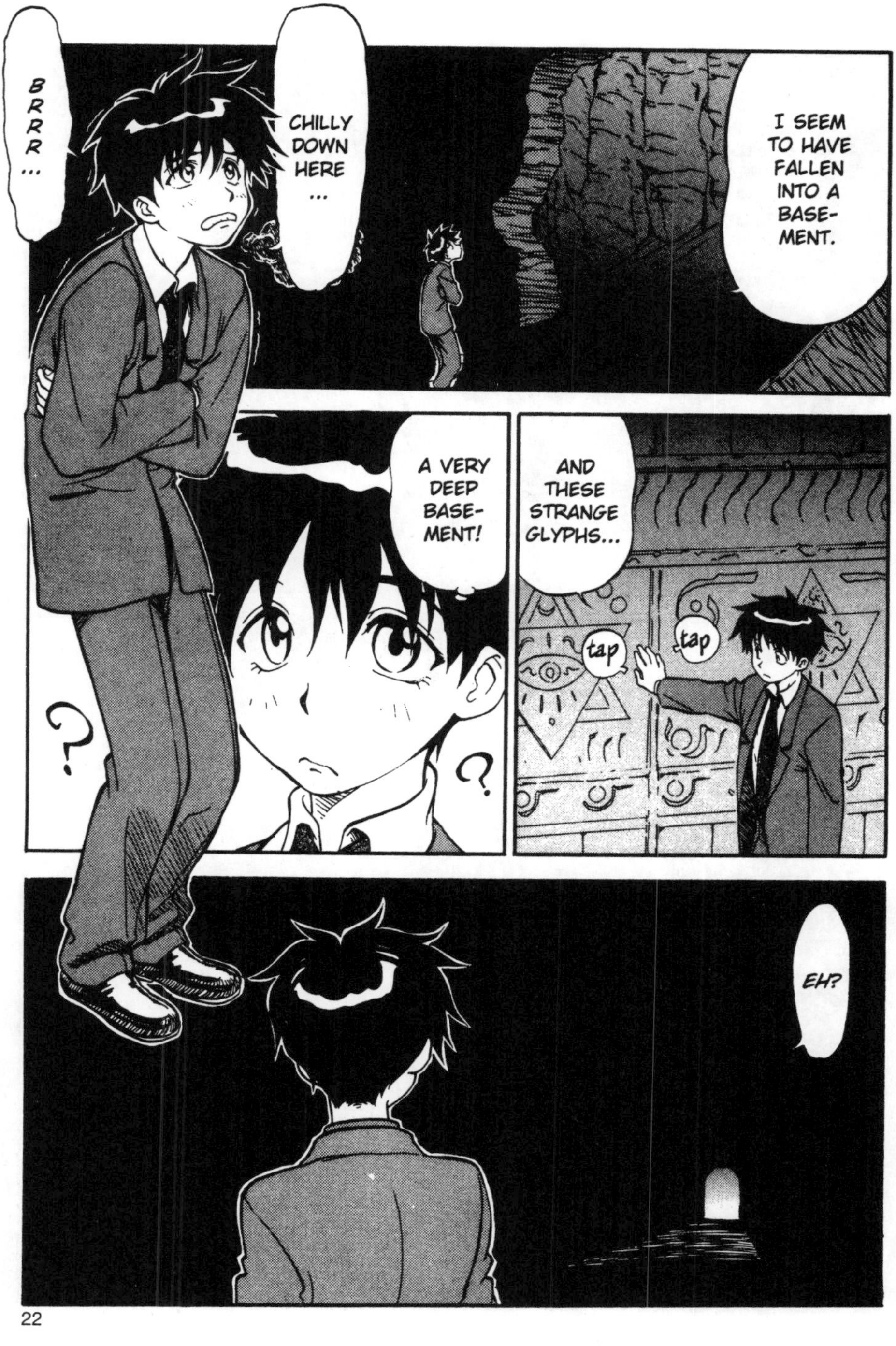
BRRR...
CHILLY DOWN HERE ...
I SEEM TO HAVE FALLEN INTO A BASEMENT.
A VERY DEEP BASEMENT!
AND THESE STRANGE GLYPHS...
tap
tap
EH?

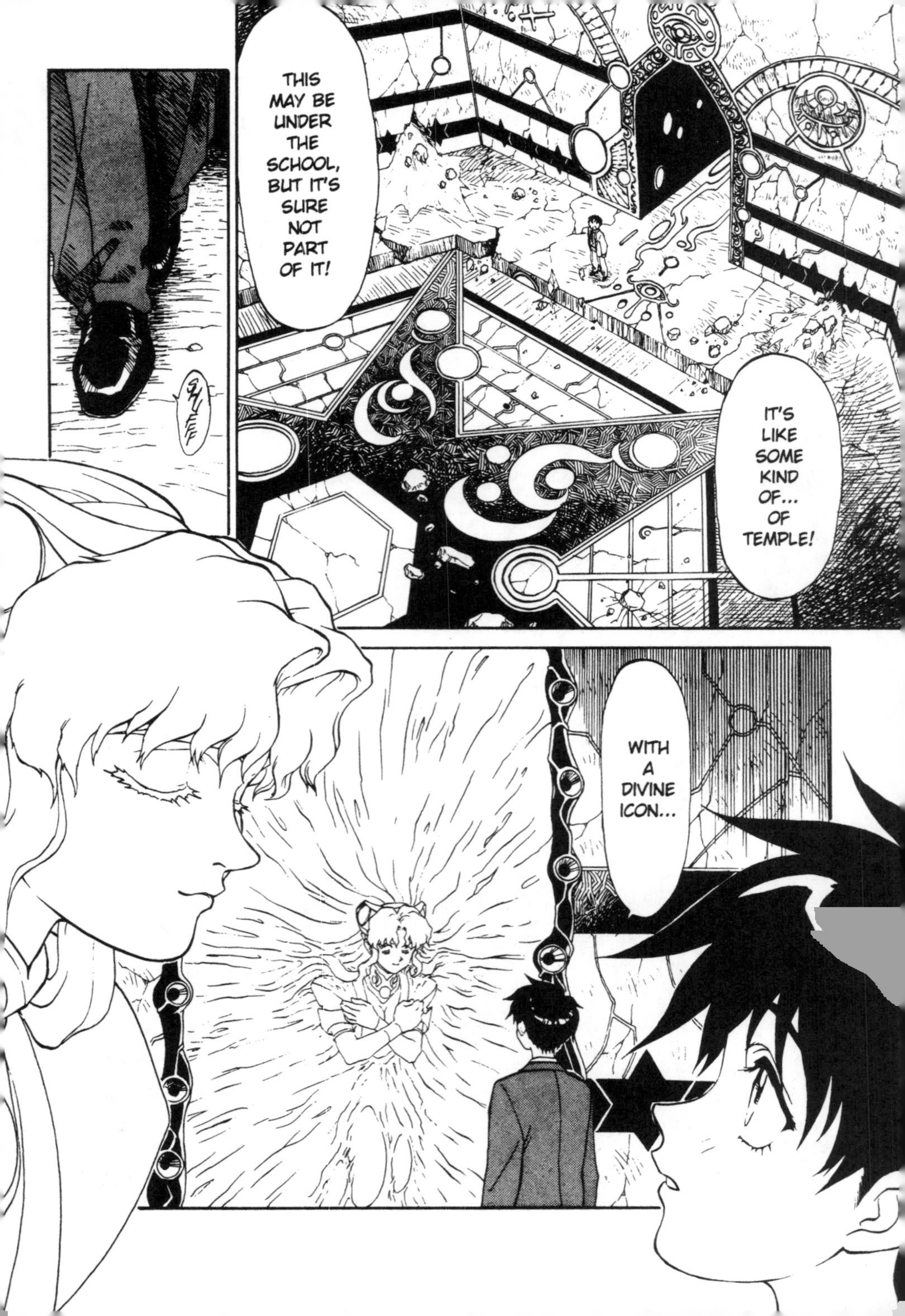
SHUFFF
THIS MAY BE UNDER THE SCHOOL, BUT IT'S SURE NOT PART OF IT!
IT'S LIKE SOME KIND OF... OF TEMPLE!
WITH A DIVINE ICON...

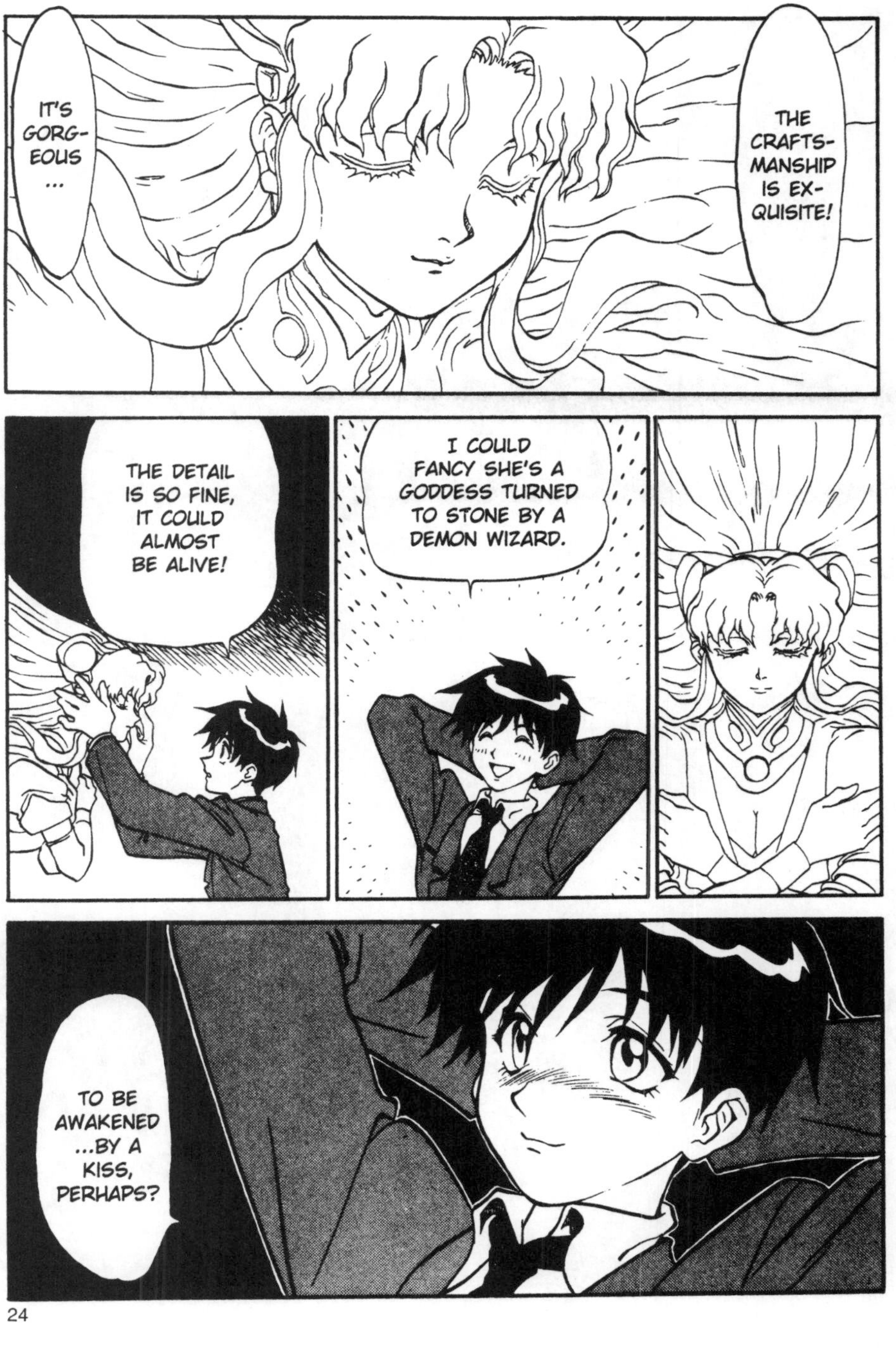
IT'S GORG-EOUS ...
THE CRAFTS-MANSHIP IS EX-QUISITE!
THE DETAIL IS SO FINE, IT COULD ALMOST BE ALIVE!
I COULD FANCY SHE'S A GODDESS TURNED TO STONE BY A DEMON WIZARD.
TO BE AWAKENED ...BY A KISS, PERHAPS?

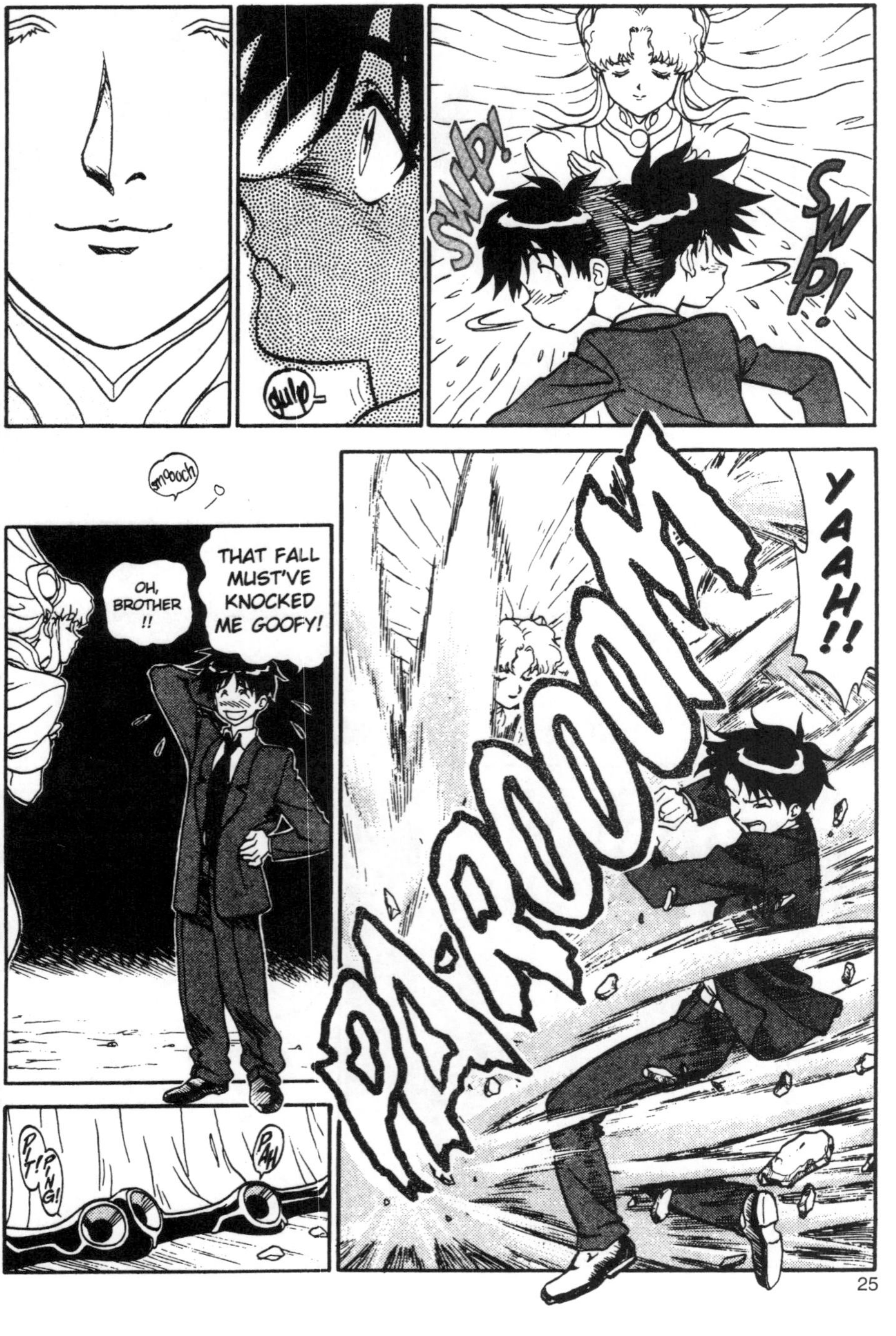
gulp
SWP!
SWP!
smooch
OH, BROTHER !!
THAT FALL MUST'VE KNOCKED ME GOOFY!
PIT! PING!
PAH
YAAAH!!
BA-ROOOM

HISSSS
WHOOO-EE!
HSSSSS
ONE KISS... STARTED THIS?
HSSSSSSSSS
GOOD GOD!
SSSSSSSS
SHUFFF

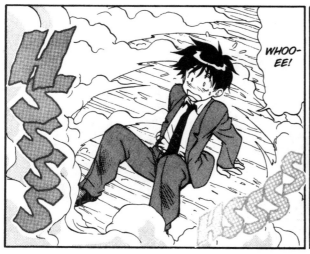

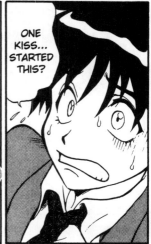

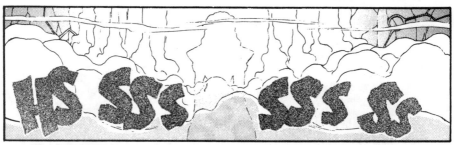

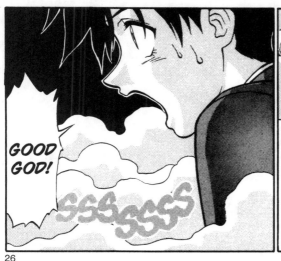

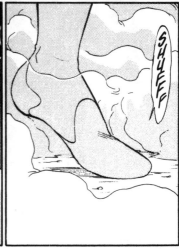

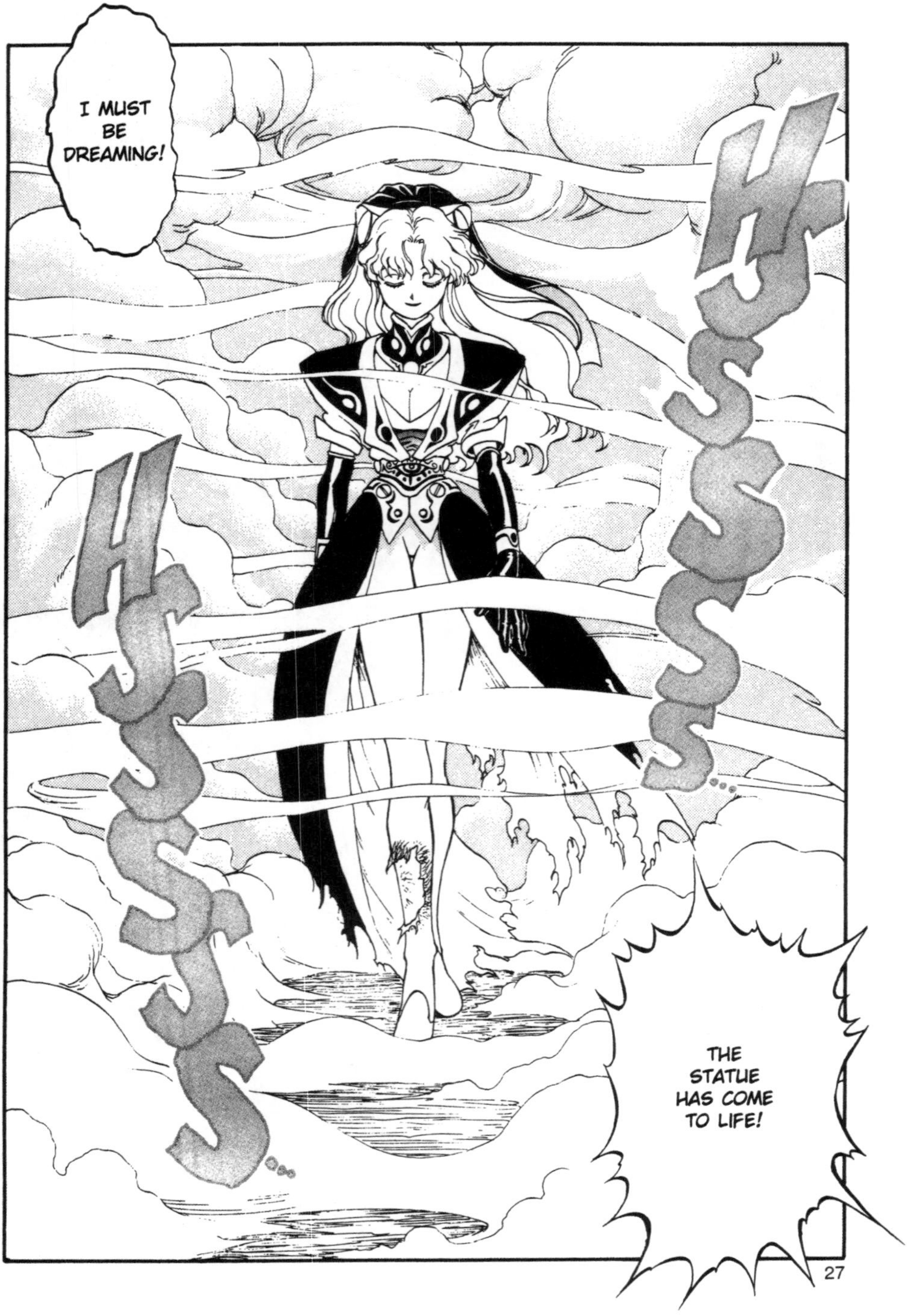
I MUST BE DREAMING!
HSSSSSS...
HSSSSSS...
THE STATUE HAS COME TO LIFE!

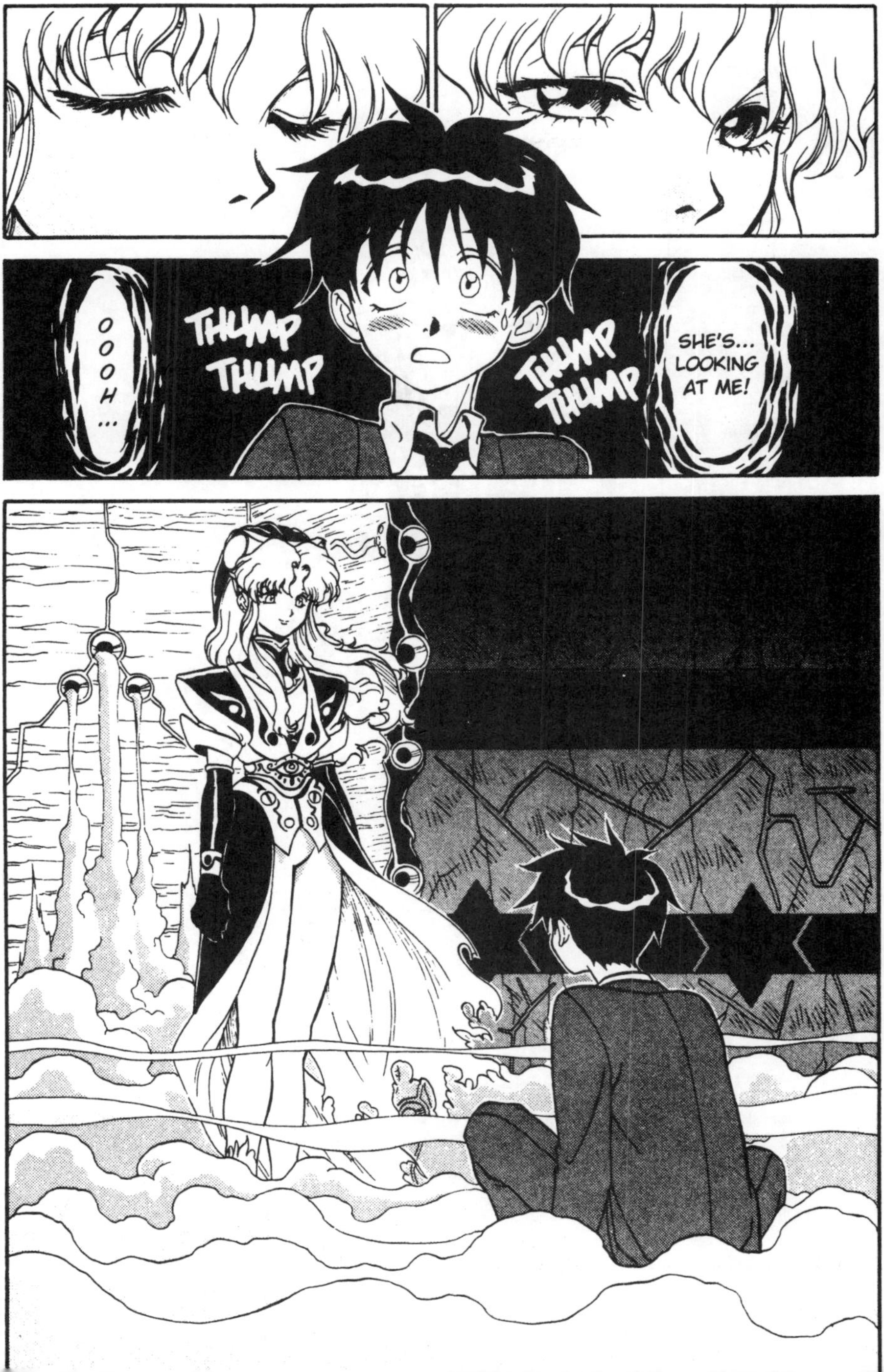
OOOH...
THUMP THUMP
THUMP THUMP
SHE'S... LOOKING AT ME!

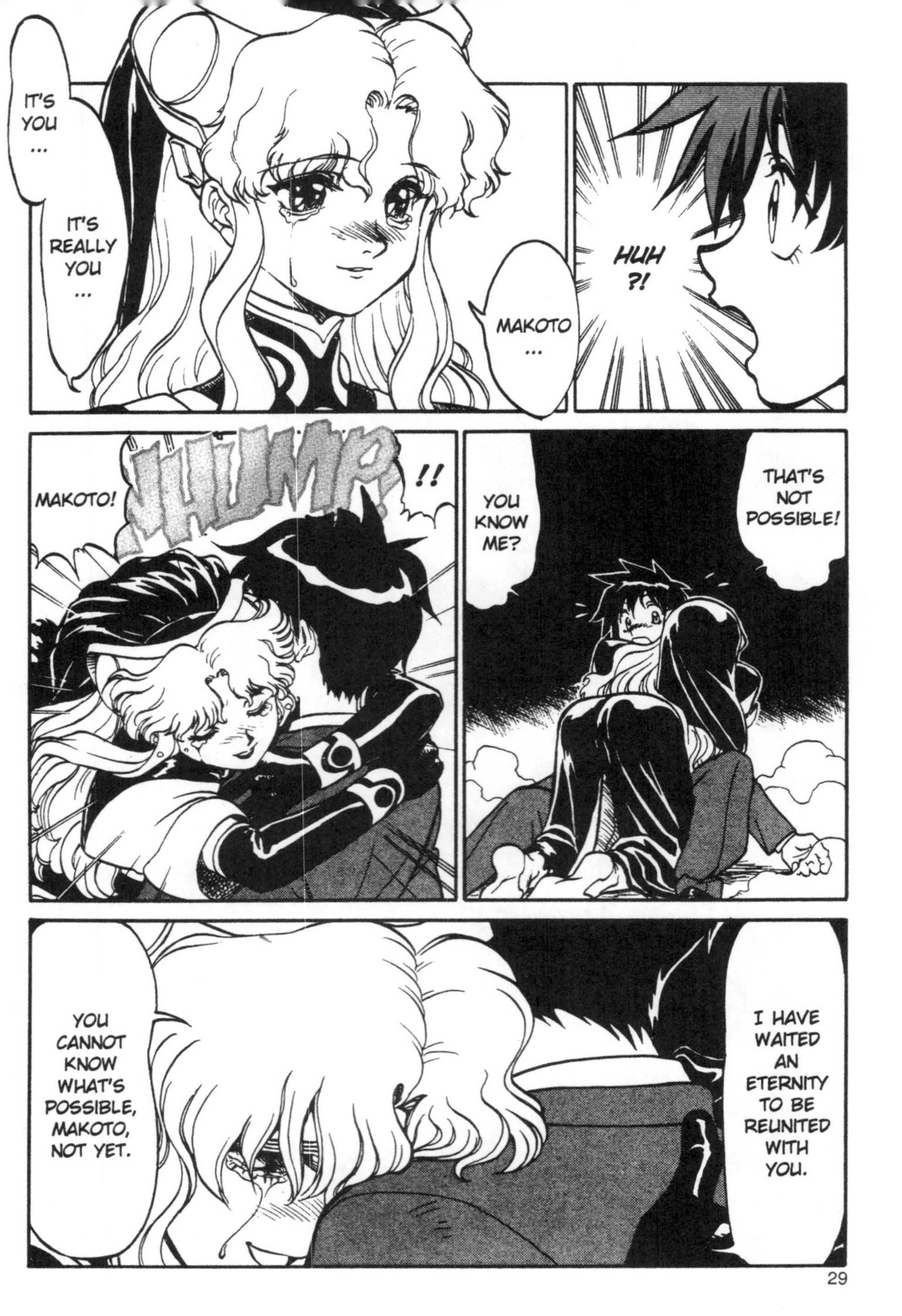
IT'S YOU ...
IT'S REALLY YOU ...
MAKOTO ...
HUH ?!
THUMP
!!
MAKOTO!
YOU KNOW ME?
THAT'S NOT POSSIBLE!
YOU CANNOT KNOW WHAT'S POSSIBLE, MAKOTO, NOT YET.
I HAVE WAITED AN ETERNITY TO BE REUNITED WITH YOU.

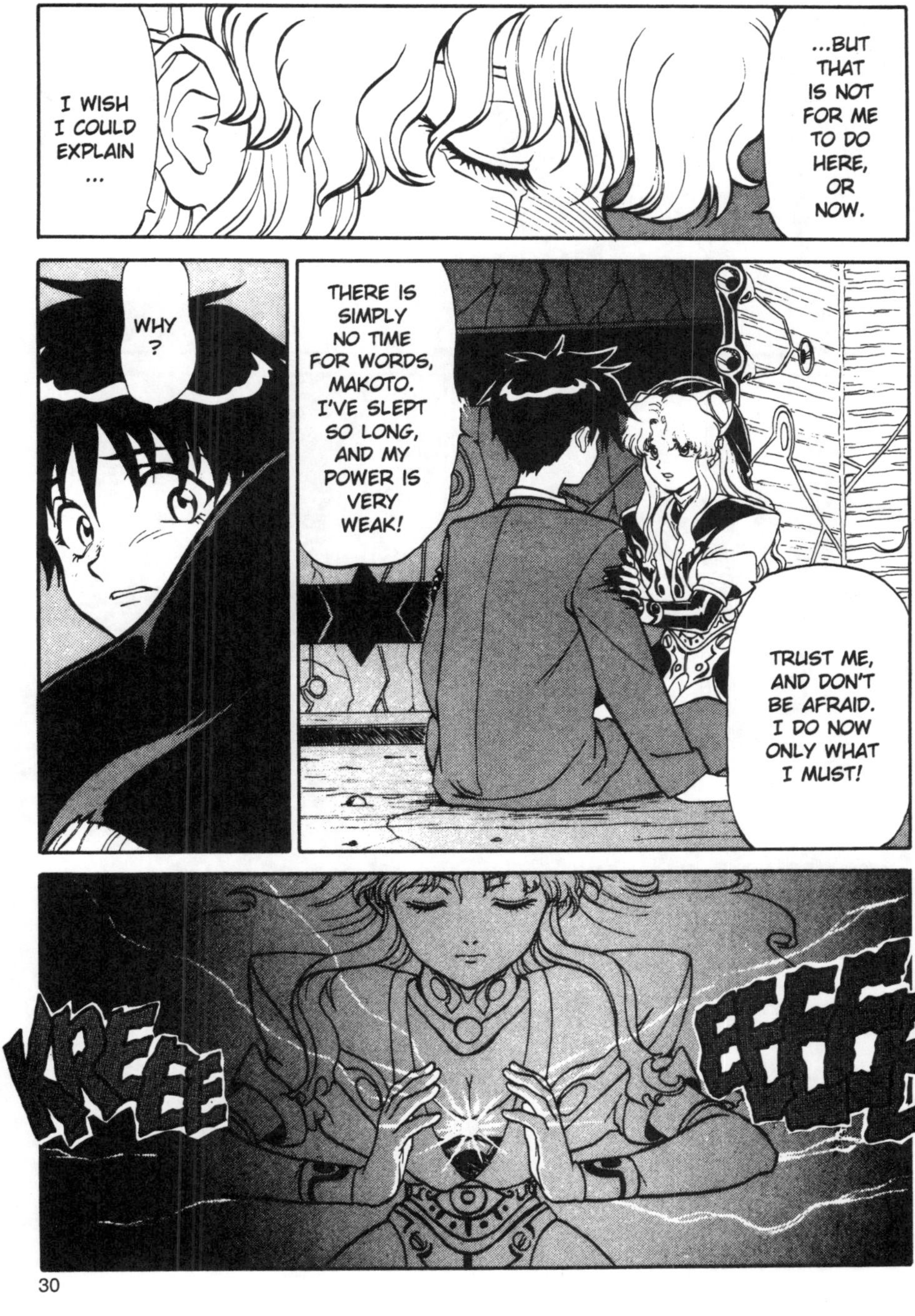
I WISH I COULD EXPLAIN ...
...BUT THAT IS NOT FOR ME TO DO HERE, OR NOW.
WHY?
THERE IS SIMPLY NO TIME FOR WORDS, MAKOTO. I'VE SLEPT SO LONG, AND MY POWER IS VERY WEAK!
TRUST ME, AND DON'T BE AFRAID. I DO NOW ONLY WHAT I MUST!
KREEEEEEEE

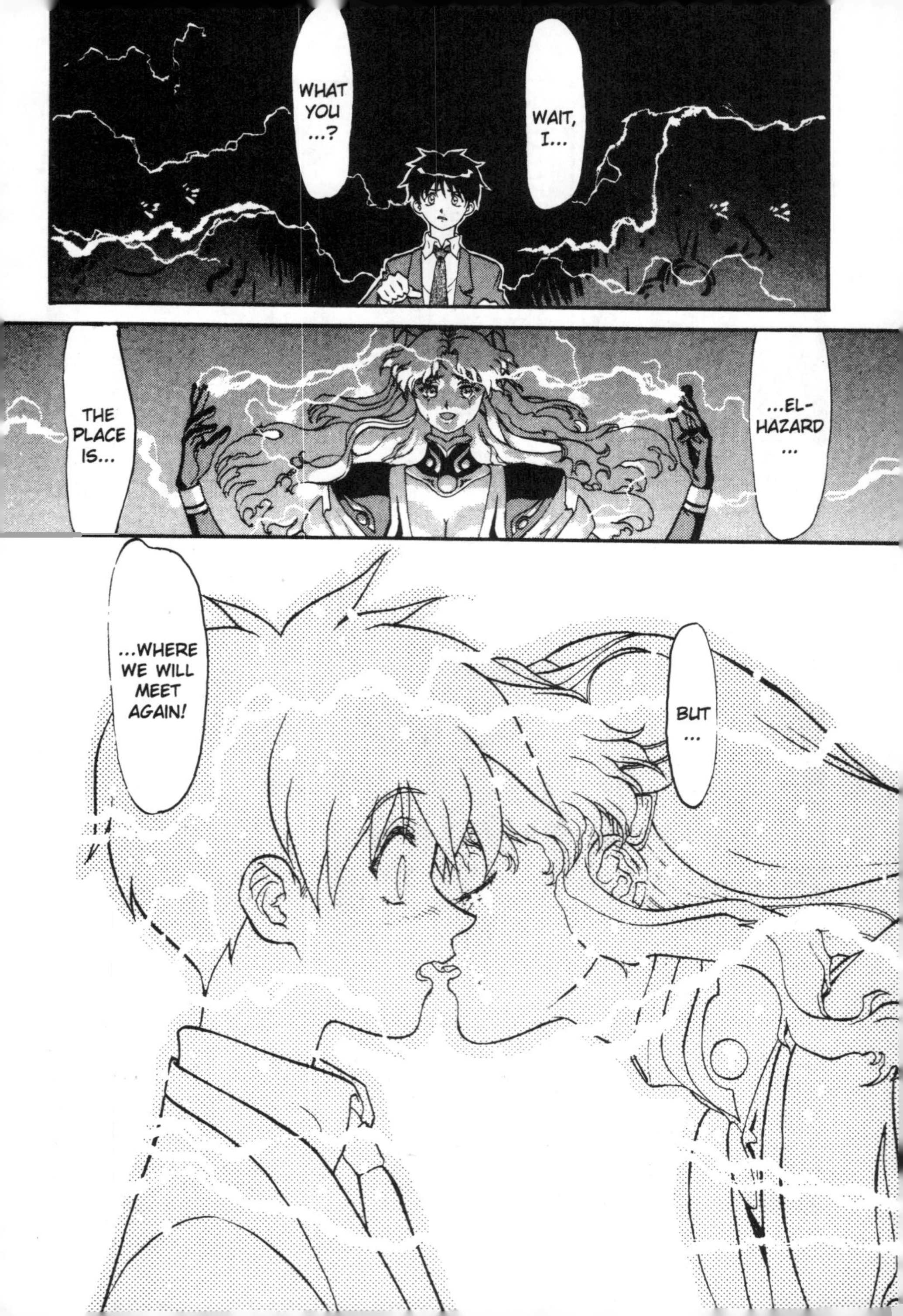
WHAT YOU ...?
WAIT, I...
THE PLACE IS...
...EL-HAZARD ...
...WHERE WE WILL MEET AGAIN!
BUT ...

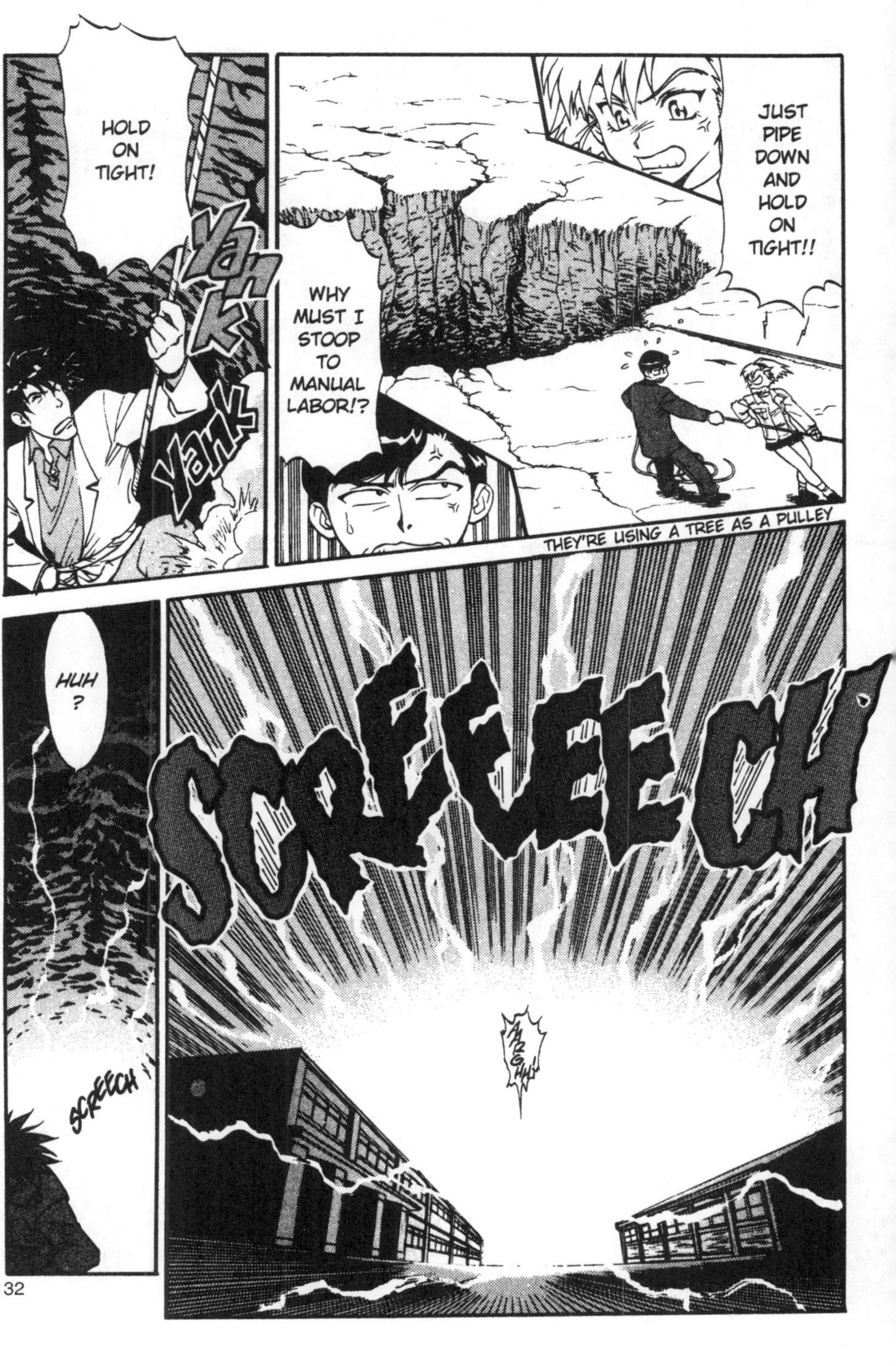
HOLD ON TIGHT!
YANK
YANK
JUST PIPE DOWN AND HOLD ON TIGHT!!
WHY MUST I STOOP TO MANUAL LABOR!?
THEY'RE USING A TREE AS A PULLEY
HUH?
SCREECH
SCREEECH
AARGHH!

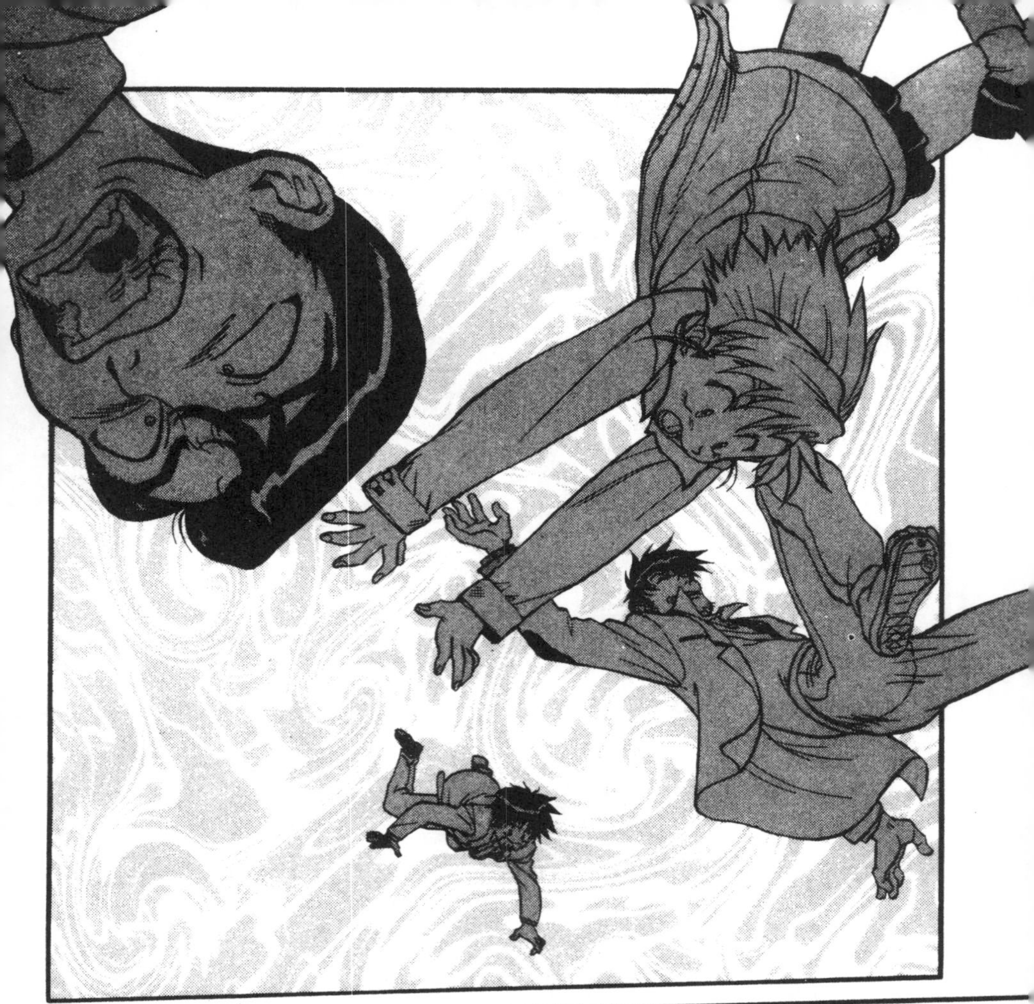

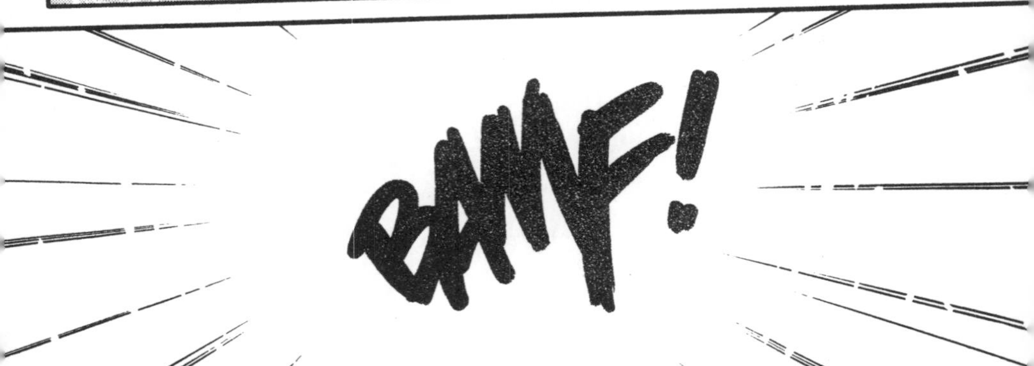
BAMF!

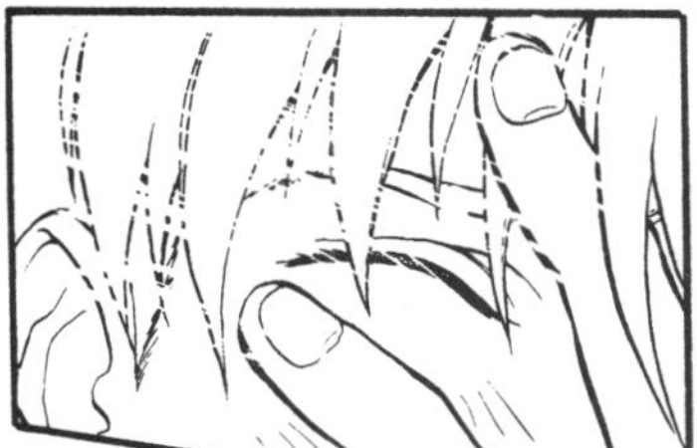

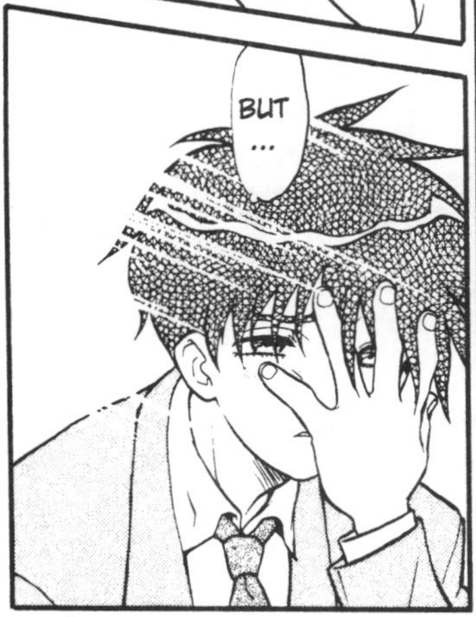
BUT ...

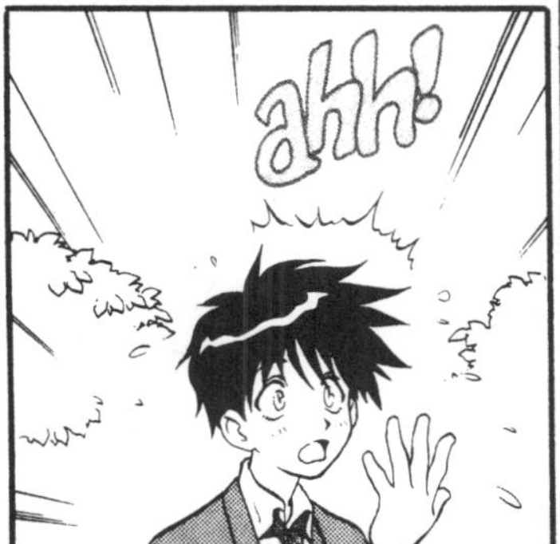
ahh!

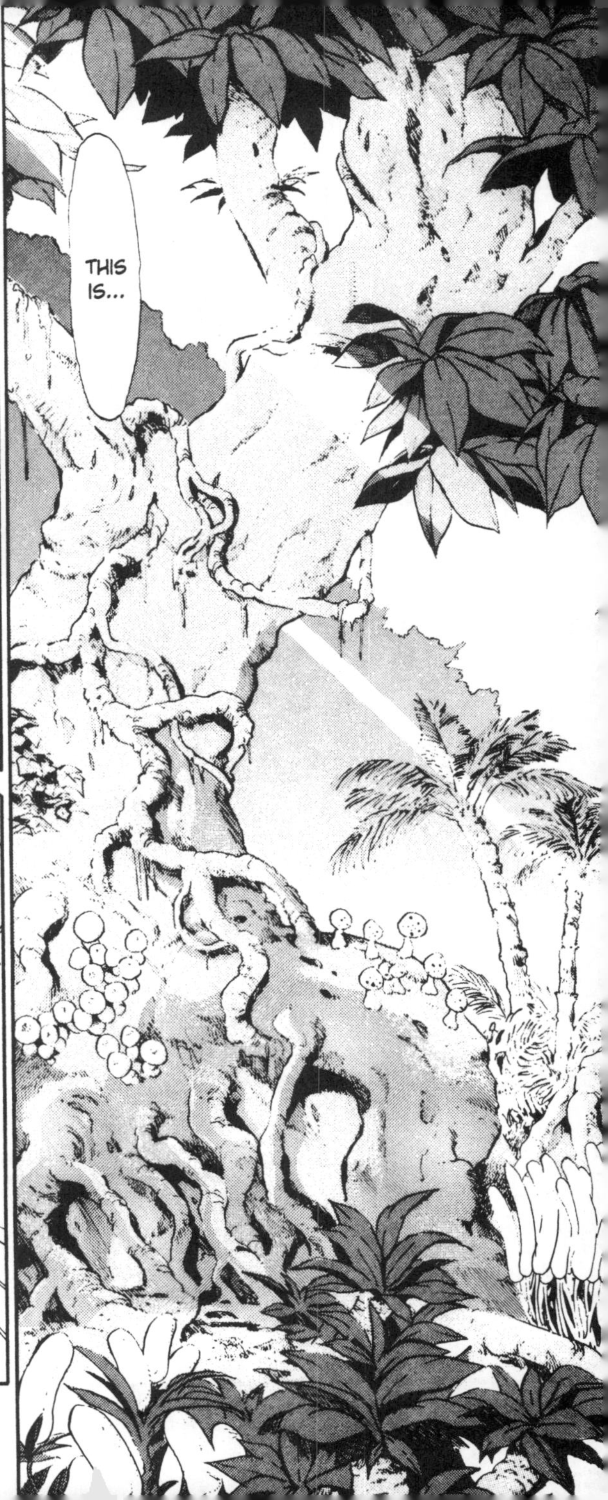
THIS IS...

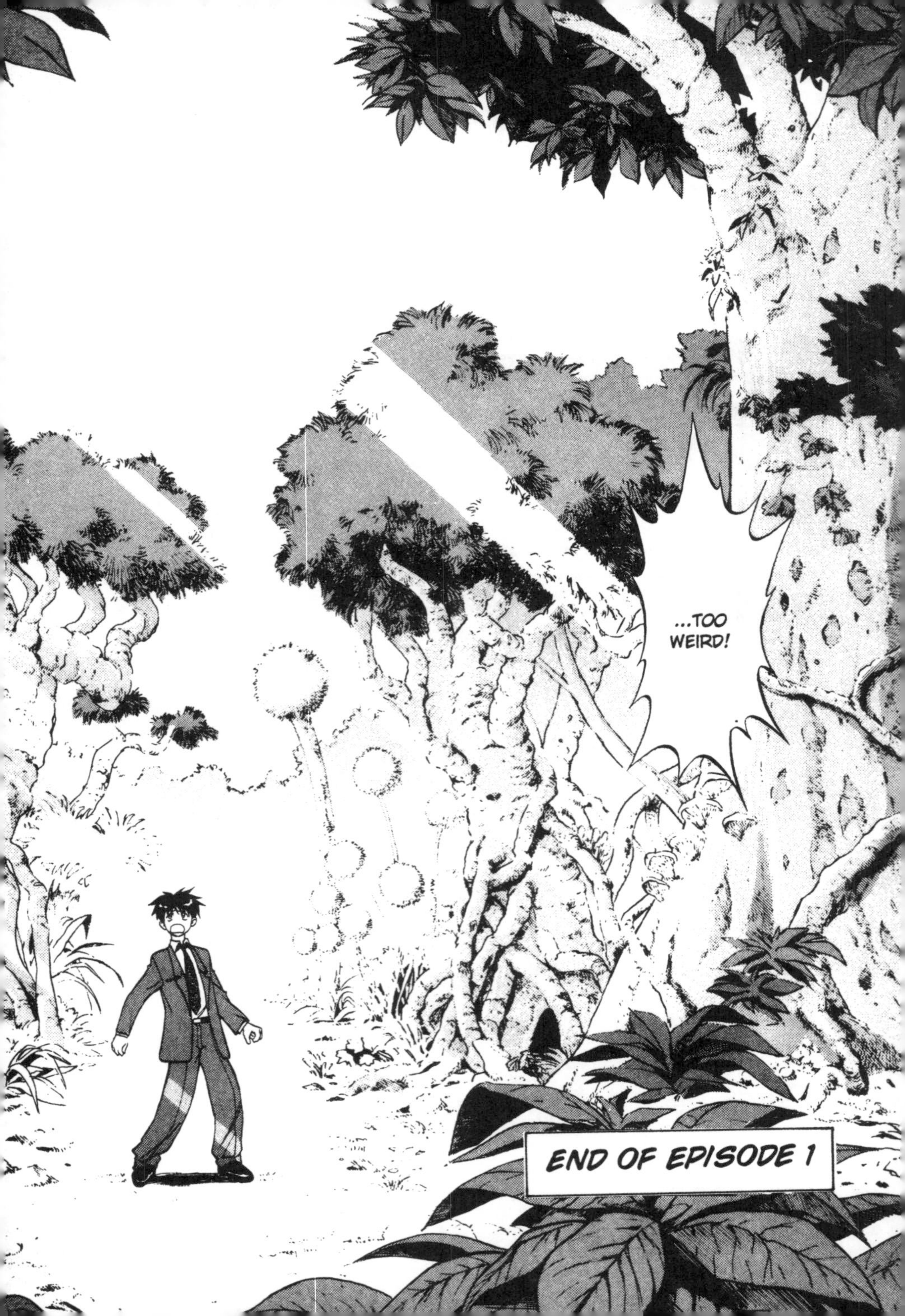
...TOO
WEIRD!
END OF EPISODE 1

EPISODE 2

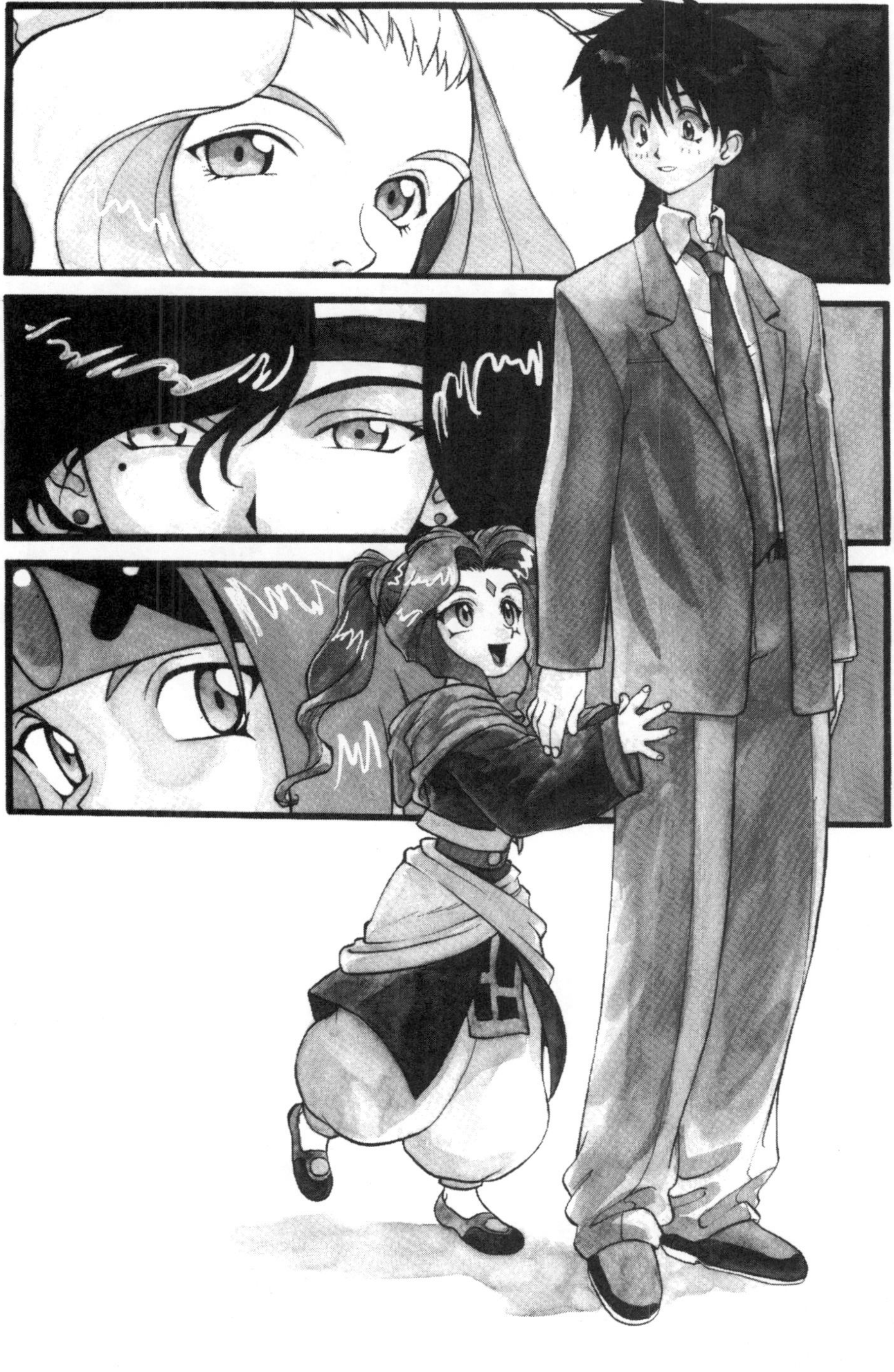

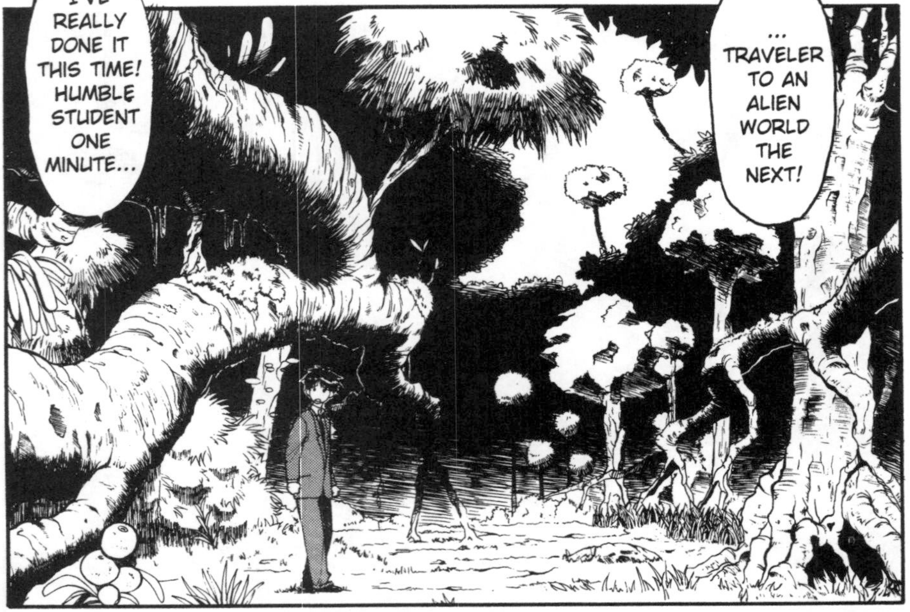
I'VE REALLY DONE IT THIS TIME! HUMBLE STUDENT ONE MINUTE...
... TRAVELER TO AN ALIEN WORLD THE NEXT!

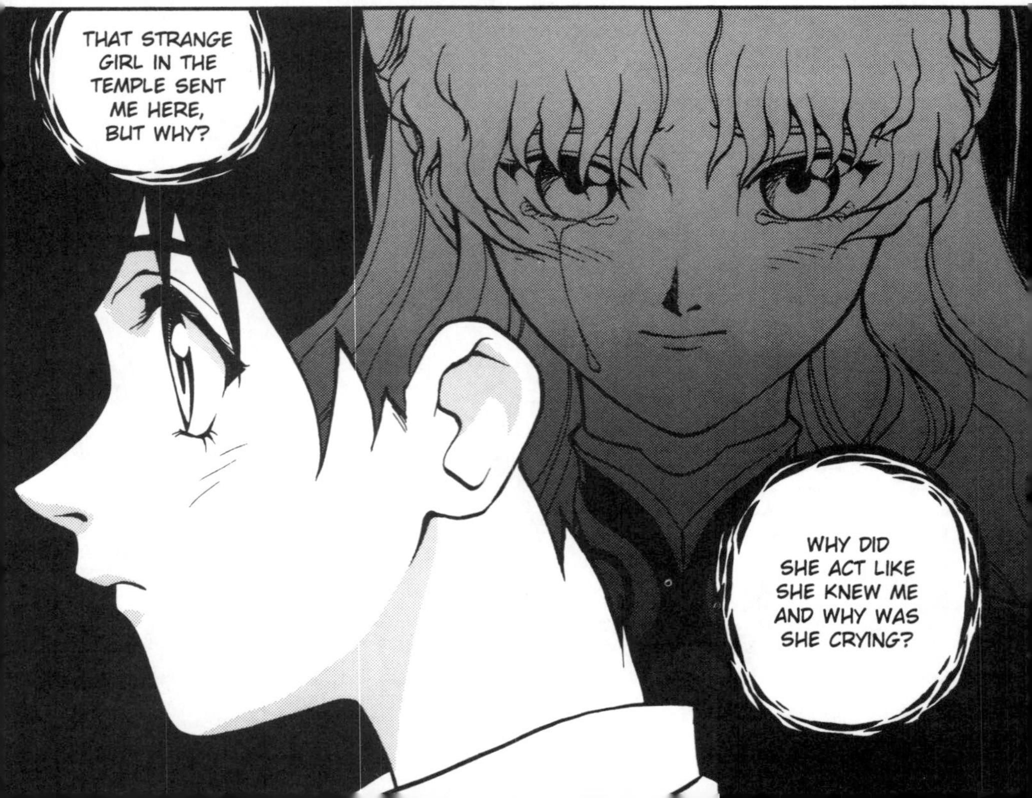
THAT STRANGE GIRL IN THE TEMPLE SENT ME HERE, BUT WHY?
WHY DID SHE ACT LIKE SHE KNEW ME AND WHY WAS SHE CRYING?

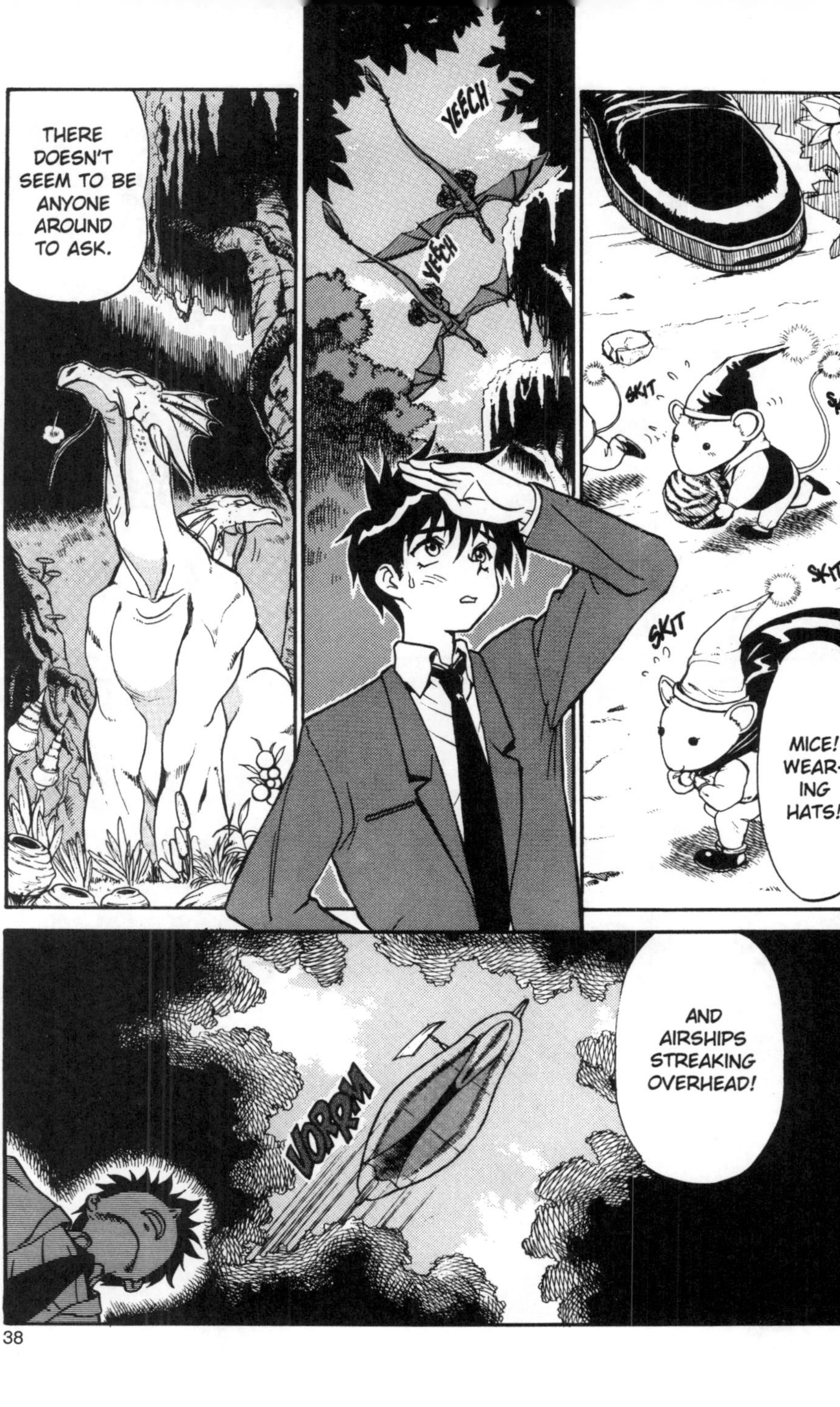

THERE DOESN'T SEEM TO BE ANYONE AROUND TO ASK.
YEECH
YEECH
SKIT
SKIT
SKIT
SKIT
MICE! WEAR-ING HATS!
VORRM
AND AIRSHIPS STREAKING OVERHEAD!

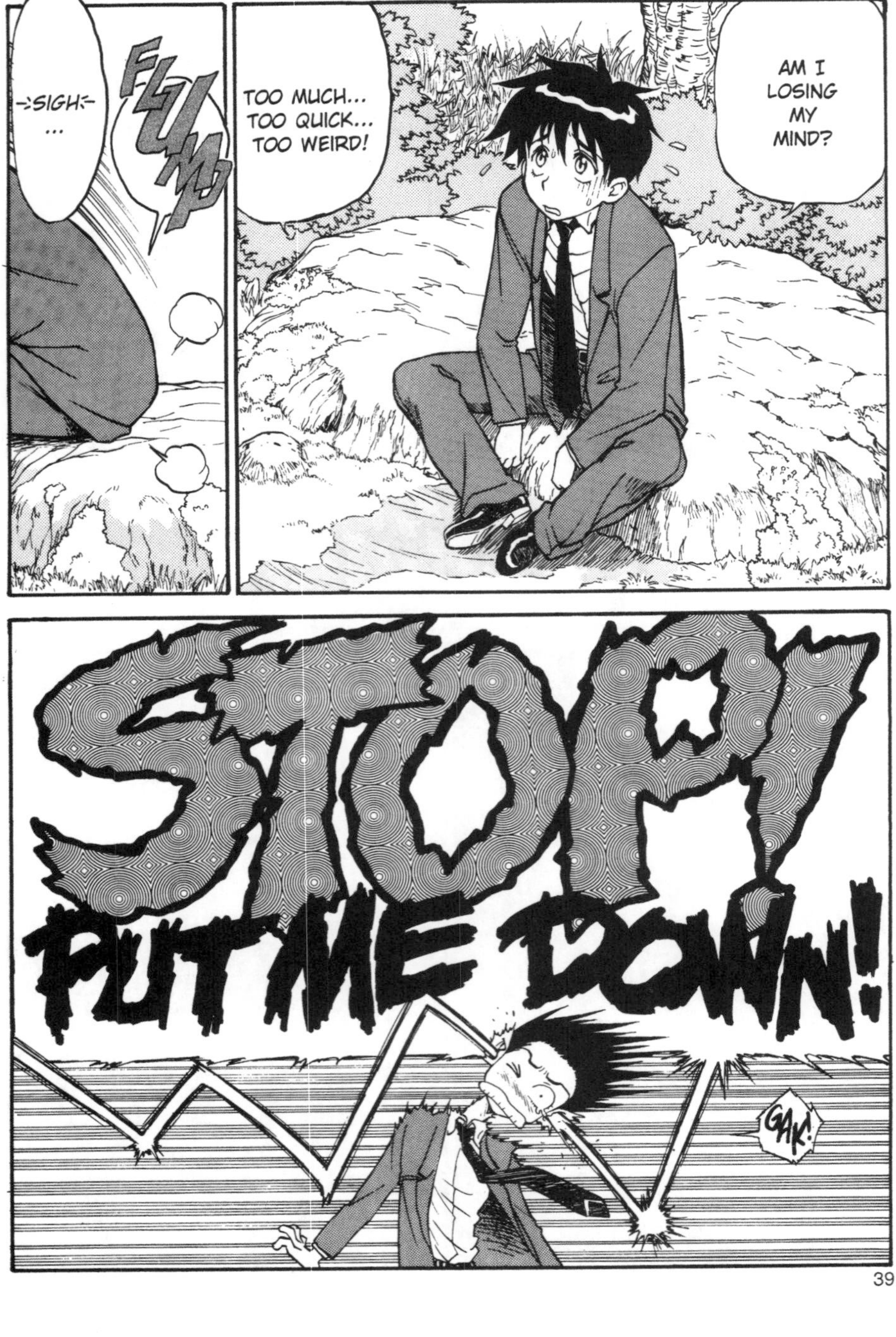
-SIGH-
...
FLUMP
TOO MUCH... TOO QUICK... TOO WEIRD!
AM I LOSING MY MIND?
STOP!
PUT ME DOWN!
GAK!

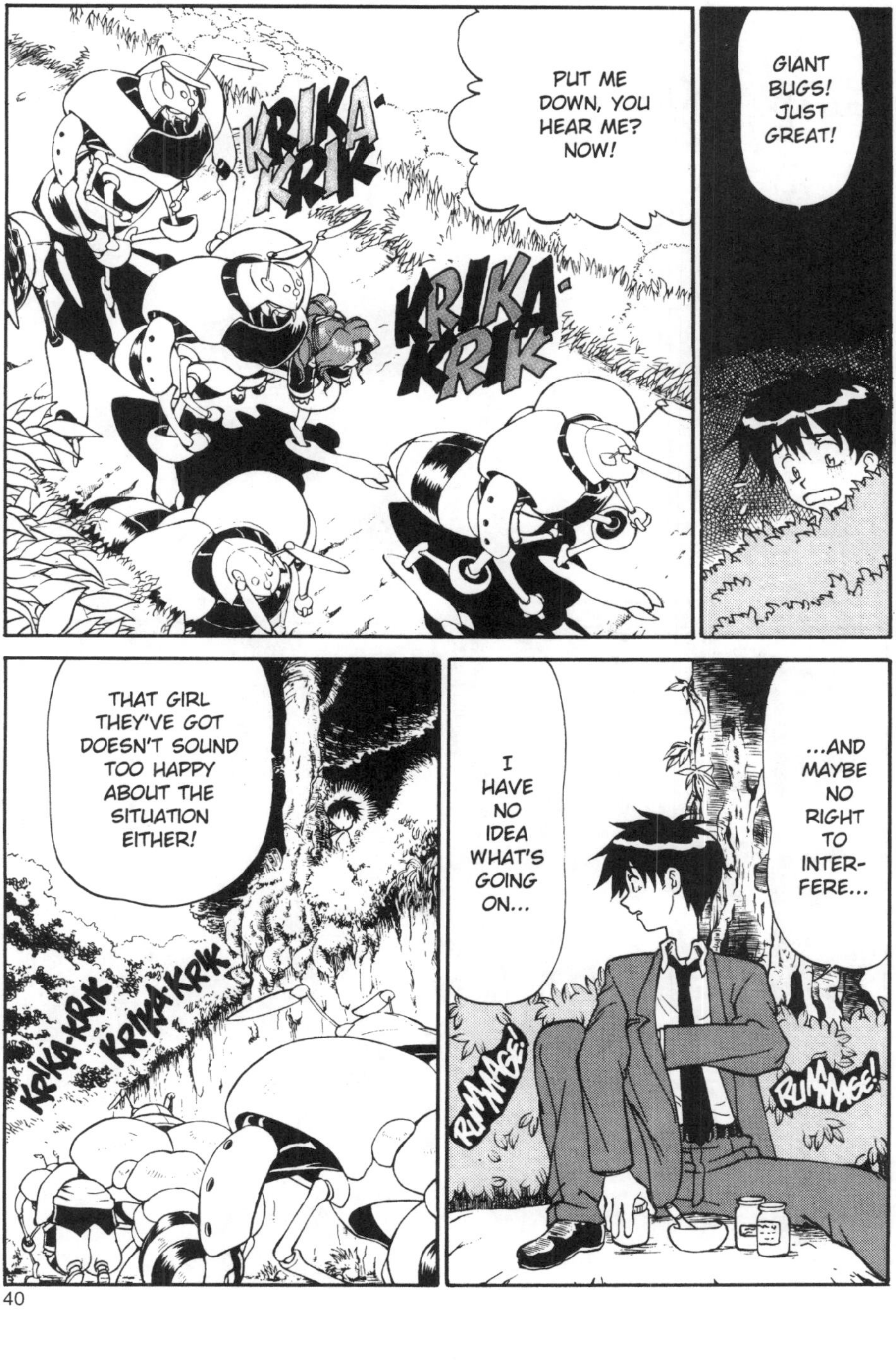

KRIKA-KRIK
PUT ME DOWN, YOU HEAR ME? NOW!
KRIKA-KRIK
GIANT BUGS! JUST GREAT!
THAT GIRL THEY'VE GOT DOESN'T SOUND TOO HAPPY ABOUT THE SITUATION EITHER!
KRIKA-KRIK
KRIKA-KRIK
I HAVE NO IDEA WHAT'S GOING ON...
...AND MAYBE NO RIGHT TO INTER-FERE...
RUMMAGE!
RUMMAGE!

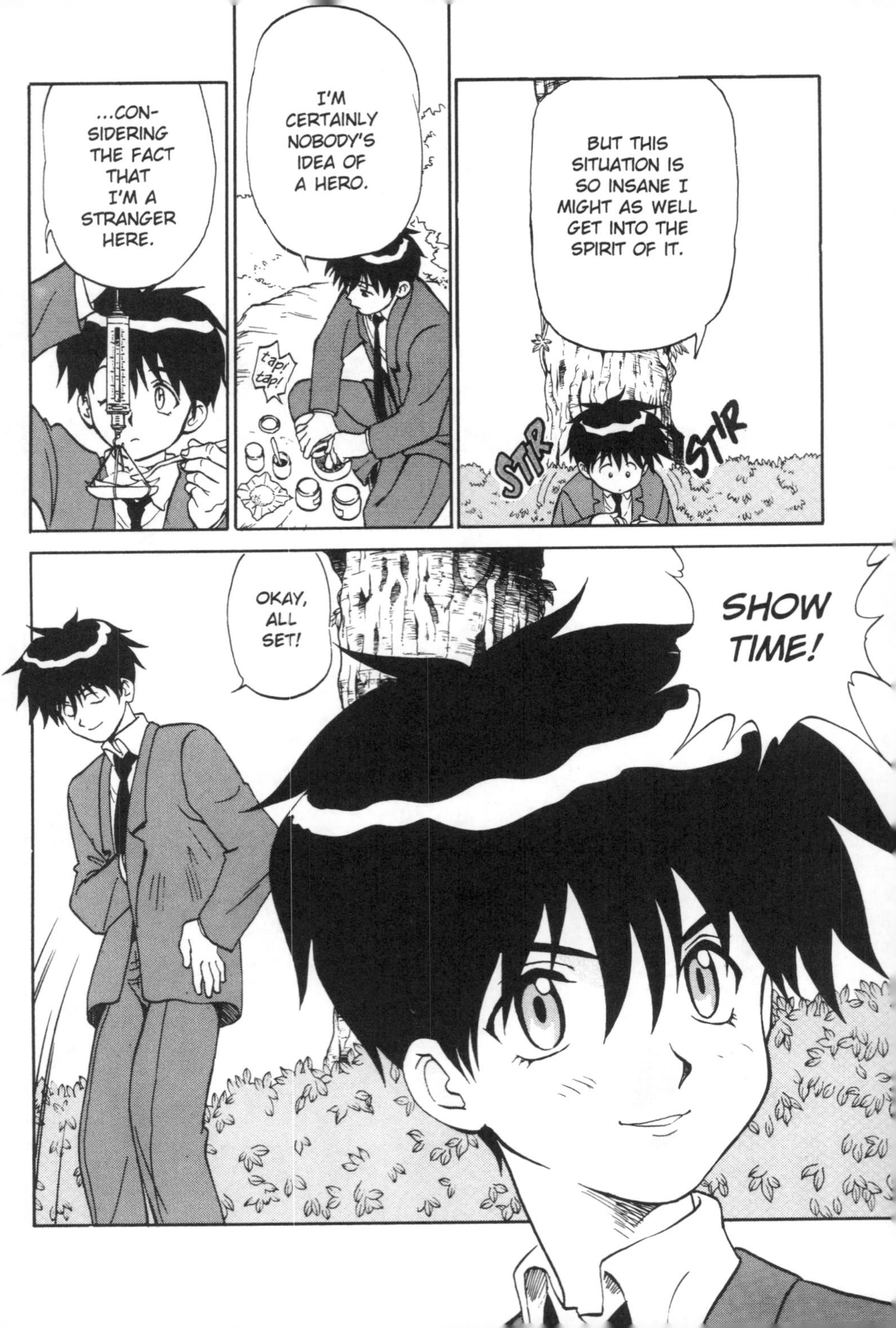
...CON- SIDERING THE FACT THAT I'M A STRANGER HERE.
I'M CERTAINLY NOBODY'S IDEA OF A HERO.
tap! tap!
BUT THIS SITUATION IS SO INSANE I MIGHT AS WELL GET INTO THE SPIRIT OF IT.
STIR STIR
OKAY, ALL SET!
SHOW TIME!

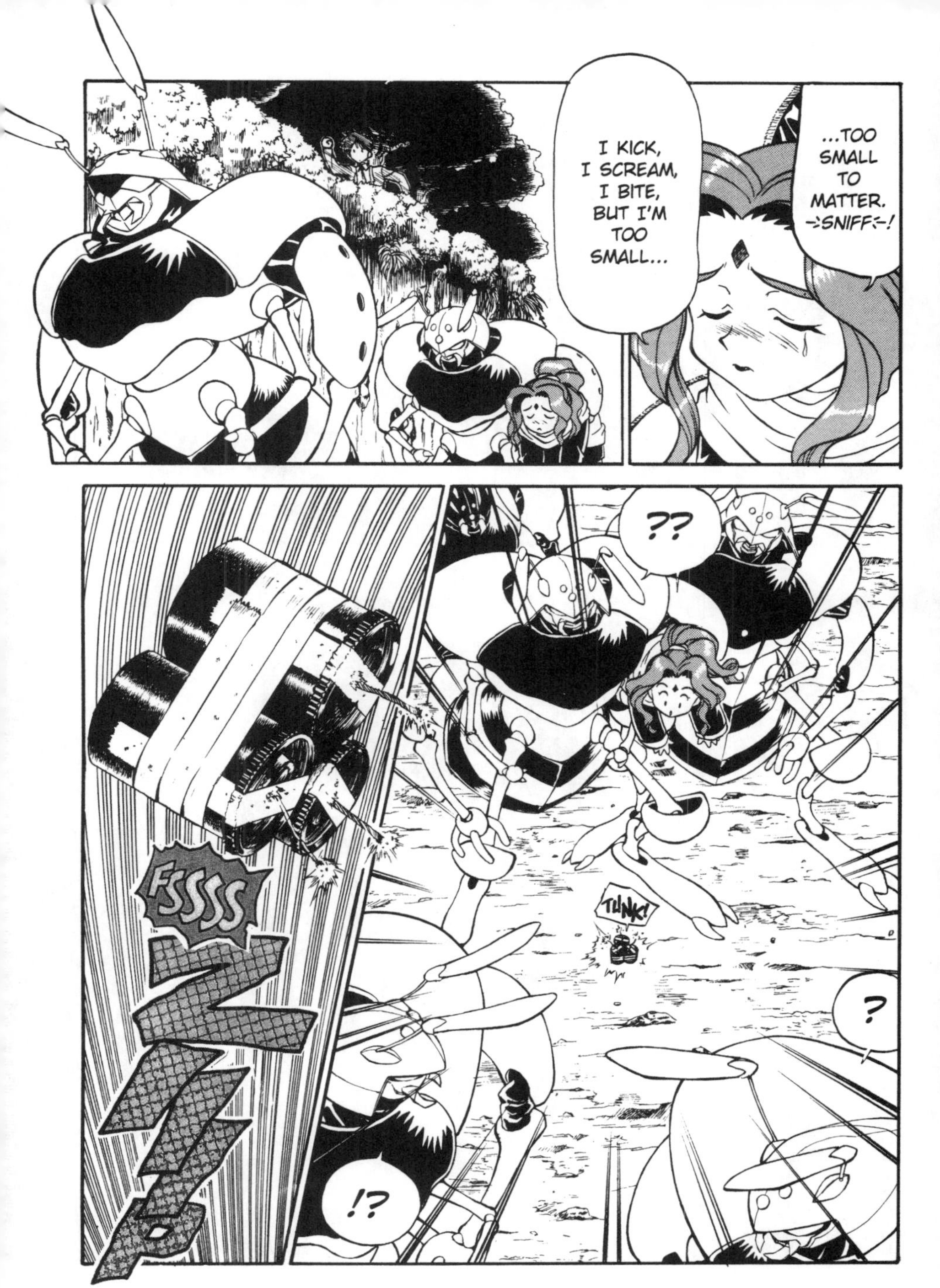
I KICK, I SCREAM, I BITE, BUT I'M TOO SMALL...
...TOO SMALL TO MATTER. -SNIFF-!
FSSSS
??
TUNK!
?
!?

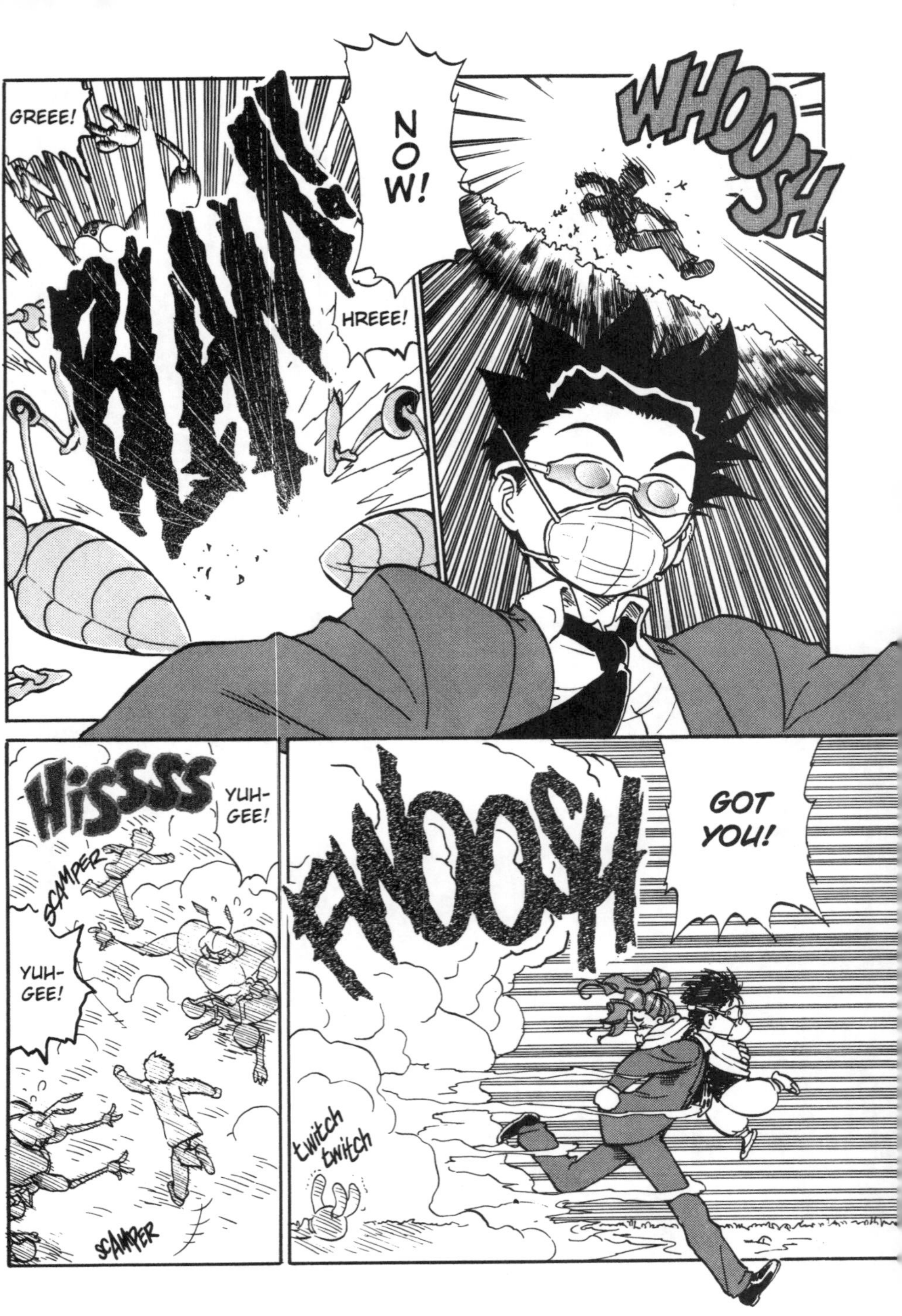
GREEE!
BLAM!
NOW!
HREEE!
WHOOSH
HISSSS
YUH-GEE!
SCAMPER
YUH-GEE!
SCAMPER
FWOOSH
GOT YOU!
twitch twitch

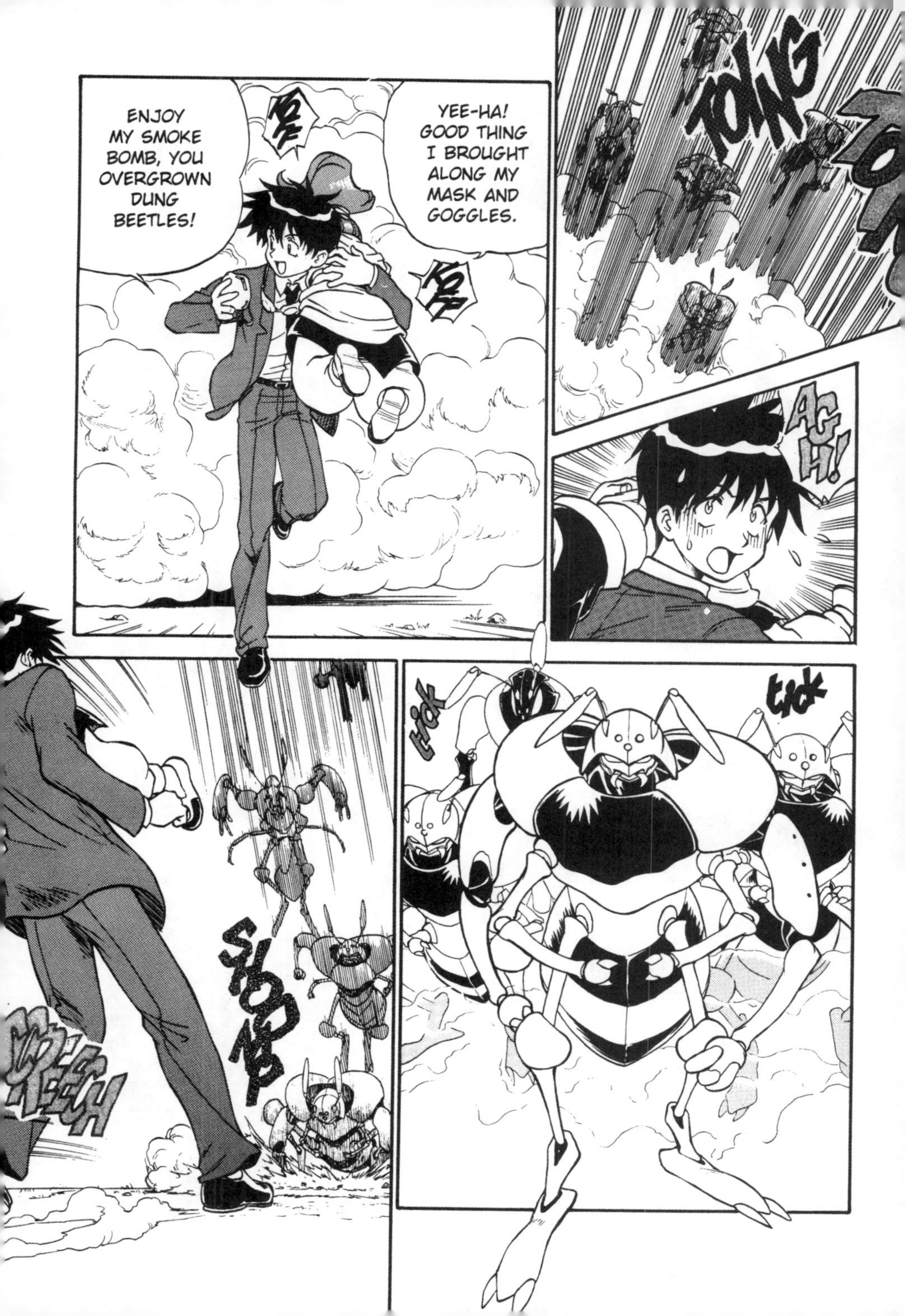
ENJOY MY SMOKE BOMB, YOU OVERGROWN DUNG BEETLES!
YEE-HA! GOOD THING I BROUGHT ALONG MY MASK AND GOGGLES.
TONG
AGH!
tick
tick

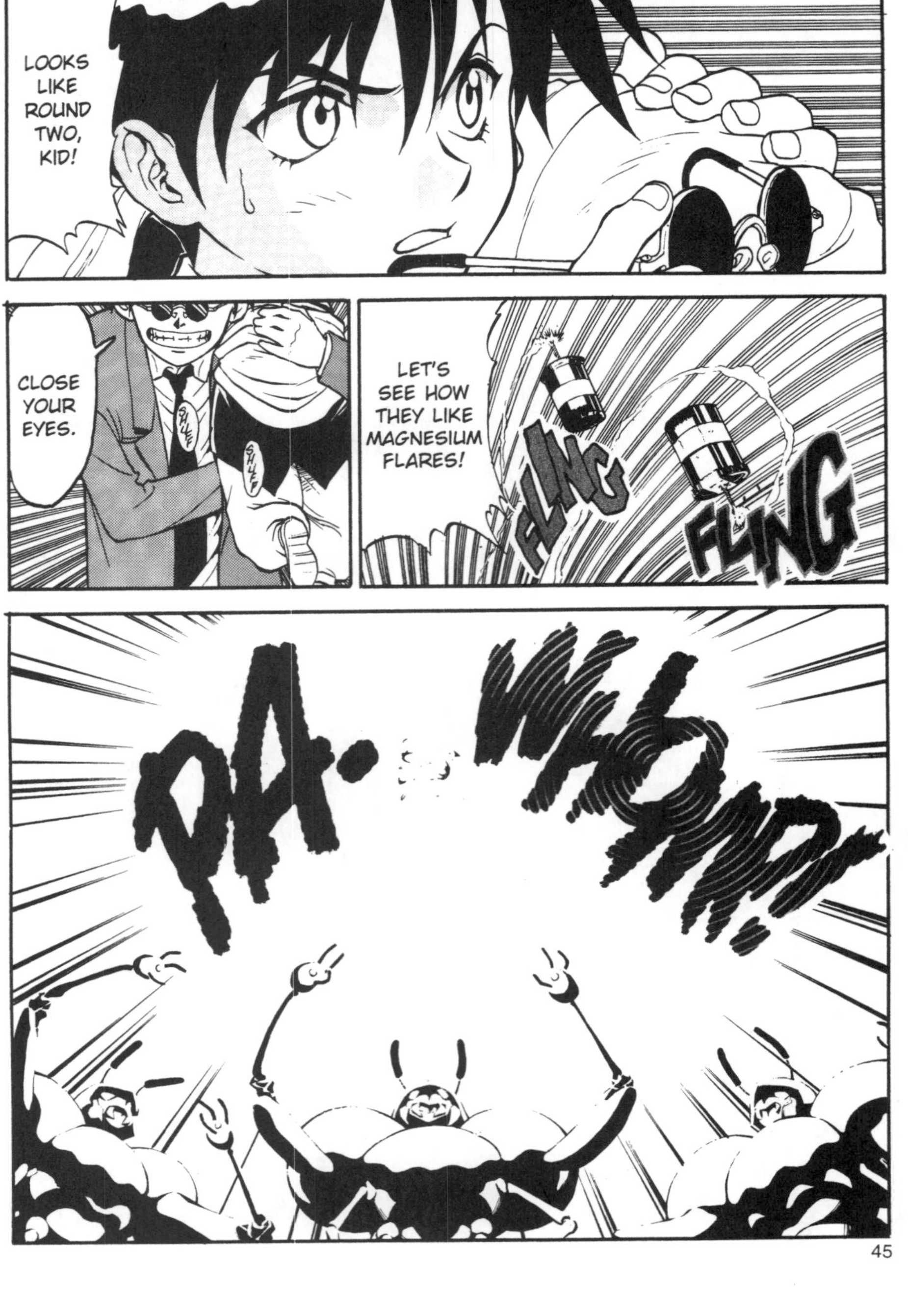
LOOKS LIKE ROUND TWO, KID!
CLOSE YOUR EYES.
SHUFF
SHUFF
LET'S SEE HOW THEY LIKE MAGNESIUM FLARES!
FLING
FLING
BA-WHOOM!!

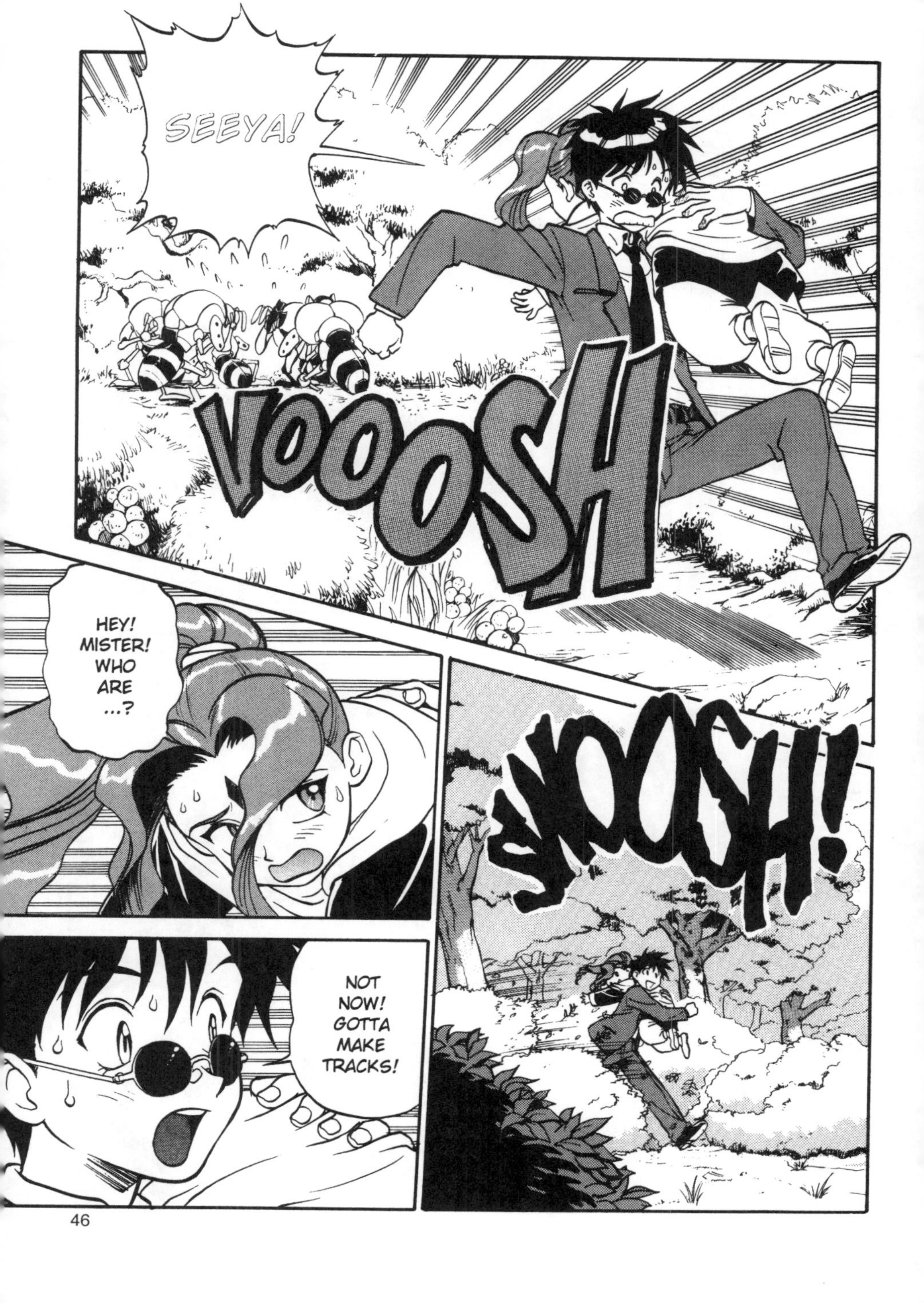
SEEYA!
VOOOSH
HEY! MISTER! WHO ARE ...?
WOOOSH!
NOT NOW! GOTTA MAKE TRACKS!

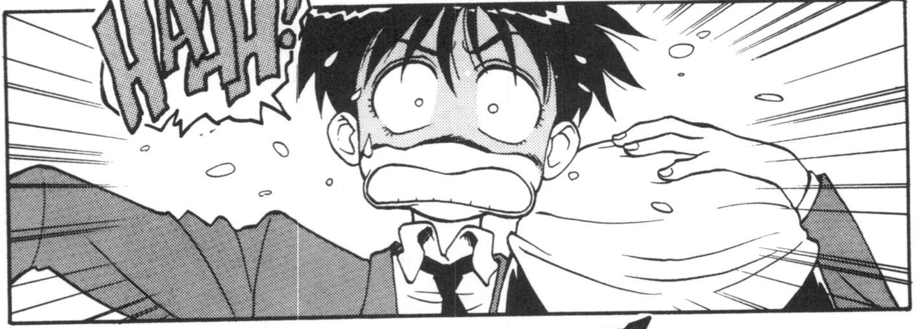
HAAH!

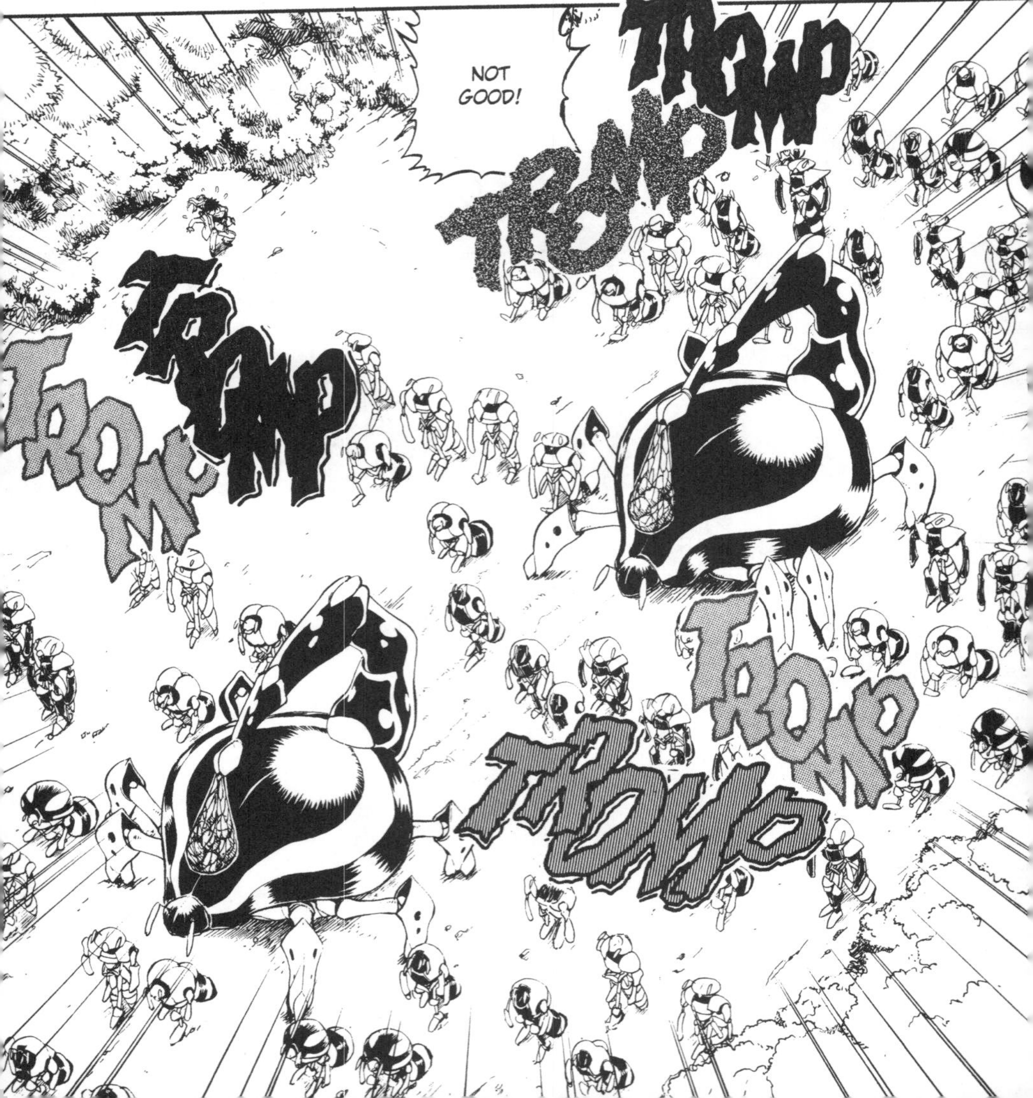
NOT GOOD!
TROMP
TROMP
TROMP
TROMP
TROMP
TROMP

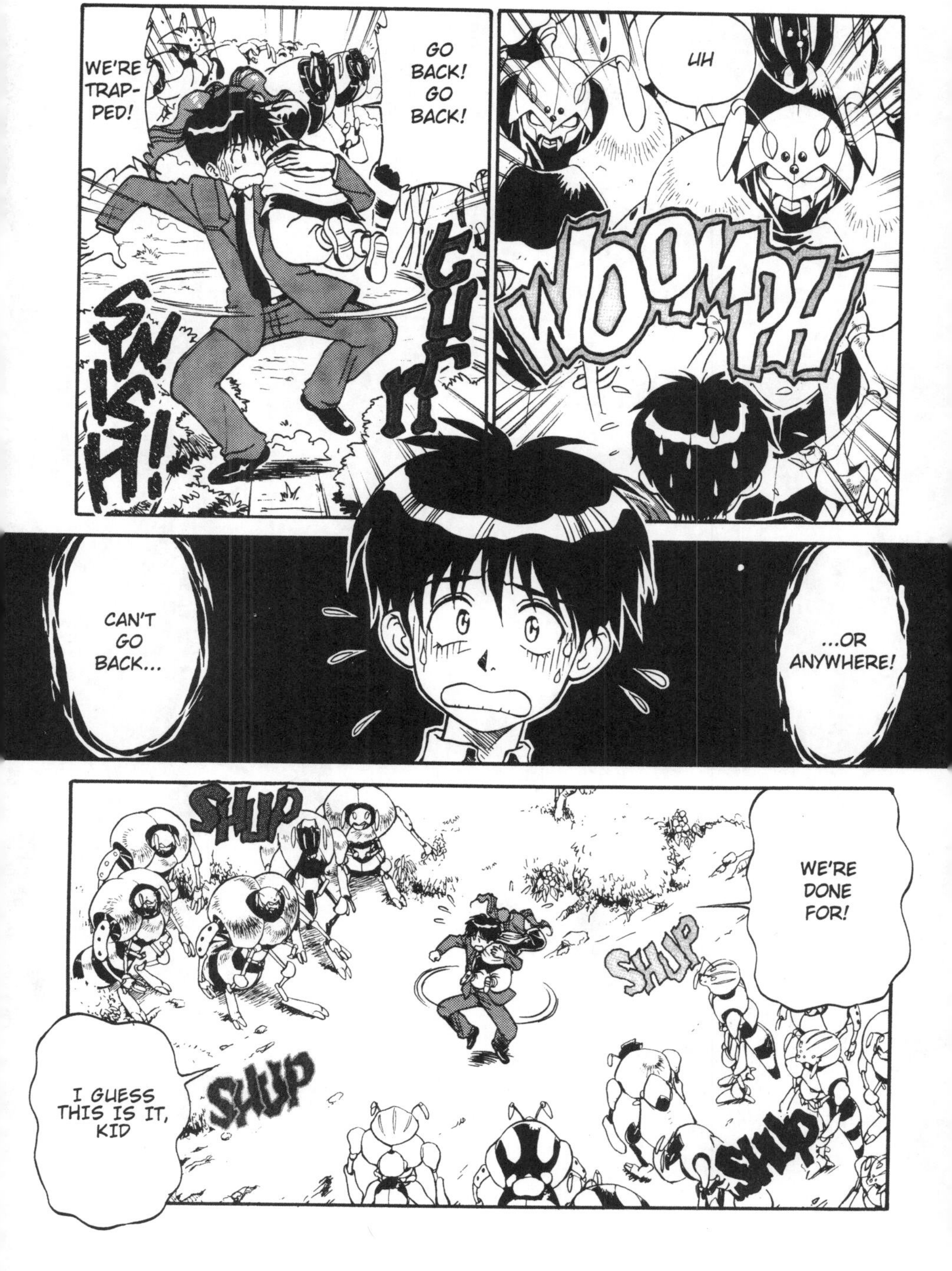

WE'RE TRAP-PED!
GO BACK! GO BACK!
SWISH!
UH
WOOMPH
CAN'T GO BACK...
...OR ANYWHERE!
SHUP
WE'RE DONE FOR!
SHUP
I GUESS THIS IS IT, KID
SHUP
SHUP

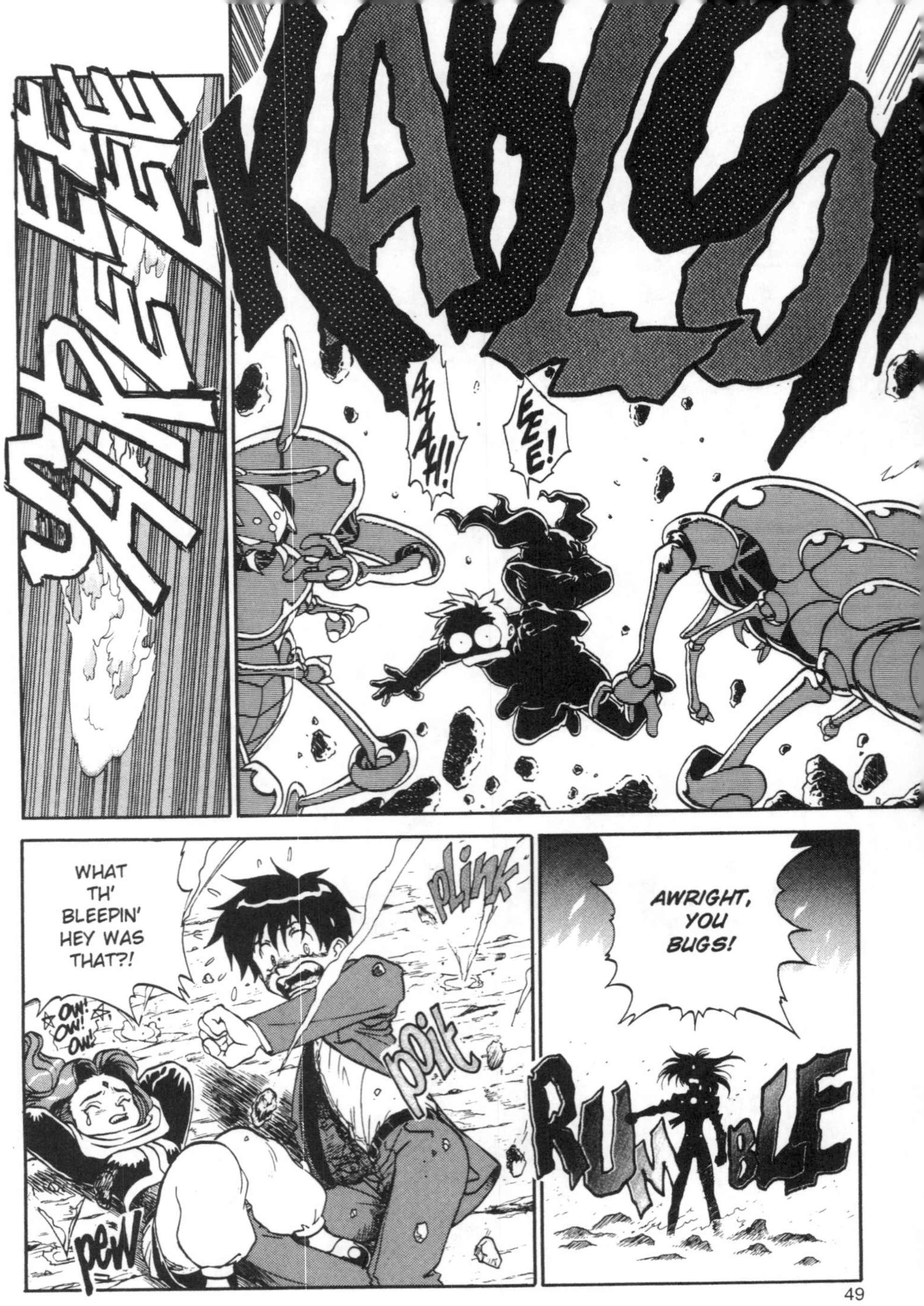
EEEE!
WHAT TH' BLEEPIN' HEY WAS THAT?!
plink
OW! OW! OW!
poit
peiw
AWRIGHT, YOU BUGS!
RUMBLE

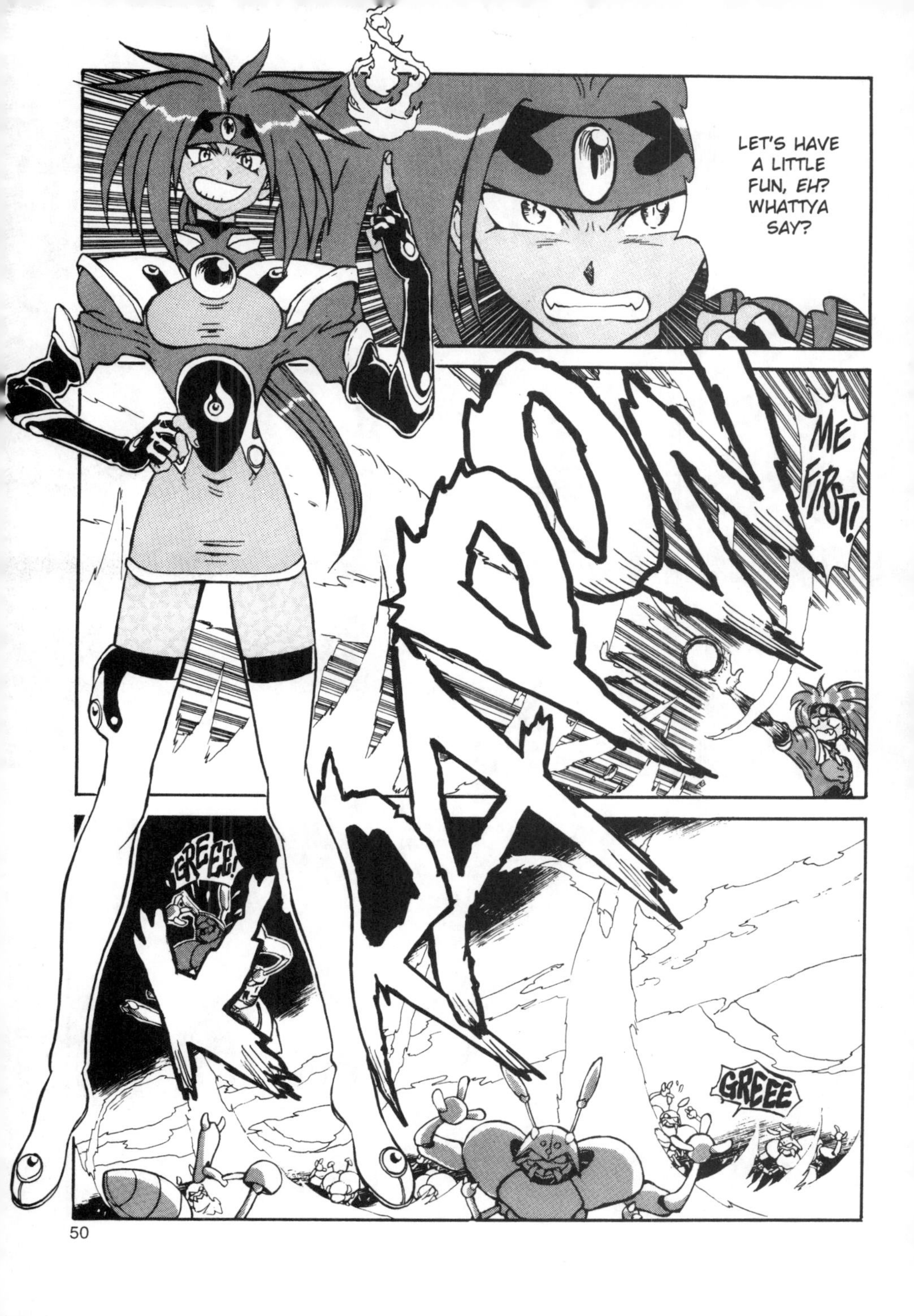
LET'S HAVE A LITTLE FUN, EH? WHATTYA SAY?
ME FIRST!
BOOM
KRAK
GREEE!
GREEE

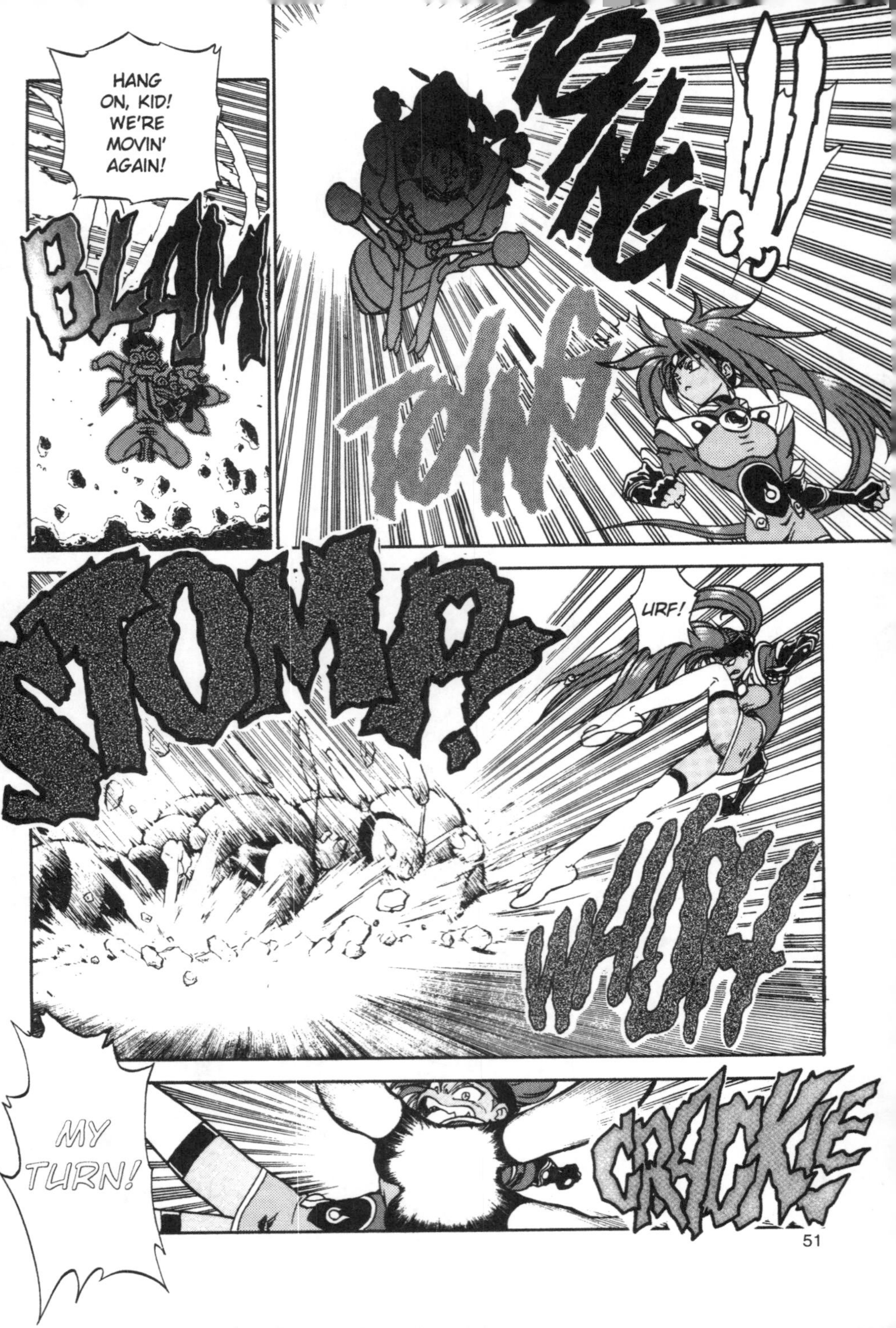
HANG ON, KID! WE'RE MOVIN' AGAIN!
BLAM
TOING
TOING
STOMP
URF!
WHUCK
MY TURN!
CRACKLE

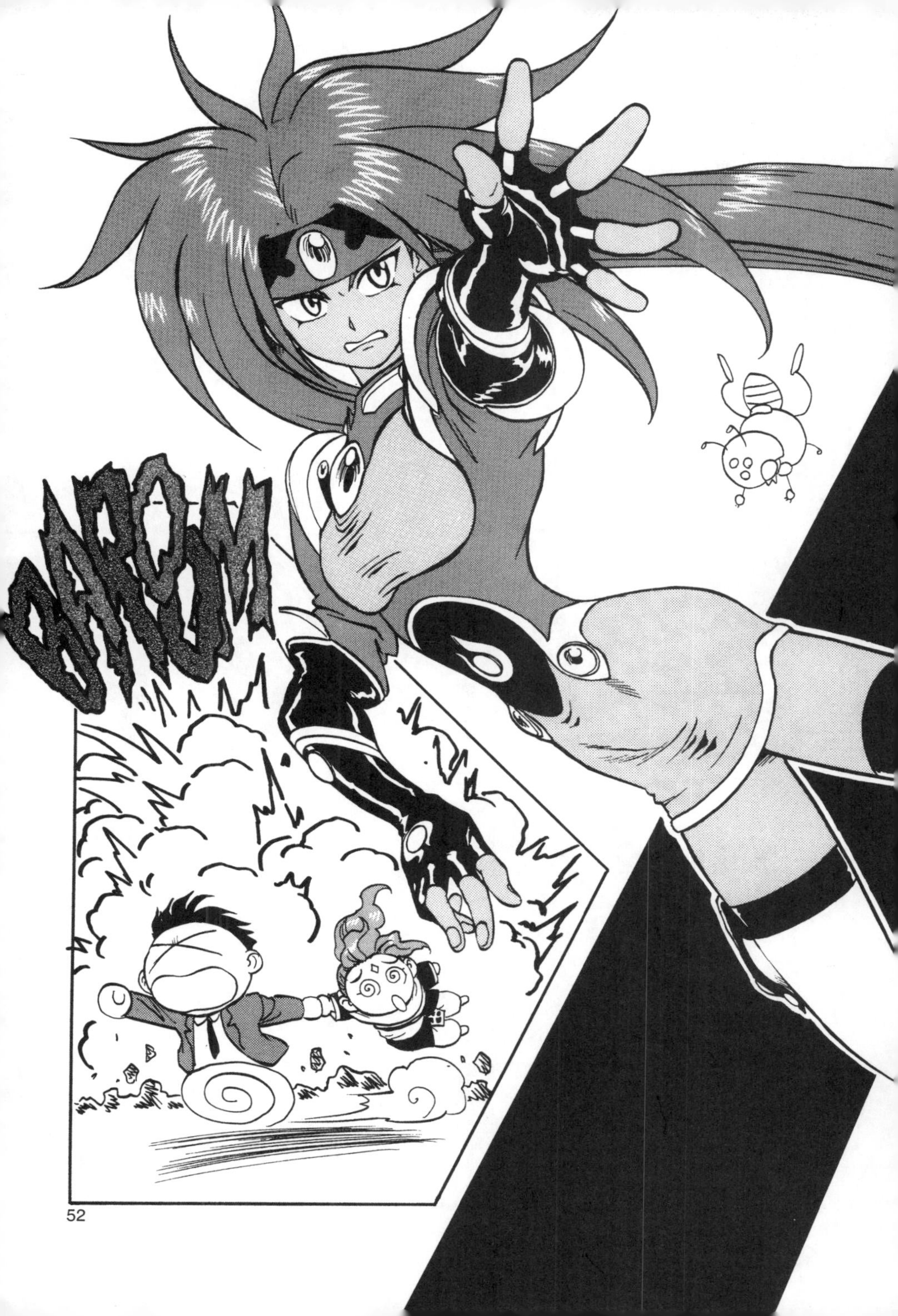
CAROOM

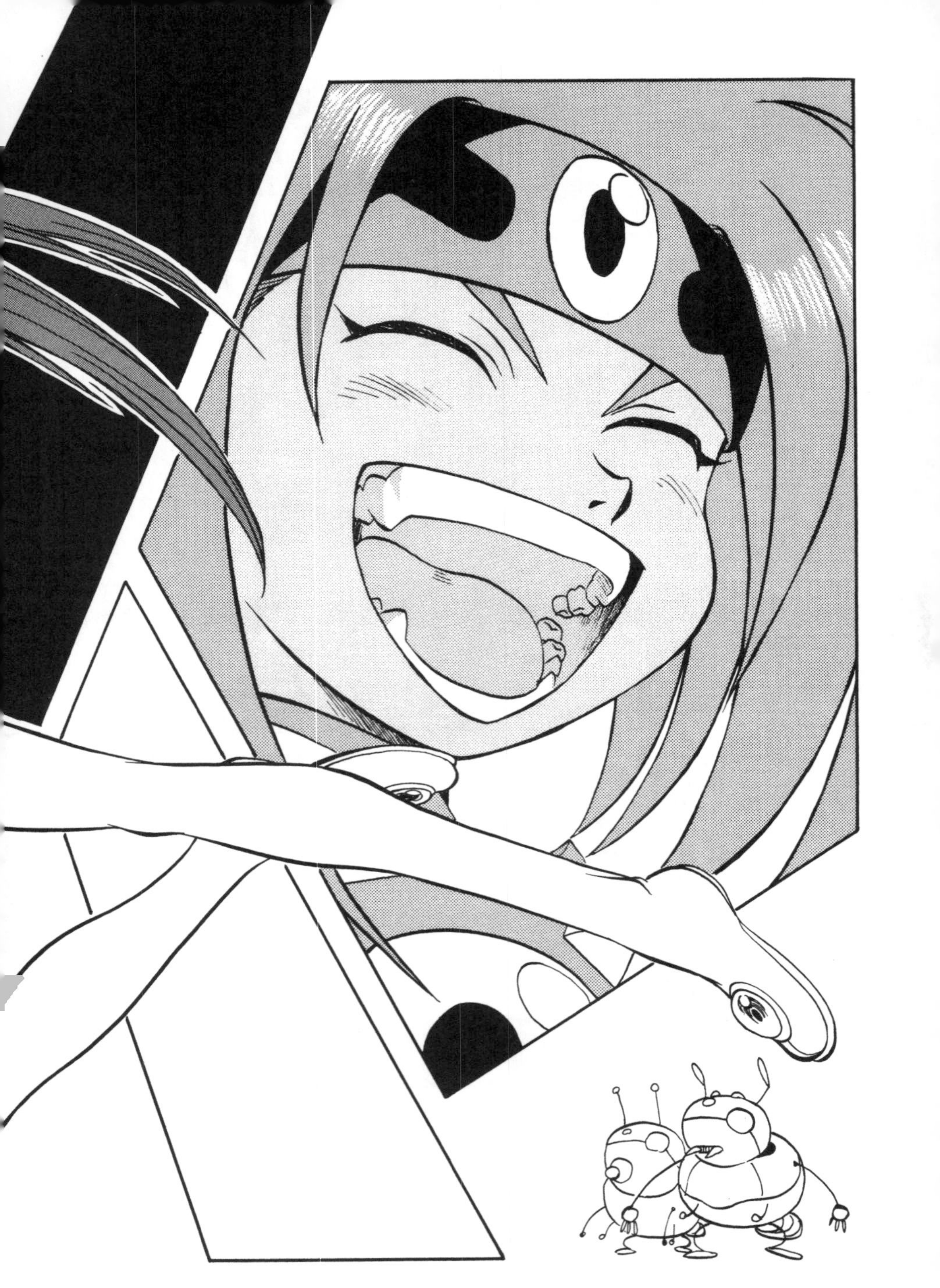

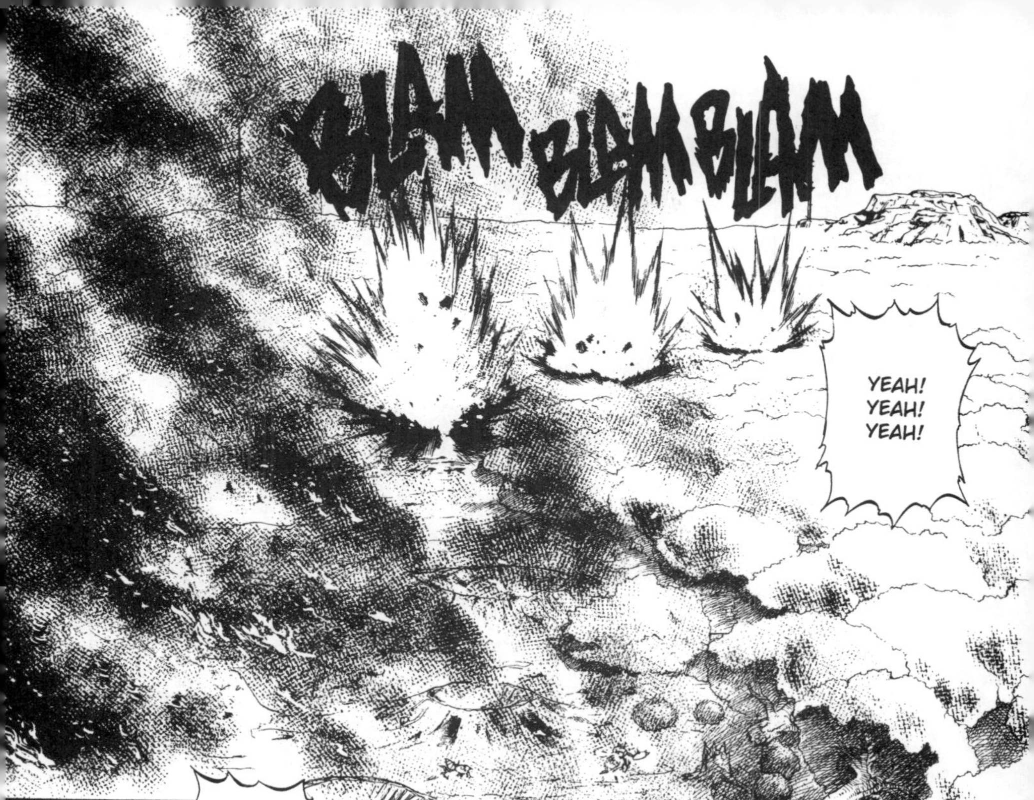
BLAM BLAM BLAM
YEAH! YEAH! YEAH!

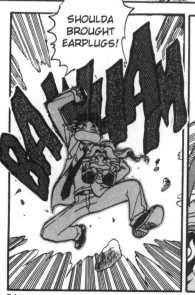

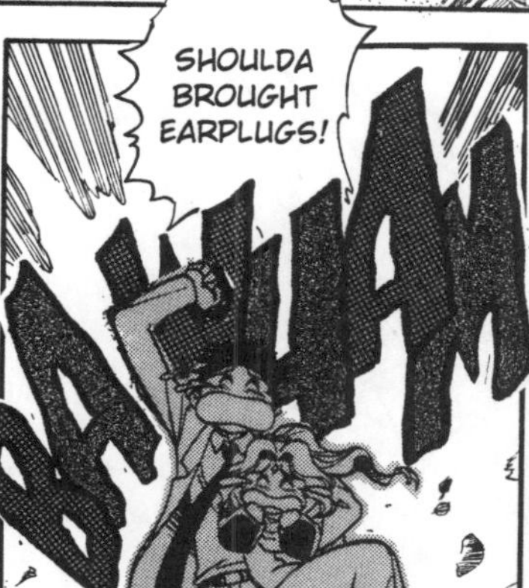
SHOULDA BROUGHT EARPLUGS!

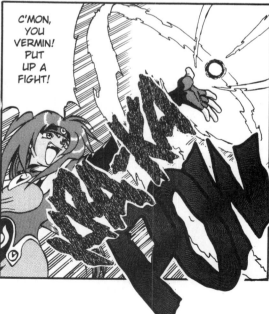

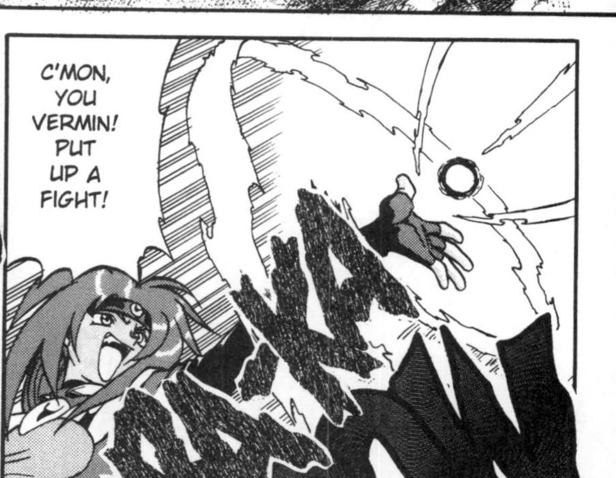
C'MON, YOU VERMIN! PUT UP A FIGHT!

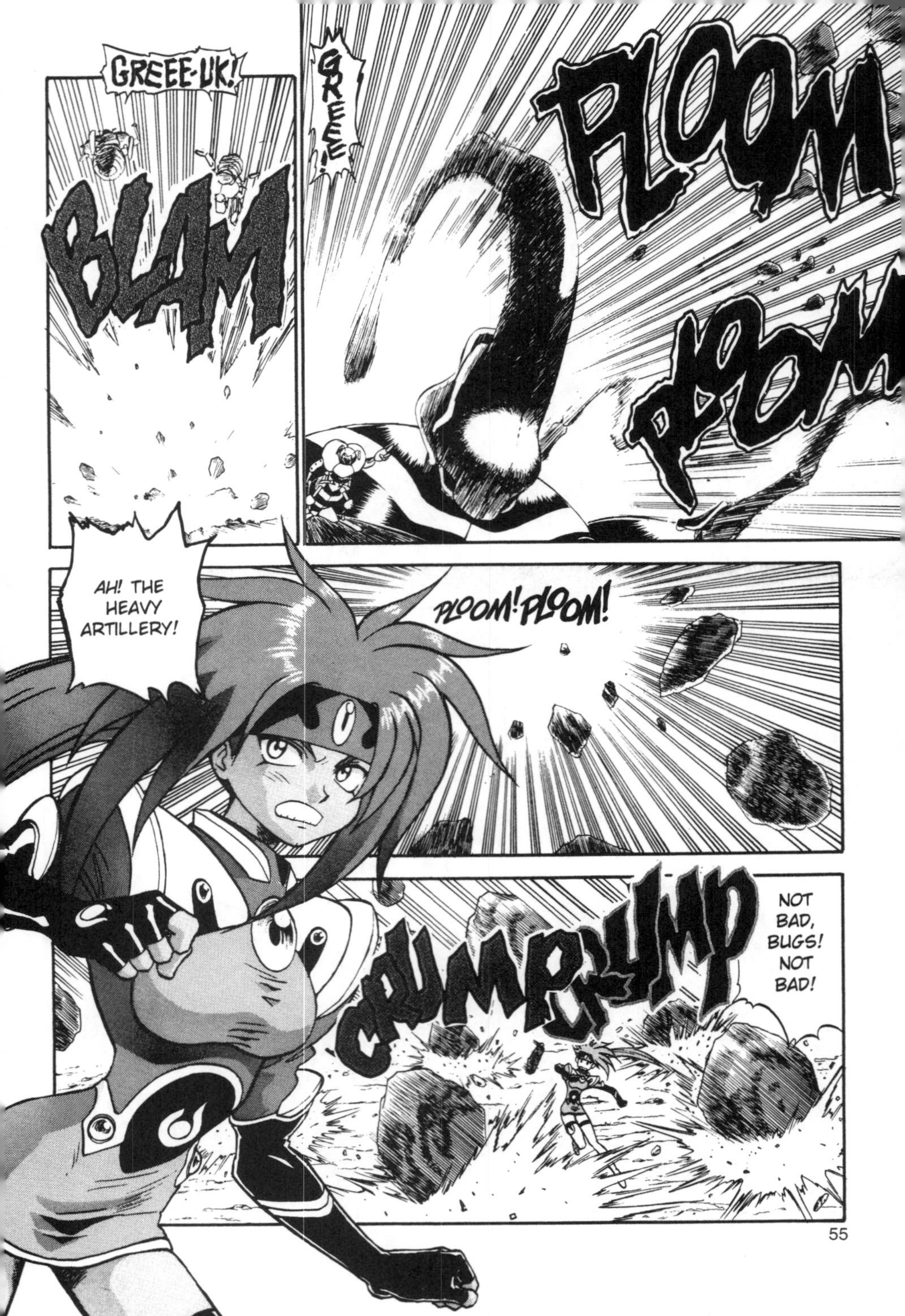
GREEE-UK!
BLAM
GREEE!
PLOOM
PLOOM
AH! THE HEAVY ARTILLERY!
PLOOM! PLOOM!
CRUMP CRUMP
NOT BAD, BUGS! NOT BAD!

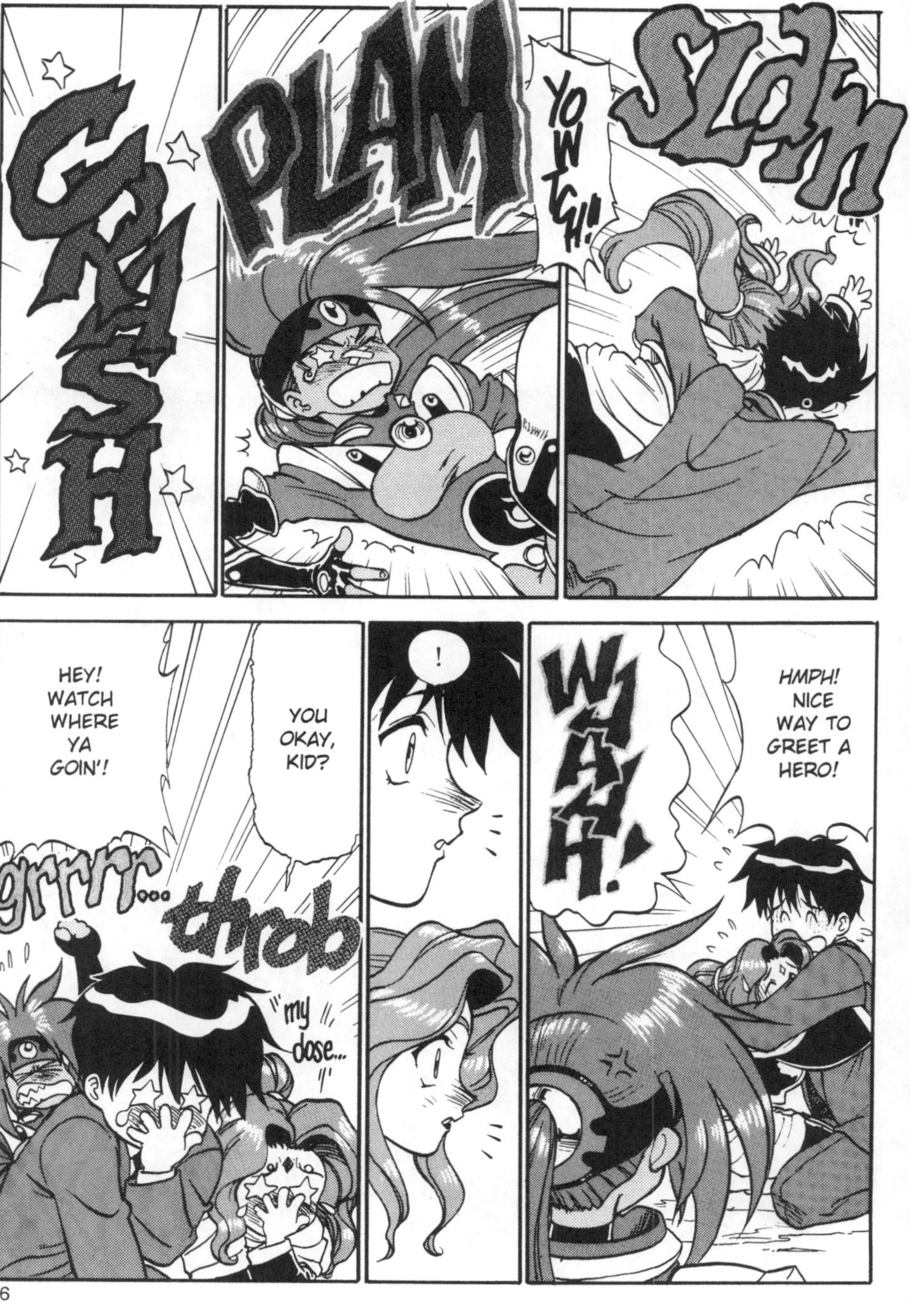
CRASH
PLAM
YOWTCH!!
SLAM
HEY! WATCH WHERE YA GOIN'!
YOU OKAY, KID?
grrrr...
throb
my dose...
!
WHAAH!
HMPH! NICE WAY TO GREET A HERO!

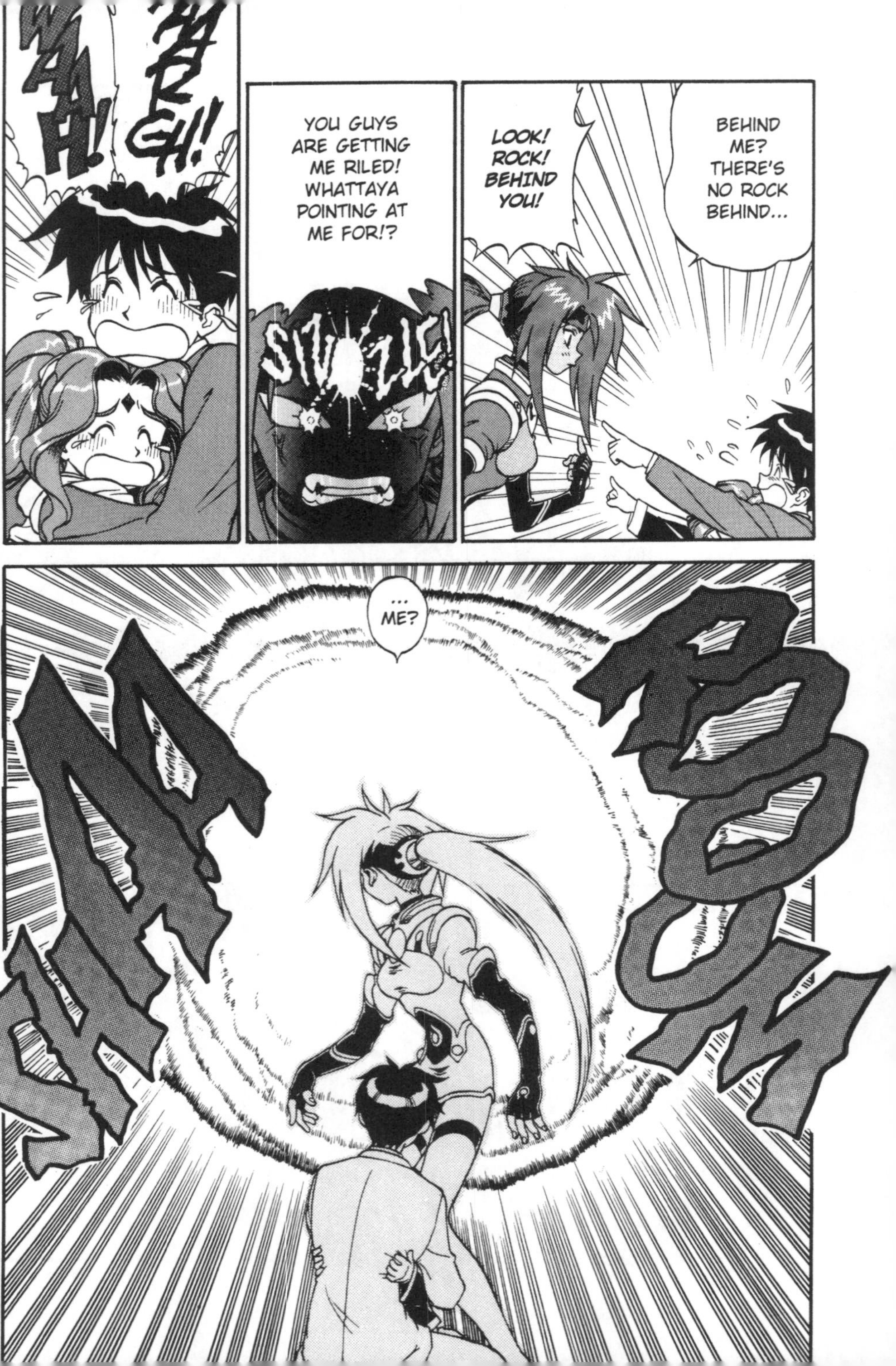
WAAH!
WAARGH!
YOU GUYS ARE GETTING ME RILED! WHATTAYA POINTING AT ME FOR!?
SIZZLE!
LOOK! ROCK! BEHIND YOU!
BEHIND ME? THERE'S NO ROCK BEHIND...
...ME?
SHA
BOOM

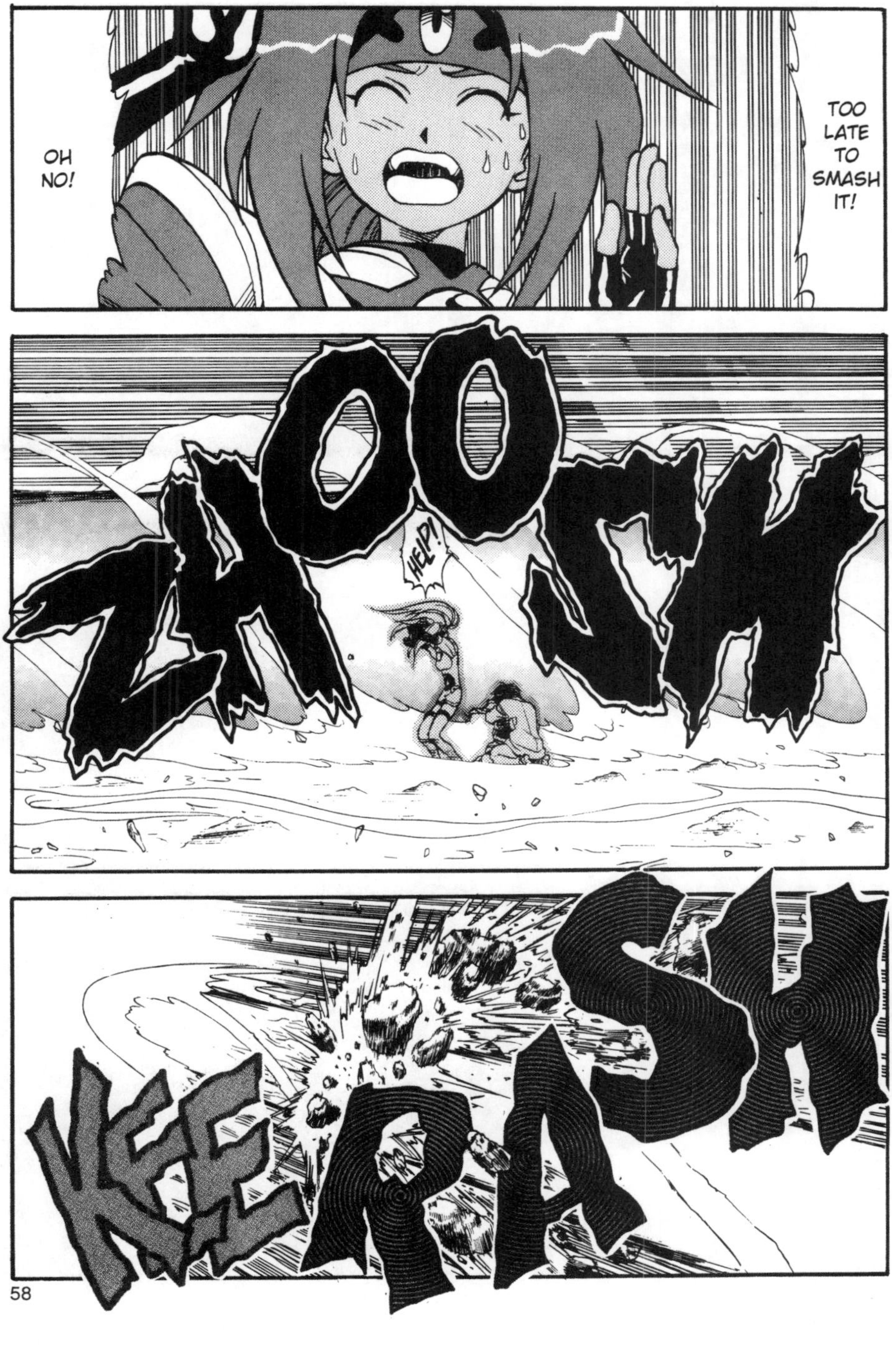
OH NO!
TOO LATE TO SMASH IT!
HELP!

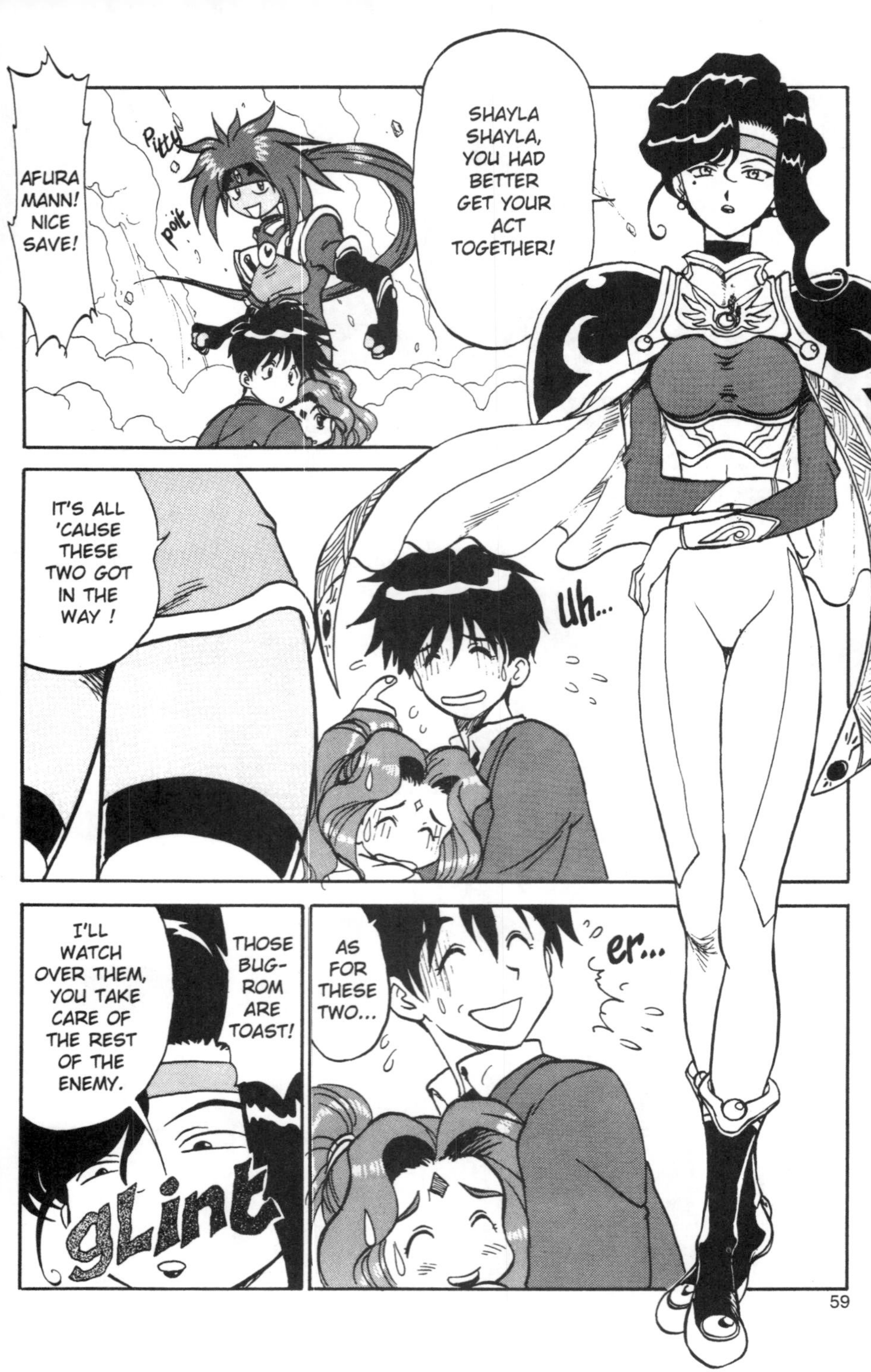
AFURA MANN! NICE SAVE!
Pitty
poit
SHAYLA SHAYLA, YOU HAD BETTER GET YOUR ACT TOGETHER!
IT'S ALL 'CAUSE THESE TWO GOT IN THE WAY !
uh...
I'LL WATCH OVER THEM, YOU TAKE CARE OF THE REST OF THE ENEMY.
gLint
THOSE BUG-ROM ARE TOAST!
AS FOR THESE TWO...
er...

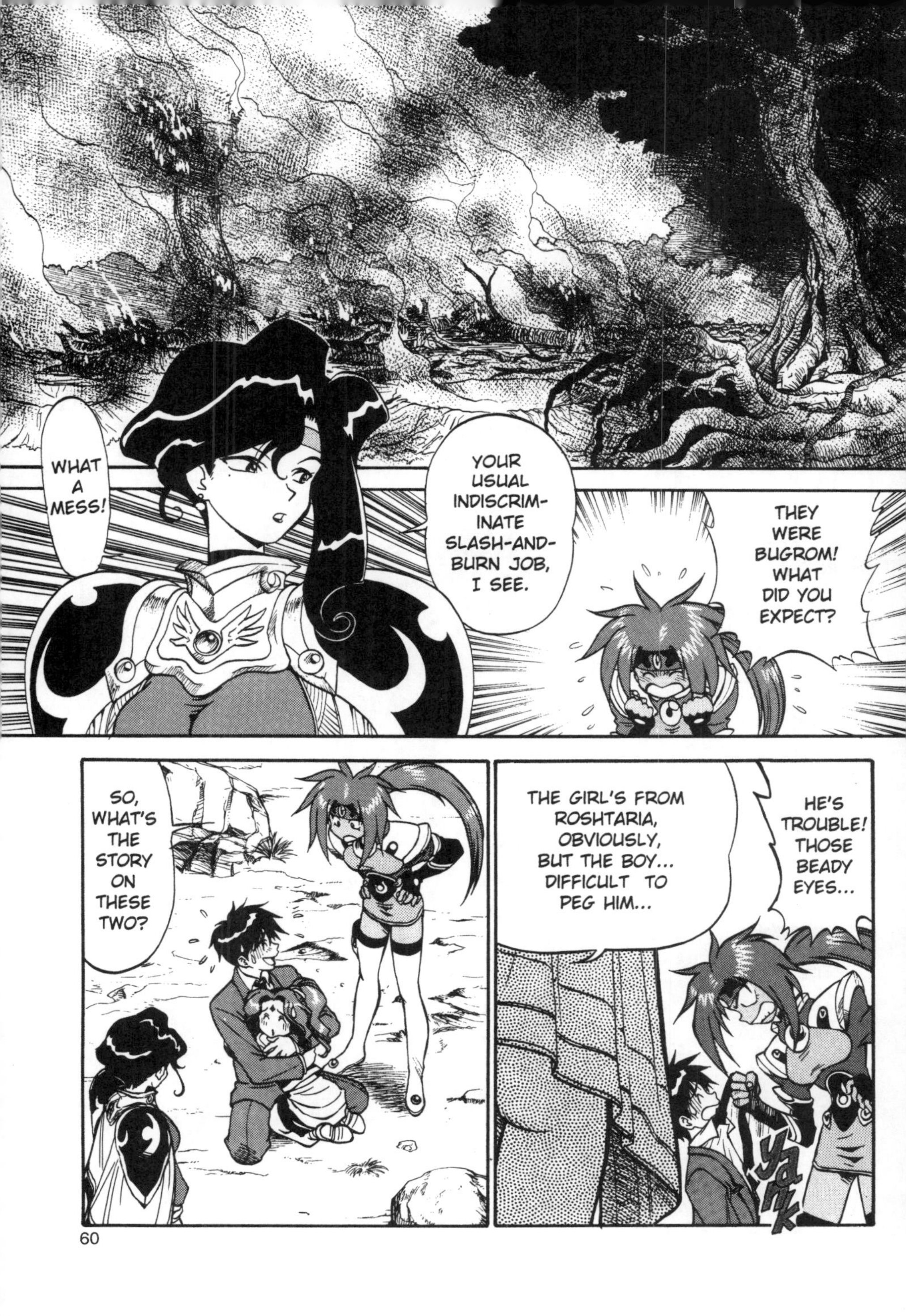
WHAT A MESS!
YOUR USUAL INDISCRIM-INATE SLASH-AND-BURN JOB, I SEE.
THEY WERE BUGROM! WHAT DID YOU EXPECT?
SO, WHAT'S THE STORY ON THESE TWO?
THE GIRL'S FROM ROSHTARIA, OBVIOUSLY, BUT THE BOY... DIFFICULT TO PEG HIM...
HE'S TROUBLE! THOSE BEADY EYES...
yank

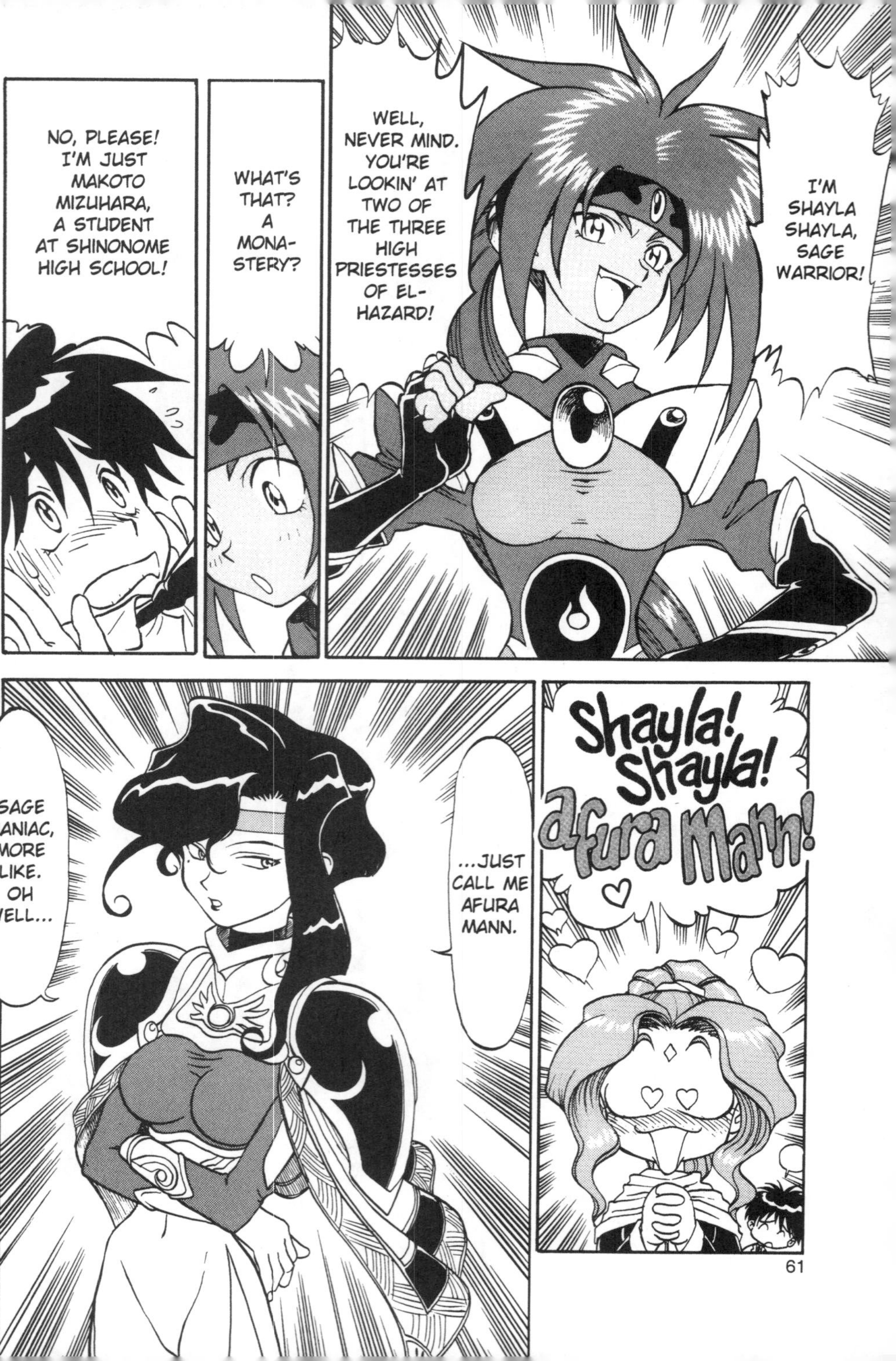
NO, PLEASE! I'M JUST MAKOTO MIZUHARA, A STUDENT AT SHINONOME HIGH SCHOOL!
WHAT'S THAT? A MONA-STERY?
WELL, NEVER MIND. YOU'RE LOOKIN' AT TWO OF THE THREE HIGH PRIESTESSES OF EL-HAZARD!
I'M SHAYLA SHAYLA, SAGE WARRIOR!
SAGE MANIAC, MORE LIKE. OH WELL...
...JUST CALL ME AFURA MANN.
Shayla! Shayla! afura Mann!

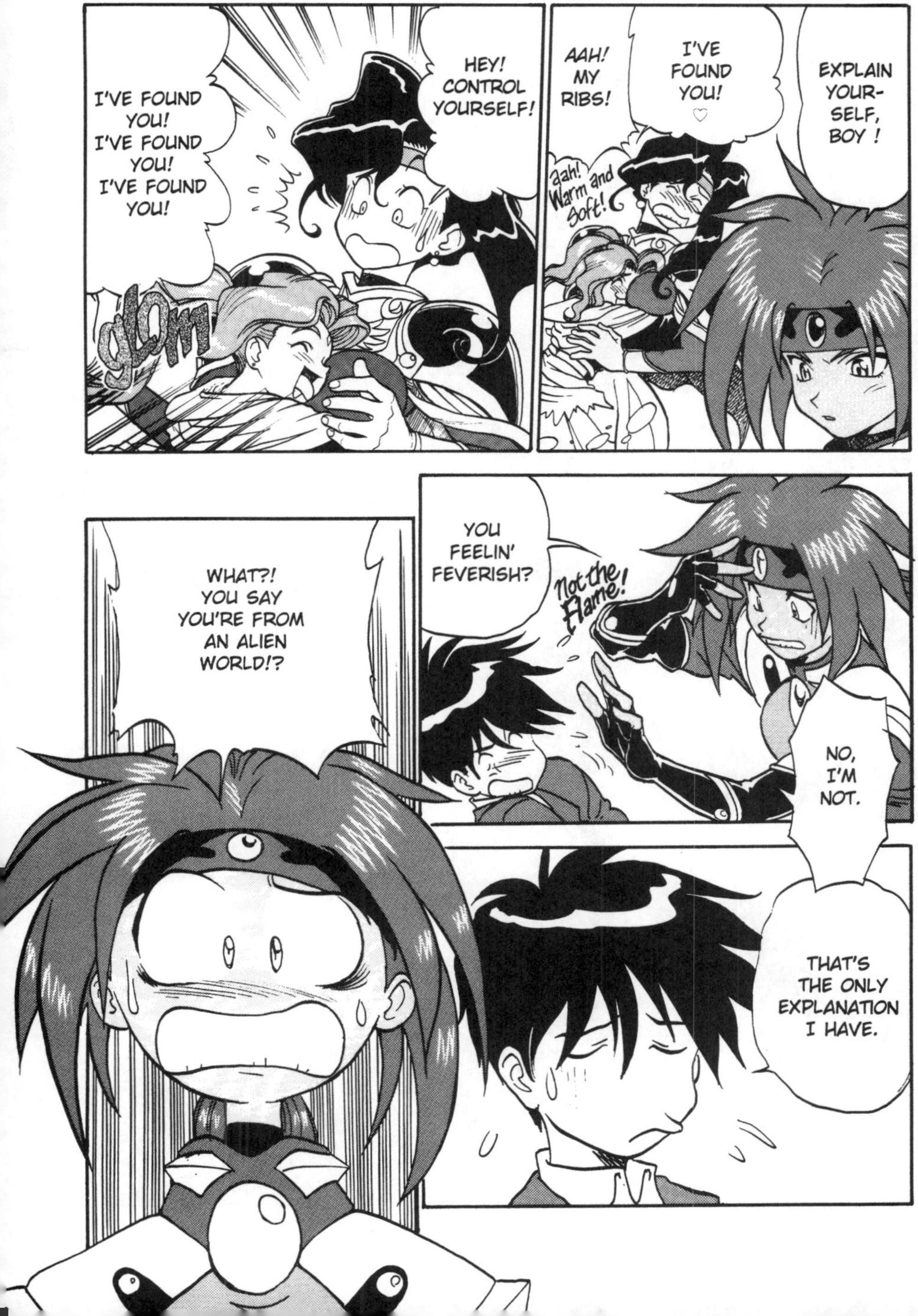
I'VE FOUND YOU! I'VE FOUND YOU! I'VE FOUND YOU!
glom
HEY! CONTROL YOURSELF!
AAH! MY RIBS!
Aah! Warm and Soft!
I'VE FOUND YOU! ♡
EXPLAIN YOUR-SELF, BOY !
WHAT?! YOU SAY YOU'RE FROM AN ALIEN WORLD!?
YOU FEELIN' FEVERISH?
Not the Flame!
NO, I'M NOT.
THAT'S THE ONLY EXPLANATION I HAVE.

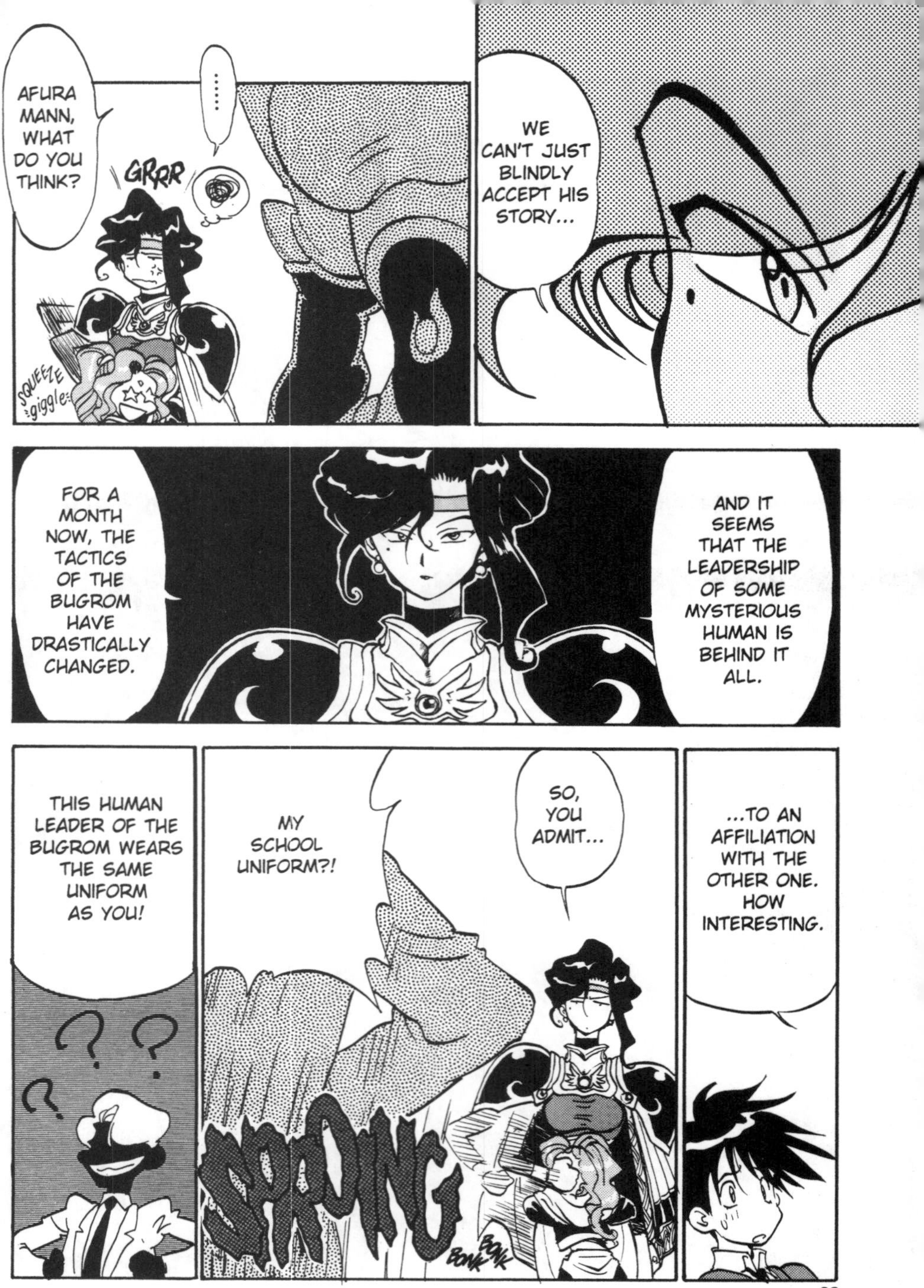
AFURA MANN, WHAT DO YOU THINK?
......
GRRR
SQUEEZE
giggle
WE CAN'T JUST BLINDLY ACCEPT HIS STORY...
FOR A MONTH NOW, THE TACTICS OF THE BUGROM HAVE DRASTICALLY CHANGED.
AND IT SEEMS THAT THE LEADERSHIP OF SOME MYSTERIOUS HUMAN IS BEHIND IT ALL.
THIS HUMAN LEADER OF THE BUGROM WEARS THE SAME UNIFORM AS YOU!
? ? ?
MY SCHOOL UNIFORM?!
SO, YOU ADMIT...
SPROING
BONK BONK
...TO AN AFFILIATION WITH THE OTHER ONE. HOW INTERESTING.

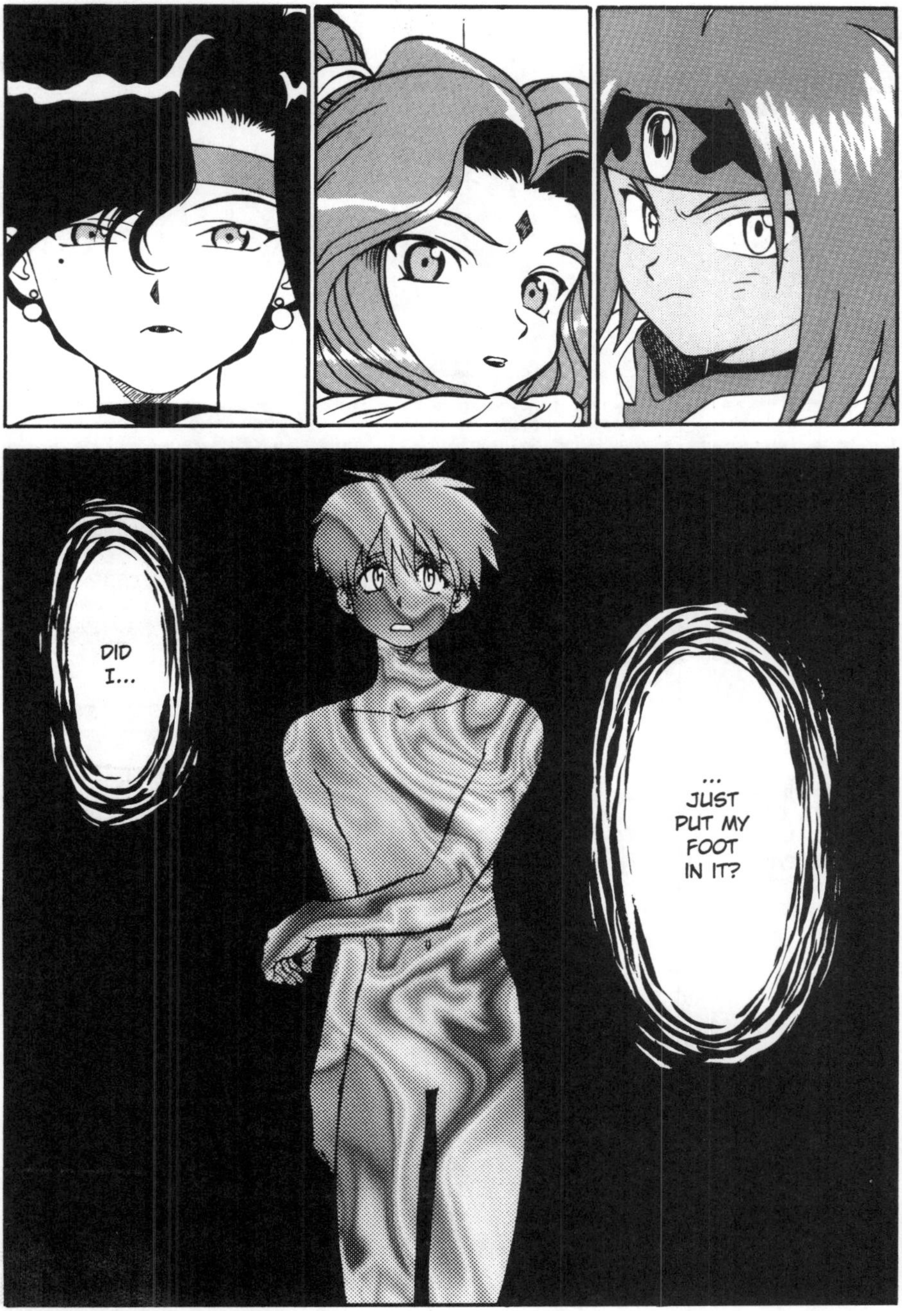
DID I...
... JUST PUT MY FOOT IN IT?

END OF EPISODE 2

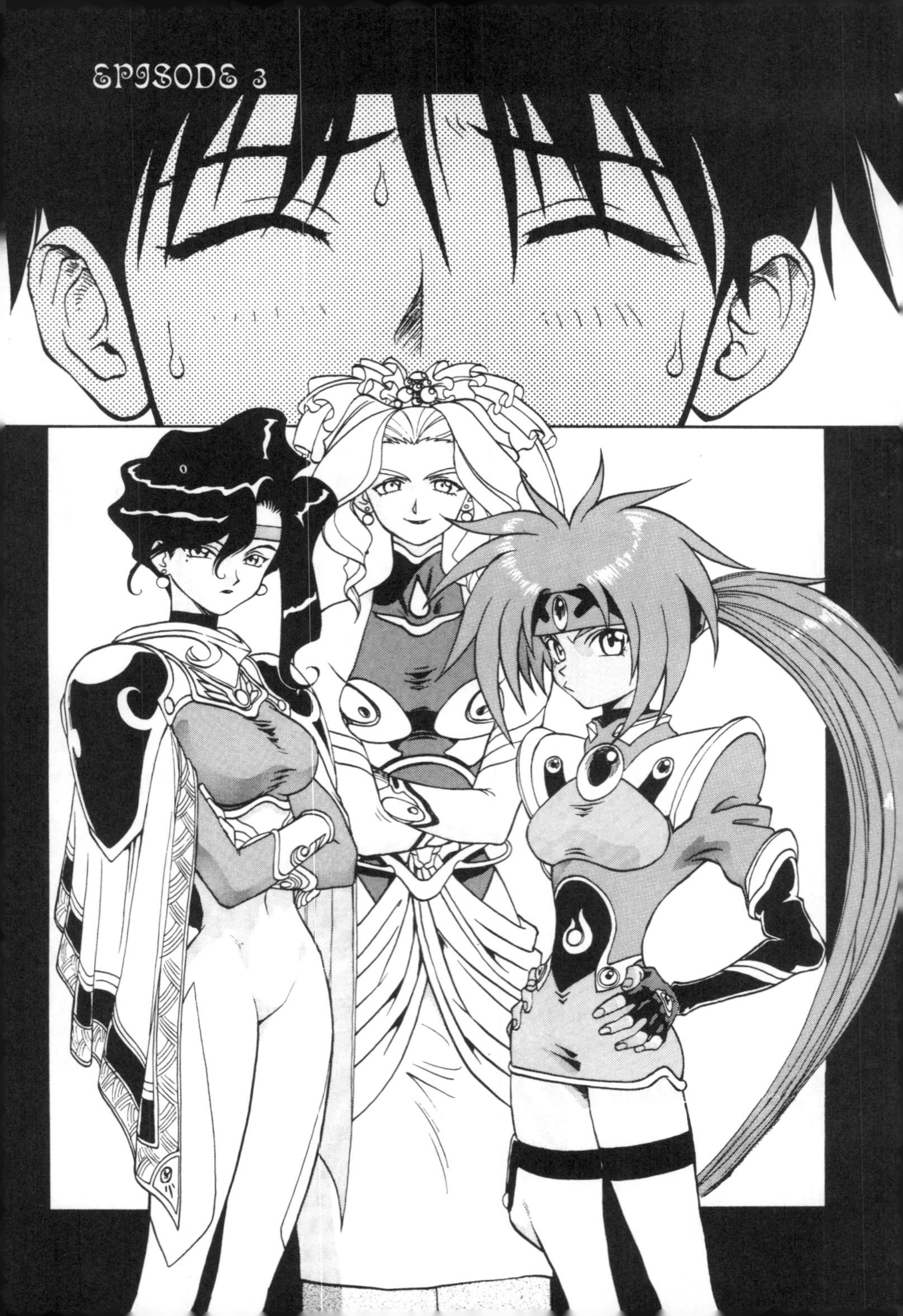
EPISODE 3

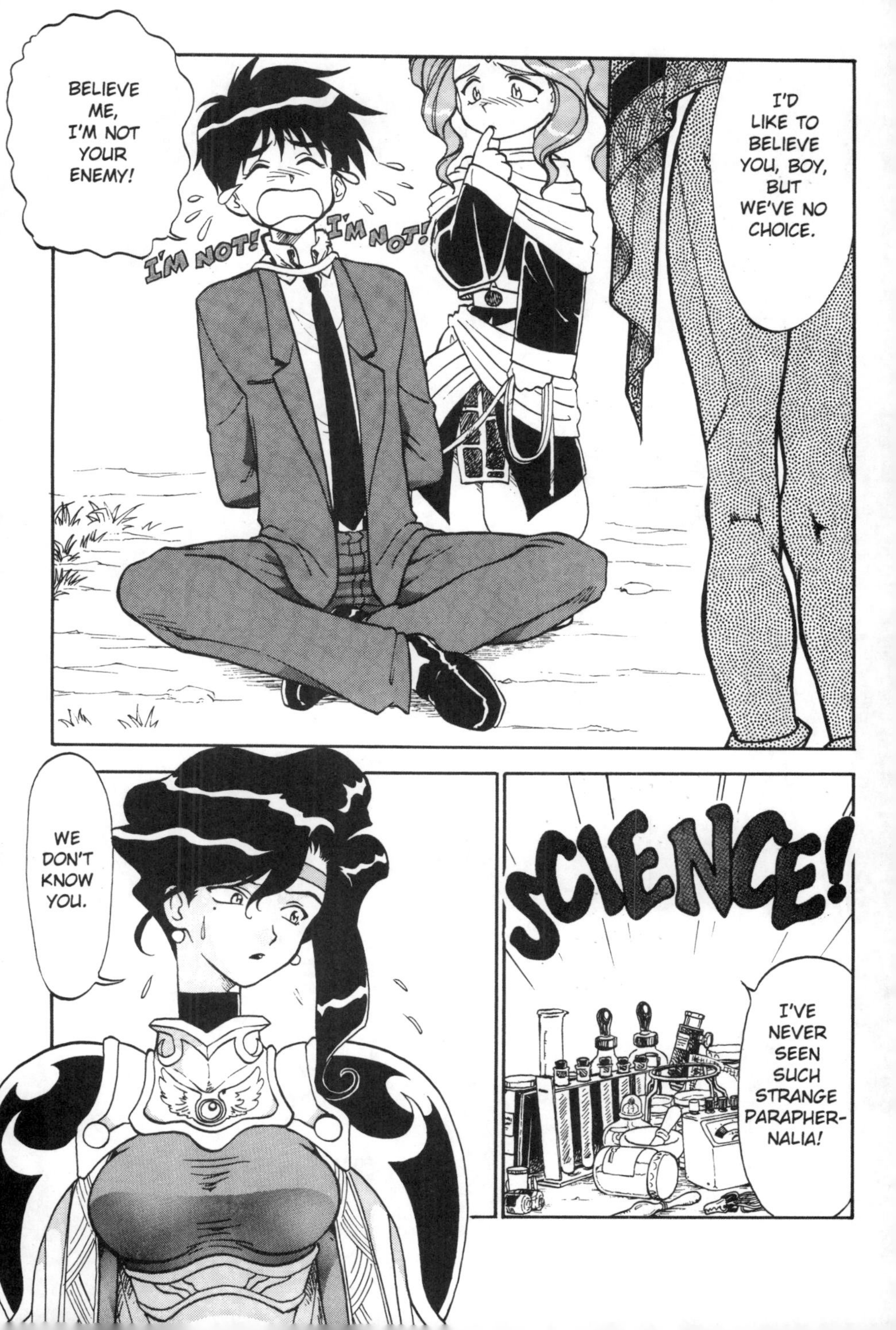
BELIEVE ME, I'M NOT YOUR ENEMY!
I'M NOT! I'M NOT!
I'D LIKE TO BELIEVE YOU, BOY, BUT WE'VE NO CHOICE.
WE DON'T KNOW YOU.
SCIENCE!
I'VE NEVER SEEN SUCH STRANGE PARAPHER-NALIA!

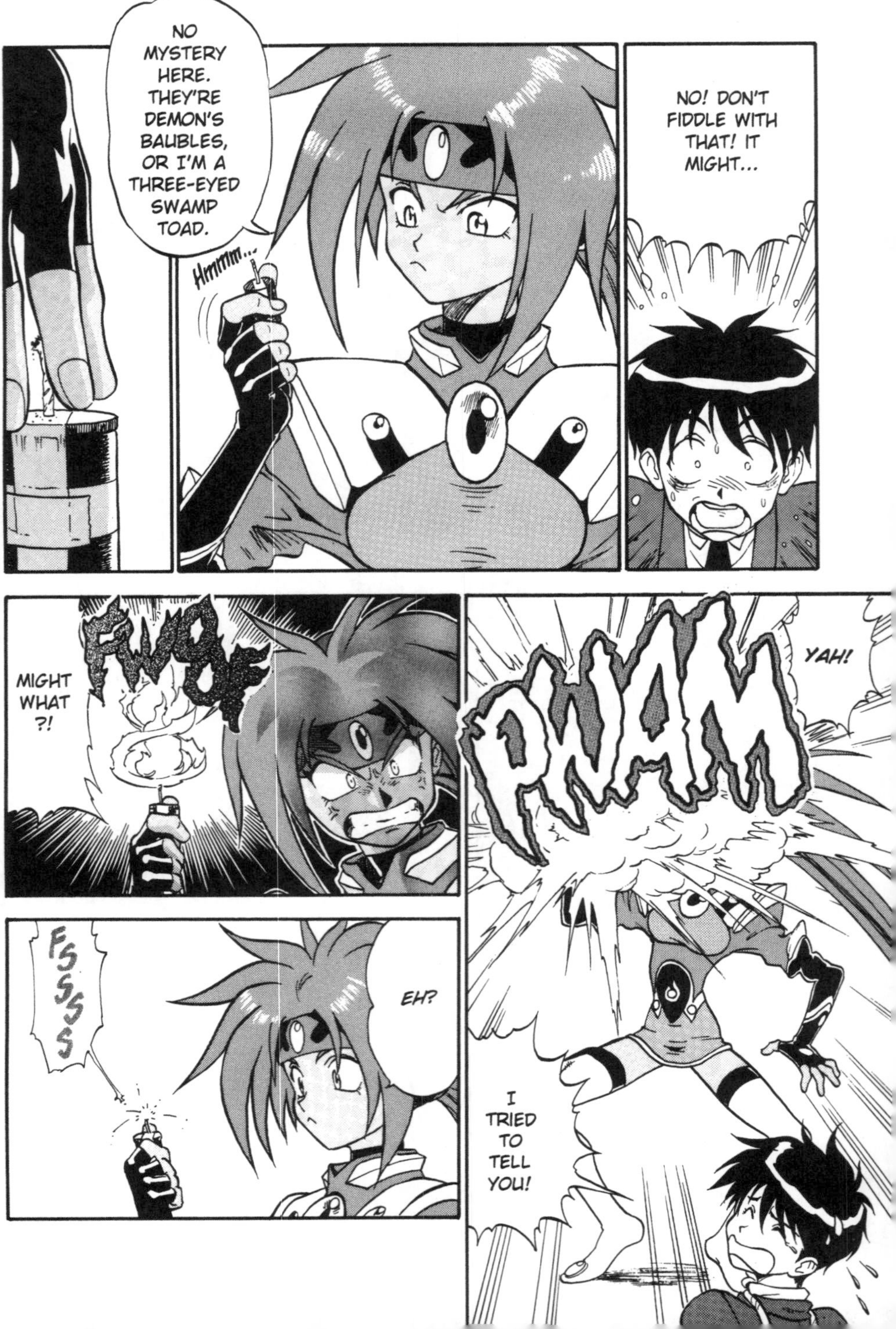
NO MYSTERY HERE. THEY'RE DEMON'S BAUBLES, OR I'M A THREE-EYED SWAMP TOAD.
Hmmm...
NO! DON'T FIDDLE WITH THAT! IT MIGHT...
FWOOF
MIGHT WHAT?!
FSSSS
EH?
PWAM
YAH!
I TRIED TO TELL YOU!

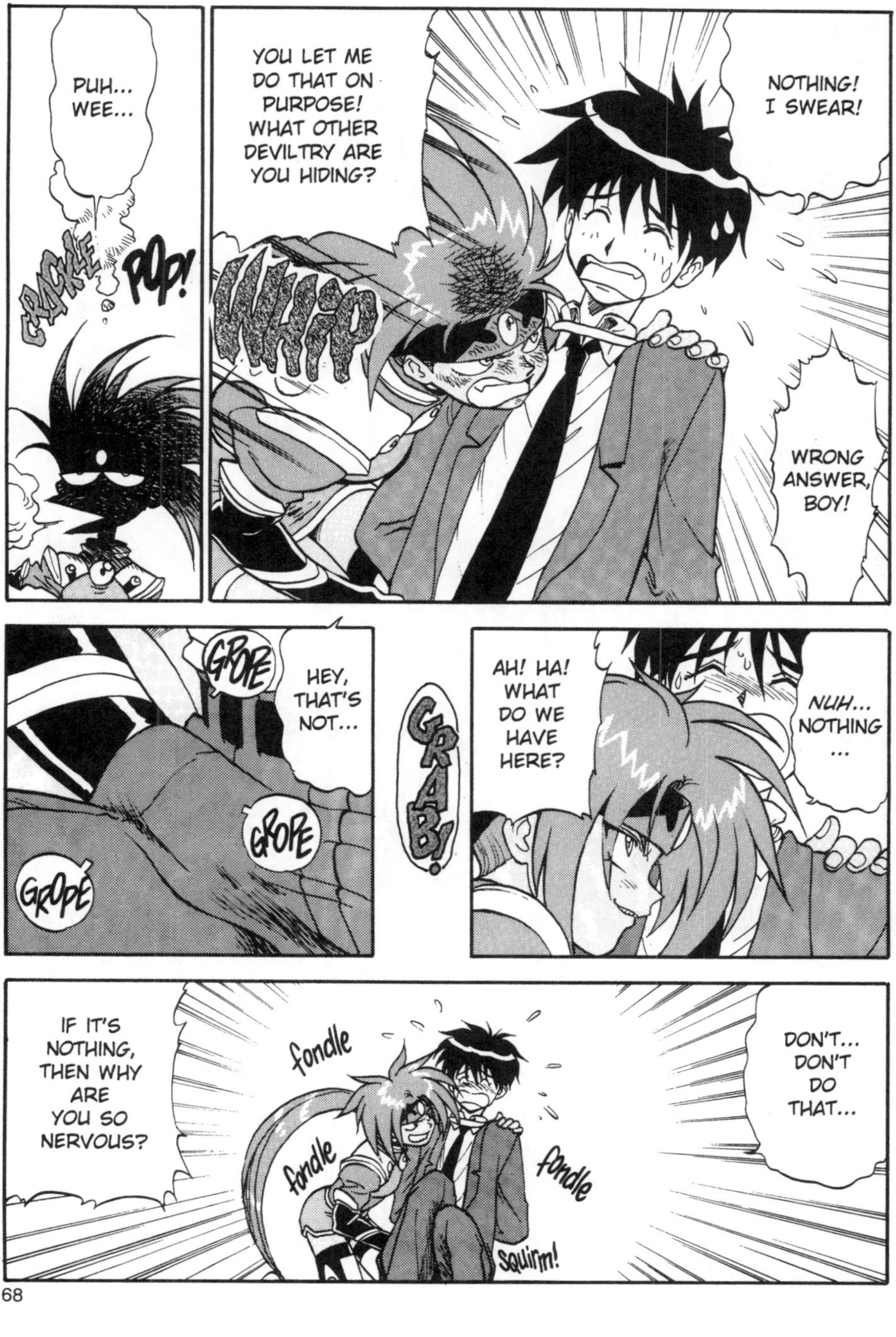
PUH... WEE...
CRACKLE
POP!
YOU LET ME DO THAT ON PURPOSE! WHAT OTHER DEVILTRY ARE YOU HIDING?
WHIP
NOTHING! I SWEAR!
WRONG ANSWER, BOY!
GROPE
HEY, THAT'S NOT...
GROPE
GROPE
GRAB!
AH! HA! WHAT DO WE HAVE HERE?
NUH... NOTHING...
IF IT'S NOTHING, THEN WHY ARE YOU SO NERVOUS?
fondle
fondle
DON'T... DON'T DO THAT...
fondle
squirm!

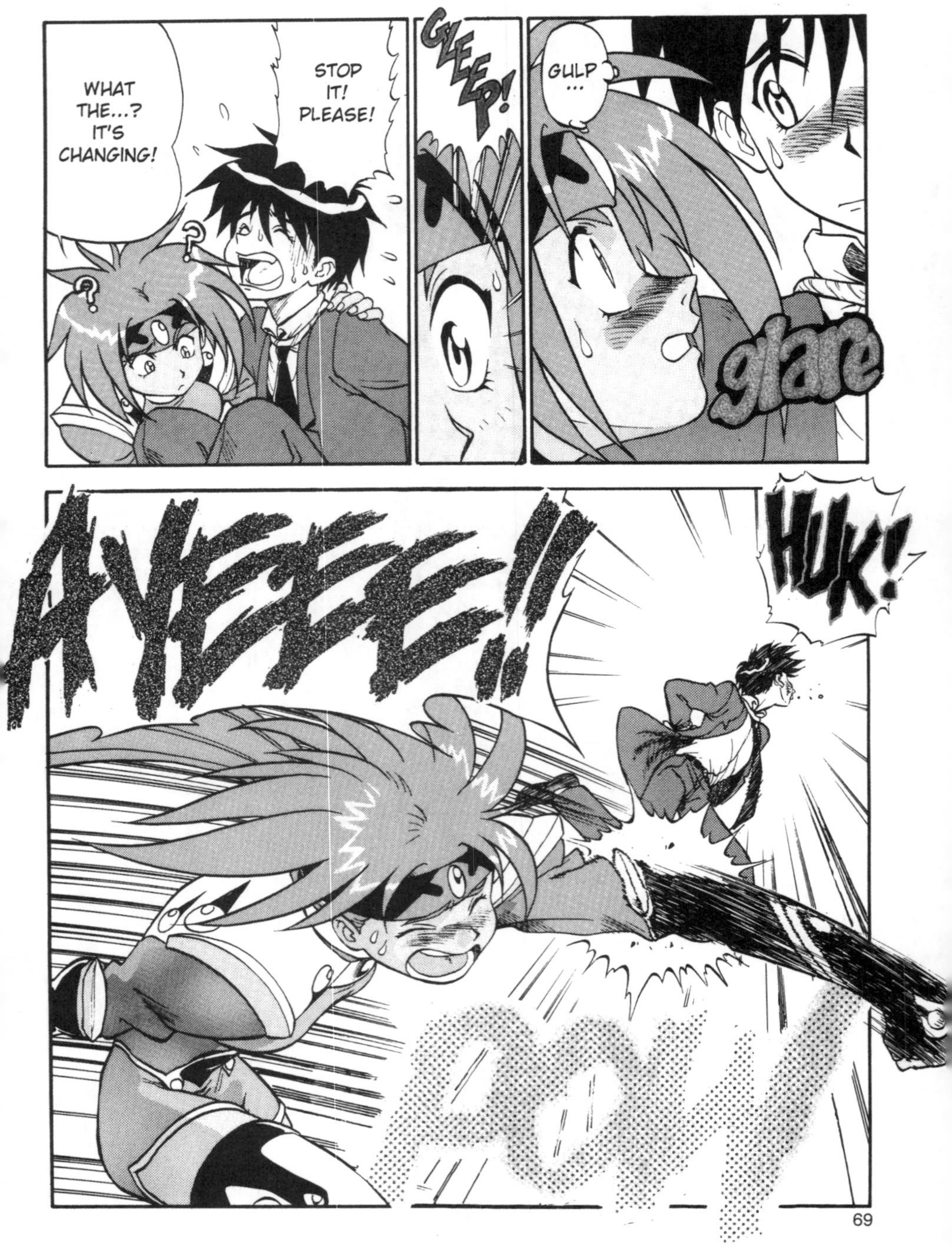
WHAT THE...? IT'S CHANGING!
STOP IT! PLEASE!
GLEEP!
GULP ...
glare
AYEEE!!
HUK!
POW!

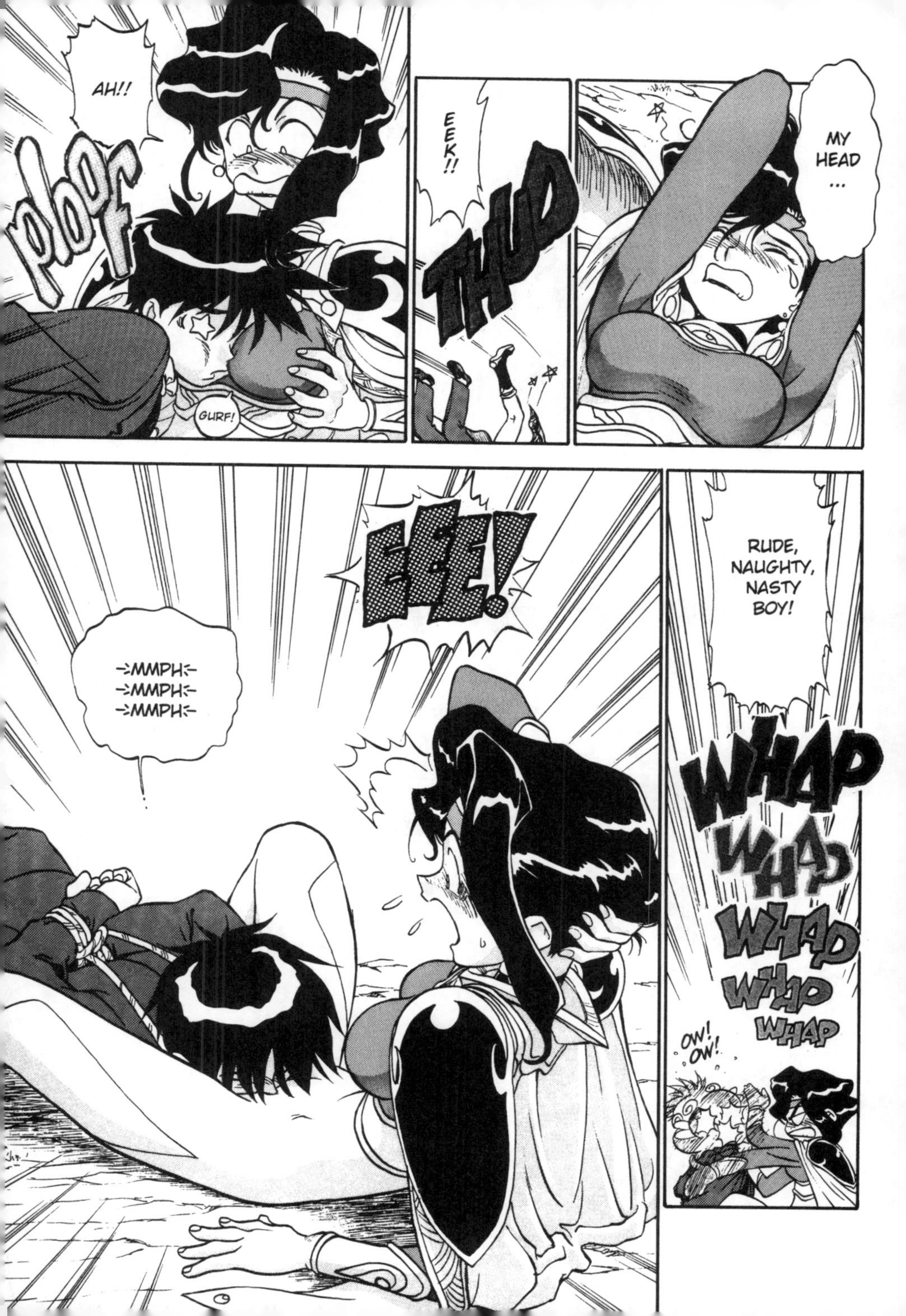
AH!!
ploof
GURF!
EEK!!
THUD
MY HEAD ...
EEE!
-MMPH-
-MMPH-
-MMPH-
RUDE, NAUGHTY, NASTY BOY!
WHAP
WHAP
WHAP
WHAP
WHAP
OW! OW!

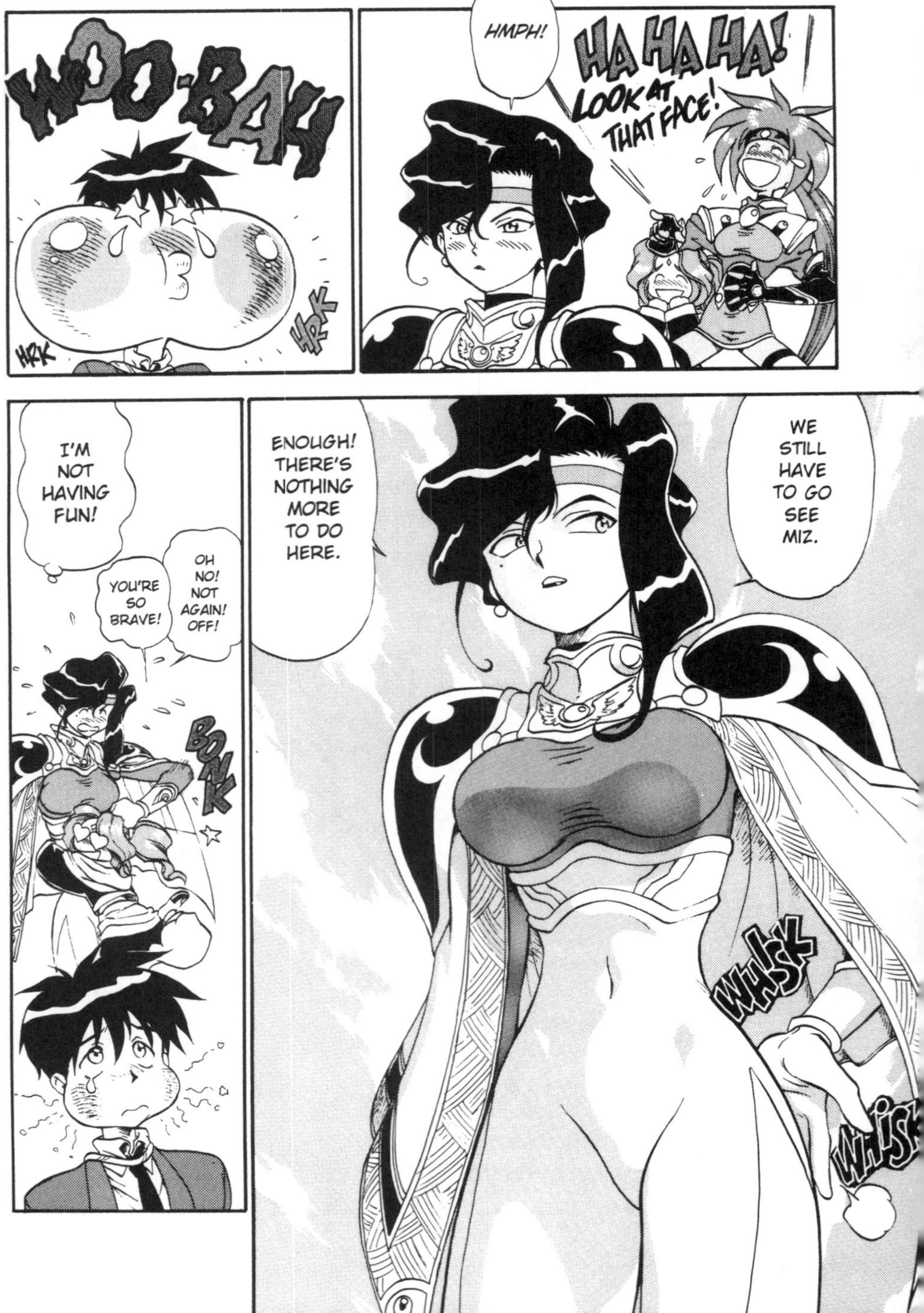
WOO-BAH
HRK
HRK
HMPH!
HA HA HA!
LOOK AT THAT FACE!
I'M NOT HAVING FUN!
YOU'RE SO BRAVE!
OH NO! NOT AGAIN! OFF!
BONK
ENOUGH! THERE'S NOTHING MORE TO DO HERE.
WE STILL HAVE TO GO SEE MIZ.
WHISK
WHISK

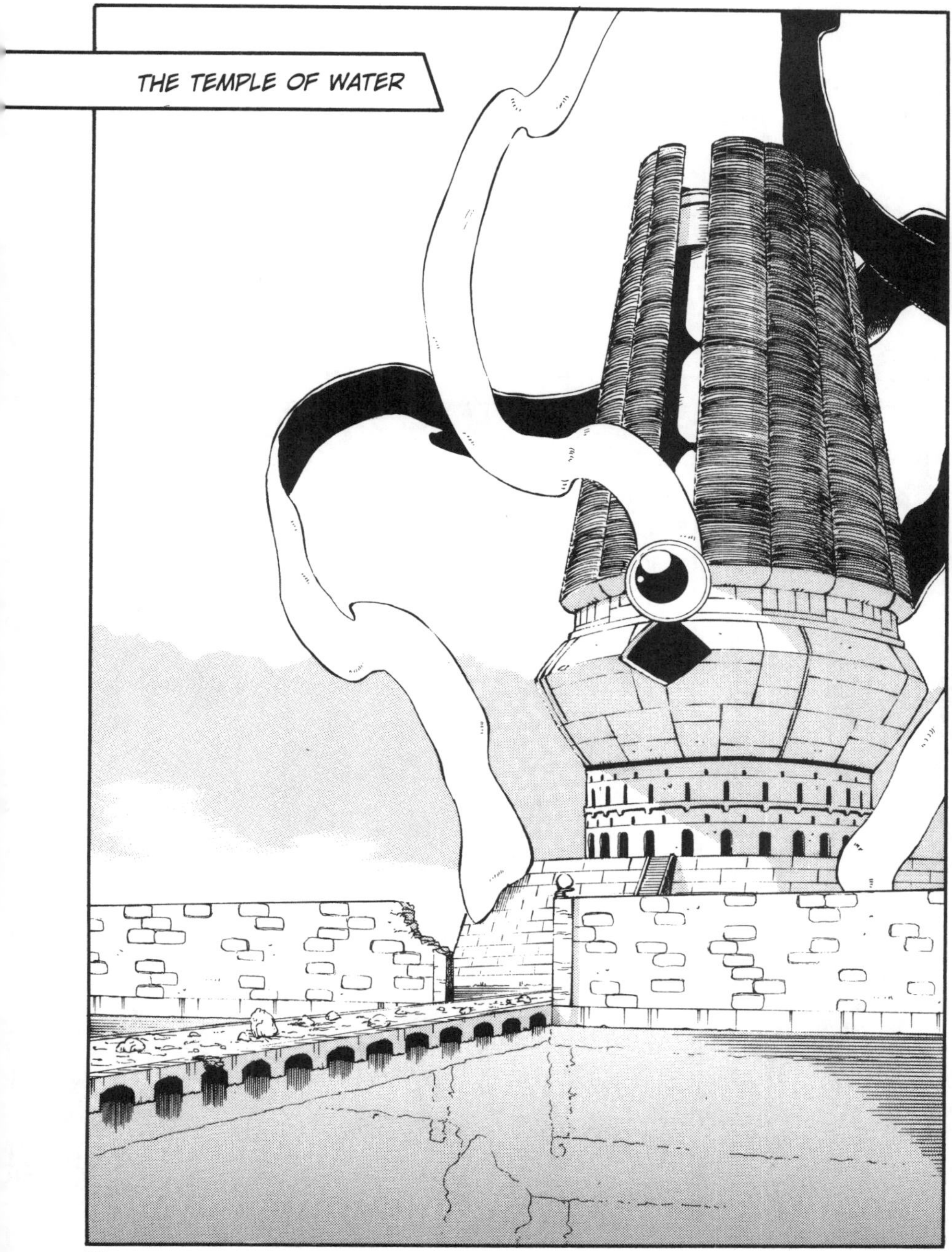
THE TEMPLE OF WATER

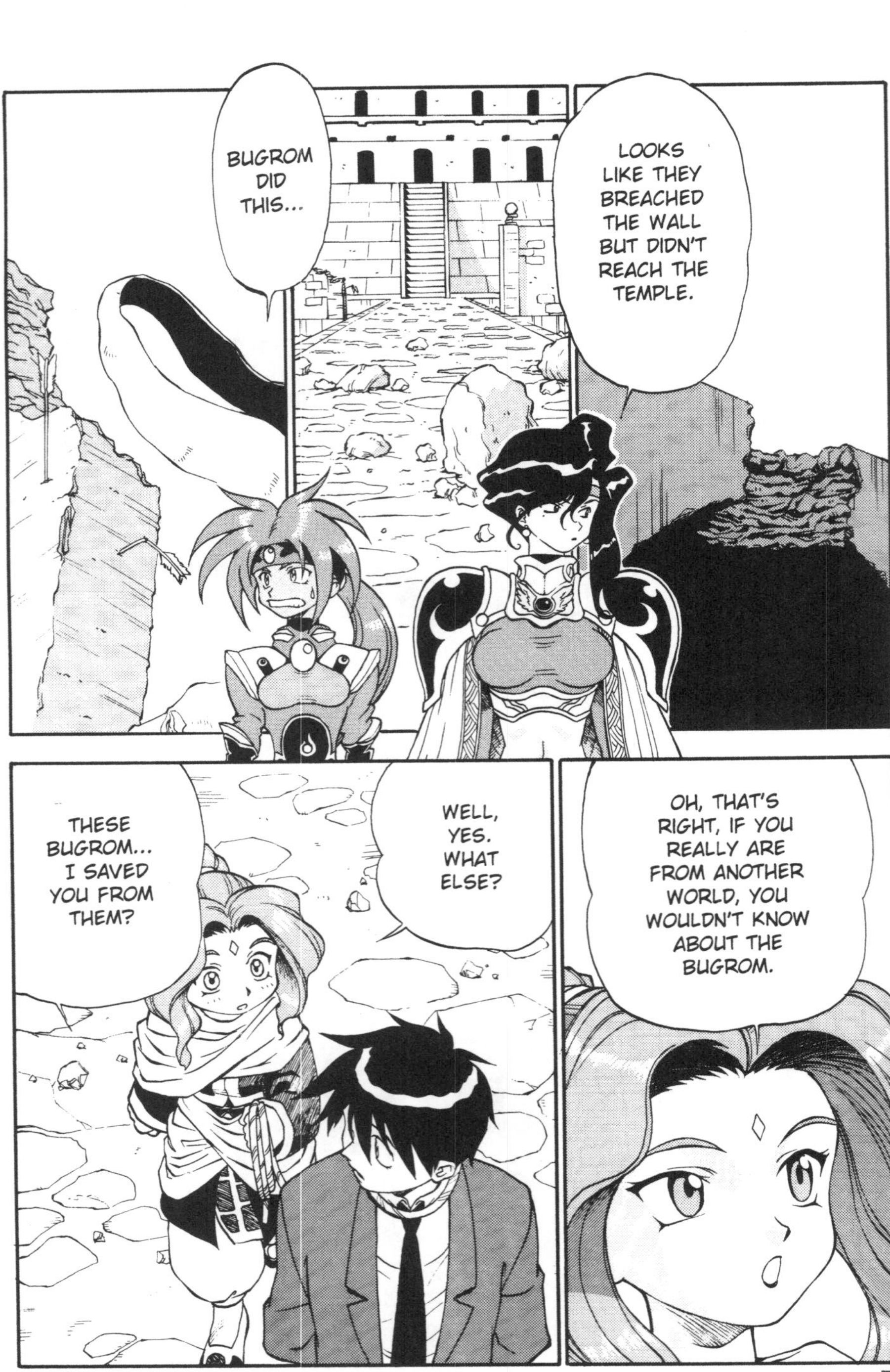
BUGROM DID THIS...
LOOKS LIKE THEY BREACHED THE WALL BUT DIDN'T REACH THE TEMPLE.
THESE BUGROM... I SAVED YOU FROM THEM?
WELL, YES. WHAT ELSE?
OH, THAT'S RIGHT, IF YOU REALLY ARE FROM ANOTHER WORLD, YOU WOULDN'T KNOW ABOUT THE BUGROM.

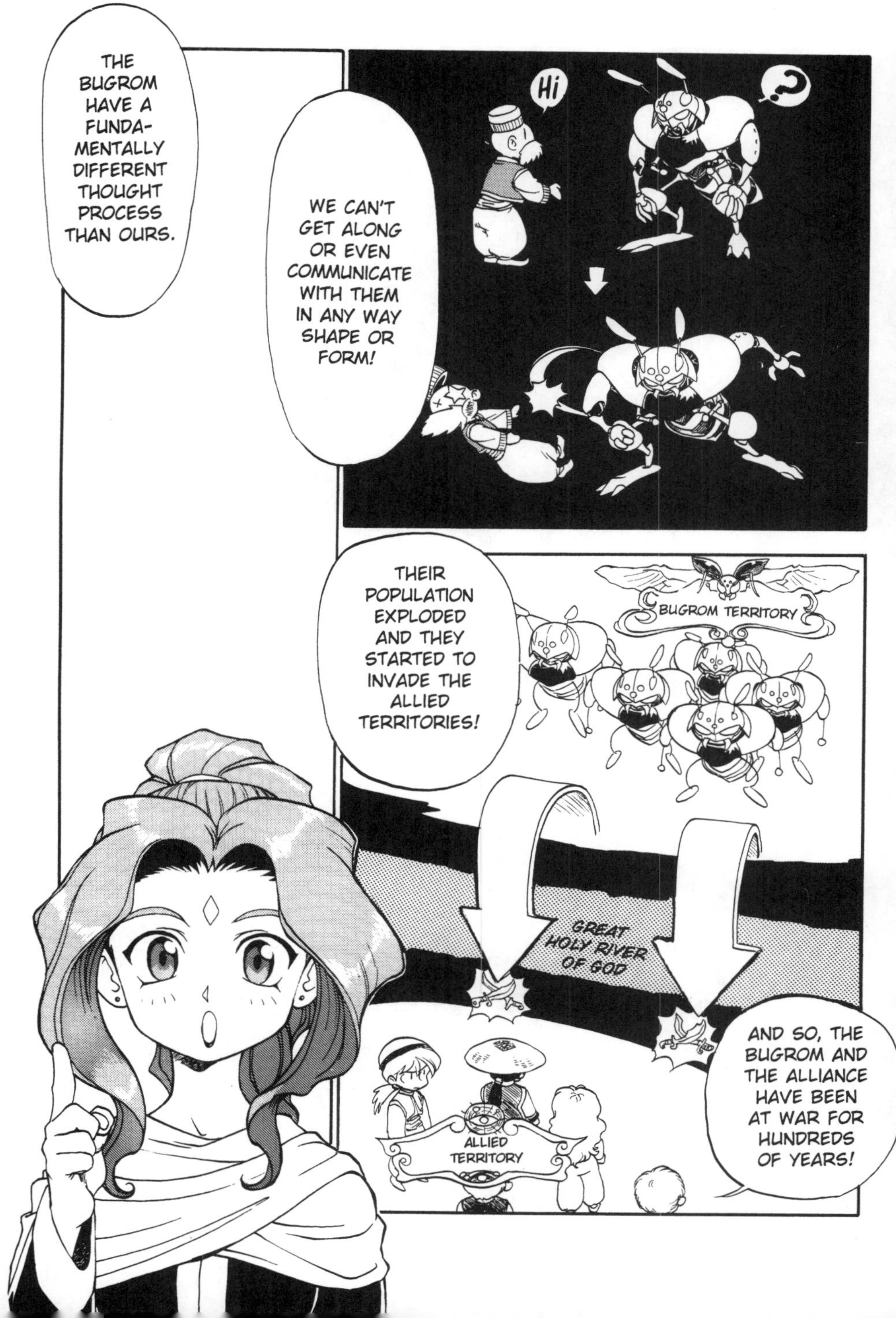
THE BUGROM HAVE A FUNDA-MENTALLY DIFFERENT THOUGHT PROCESS THAN OURS.
Hi
?
WE CAN'T GET ALONG OR EVEN COMMUNICATE WITH THEM IN ANY WAY SHAPE OR FORM!
THEIR POPULATION EXPLODED AND THEY STARTED TO INVADE THE ALLIED TERRITORIES!
BUGROM TERRITORY
GREAT HOLY RIVER OF GOD
ALLIED TERRITORY
AND SO, THE BUGROM AND THE ALLIANCE HAVE BEEN AT WAR FOR HUNDREDS OF YEARS!

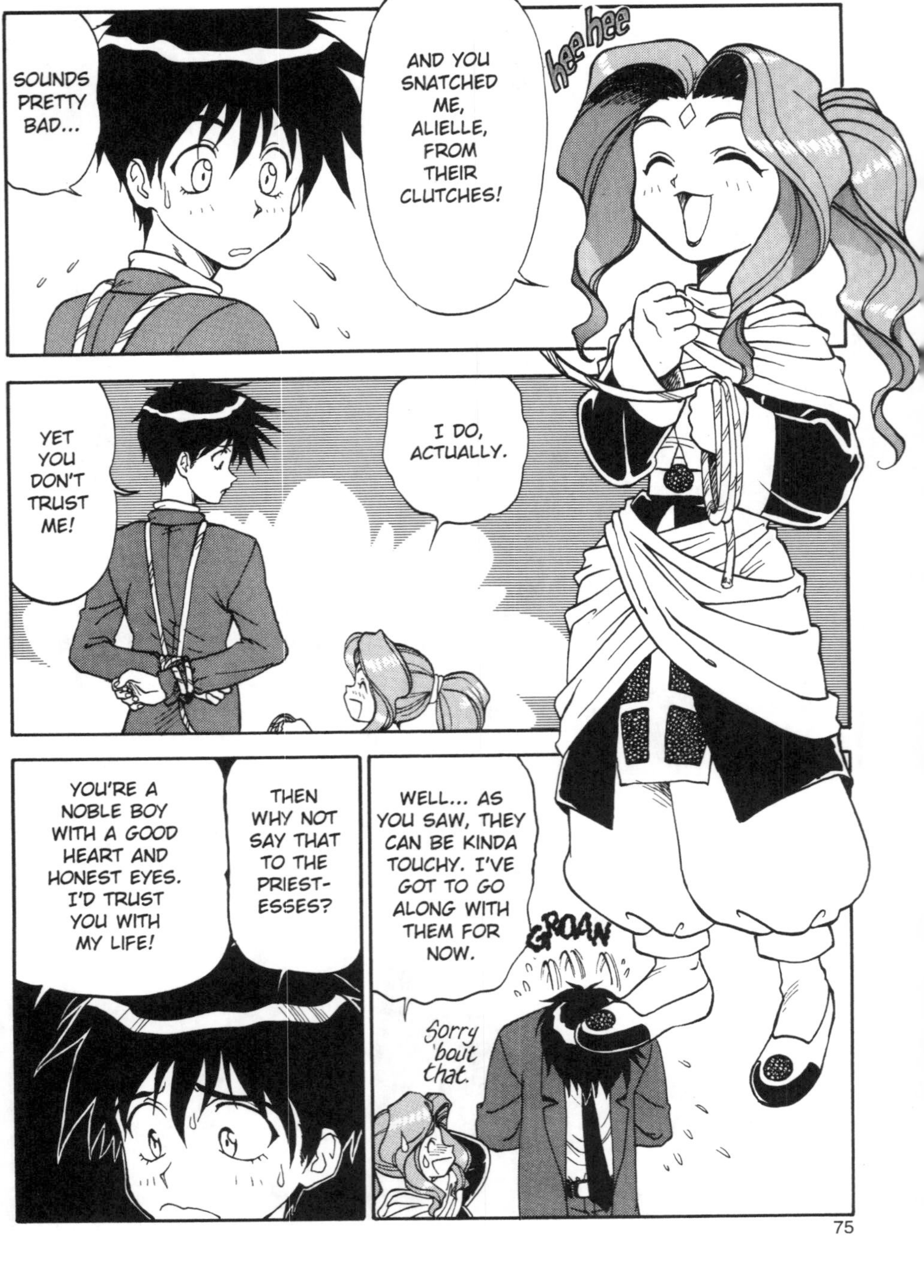
SOUNDS PRETTY BAD...
AND YOU SNATCHED ME, ALIELLE, FROM THEIR CLUTCHES!
hee hee
YET YOU DON'T TRUST ME!
I DO, ACTUALLY.
YOU'RE A NOBLE BOY WITH A GOOD HEART AND HONEST EYES. I'D TRUST YOU WITH MY LIFE!
THEN WHY NOT SAY THAT TO THE PRIEST-ESSES?
WELL... AS YOU SAW, THEY CAN BE KINDA TOUCHY. I'VE GOT TO GO ALONG WITH THEM FOR NOW.
GROAN
Sorry 'bout that.

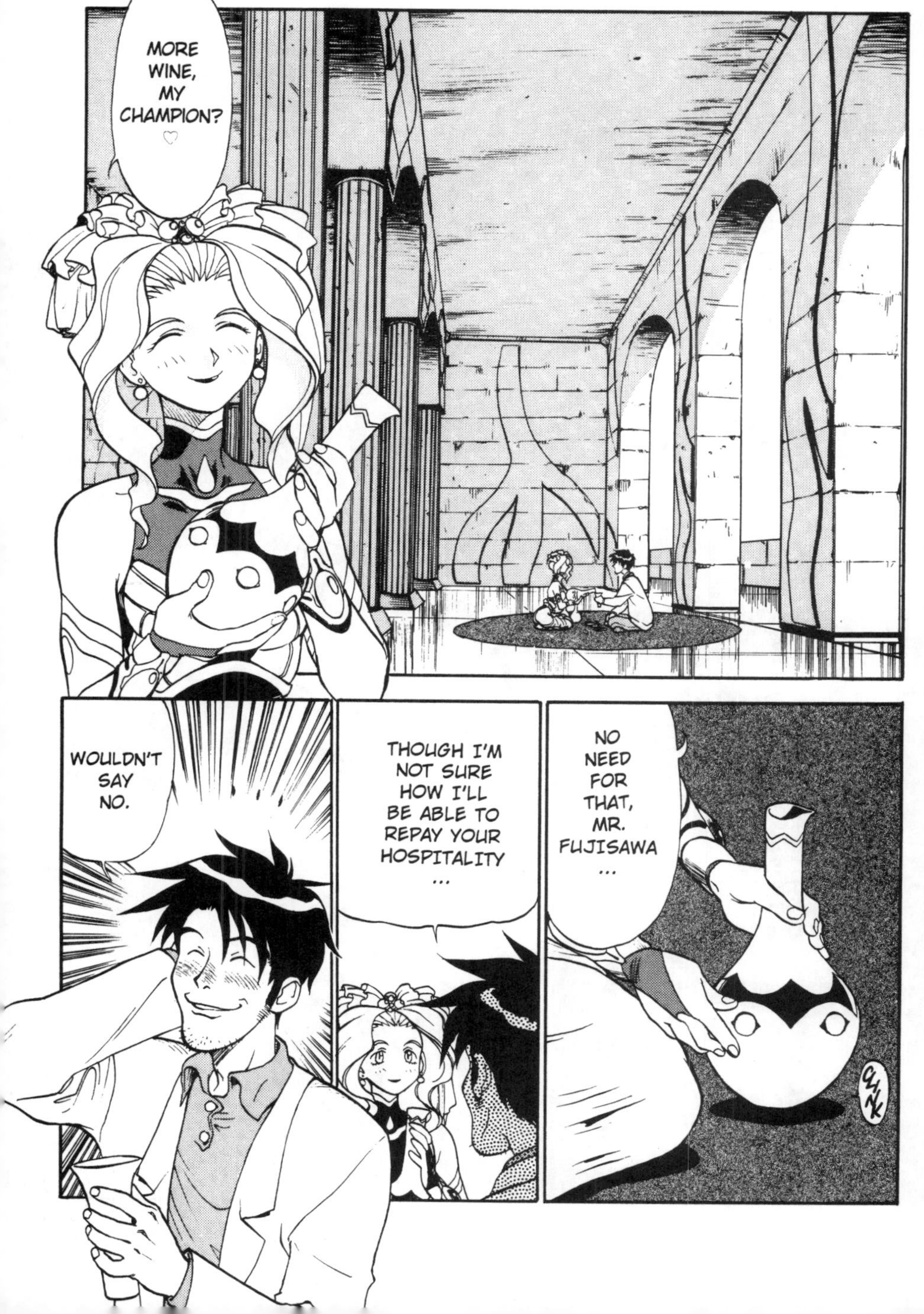
MORE WINE, MY CHAMPION? ♡
WOULDN'T SAY NO.
THOUGH I'M NOT SURE HOW I'LL BE ABLE TO REPAY YOUR HOSPITALITY ...
NO NEED FOR THAT, MR. FUJISAWA ...
CLINK

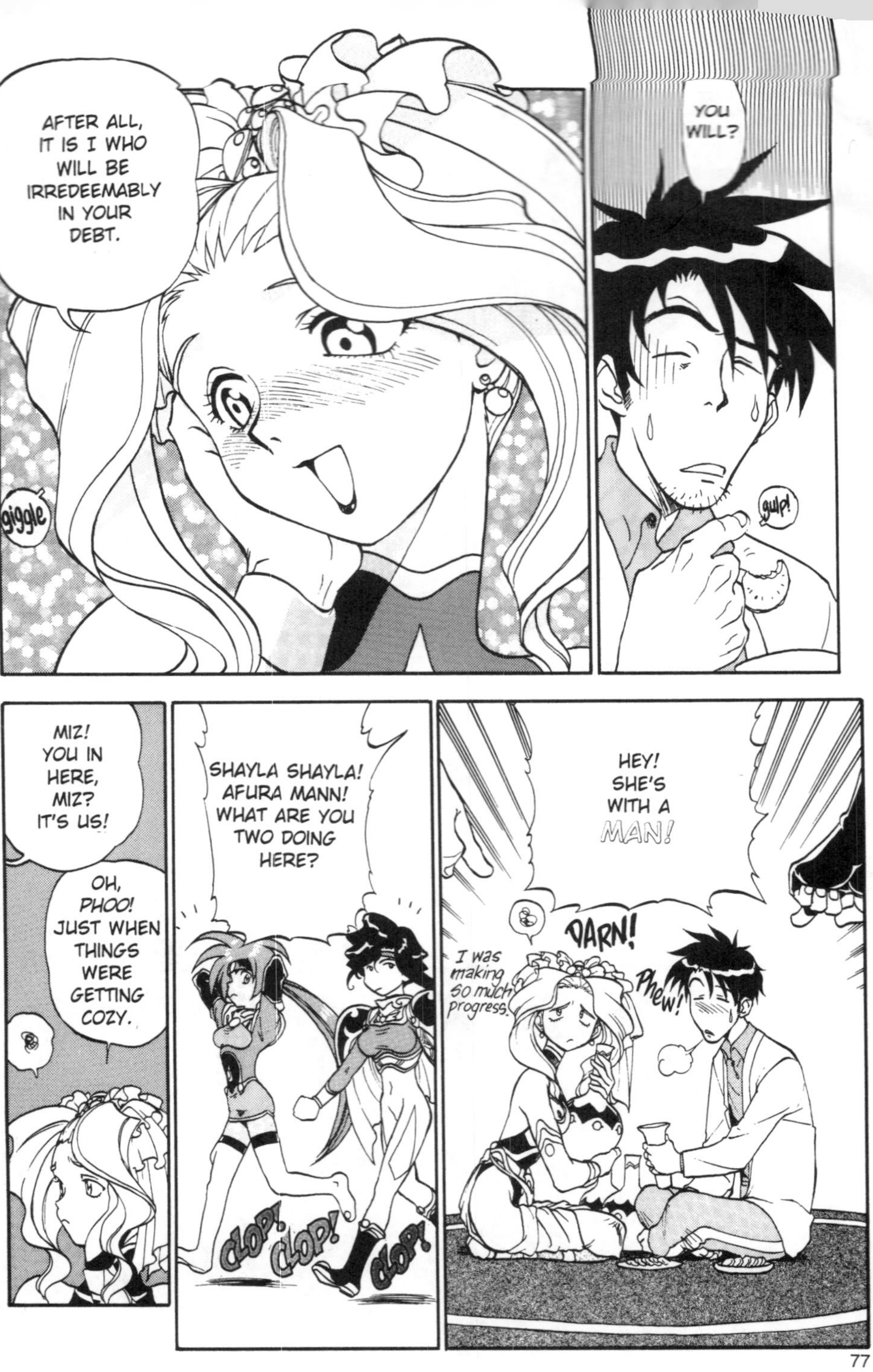
AFTER ALL, IT IS I WHO WILL BE IRREDEEMABLY IN YOUR DEBT.
giggle
YOU WILL?
gulp!
MIZ! YOU IN HERE, MIZ? IT'S US!
OH, PHOO! JUST WHEN THINGS WERE GETTING COZY.
SHAYLA SHAYLA! AFURA MANN! WHAT ARE YOU TWO DOING HERE?
CLOP! CLOP! CLOP!
HEY! SHE'S WITH A MAN!
DARN!
I was making so much progress.
Phew!

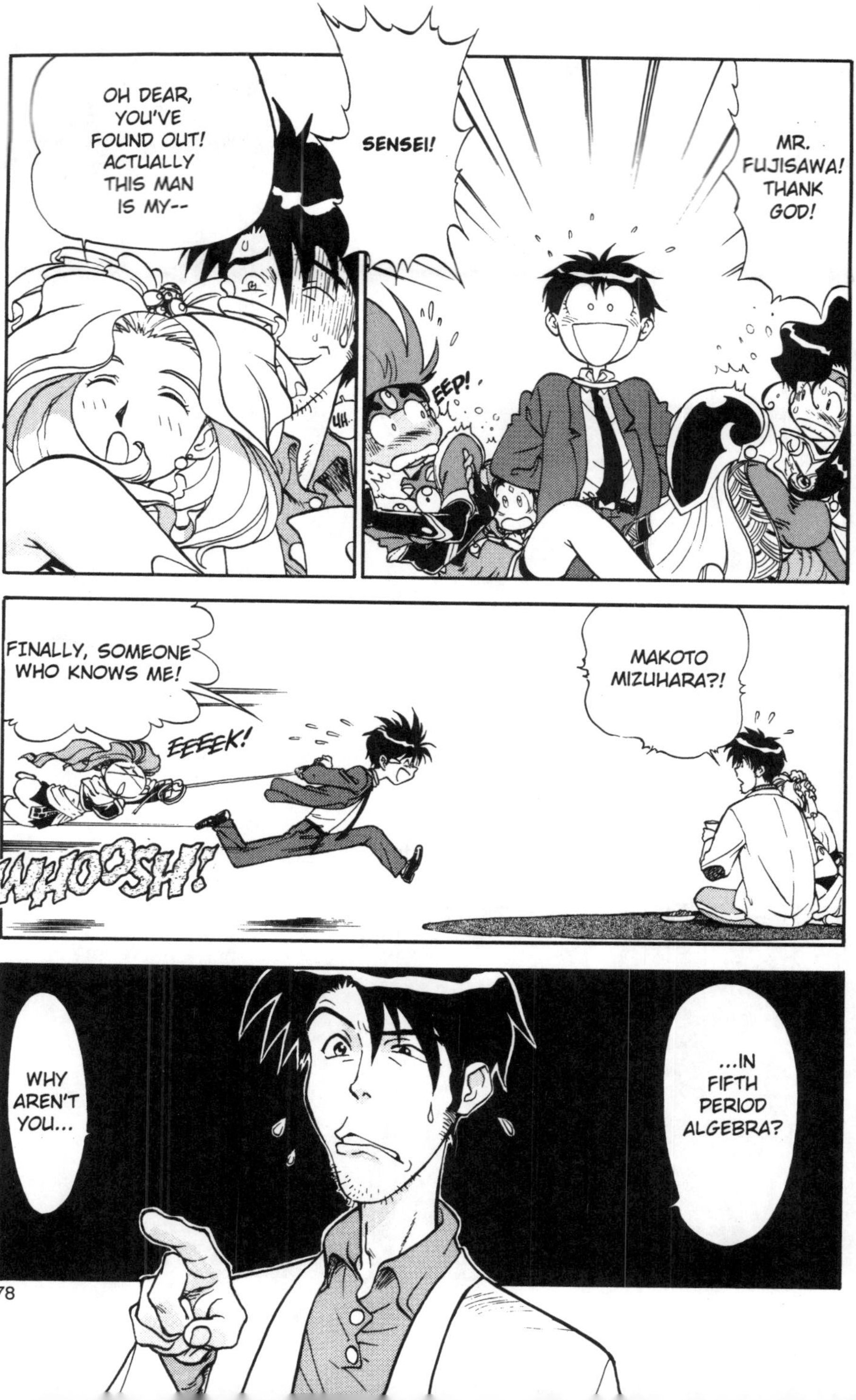
OH DEAR, YOU'VE FOUND OUT! ACTUALLY THIS MAN IS MY--
UH...
SENSEI!
MR. FUJISAWA! THANK GOD!
EEP!
FINALLY, SOMEONE WHO KNOWS ME!
EEEEK!
WHOOSH!
MAKOTO MIZUHARA?!
WHY AREN'T YOU...
...IN FIFTH PERIOD ALGEBRA?

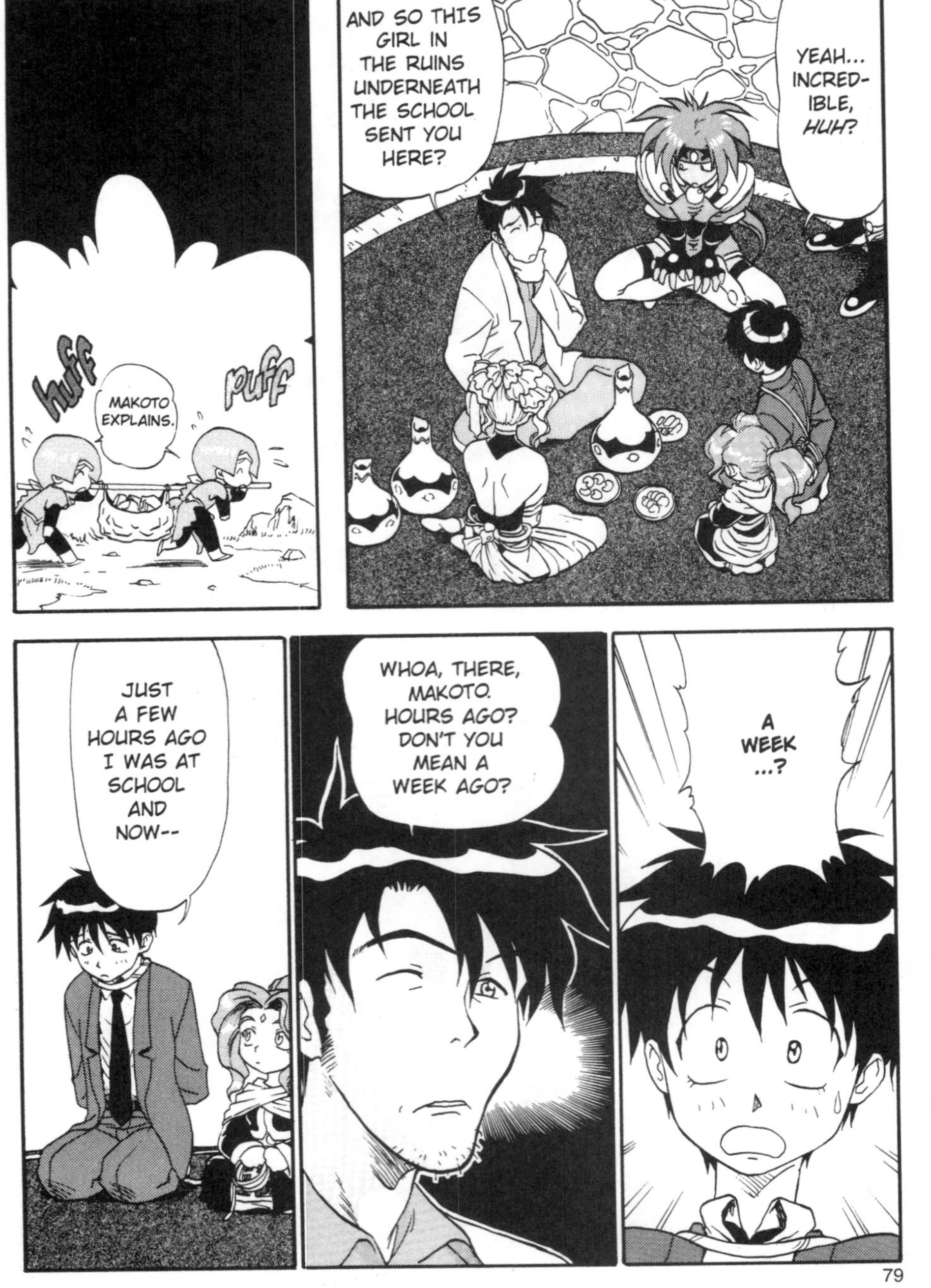
huff
MAKOTO EXPLAINS.
puff
AND SO THIS GIRL IN THE RUINS UNDERNEATH THE SCHOOL SENT YOU HERE?
YEAH... INCRED-IBLE, HUH?
JUST A FEW HOURS AGO I WAS AT SCHOOL AND NOW--
WHOA, THERE, MAKOTO. HOURS AGO? DON'T YOU MEAN A WEEK AGO?
A WEEK ...?

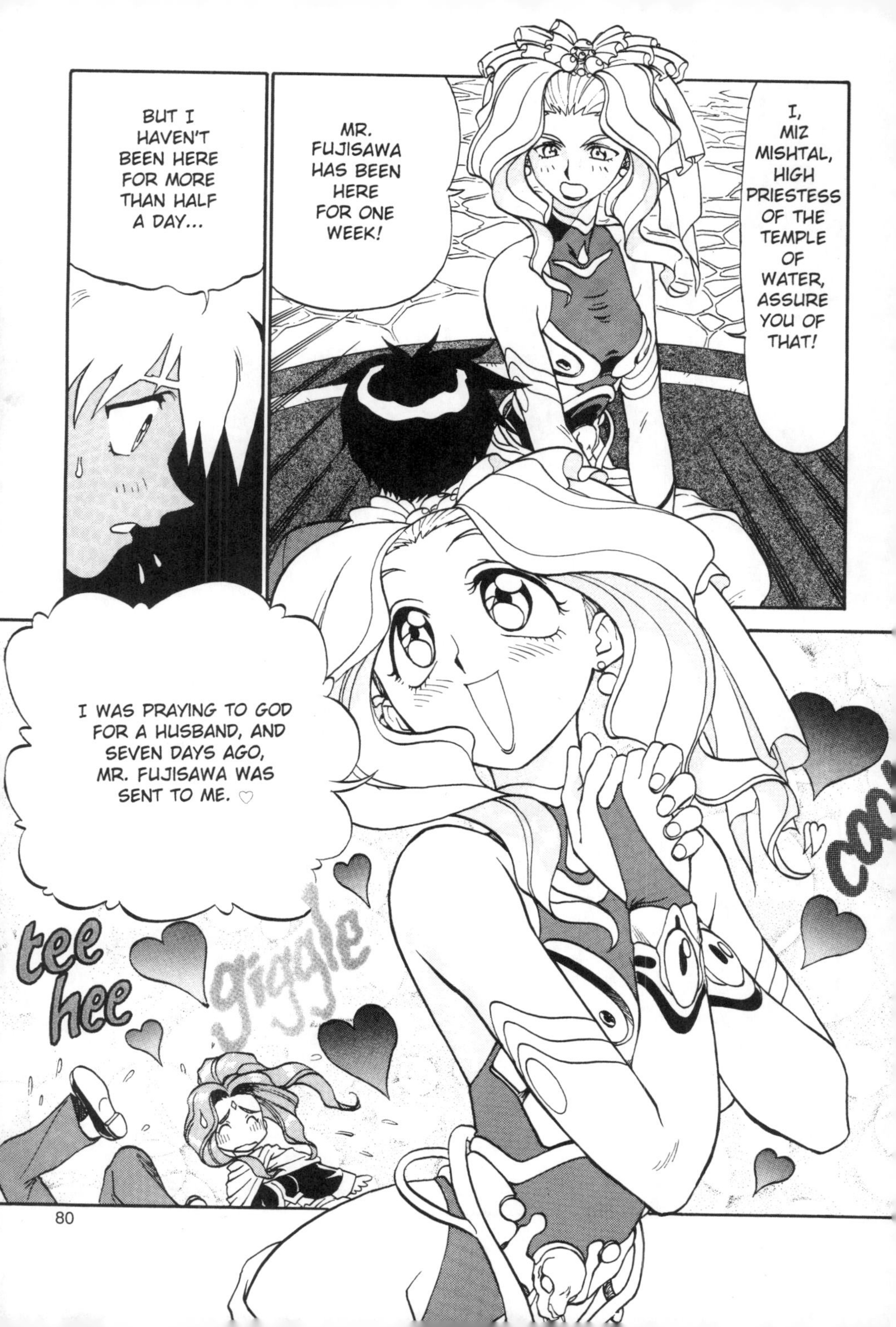
BUT I HAVEN'T BEEN HERE FOR MORE THAN HALF A DAY...
MR. FUJISAWA HAS BEEN HERE FOR ONE WEEK!
I, MIZ MISHTAL, HIGH PRIESTESS OF THE TEMPLE OF WATER, ASSURE YOU OF THAT!
I WAS PRAYING TO GOD FOR A HUSBAND, AND SEVEN DAYS AGO, MR. FUJISAWA WAS SENT TO ME. ♡
tee hee
giggle
coo

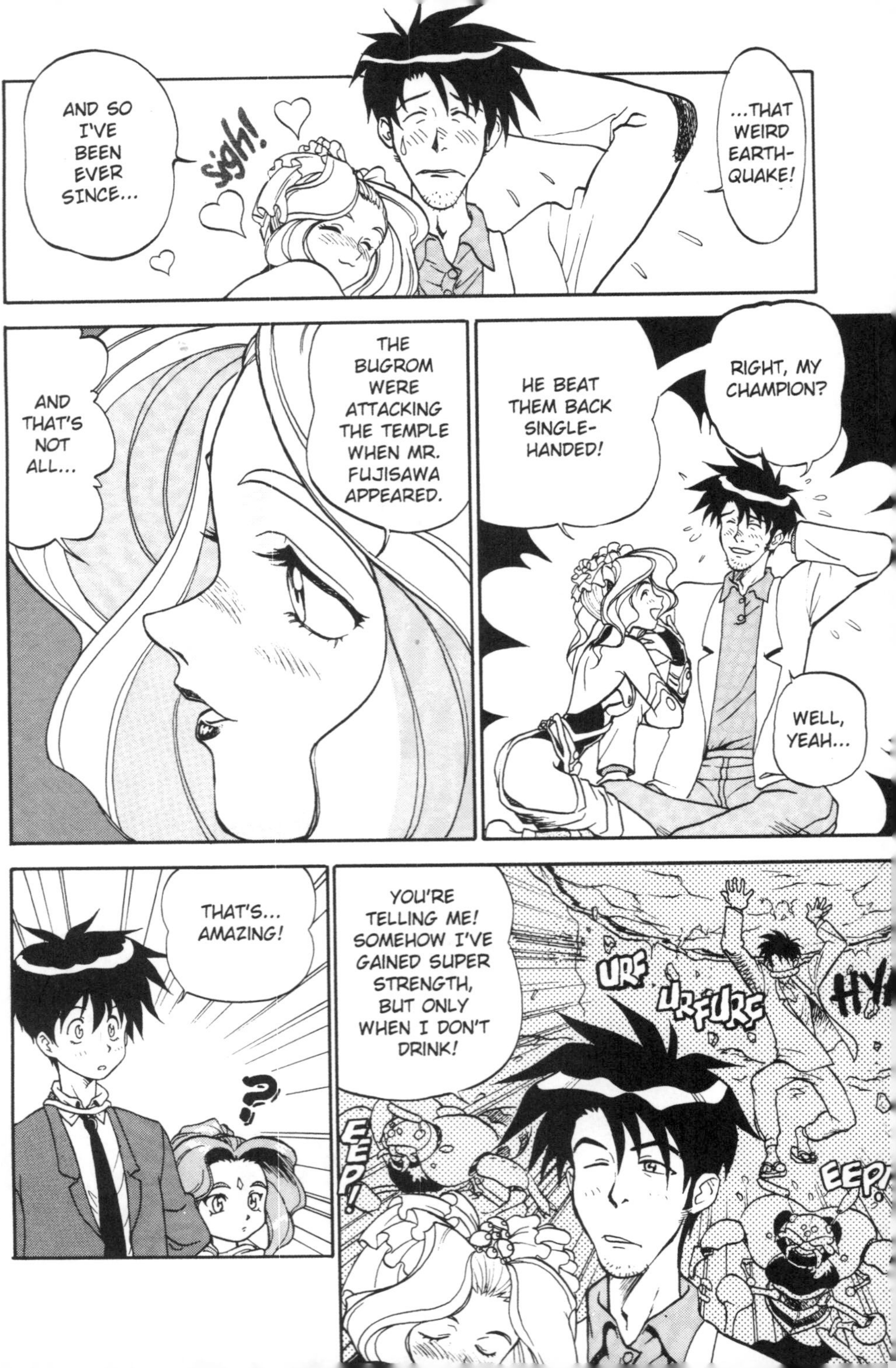
AND SO I'VE BEEN EVER SINCE...
sigh!
...THAT WEIRD EARTH-QUAKE!
AND THAT'S NOT ALL...
THE BUGROM WERE ATTACKING THE TEMPLE WHEN MR. FUJISAWA APPEARED.
HE BEAT THEM BACK SINGLE-HANDED!
RIGHT, MY CHAMPION?
WELL, YEAH...
THAT'S... AMAZING!
?
YOU'RE TELLING ME! SOMEHOW I'VE GAINED SUPER STRENGTH, BUT ONLY WHEN I DON'T DRINK!
URF
URFURF
EEP!
EEP!

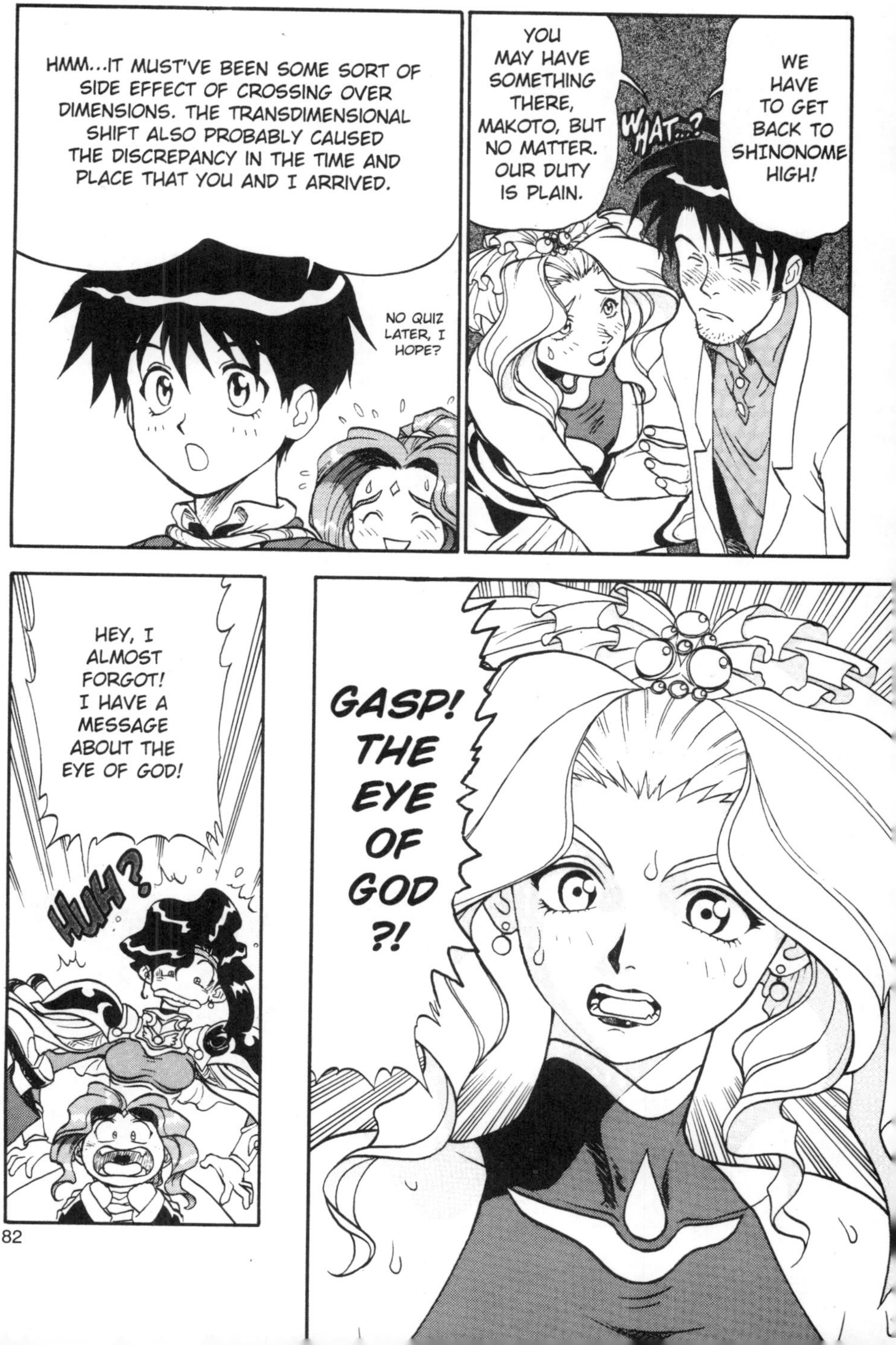
HMM...IT MUST'VE BEEN SOME SORT OF SIDE EFFECT OF CROSSING OVER DIMENSIONS. THE TRANSDIMENSIONAL SHIFT ALSO PROBABLY CAUSED THE DISCREPANCY IN THE TIME AND PLACE THAT YOU AND I ARRIVED.
NO QUIZ LATER, I HOPE?
YOU MAY HAVE SOMETHING THERE, MAKOTO, BUT NO MATTER. OUR DUTY IS PLAIN.
WHAT...?
WE HAVE TO GET BACK TO SHINONOME HIGH!
HEY, I ALMOST FORGOT! I HAVE A MESSAGE ABOUT THE EYE OF GOD!
HUH?
GASP! THE EYE OF GOD ?!

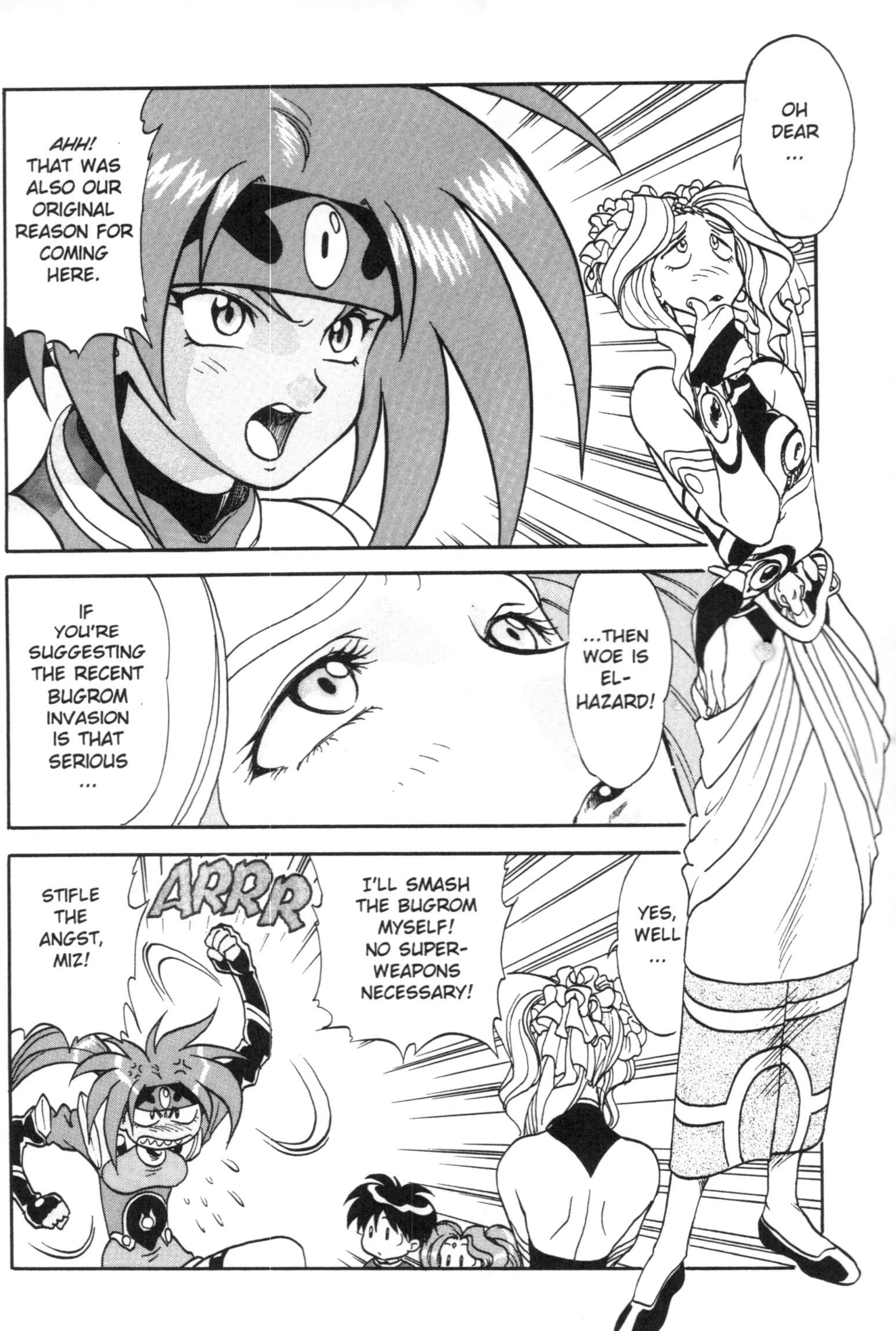
AHH! THAT WAS ALSO OUR ORIGINAL REASON FOR COMING HERE.
OH DEAR ...
IF YOU'RE SUGGESTING THE RECENT BUGROM INVASION IS THAT SERIOUS ...
...THEN WOE IS EL-HAZARD!
STIFLE THE ANGST, MIZ!
ARRR
I'LL SMASH THE BUGROM MYSELF! NO SUPER-WEAPONS NECESSARY!
YES, WELL ...

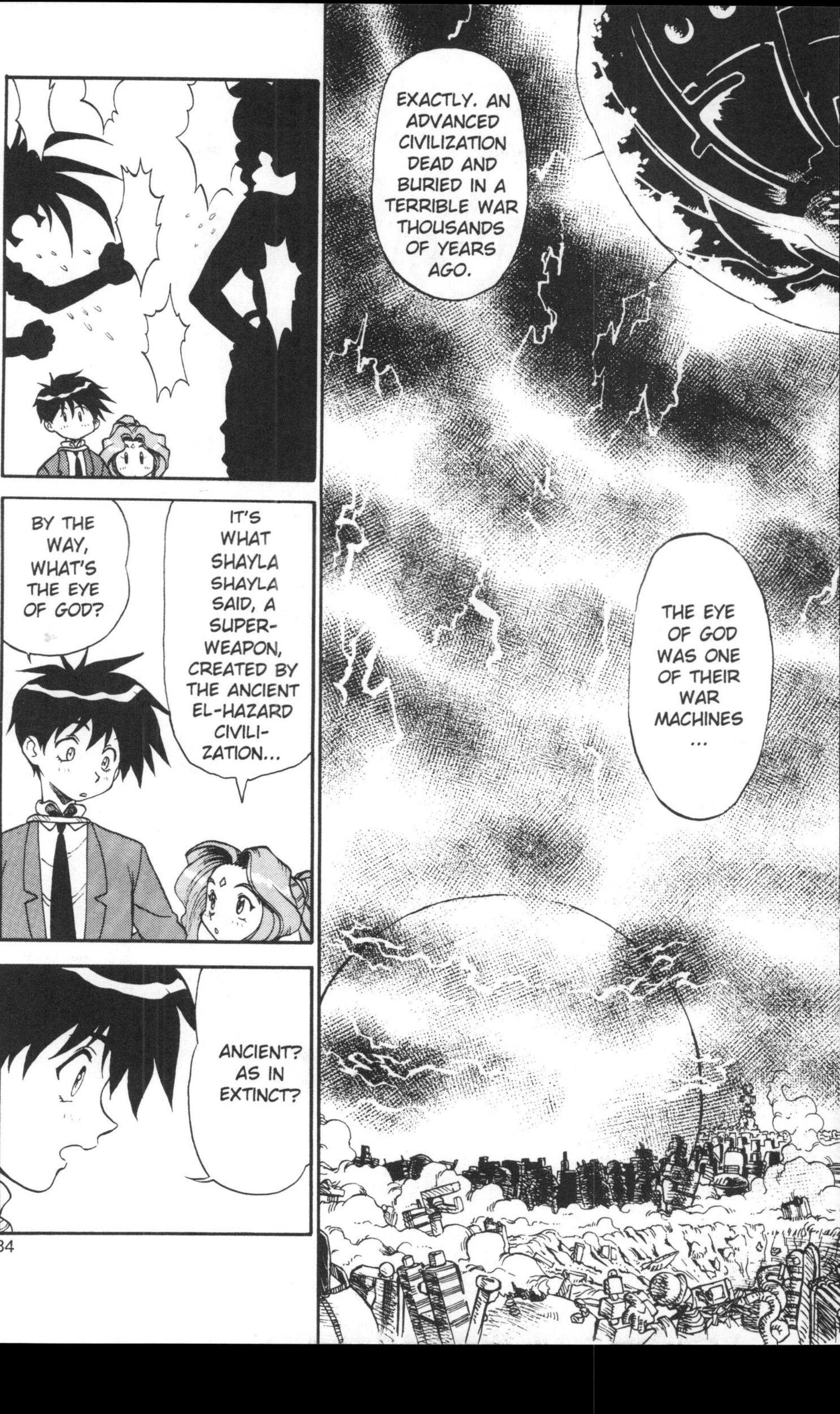
BY THE WAY, WHAT'S THE EYE OF GOD?
IT'S WHAT SHAYLA SHAYLA SAID, A SUPER-WEAPON, CREATED BY THE ANCIENT EL-HAZARD CIVILI-ZATION...
ANCIENT? AS IN EXTINCT?
EXACTLY. AN ADVANCED CIVILIZATION DEAD AND BURIED IN A TERRIBLE WAR THOUSANDS OF YEARS AGO.
THE EYE OF GOD WAS ONE OF THEIR WAR MACHINES ...

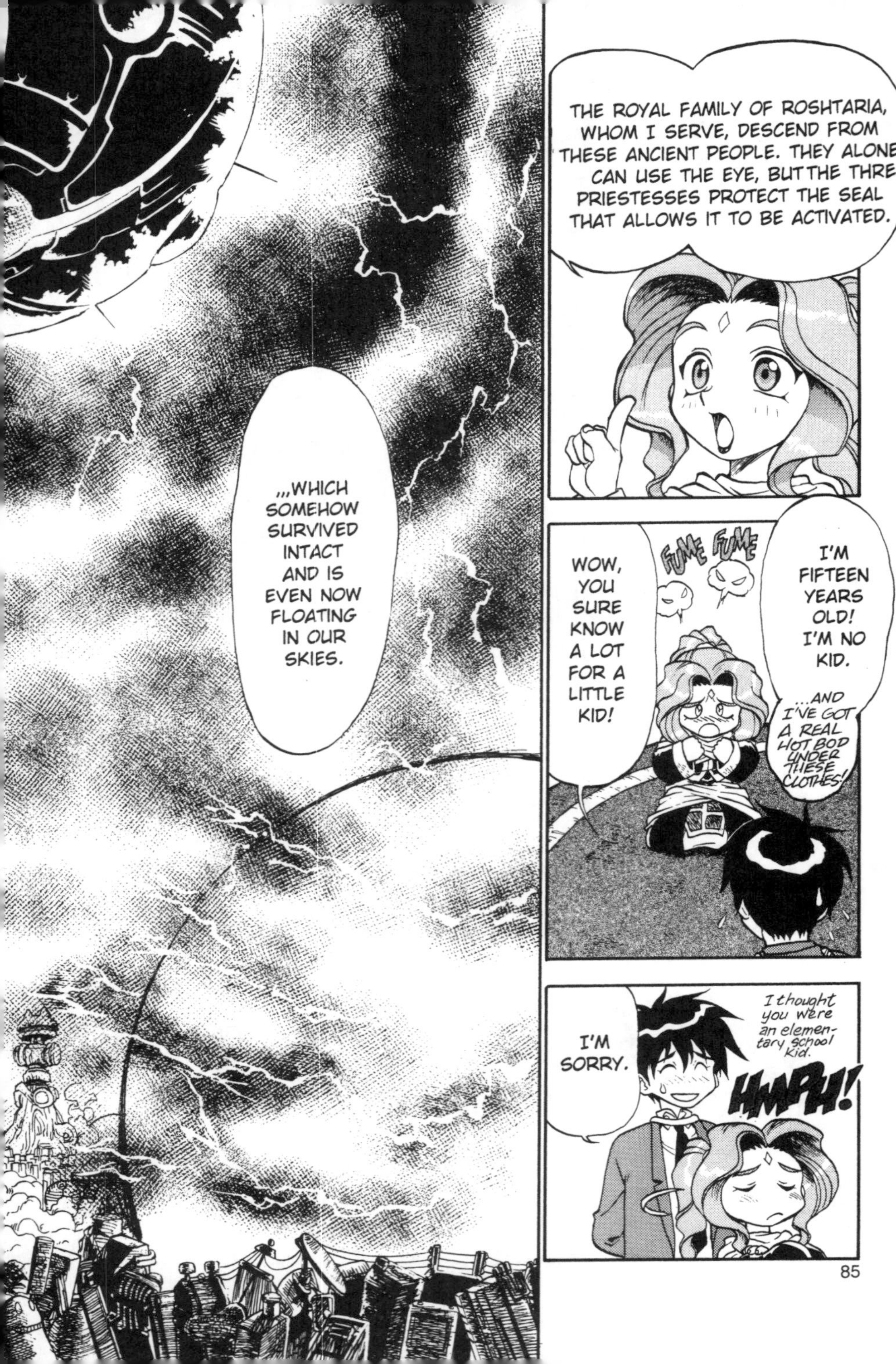
...WHICH SOMEHOW SURVIVED INTACT AND IS EVEN NOW FLOATING IN OUR SKIES.
THE ROYAL FAMILY OF ROSHTARIA, WHOM I SERVE, DESCEND FROM THESE ANCIENT PEOPLE. THEY ALONE CAN USE THE EYE, BUT THE THREE PRIESTESSES PROTECT THE SEAL THAT ALLOWS IT TO BE ACTIVATED.
WOW, YOU SURE KNOW A LOT FOR A LITTLE KID!
FUME FUME
I'M FIFTEEN YEARS OLD! I'M NO KID.
...AND I'VE GOT A REAL HOT BOD UNDER THESE CLOTHES!
I'M SORRY.
I thought you were an elementary school kid.
HMPH!

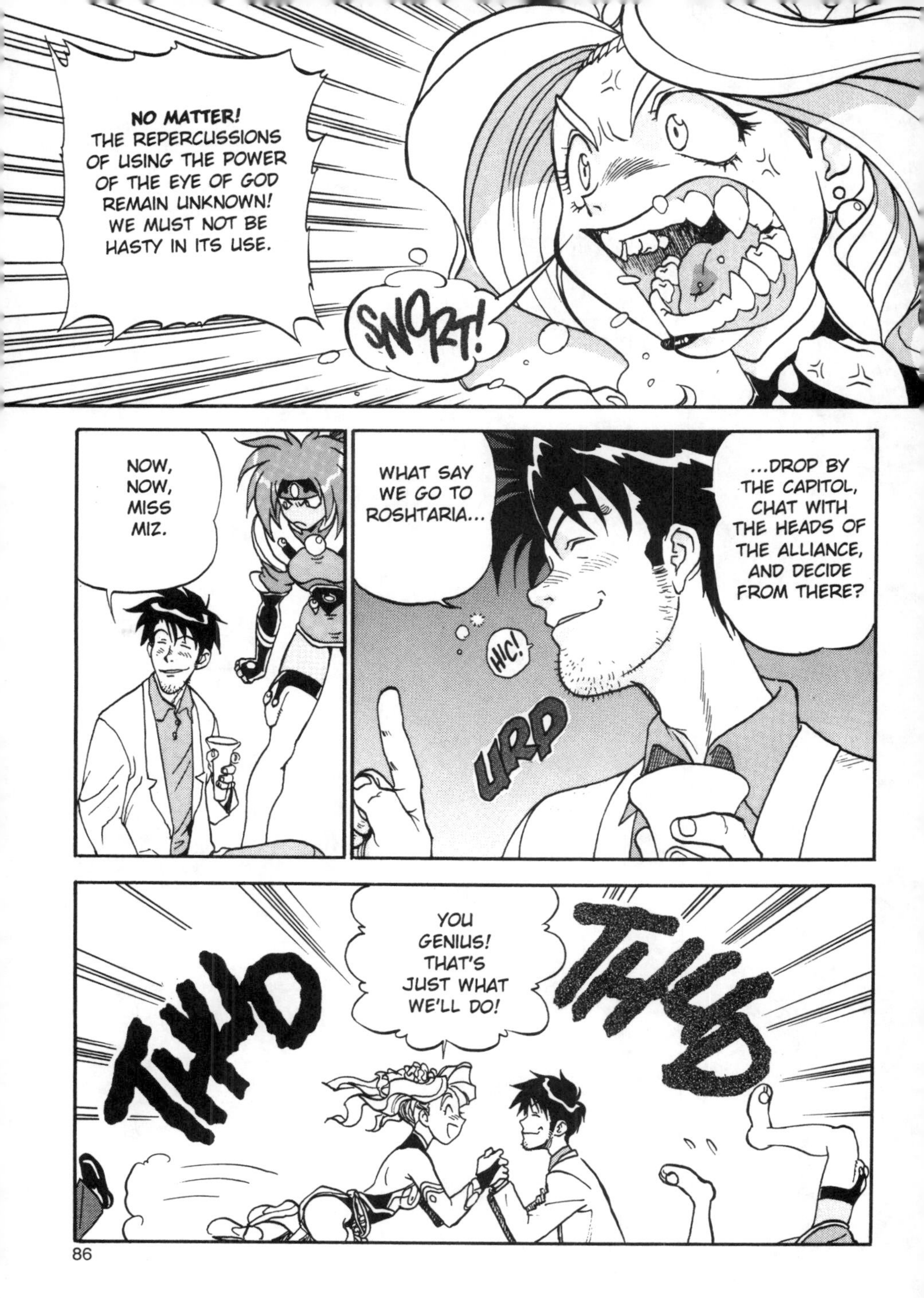
NO MATTER! THE REPERCUSSIONS OF USING THE POWER OF THE EYE OF GOD REMAIN UNKNOWN! WE MUST NOT BE HASTY IN ITS USE.
SNORT!
NOW, NOW, MISS MIZ.
WHAT SAY WE GO TO ROSHTARIA...
HIC!
URP
...DROP BY THE CAPITOL, CHAT WITH THE HEADS OF THE ALLIANCE, AND DECIDE FROM THERE?
THUD
YOU GENIUS! THAT'S JUST WHAT WE'LL DO!
THUD

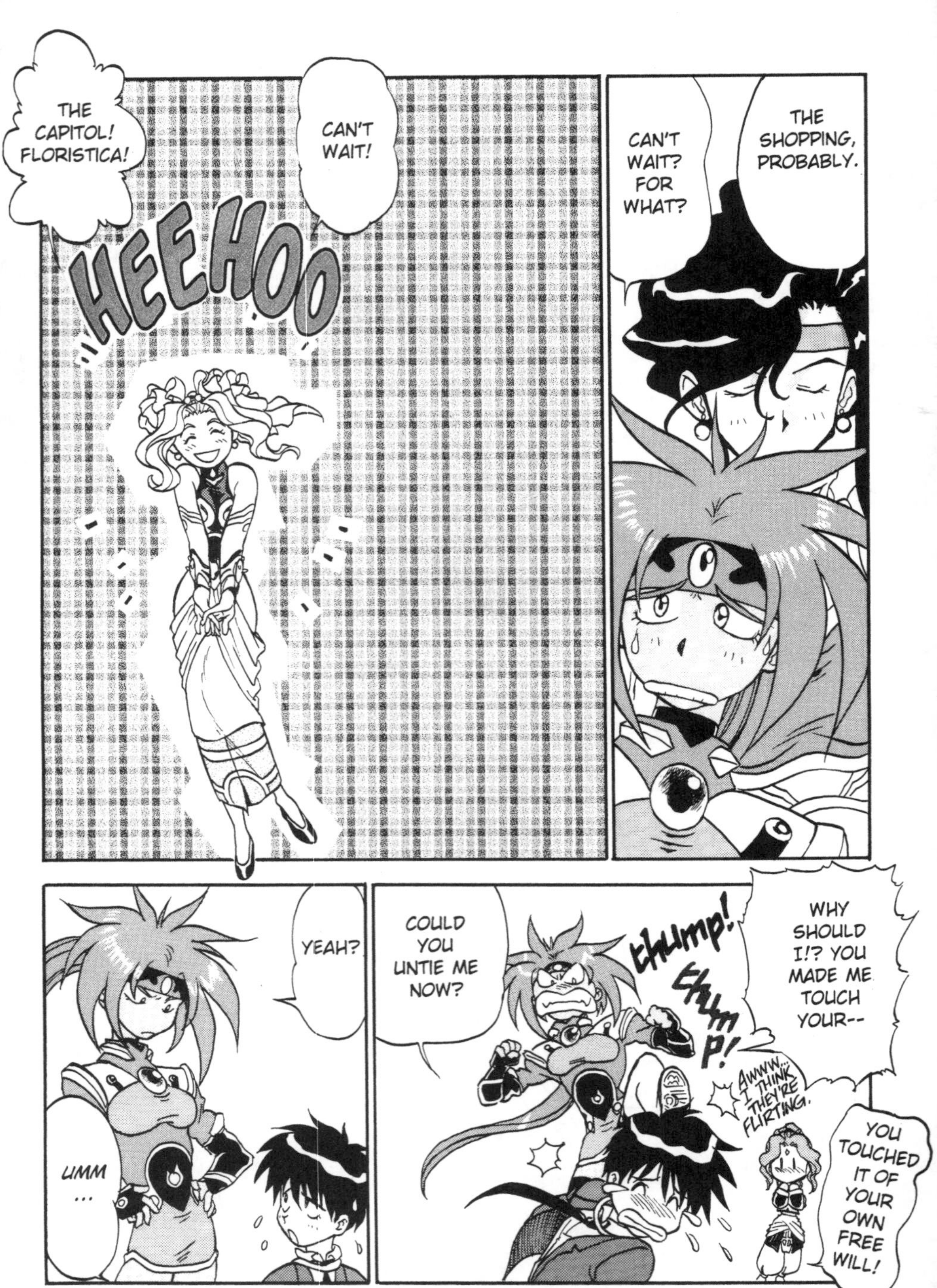
THE CAPITOL! FLORISTICA!
CAN'T WAIT!
HEEHOO
CAN'T WAIT? FOR WHAT?
THE SHOPPING, PROBABLY.
YEAH?
UMM ...
COULD YOU UNTIE ME NOW?
thump! thump!
WHY SHOULD I!? YOU MADE ME TOUCH YOUR--
AWWW... I THINK THEY'RE FLIRTING.
YOU TOUCHED IT OF YOUR OWN FREE WILL!

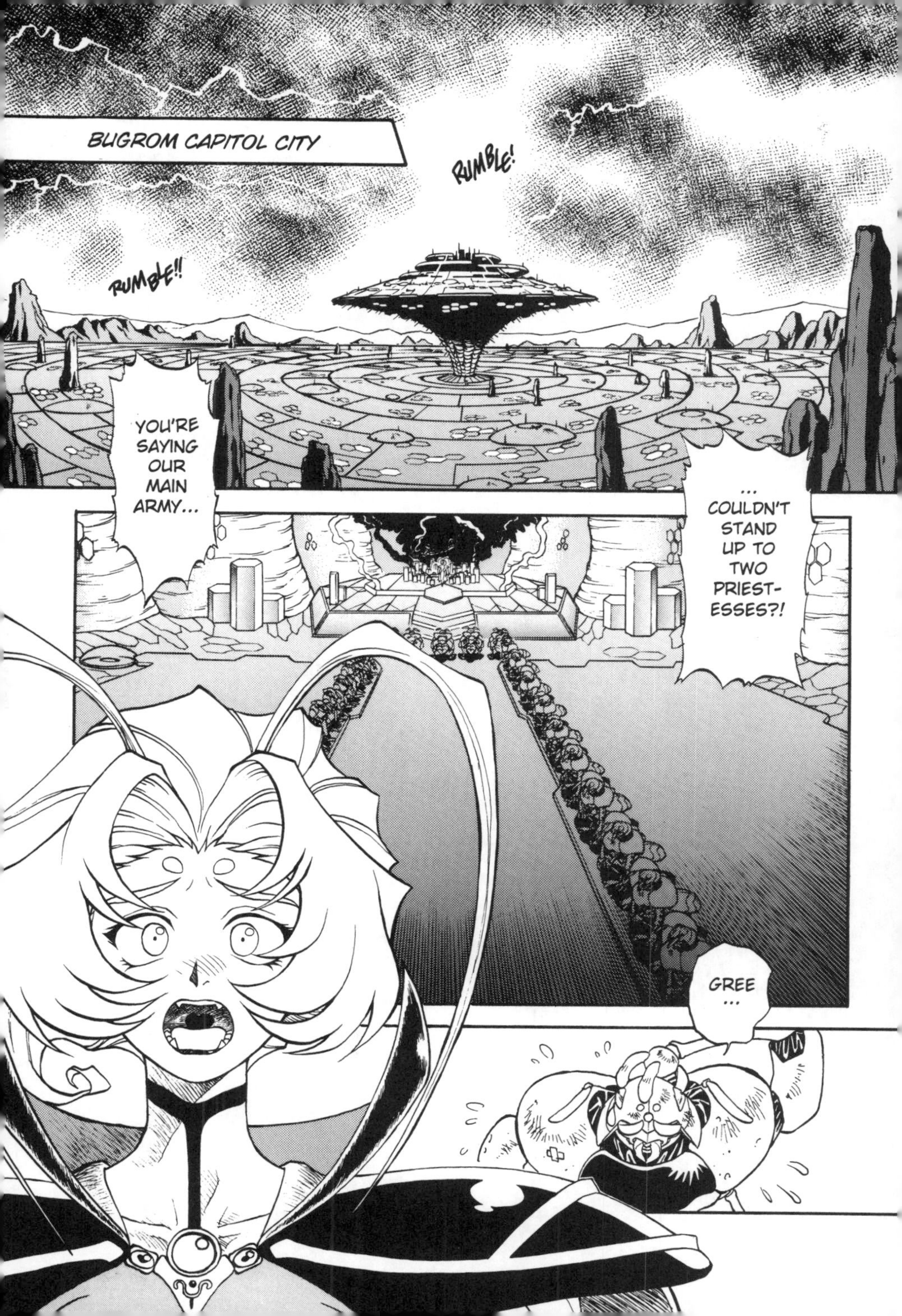
BUGROM CAPITOL CITY
RUMBLE!
RUMBLE!!
YOU'RE SAYING OUR MAIN ARMY...
... COULDN'T STAND UP TO TWO PRIEST-ESSES?!
GREE ...

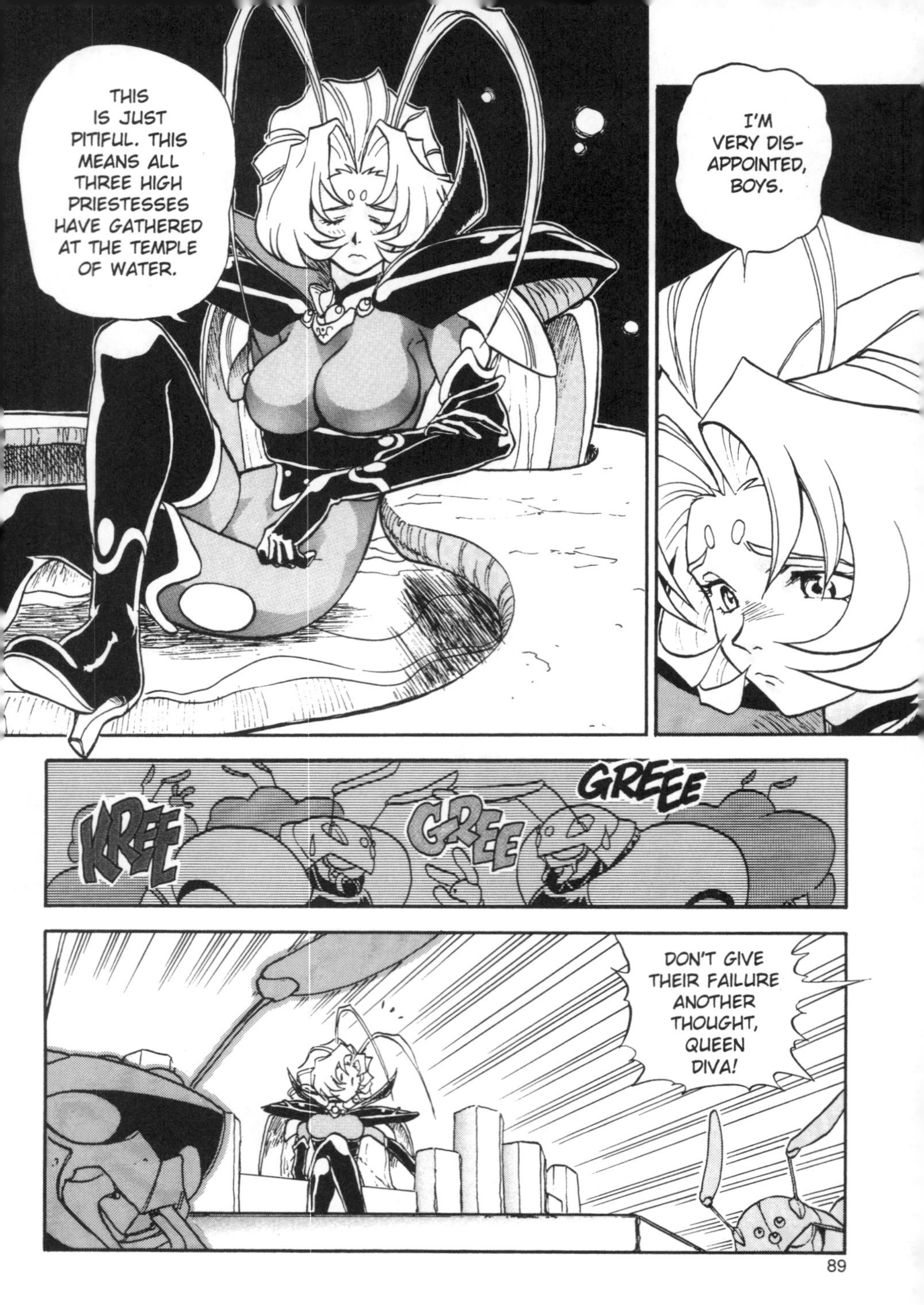
THIS IS JUST PITIFUL. THIS MEANS ALL THREE HIGH PRIESTESSES HAVE GATHERED AT THE TEMPLE OF WATER.
I'M VERY DIS-APPOINTED, BOYS.
KREE
GREE
GREEE
DON'T GIVE THEIR FAILURE ANOTHER THOUGHT, QUEEN DIVA!

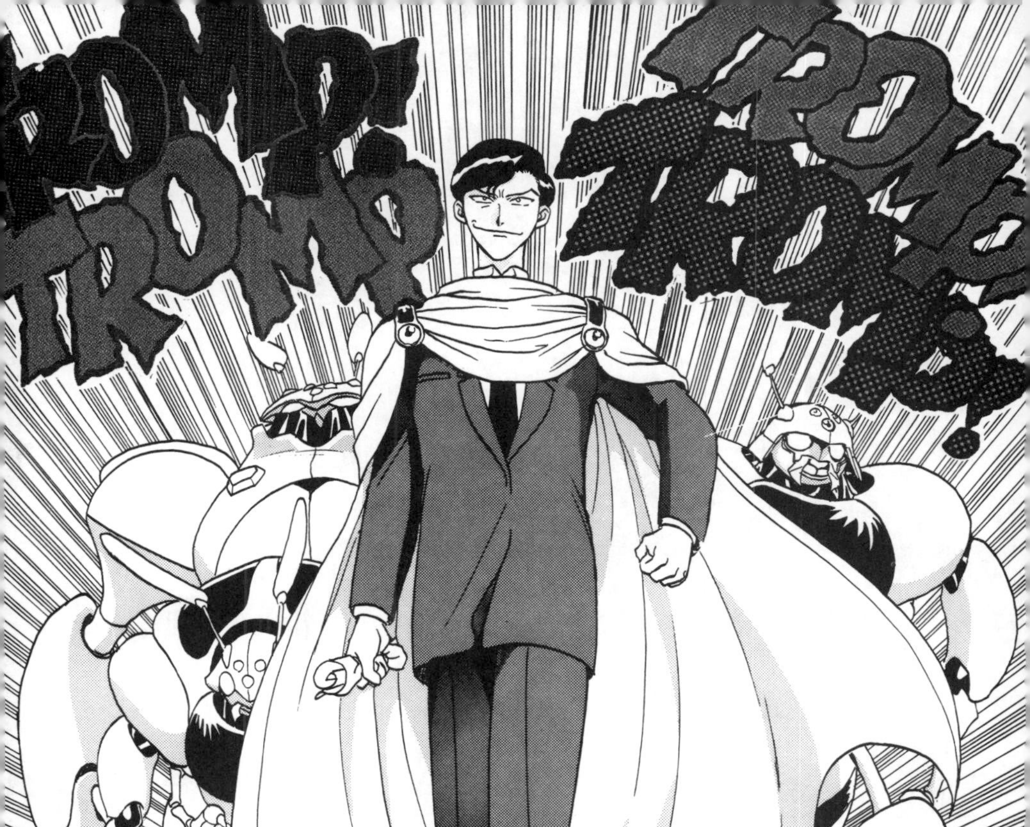
TROMP! TROMP
TROMP TROMP!

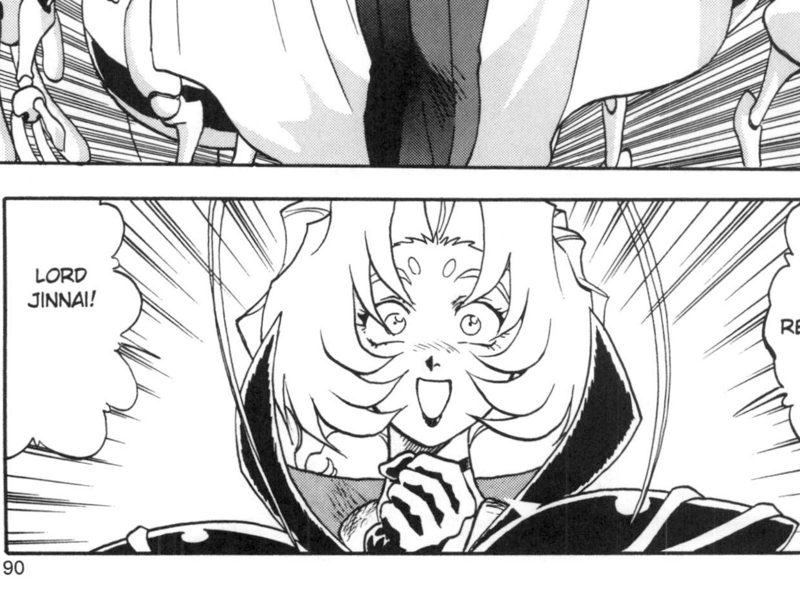
LORD JINNAI!
YOU HAVE RETURNED! ♡

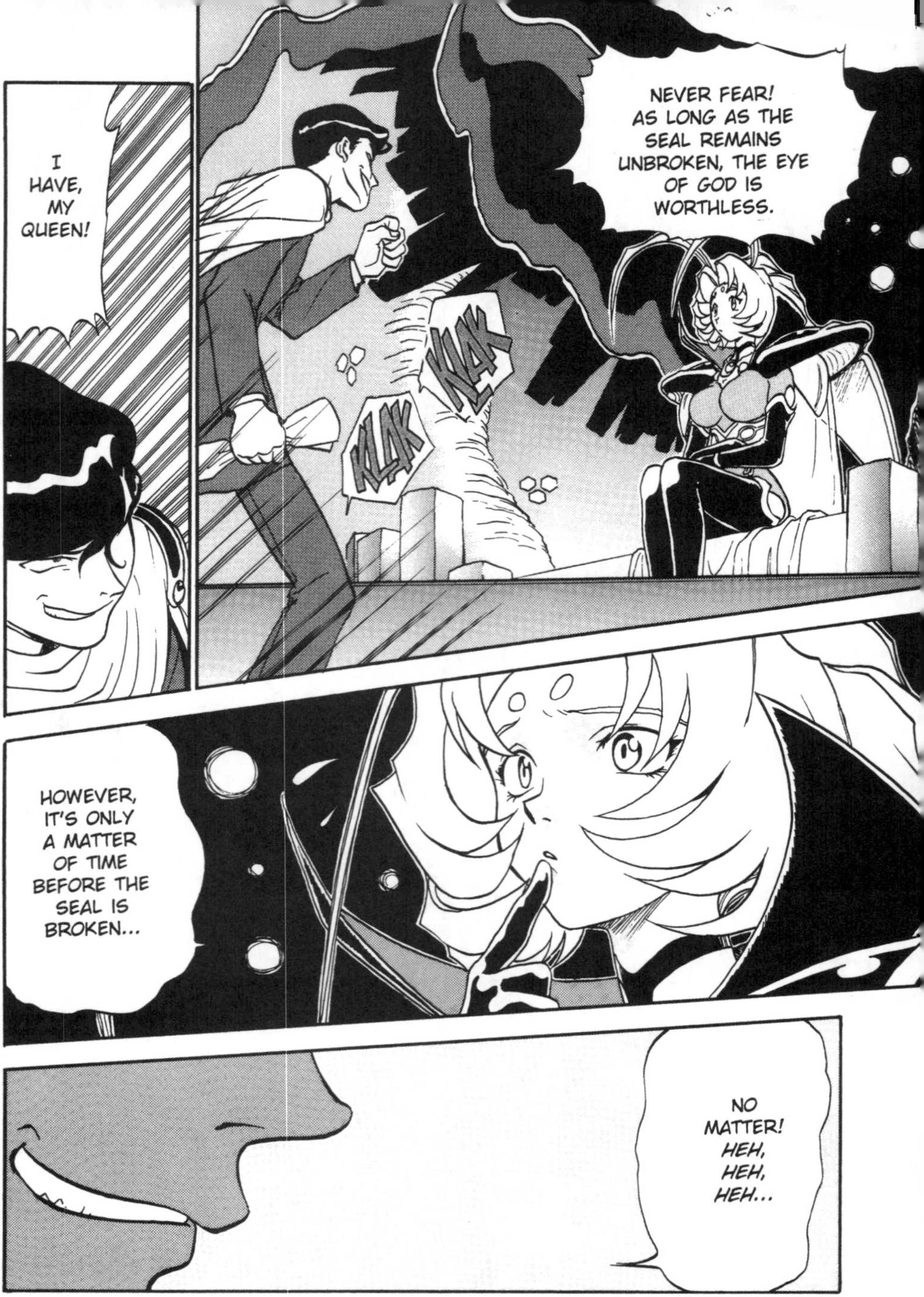
I HAVE, MY QUEEN!
NEVER FEAR! AS LONG AS THE SEAL REMAINS UNBROKEN, THE EYE OF GOD IS WORTHLESS.
KLAK
KLAK
HOWEVER, IT'S ONLY A MATTER OF TIME BEFORE THE SEAL IS BROKEN...
NO MATTER! *HEH, HEH, HEH...*

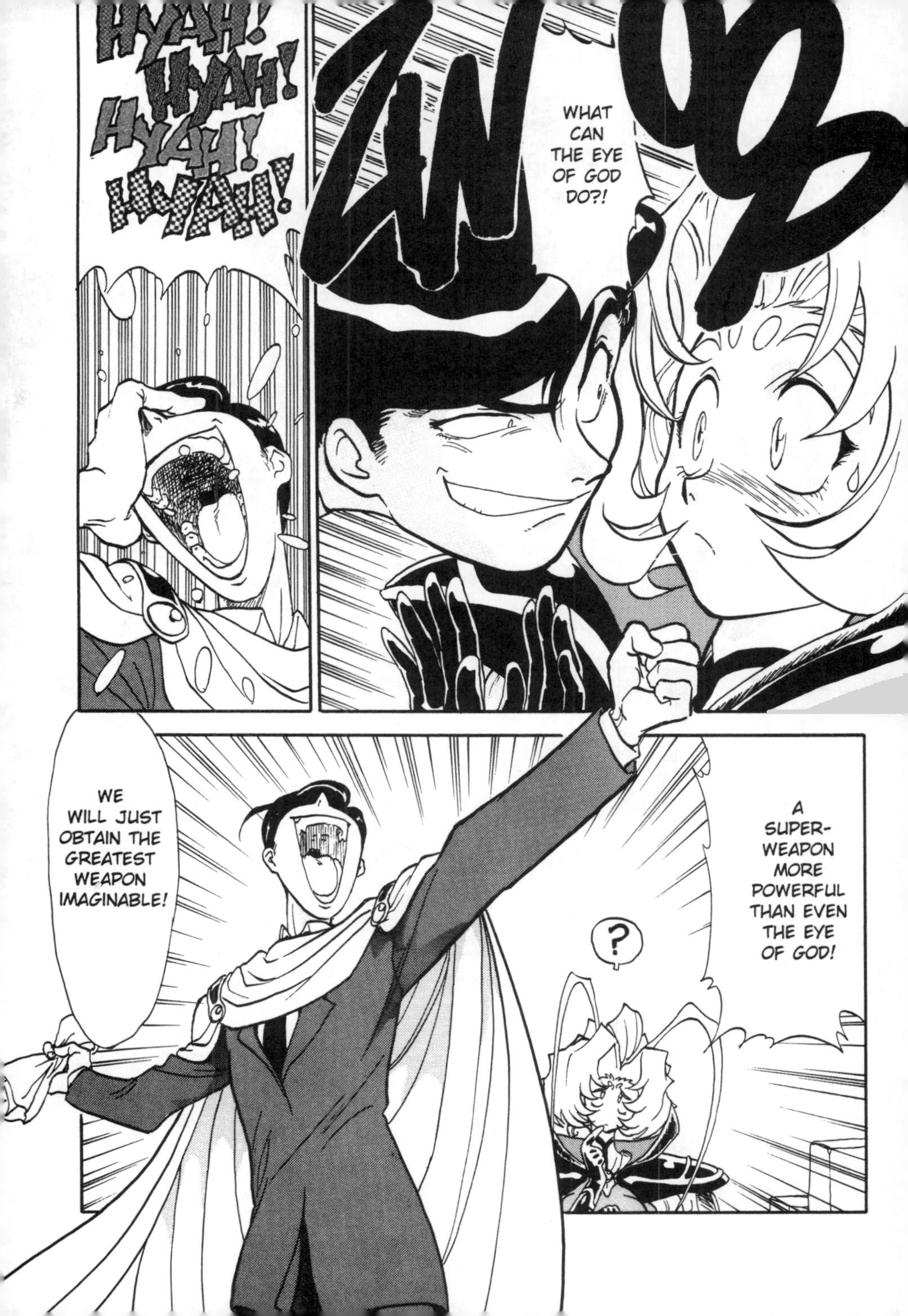
HYAH! HYAH! HYAH! HYAH!
ZWOOB
WHAT CAN THE EYE OF GOD DO?!
WE WILL JUST OBTAIN THE GREATEST WEAPON IMAGINABLE!
?
A SUPER-WEAPON MORE POWERFUL THAN EVEN THE EYE OF GOD!

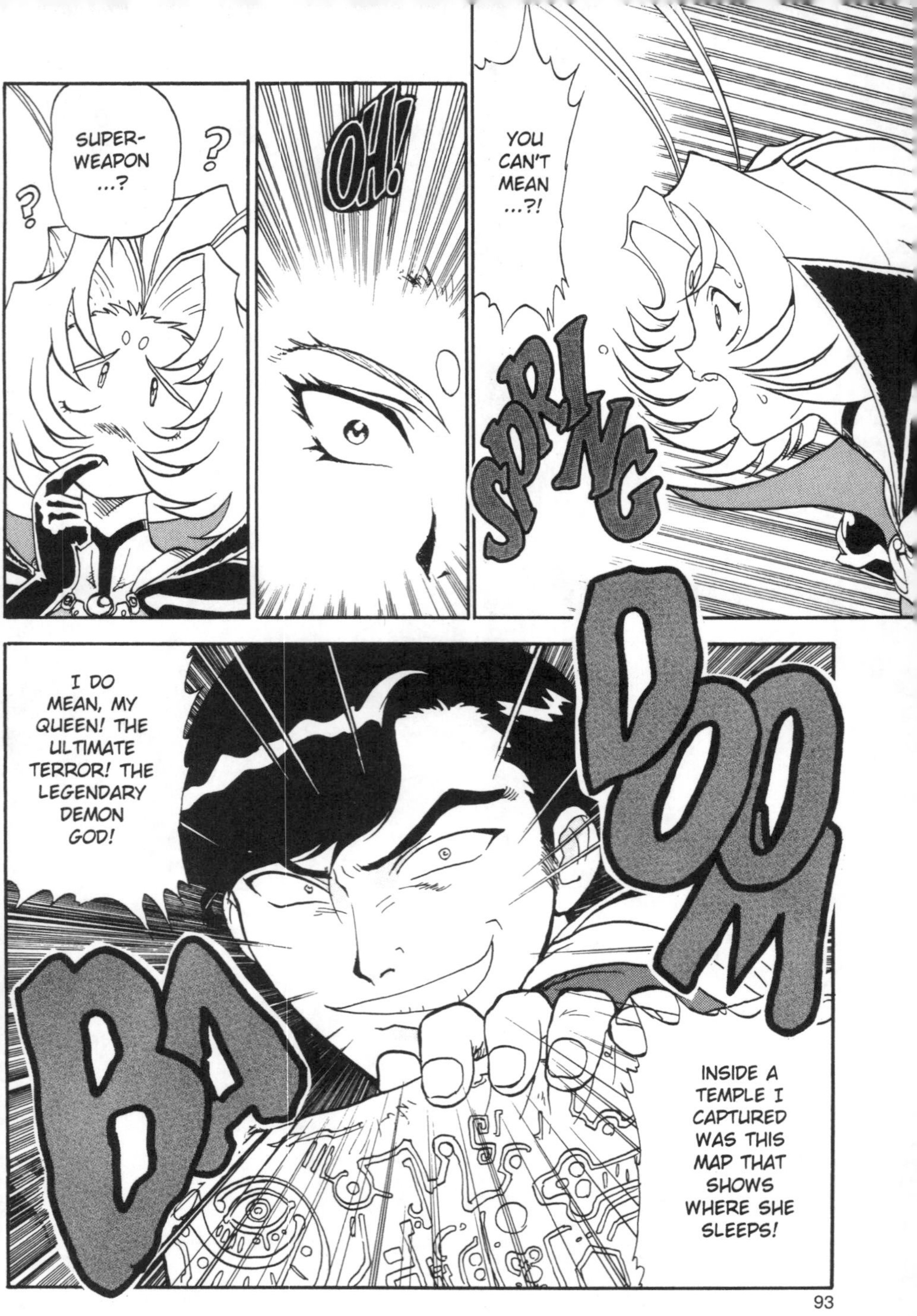
SUPER-WEAPON ...?
?
?
OH!
YOU CAN'T MEAN ...?!
SPRING
I DO MEAN, MY QUEEN! THE ULTIMATE TERROR! THE LEGENDARY DEMON GOD!
DOOM
BA
INSIDE A TEMPLE I CAPTURED WAS THIS MAP THAT SHOWS WHERE SHE SLEEPS!

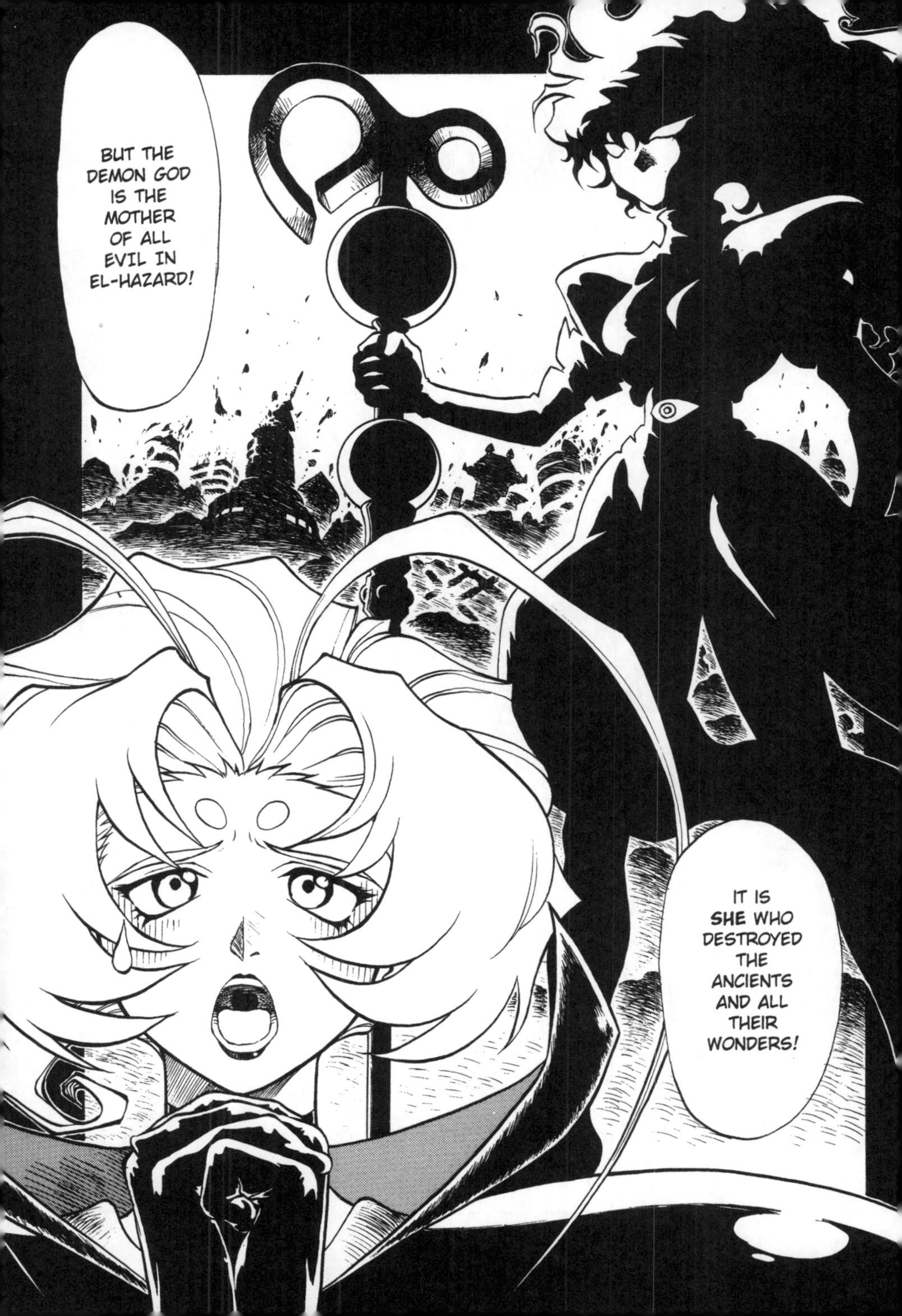
BUT THE DEMON GOD IS THE MOTHER OF ALL EVIL IN EL-HAZARD!
IT IS SHE WHO DESTROYED THE ANCIENTS AND ALL THEIR WONDERS!

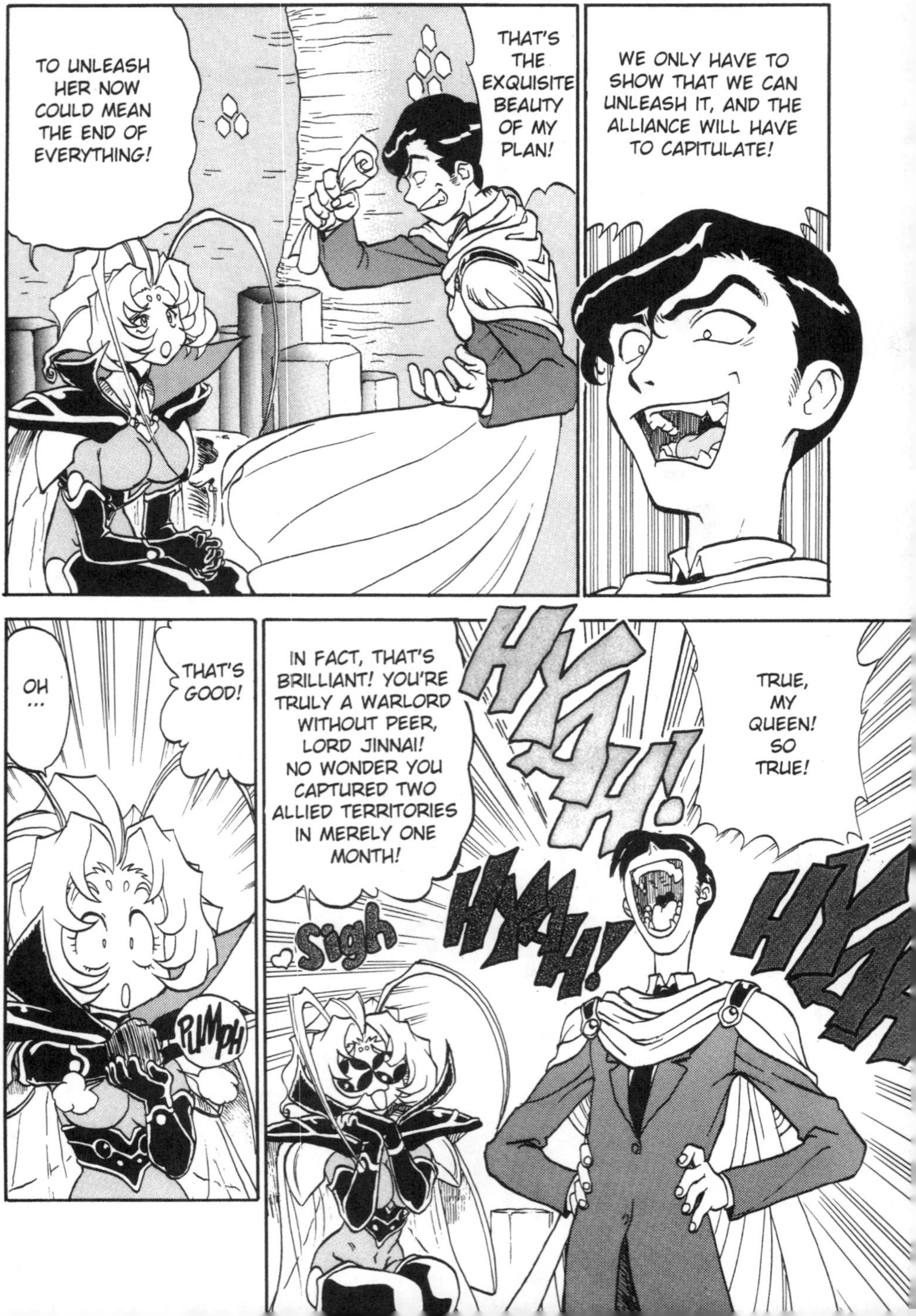
TO UNLEASH HER NOW COULD MEAN THE END OF EVERYTHING!
THAT'S THE EXQUISITE BEAUTY OF MY PLAN!
WE ONLY HAVE TO SHOW THAT WE CAN UNLEASH IT, AND THE ALLIANCE WILL HAVE TO CAPITULATE!
OH ...
THAT'S GOOD!
PUMPH
IN FACT, THAT'S BRILLIANT! YOU'RE TRULY A WARLORD WITHOUT PEER, LORD JINNAI! NO WONDER YOU CAPTURED TWO ALLIED TERRITORIES IN MERELY ONE MONTH!
Sigh
HYAH!
HYAH!
TRUE, MY QUEEN! SO TRUE!

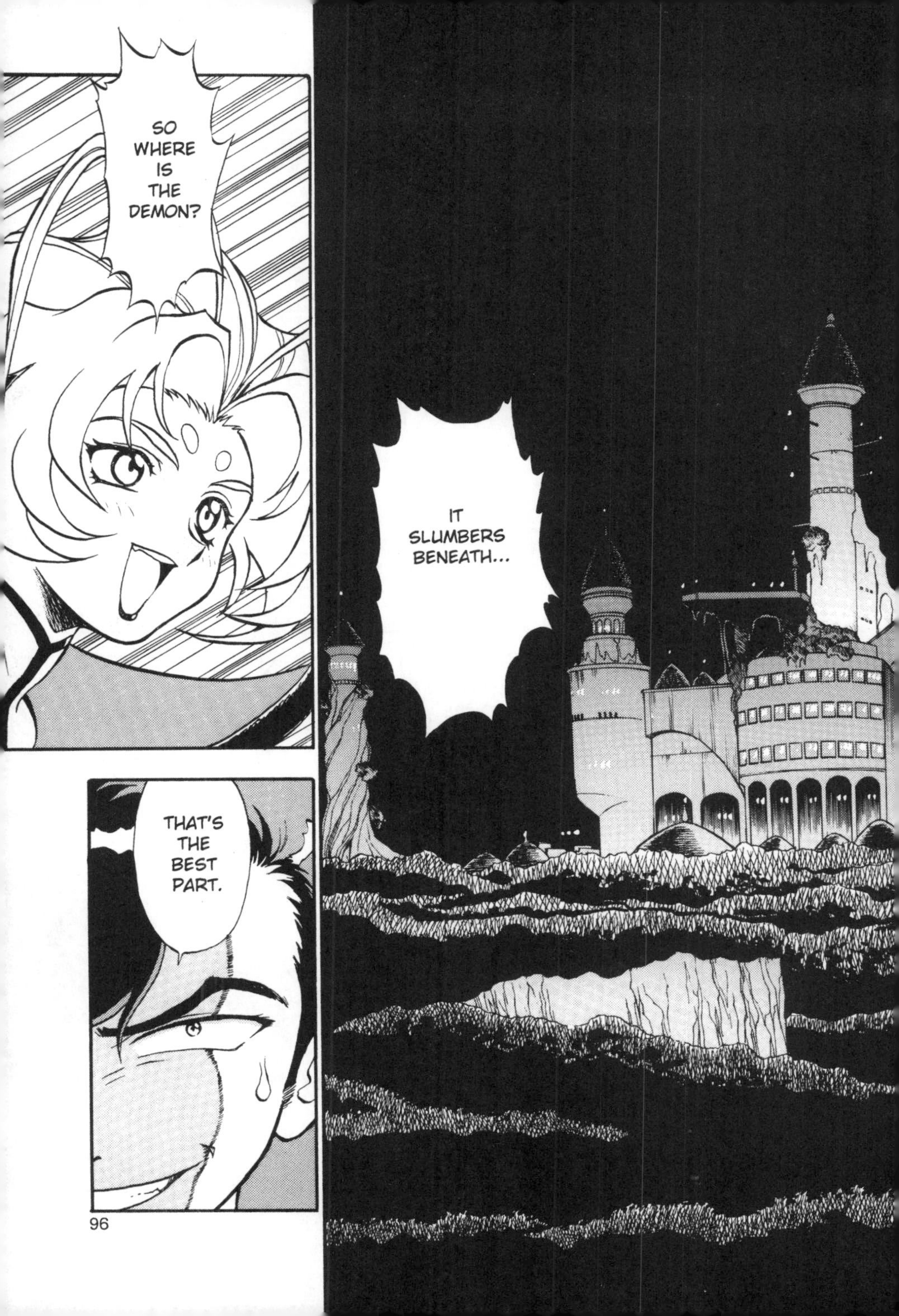
SO WHERE IS THE DEMON?
THAT'S THE BEST PART.
IT SLUMBERS BENEATH...

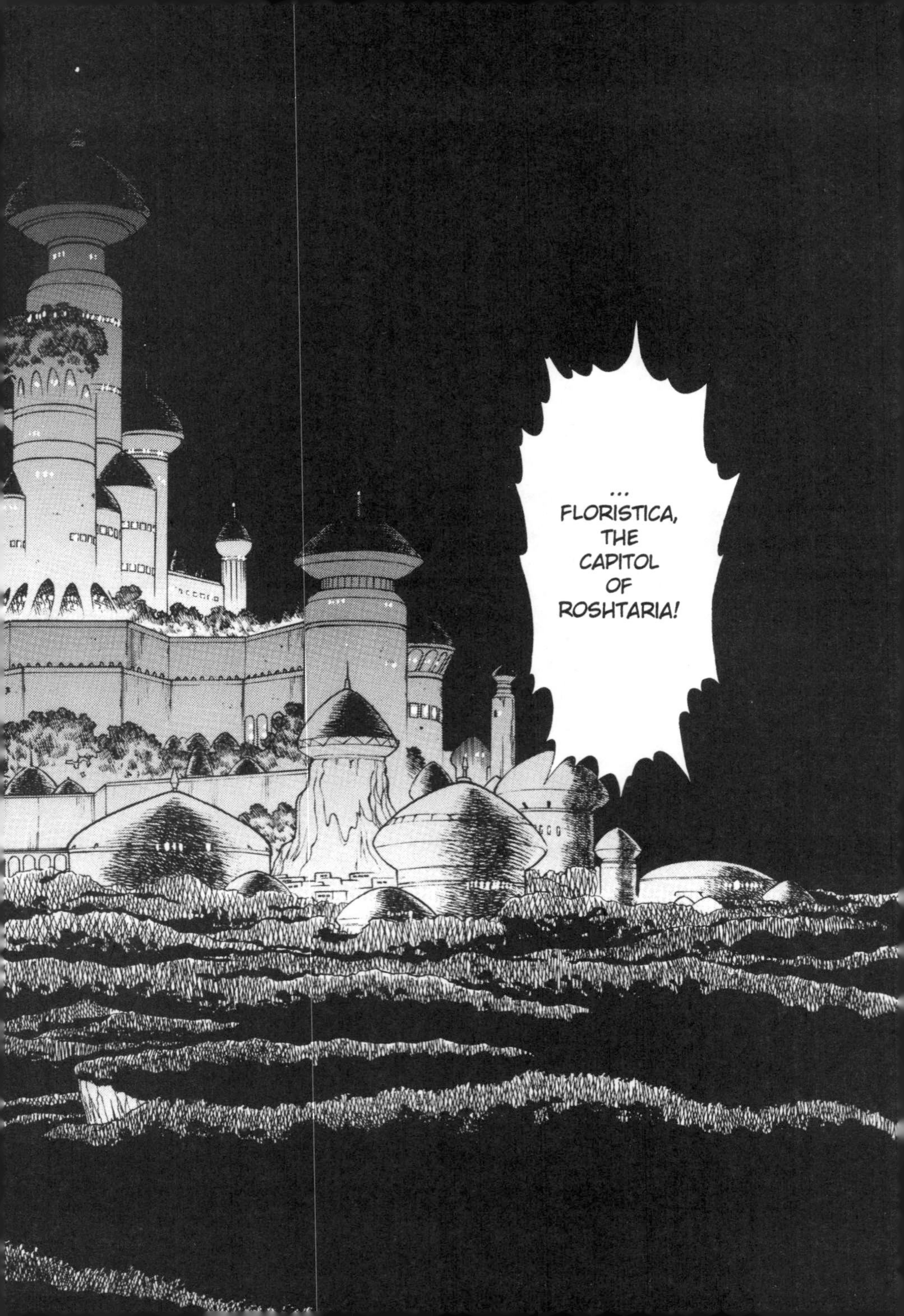
...
FLORISTICA,
THE
CAPITOL
OF
ROSHTARIA!

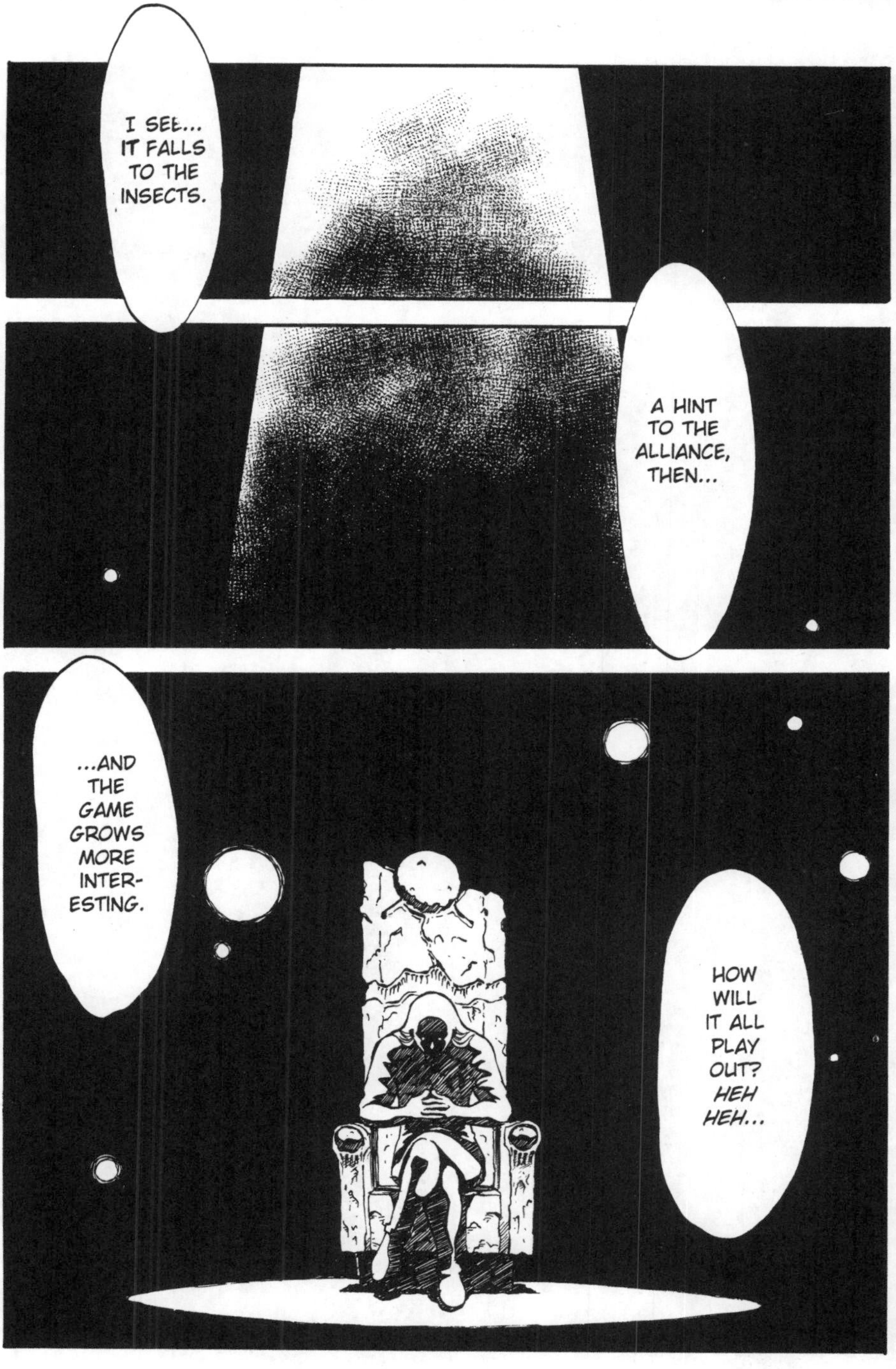
I SEE... IT FALLS TO THE INSECTS.
A HINT TO THE ALLIANCE, THEN...
...AND THE GAME GROWS MORE INTER-ESTING.
HOW WILL IT ALL PLAY OUT? HEH HEH...

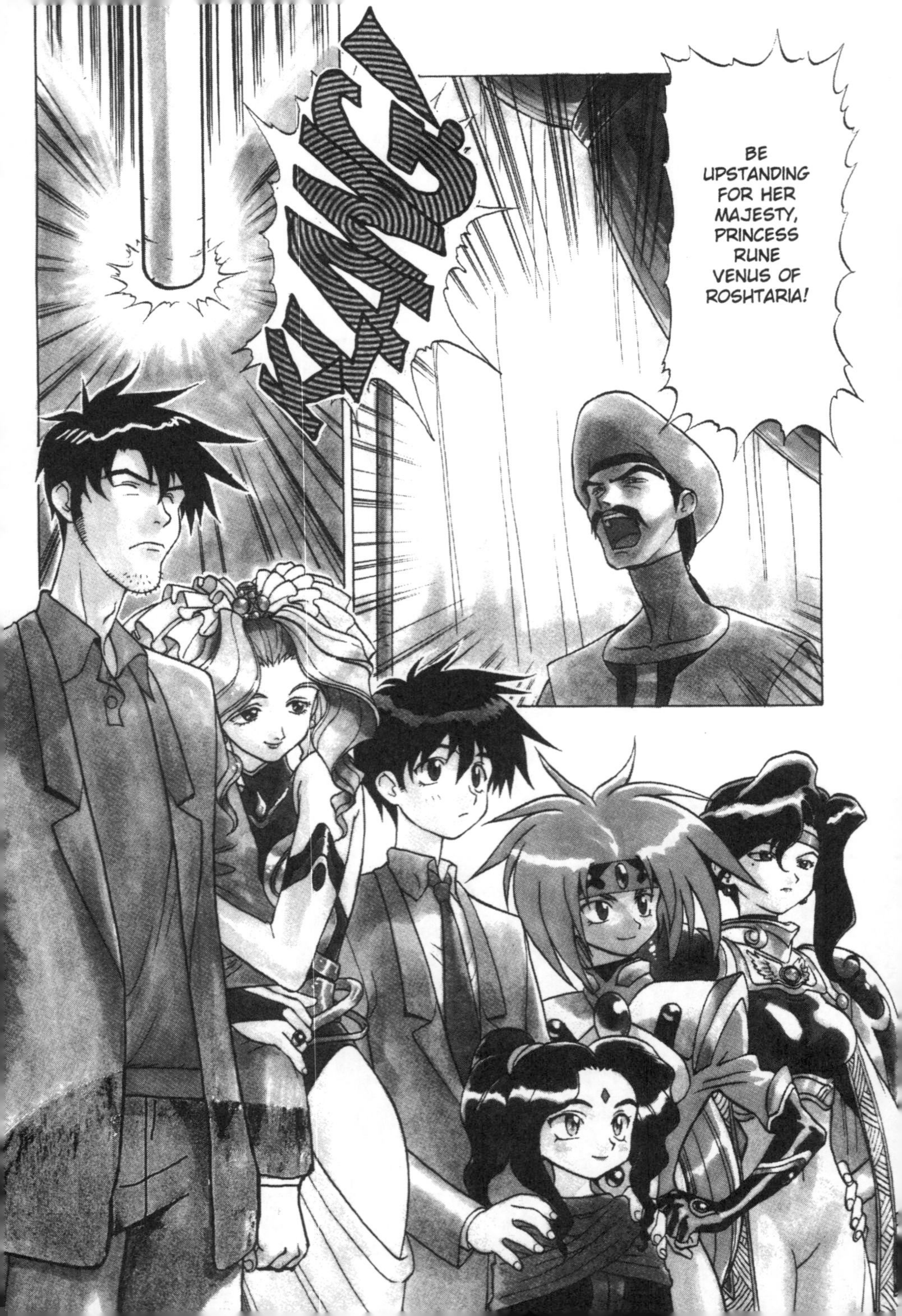
BE UPSTANDING FOR HER MAJESTY, PRINCESS RUNE VENUS OF ROSHTARIA!

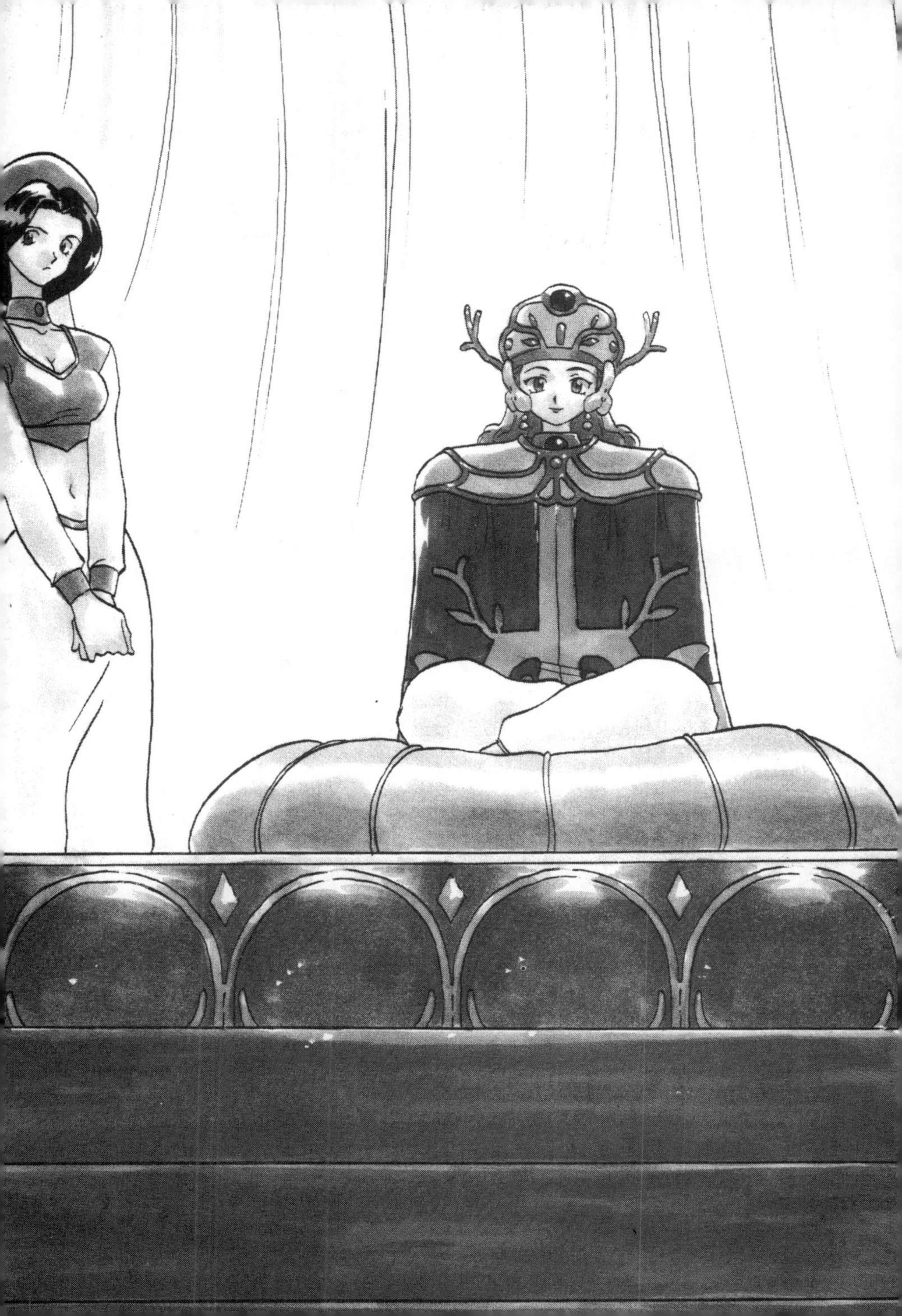

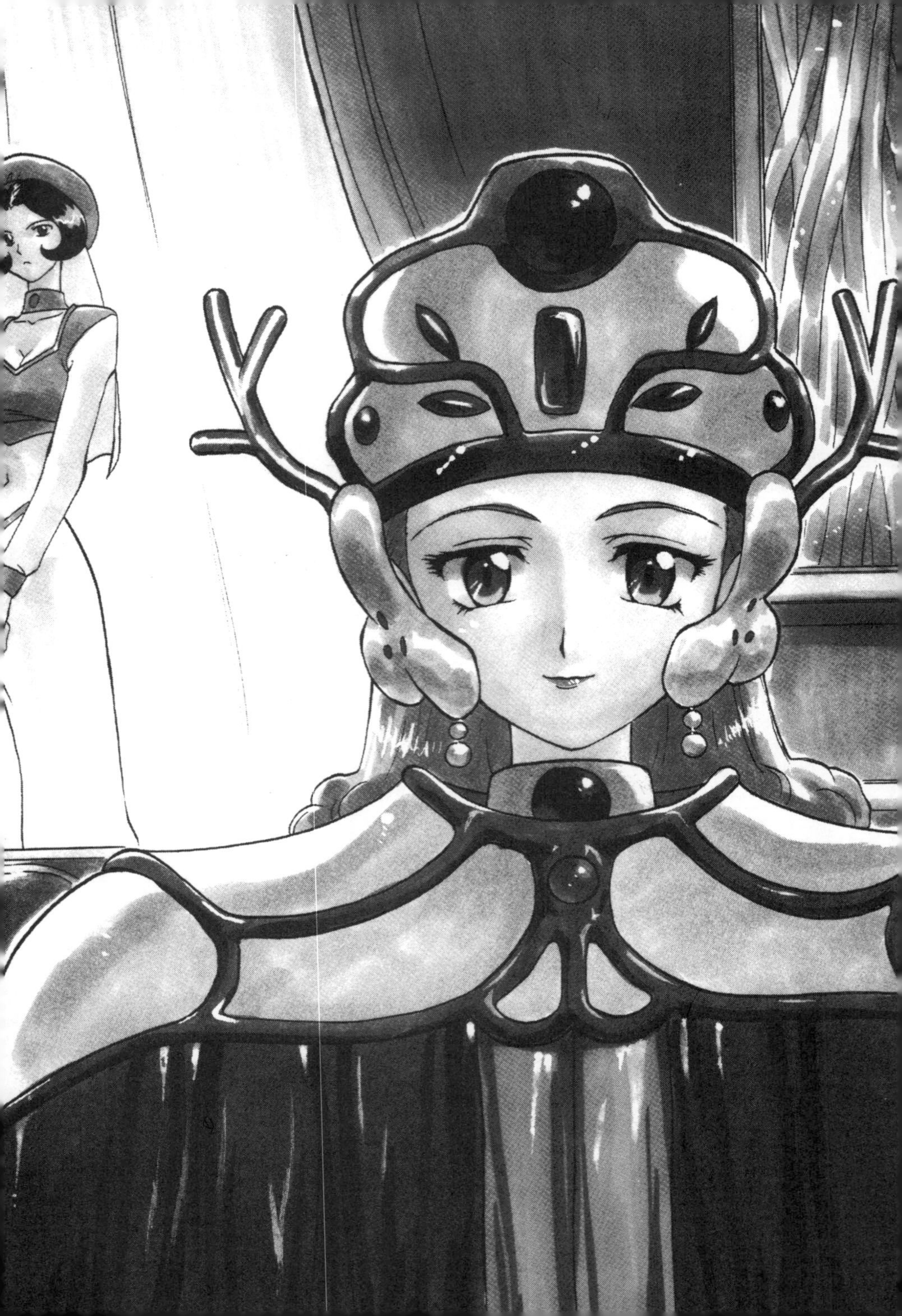

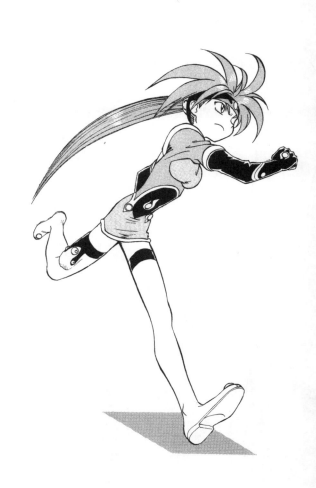

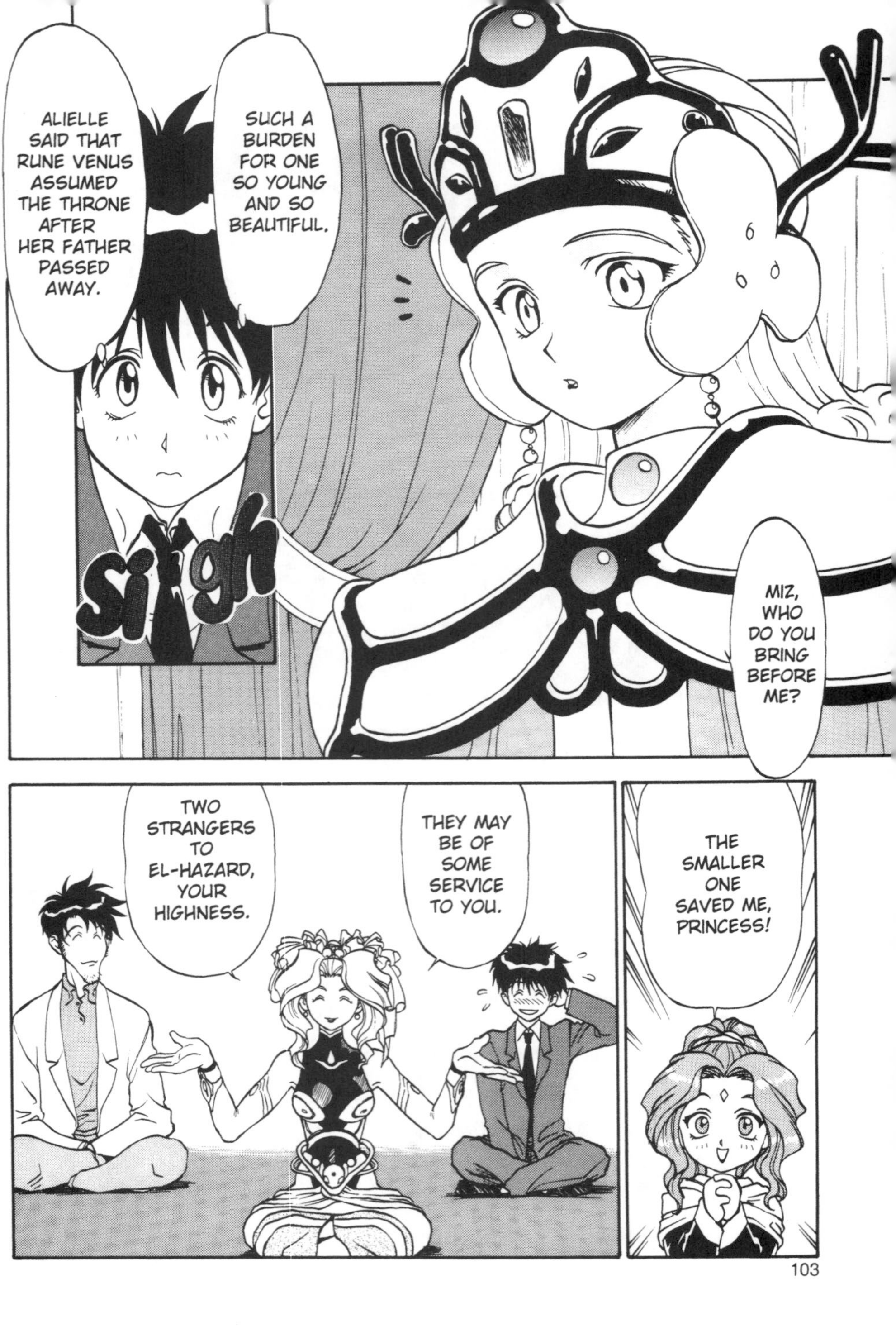
ALIELLE SAID THAT RUNE VENUS ASSUMED THE THRONE AFTER HER FATHER PASSED AWAY.
SUCH A BURDEN FOR ONE SO YOUNG AND SO BEAUTIFUL.
SIGH
MIZ, WHO DO YOU BRING BEFORE ME?
TWO STRANGERS TO EL-HAZARD, YOUR HIGHNESS.
THEY MAY BE OF SOME SERVICE TO YOU.
THE SMALLER ONE SAVED ME, PRINCESS!

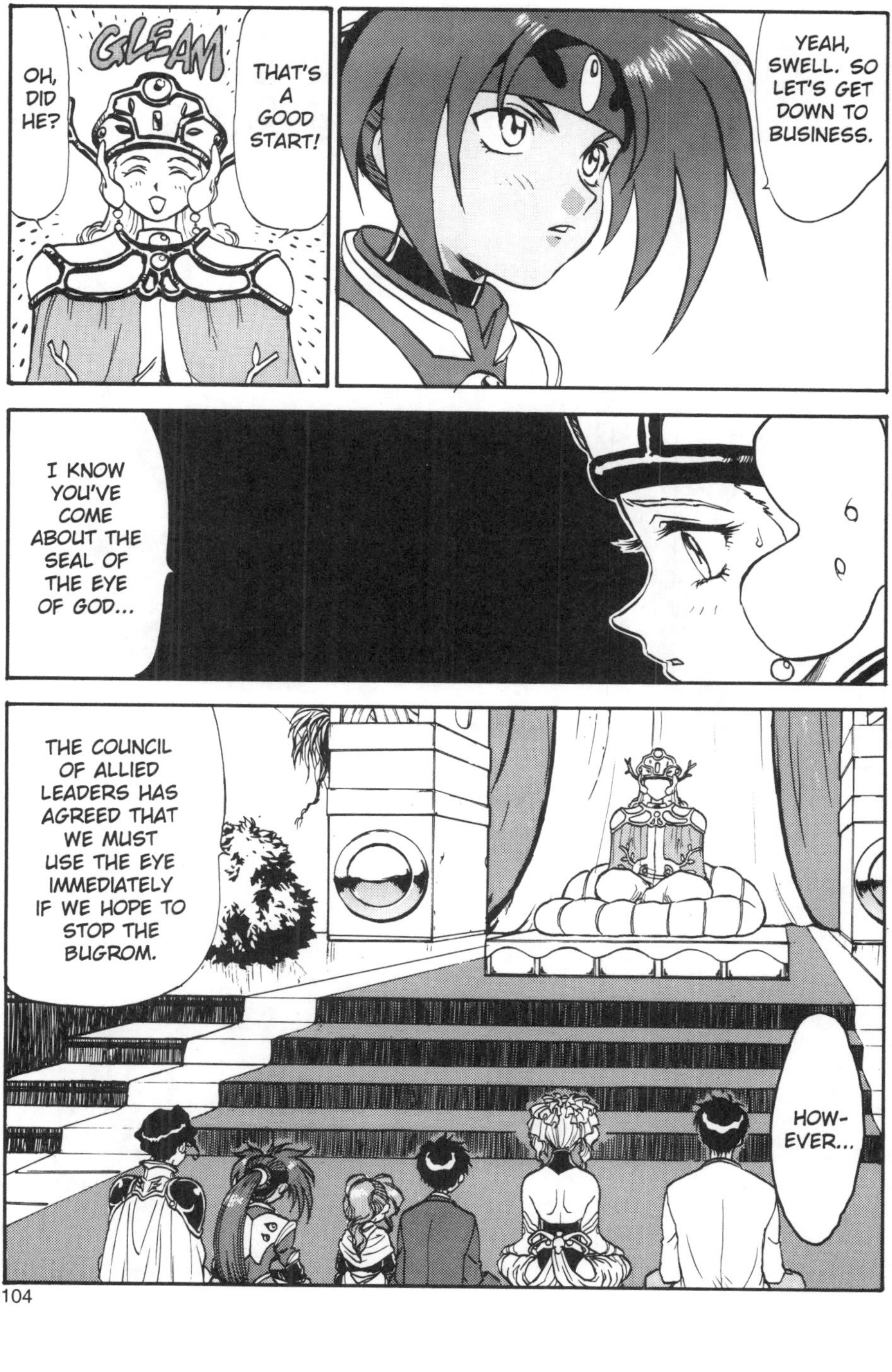
GLEAM
OH, DID HE?
THAT'S A GOOD START!
YEAH, SWELL. SO LET'S GET DOWN TO BUSINESS.
I KNOW YOU'VE COME ABOUT THE SEAL OF THE EYE OF GOD...
THE COUNCIL OF ALLIED LEADERS HAS AGREED THAT WE MUST USE THE EYE IMMEDIATELY IF WE HOPE TO STOP THE BUGROM.
HOW-EVER...

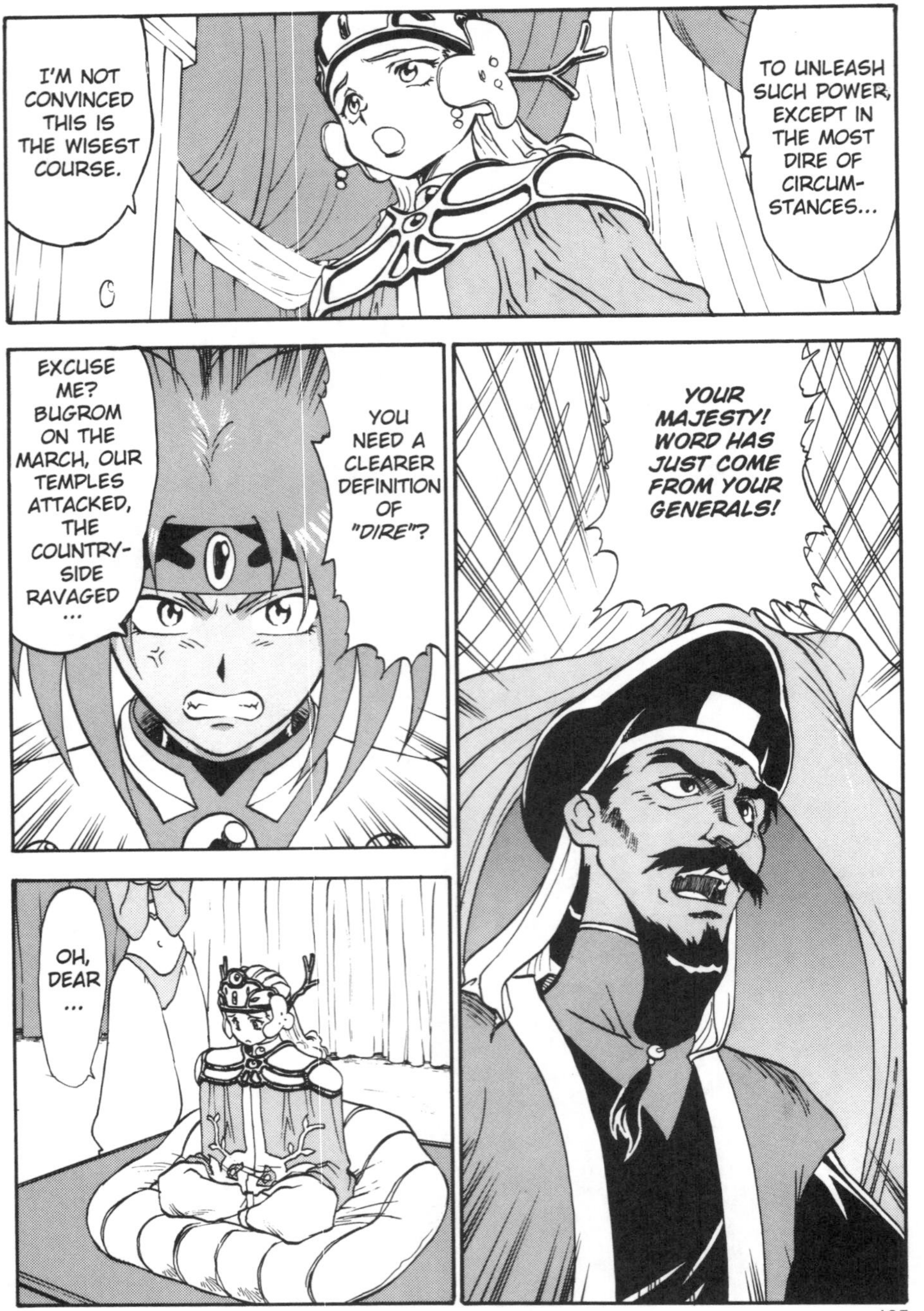
I'M NOT CONVINCED THIS IS THE WISEST COURSE.
TO UNLEASH SUCH POWER, EXCEPT IN THE MOST DIRE OF CIRCUM-STANCES...
EXCUSE ME? BUGROM ON THE MARCH, OUR TEMPLES ATTACKED, THE COUNTRY-SIDE RAVAGED...
YOU NEED A CLEARER DEFINITION OF "DIRE"?
OH, DEAR...
YOUR MAJESTY! WORD HAS JUST COME FROM YOUR GENERALS!

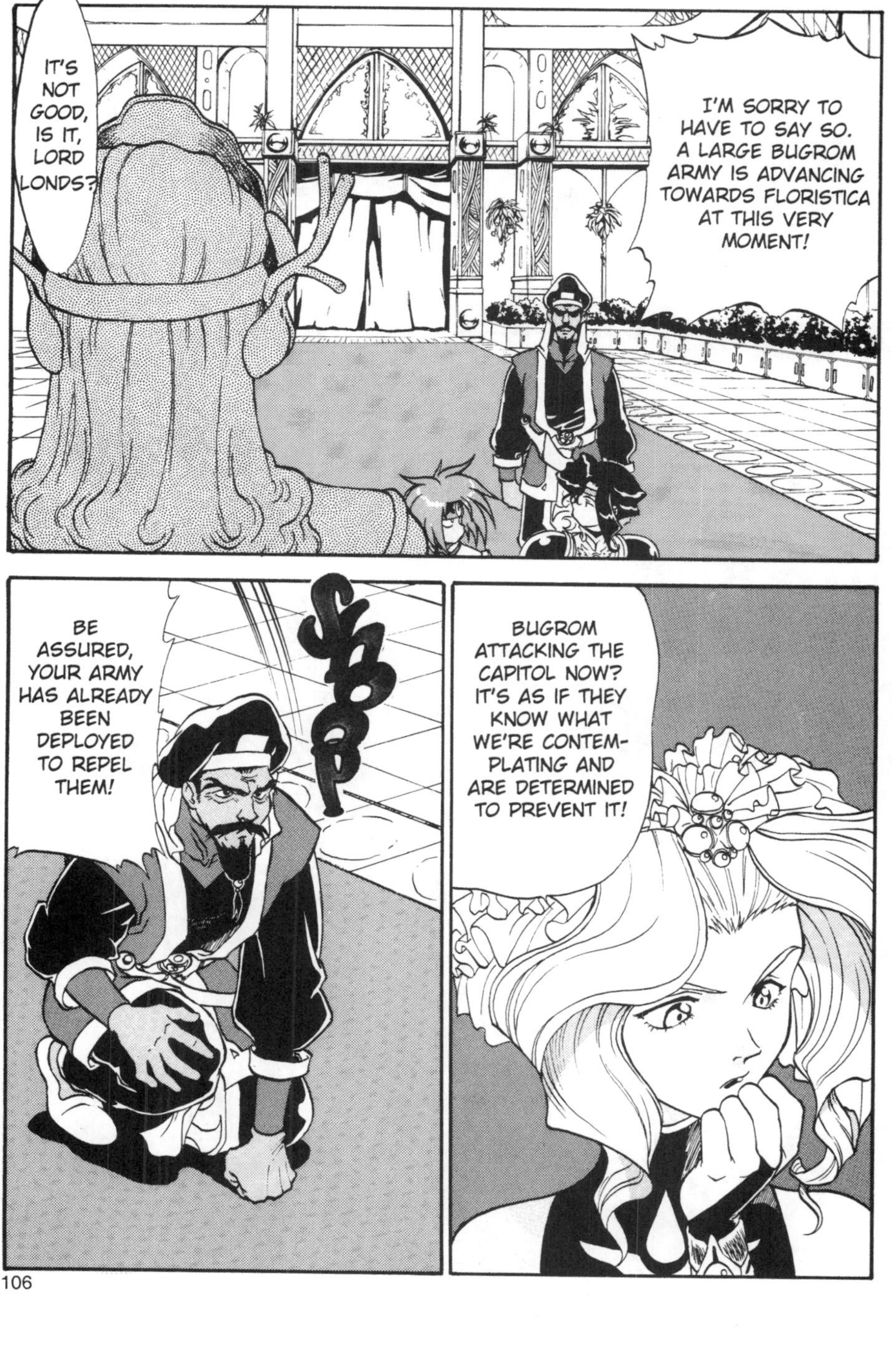
IT'S NOT GOOD, IS IT, LORD LONDS?
I'M SORRY TO HAVE TO SAY SO. A LARGE BUGROM ARMY IS ADVANCING TOWARDS FLORISTICA AT THIS VERY MOMENT!
BE ASSURED, YOUR ARMY HAS ALREADY BEEN DEPLOYED TO REPEL THEM!
BUGROM ATTACKING THE CAPITOL NOW? IT'S AS IF THEY KNOW WHAT WE'RE CONTEM-PLATING AND ARE DETERMINED TO PREVENT IT!

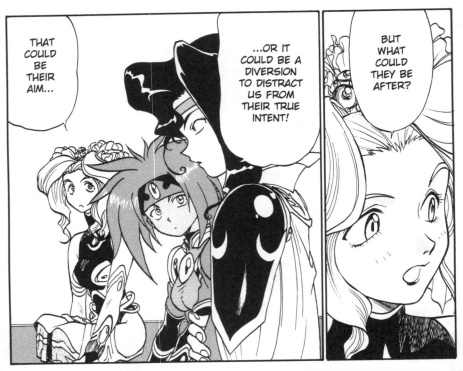

THAT COULD BE THEIR AIM...

...OR IT COULD BE A DIVERSION TO DISTRACT US FROM THEIR TRUE INTENT!

BUT WHAT COULD THEY BE AFTER?

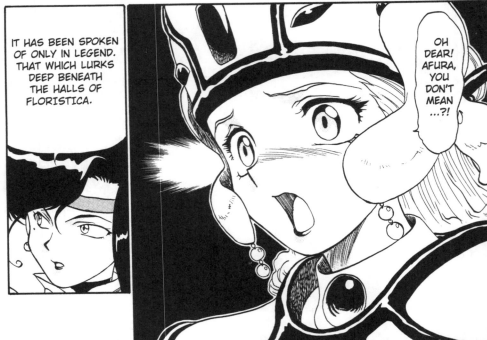

IT HAS BEEN SPOKEN OF ONLY IN LEGEND. THAT WHICH LURKS DEEP BENEATH THE HALLS OF FLORISTICA.

OH DEAR! AFURA, YOU DON'T MEAN ...?!

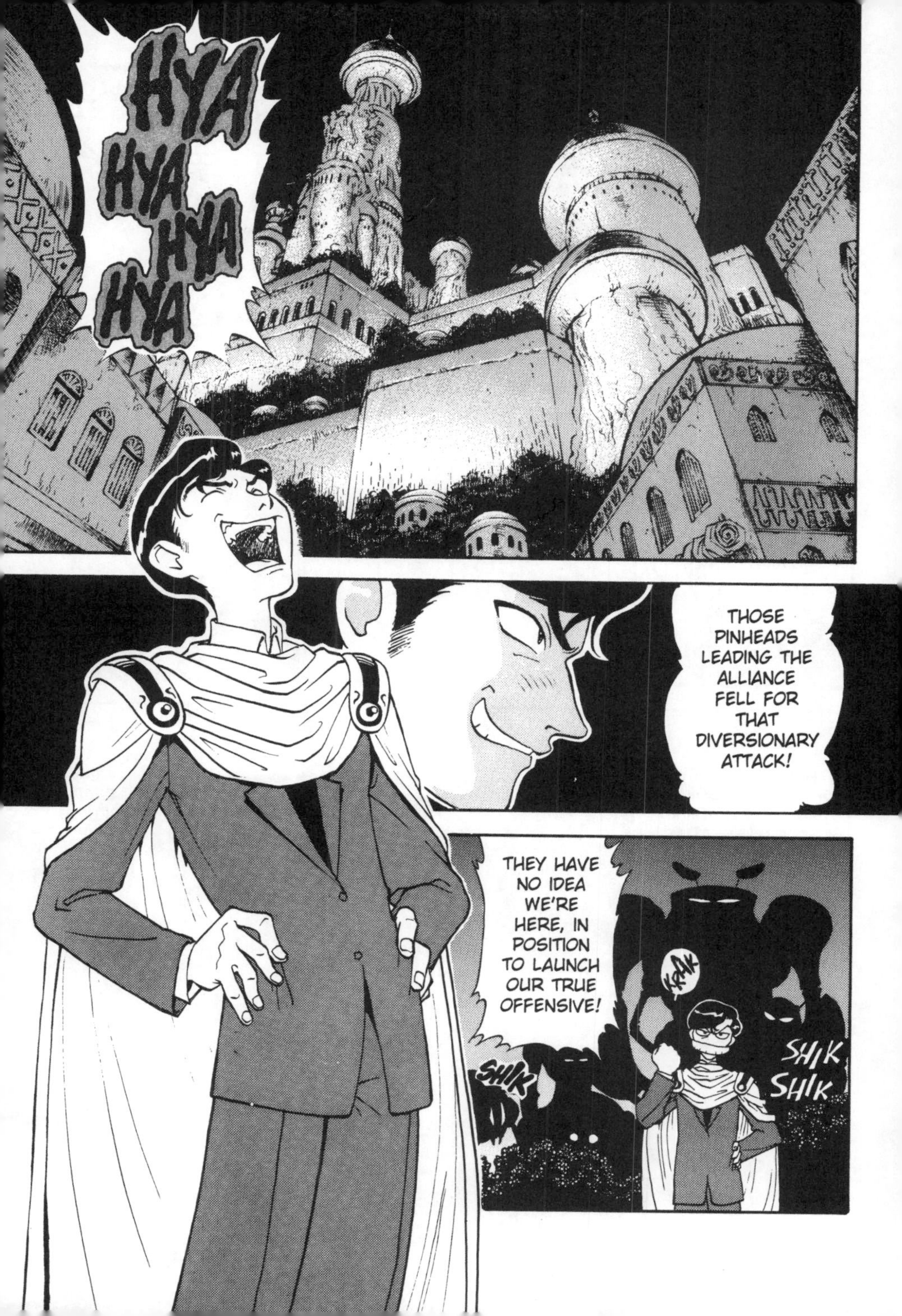
HYA HYA HYA HYA HYA
THOSE PINHEADS LEADING THE ALLIANCE FELL FOR THAT DIVERSIONARY ATTACK!
THEY HAVE NO IDEA WE'RE HERE, IN POSITION TO LAUNCH OUR TRUE OFFENSIVE!
KRAK
SHIK
SHIK SHIK

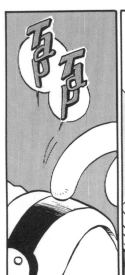

WHAT IS IT, KATSUO?

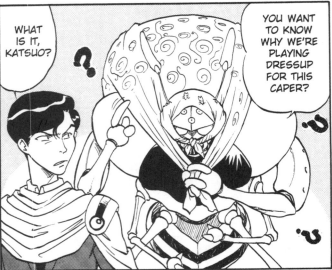

YOU WANT TO KNOW WHY WE'RE PLAYING DRESSUP FOR THIS CAPER?

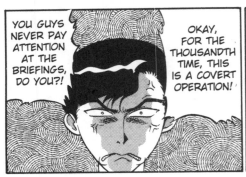

YOU GUYS NEVER PAY ATTENTION AT THE BRIEFINGS, DO YOU?!

OKAY, FOR THE THOUSANDTH TIME, THIS IS A COVERT OPERATION!

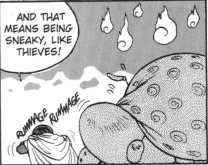

AND THAT MEANS BEING SNEAKY, LIKE THIEVES!

RUMMAGE RUMMAGE

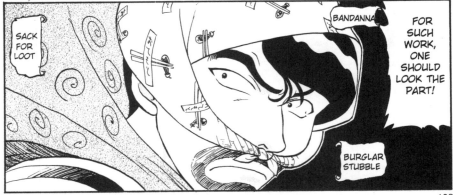

SACK FOR LOOT

BANDANNA

FOR SUCH WORK, ONE SHOULD LOOK THE PART!

BURGLAR STUBBLE

109

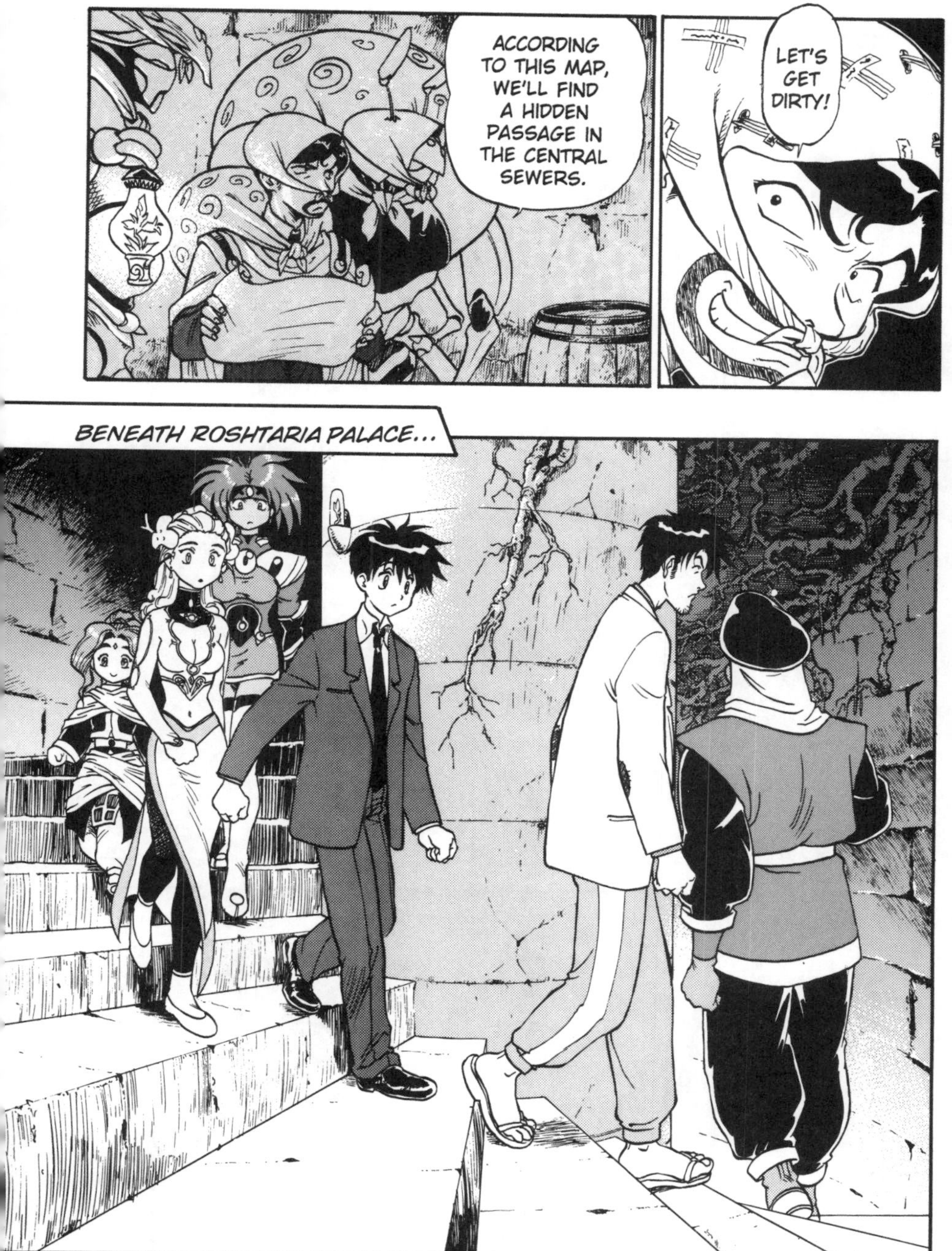
ACCORDING TO THIS MAP, WE'LL FIND A HIDDEN PASSAGE IN THE CENTRAL SEWERS.
LET'S GET DIRTY!
BENEATH ROSHTARIA PALACE...

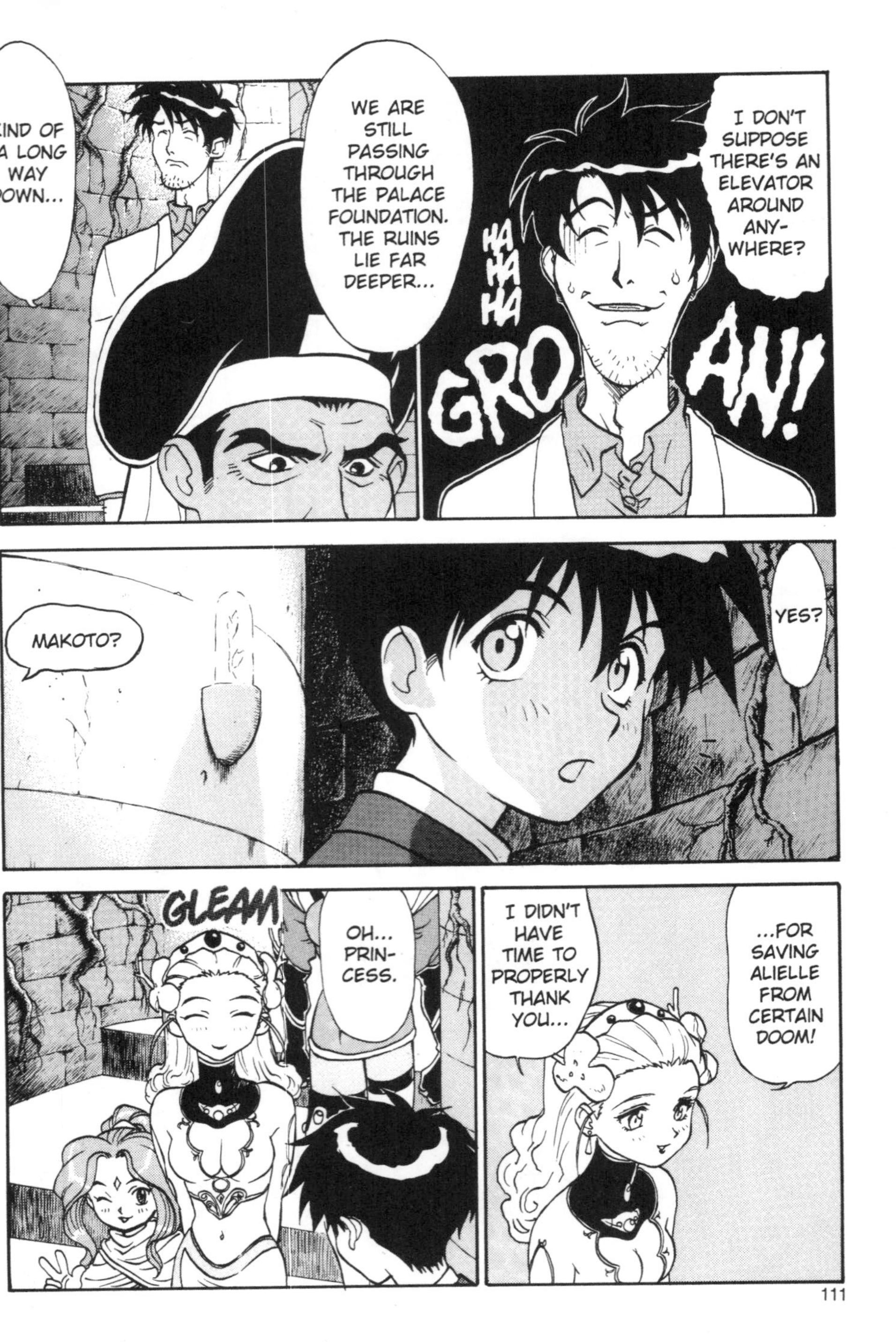
KIND OF A LONG WAY DOWN...
WE ARE STILL PASSING THROUGH THE PALACE FOUNDATION. THE RUINS LIE FAR DEEPER...
HA HA HA
I DON'T SUPPOSE THERE'S AN ELEVATOR AROUND ANY-WHERE?
GROAN!
MAKOTO?
YES?
GLEAM
OH... PRIN-CESS.
I DIDN'T HAVE TIME TO PROPERLY THANK YOU...
...FOR SAVING ALIELLE FROM CERTAIN DOOM!

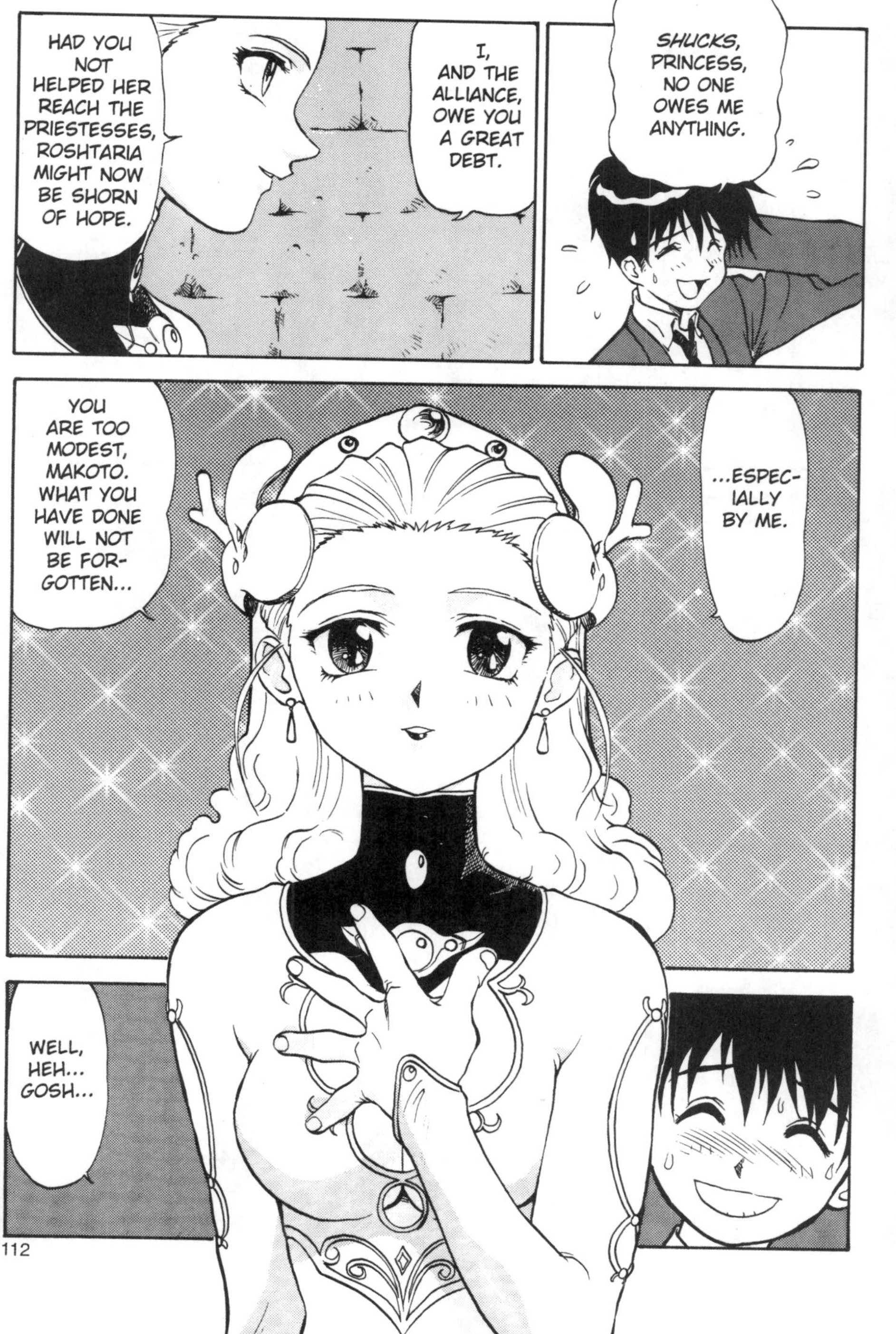
HAD YOU NOT HELPED HER REACH THE PRIESTESSES, ROSHTARIA MIGHT NOW BE SHORN OF HOPE.
I, AND THE ALLIANCE, OWE YOU A GREAT DEBT.
SHUCKS, PRINCESS, NO ONE OWES ME ANYTHING.
YOU ARE TOO MODEST, MAKOTO. WHAT YOU HAVE DONE WILL NOT BE FOR-GOTTEN...
...ESPEC-IALLY BY ME.
WELL, HEH... GOSH...

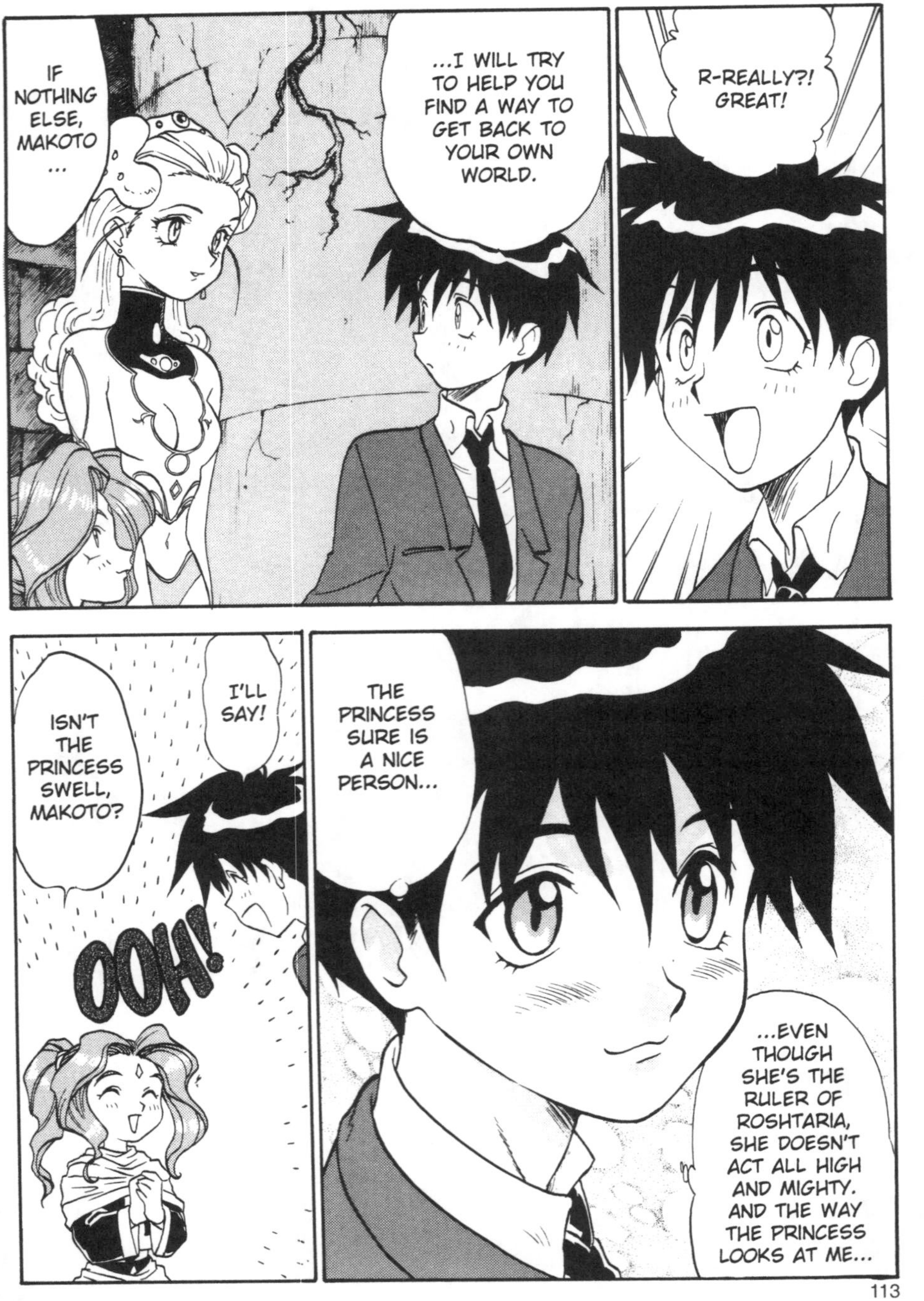

IF NOTHING ELSE, MAKOTO ...
...I WILL TRY TO HELP YOU FIND A WAY TO GET BACK TO YOUR OWN WORLD.
R-REALLY?! GREAT!
ISN'T THE PRINCESS SWELL, MAKOTO?
I'LL SAY!
OOH!
THE PRINCESS SURE IS A NICE PERSON...
...EVEN THOUGH SHE'S THE RULER OF ROSHTARIA, SHE DOESN'T ACT ALL HIGH AND MIGHTY. AND THE WAY THE PRINCESS LOOKS AT ME...

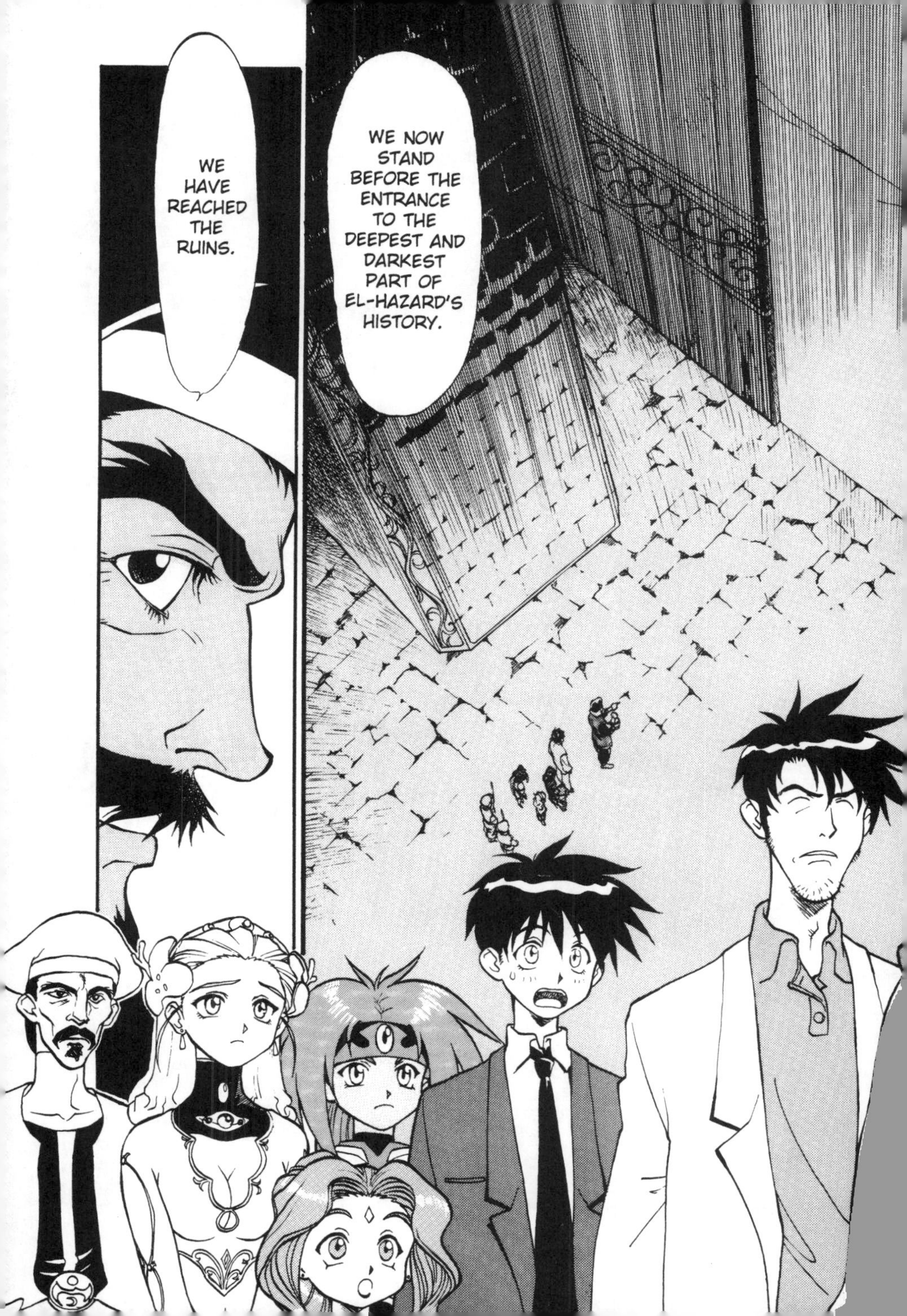
WE HAVE REACHED THE RUINS.
WE NOW STAND BEFORE THE ENTRANCE TO THE DEEPEST AND DARKEST PART OF EL-HAZARD'S HISTORY.

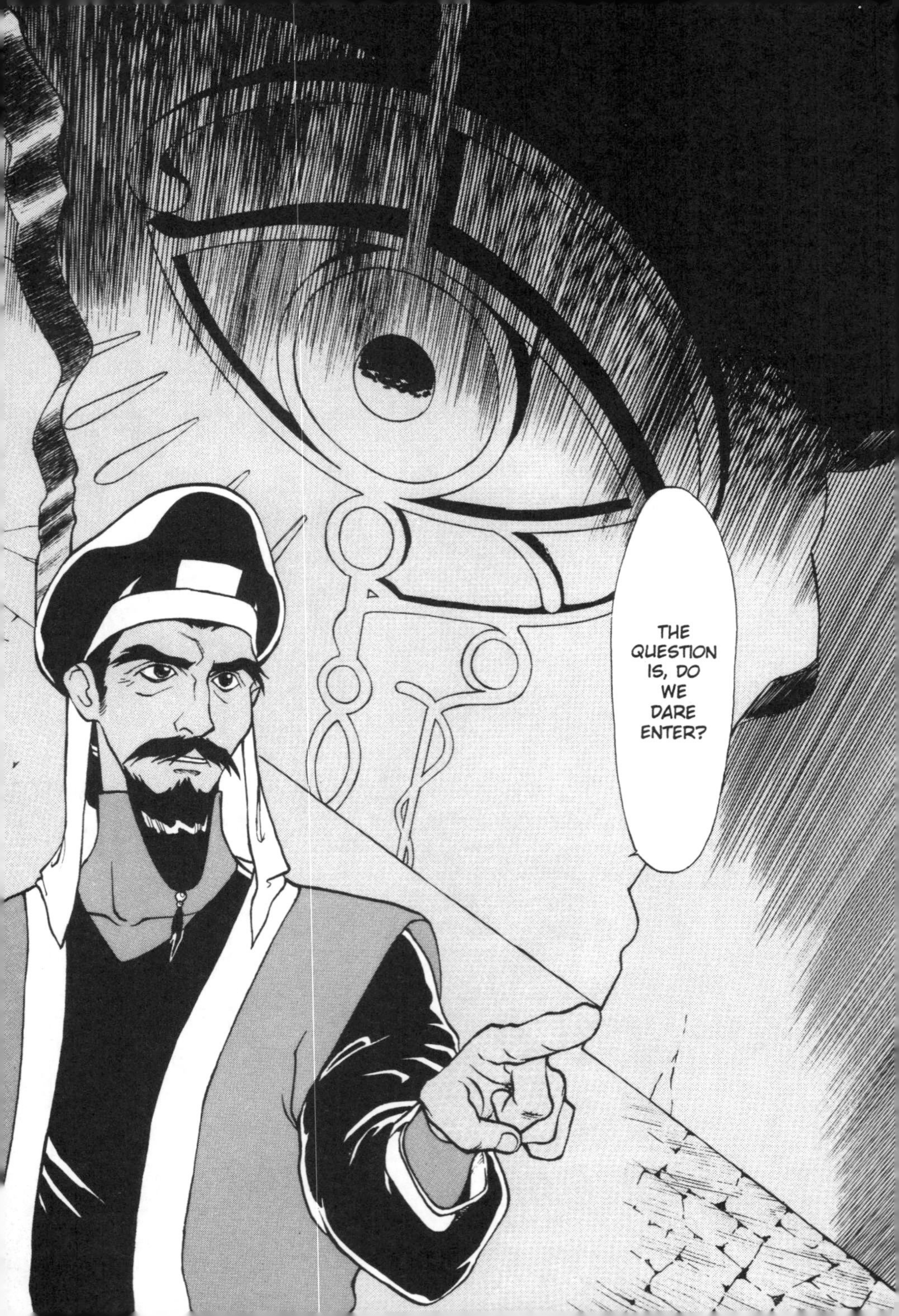
THE QUESTION IS, DO WE DARE ENTER?

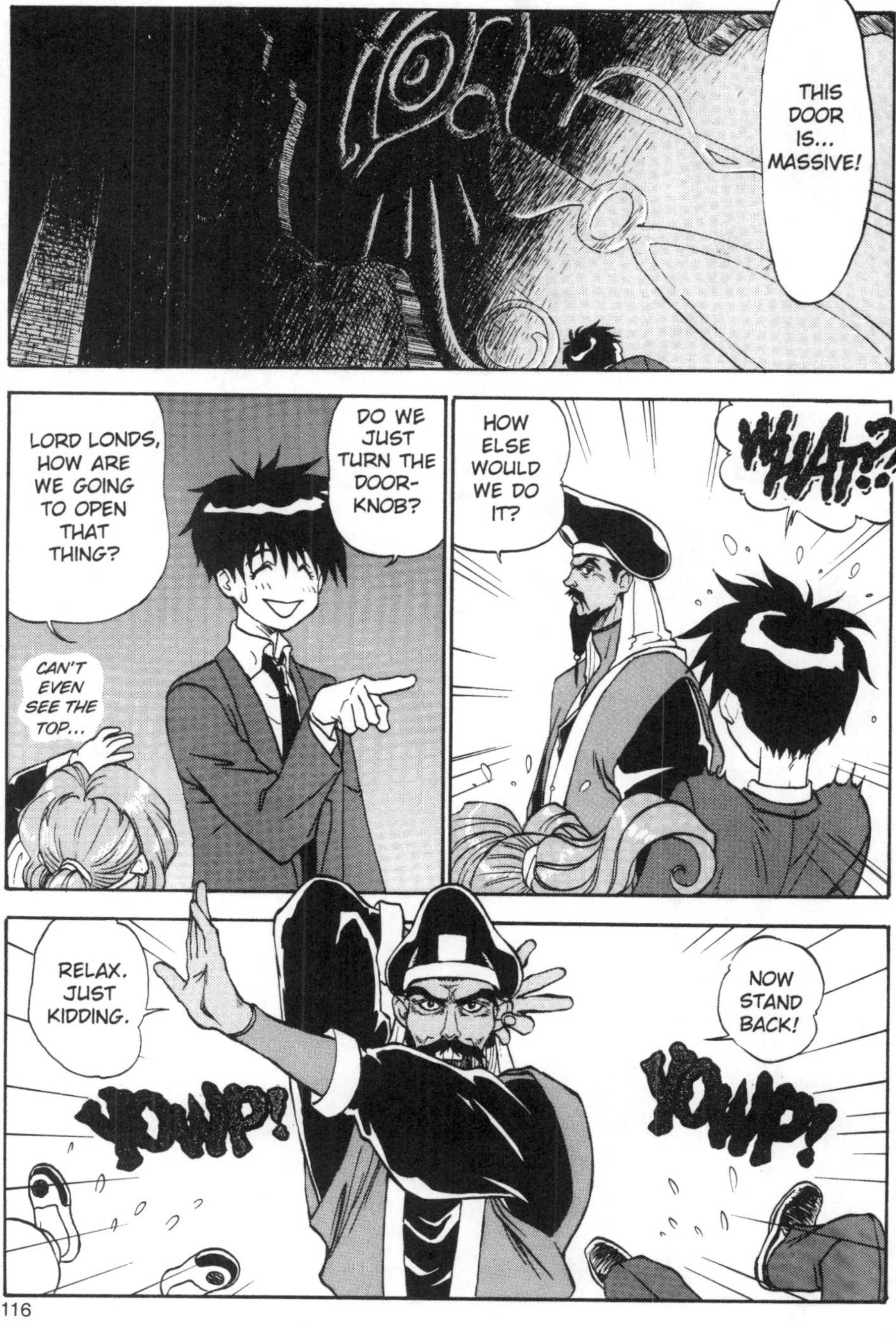
THIS DOOR IS... MASSIVE!
LORD LONDS, HOW ARE WE GOING TO OPEN THAT THING?
CAN'T EVEN SEE THE TOP...
DO WE JUST TURN THE DOOR-KNOB?
HOW ELSE WOULD WE DO IT?
WHAT?!
RELAX. JUST KIDDING.
NOW STAND BACK!
YOWP!
YOWP!

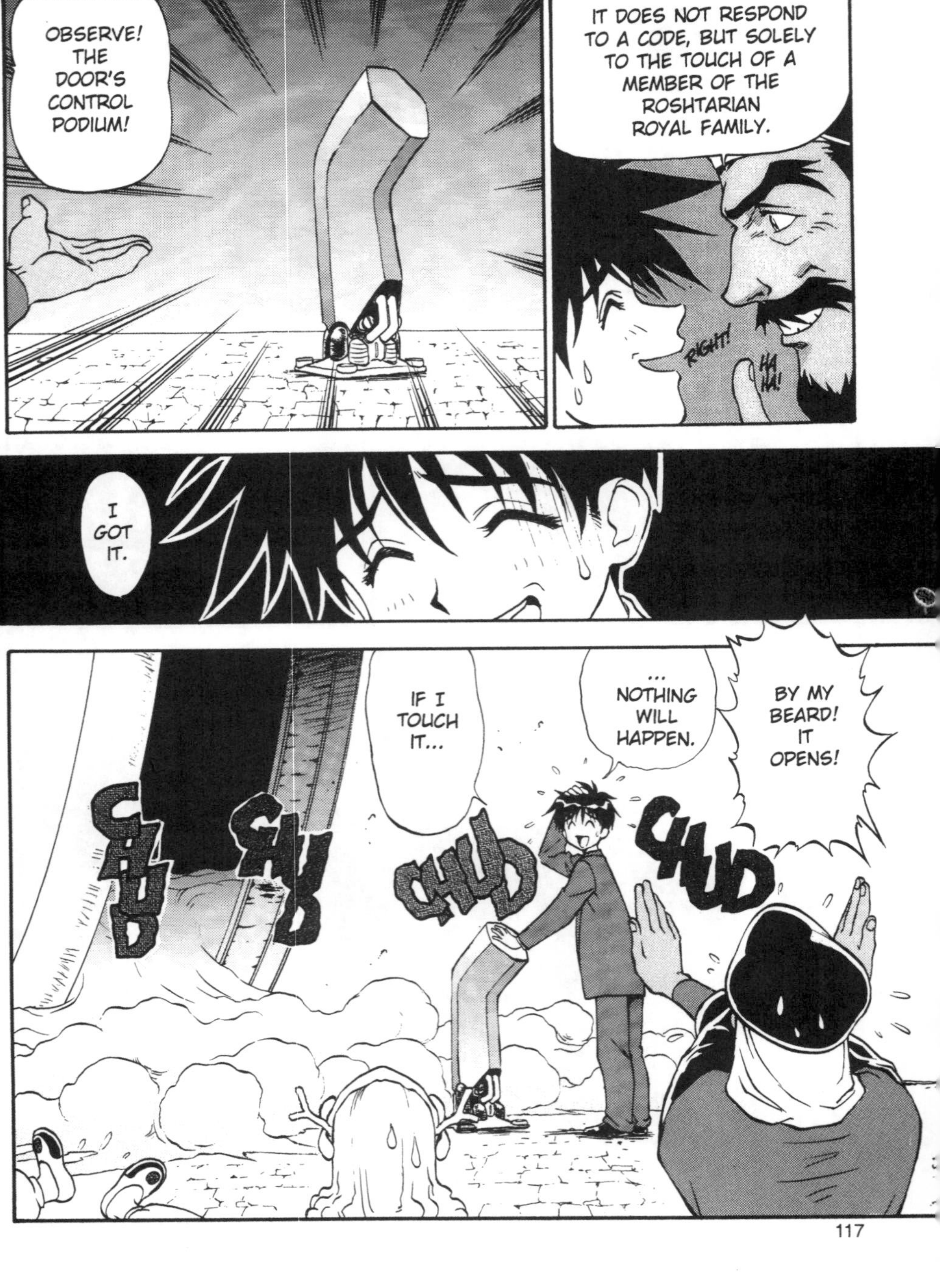
OBSERVE! THE DOOR'S CONTROL PODIUM!
IT DOES NOT RESPOND TO A CODE, BUT SOLELY TO THE TOUCH OF A MEMBER OF THE ROSHTARIAN ROYAL FAMILY.
RIGHT!
HA HA!
I GOT IT.
CHUD
CHUD
CHUD
IF I TOUCH IT...
... NOTHING WILL HAPPEN.
CHUD
BY MY BEARD! IT OPENS!

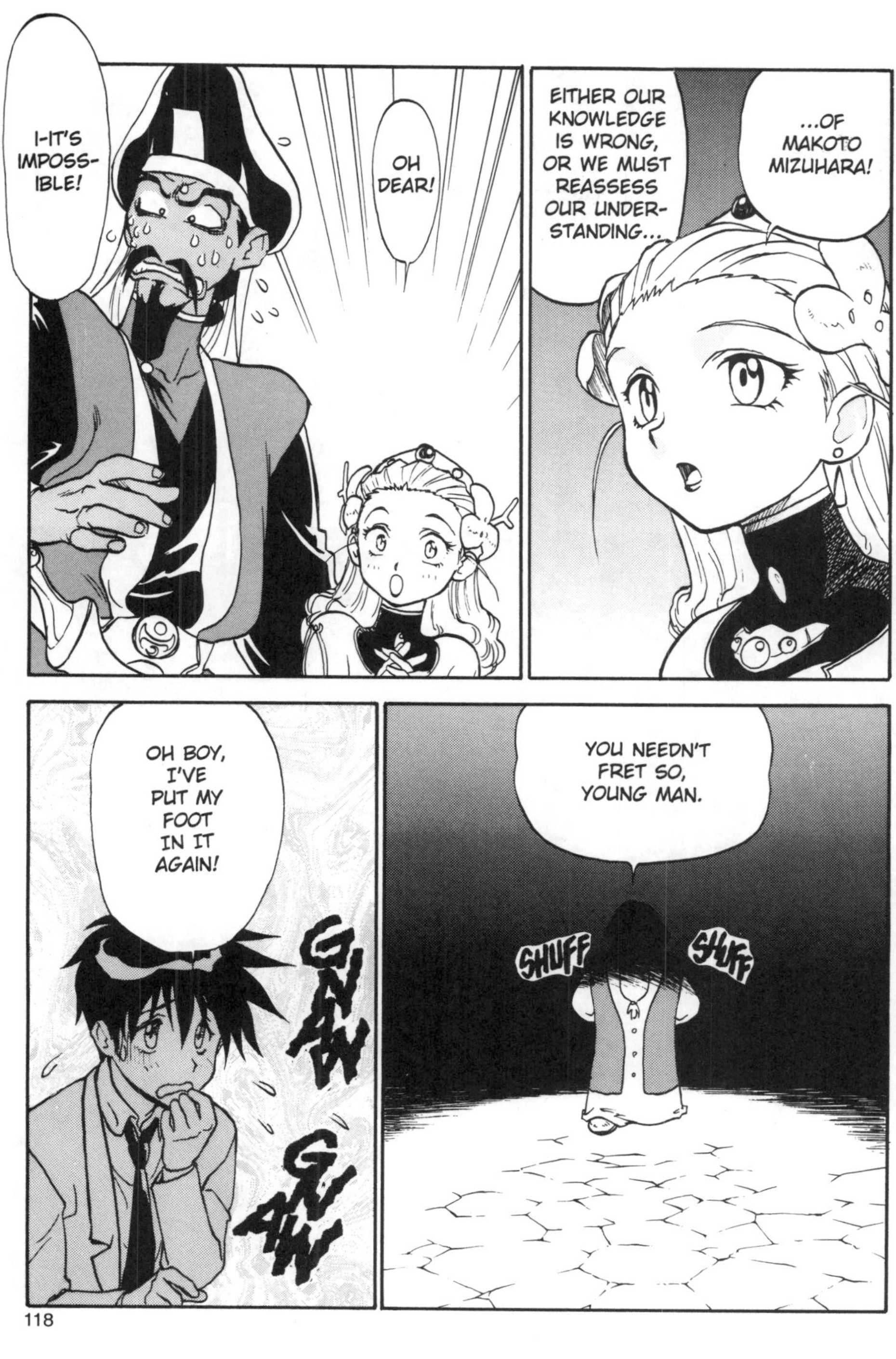
I-IT'S IMPOSS-IBLE!
OH DEAR!
EITHER OUR KNOWLEDGE IS WRONG, OR WE MUST REASSESS OUR UNDER-STANDING...
...OF MAKOTO MIZUHARA!
OH BOY, I'VE PUT MY FOOT IN IT AGAIN!
GNAW
GNAW
YOU NEEDN'T FRET SO, YOUNG MAN.
SHUFF
SHUFF

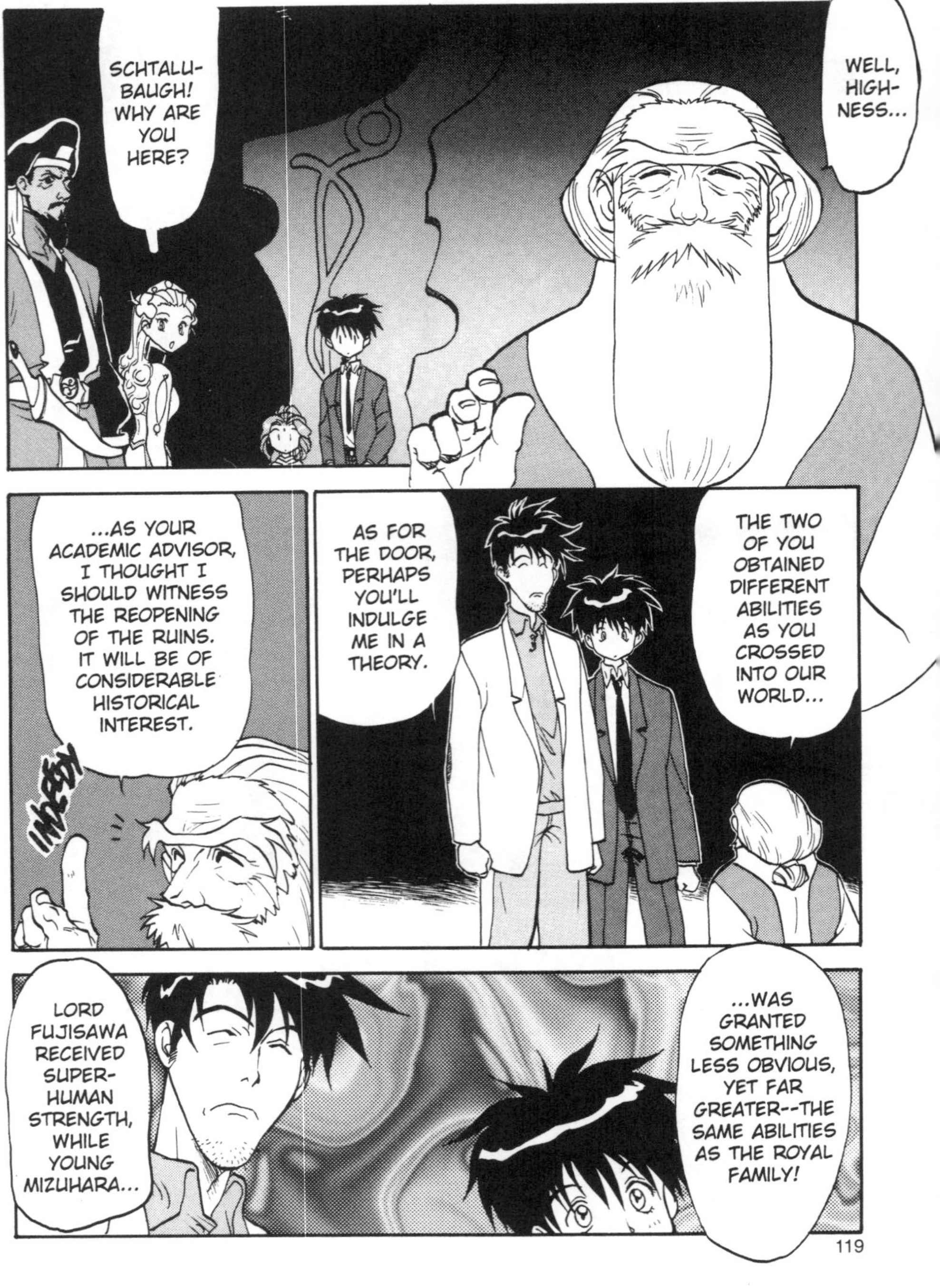
SCHTALU-BAUGH! WHY ARE YOU HERE?
WELL, HIGH-NESS...
...AS YOUR ACADEMIC ADVISOR, I THOUGHT I SHOULD WITNESS THE REOPENING OF THE RUINS. IT WILL BE OF CONSIDERABLE HISTORICAL INTEREST.
INDEEDY
AS FOR THE DOOR, PERHAPS YOU'LL INDULGE ME IN A THEORY.
THE TWO OF YOU OBTAINED DIFFERENT ABILITIES AS YOU CROSSED INTO OUR WORLD...
LORD FUJISAWA RECEIVED SUPER-HUMAN STRENGTH, WHILE YOUNG MIZUHARA...
...WAS GRANTED SOMETHING LESS OBVIOUS, YET FAR GREATER--THE SAME ABILITIES AS THE ROYAL FAMILY!

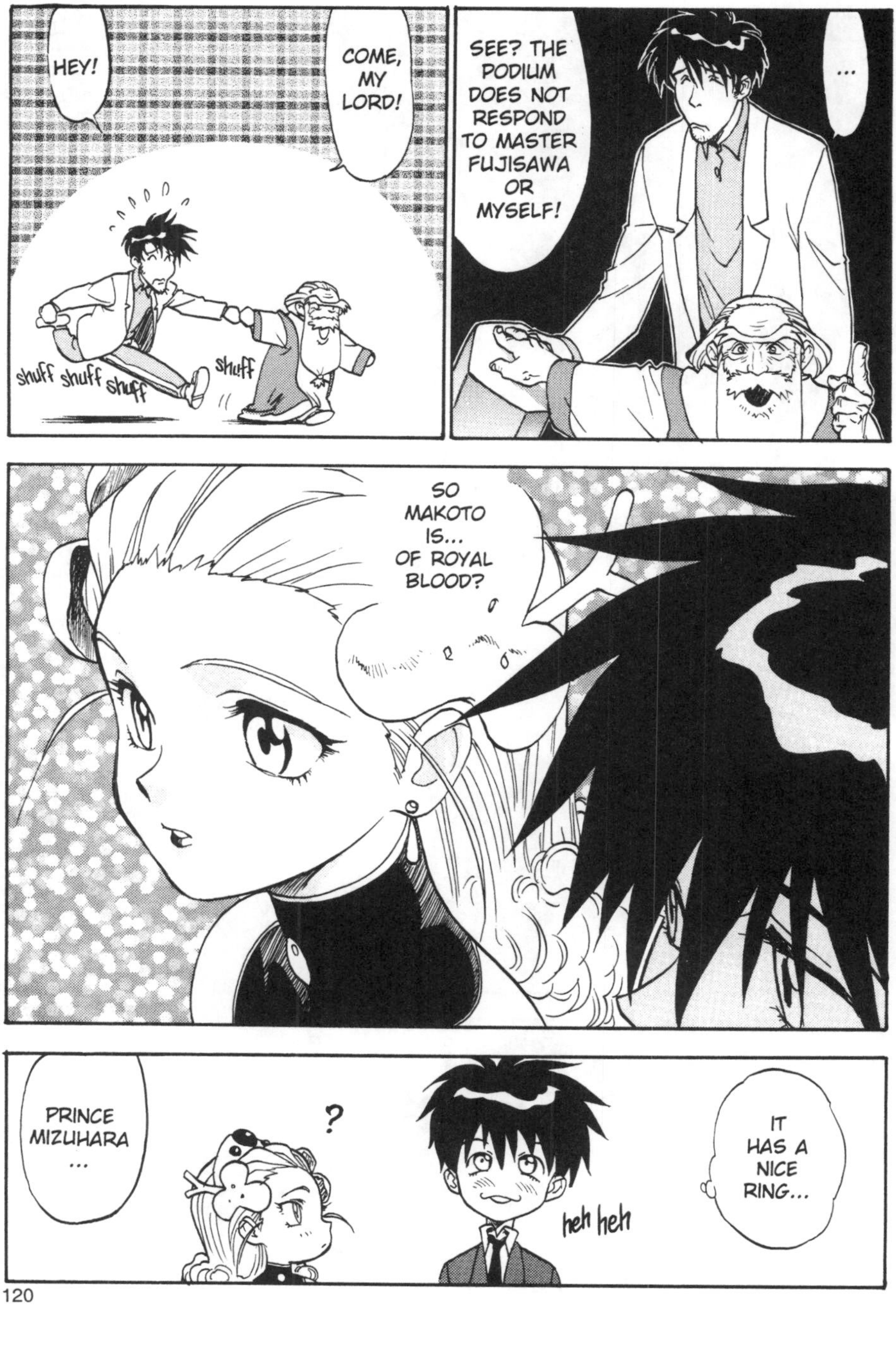
HEY!
COME, MY LORD!
shuff shuff shuff
shuff
SEE? THE PODIUM DOES NOT RESPOND TO MASTER FUJISAWA OR MYSELF!
...
SO MAKOTO IS... OF ROYAL BLOOD?
PRINCE MIZUHARA ...
?
heh heh
IT HAS A NICE RING...

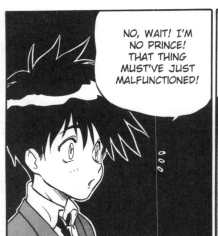

NO, WAIT! I'M NO PRINCE! THAT THING MUST'VE JUST MALFUNCTIONED!

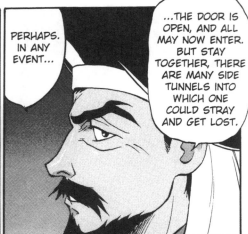

PERHAPS. IN ANY EVENT...

...THE DOOR IS OPEN, AND ALL MAY NOW ENTER. BUT STAY TOGETHER, THERE ARE MANY SIDE TUNNELS INTO WHICH ONE COULD STRAY AND GET LOST.

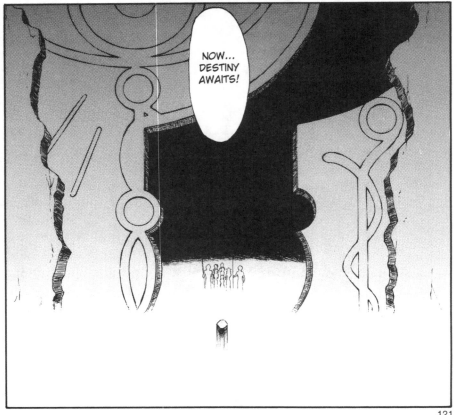

NOW... DESTINY AWAITS!

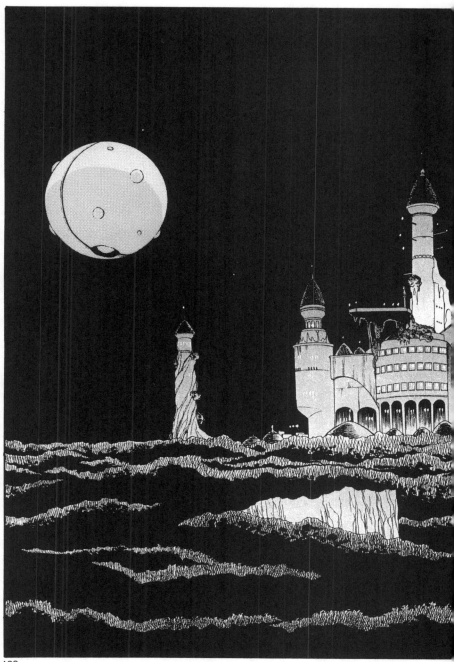

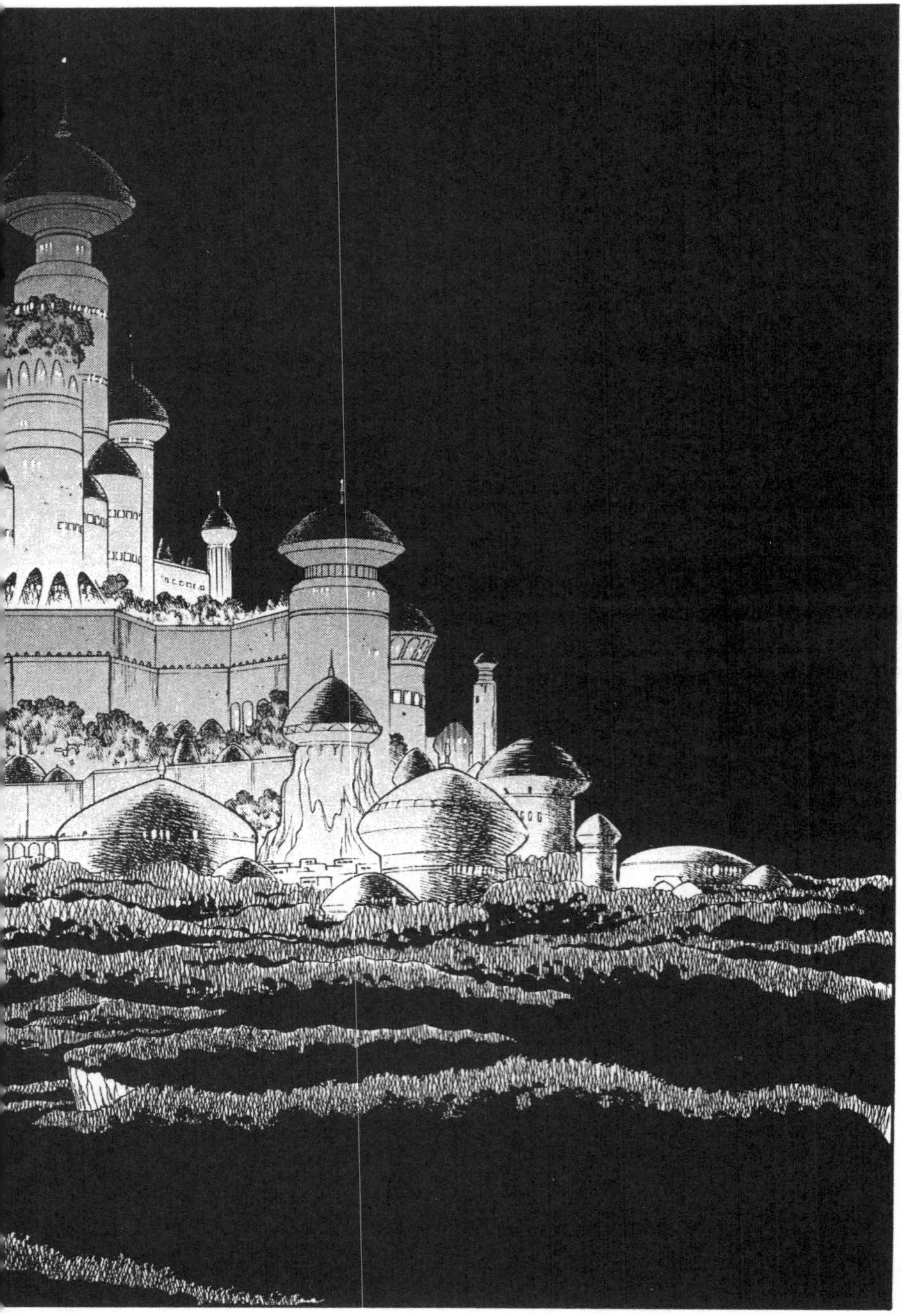

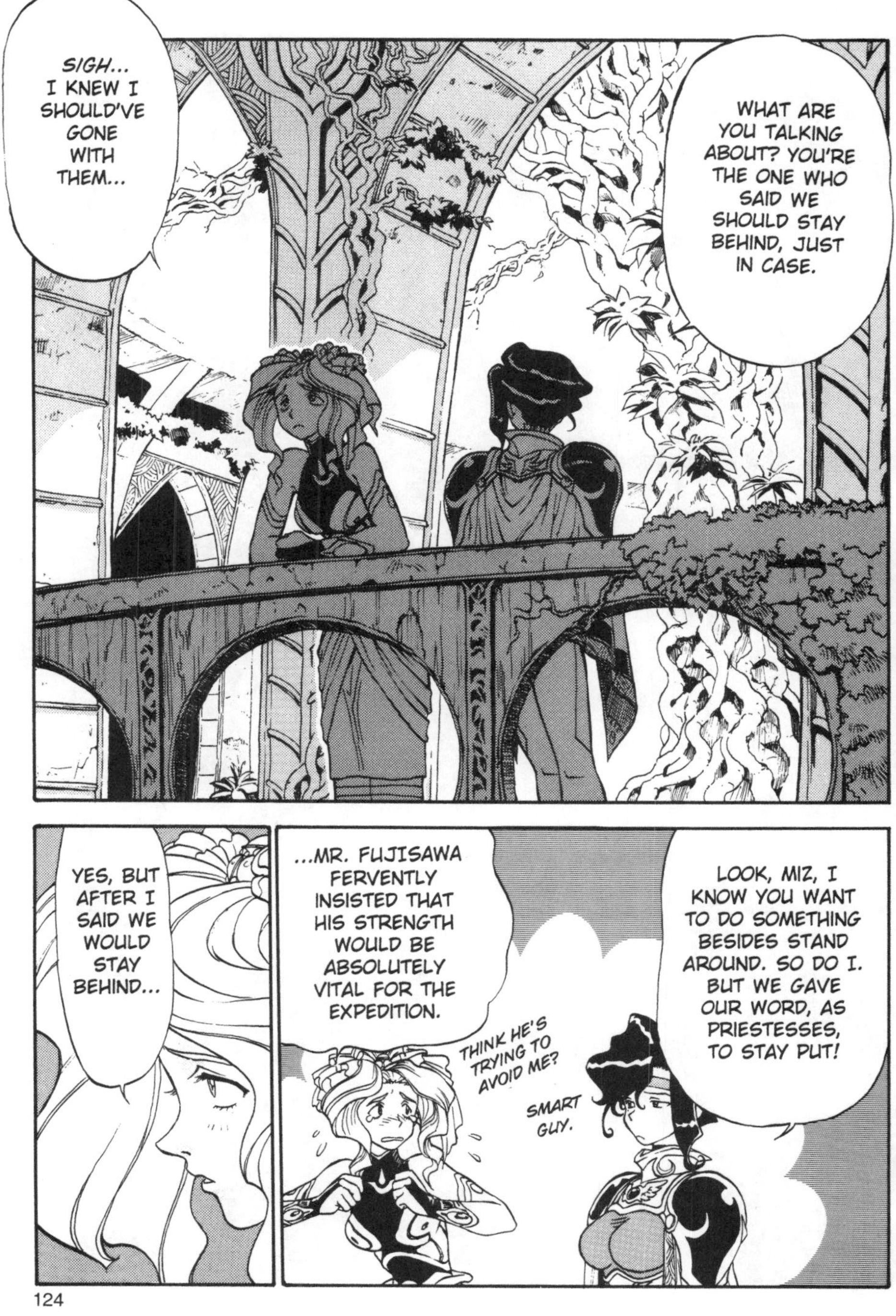

SIGH... I KNEW I SHOULD'VE GONE WITH THEM...
WHAT ARE YOU TALKING ABOUT? YOU'RE THE ONE WHO SAID WE SHOULD STAY BEHIND, JUST IN CASE.
YES, BUT AFTER I SAID WE WOULD STAY BEHIND...
...MR. FUJISAWA FERVENTLY INSISTED THAT HIS STRENGTH WOULD BE ABSOLUTELY VITAL FOR THE EXPEDITION.
THINK HE'S TRYING TO AVOID ME?
SMART GUY.
LOOK, MIZ, I KNOW YOU WANT TO DO SOMETHING BESIDES STAND AROUND. SO DO I. BUT WE GAVE OUR WORD, AS PRIESTESSES, TO STAY PUT!

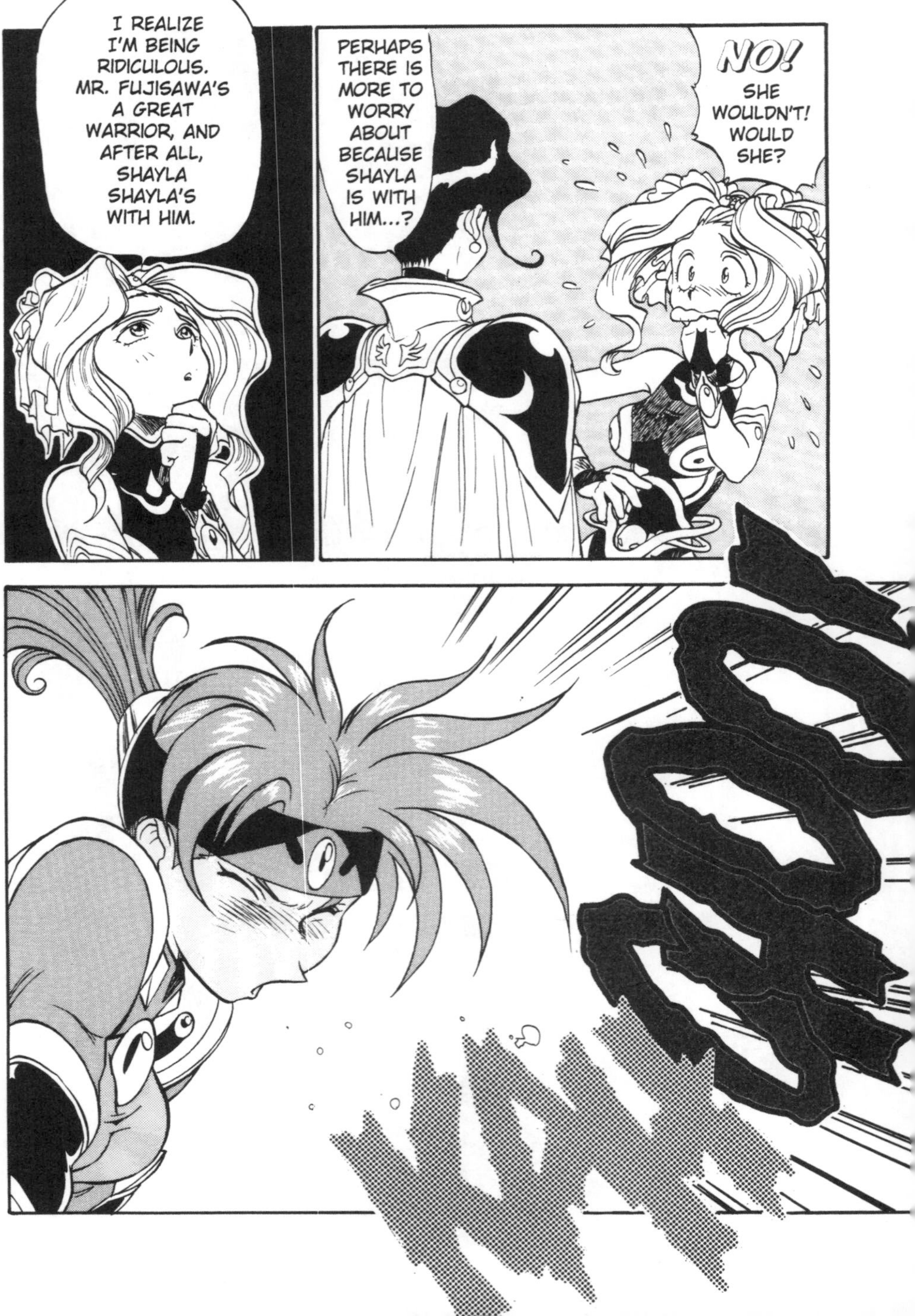
I REALIZE I'M BEING RIDICULOUS. MR. FUJISAWA'S A GREAT WARRIOR, AND AFTER ALL, SHAYLA SHAYLA'S WITH HIM.
PERHAPS THERE IS MORE TO WORRY ABOUT BECAUSE SHAYLA IS WITH HIM...?
NO!
SHE WOULDN'T! WOULD SHE?

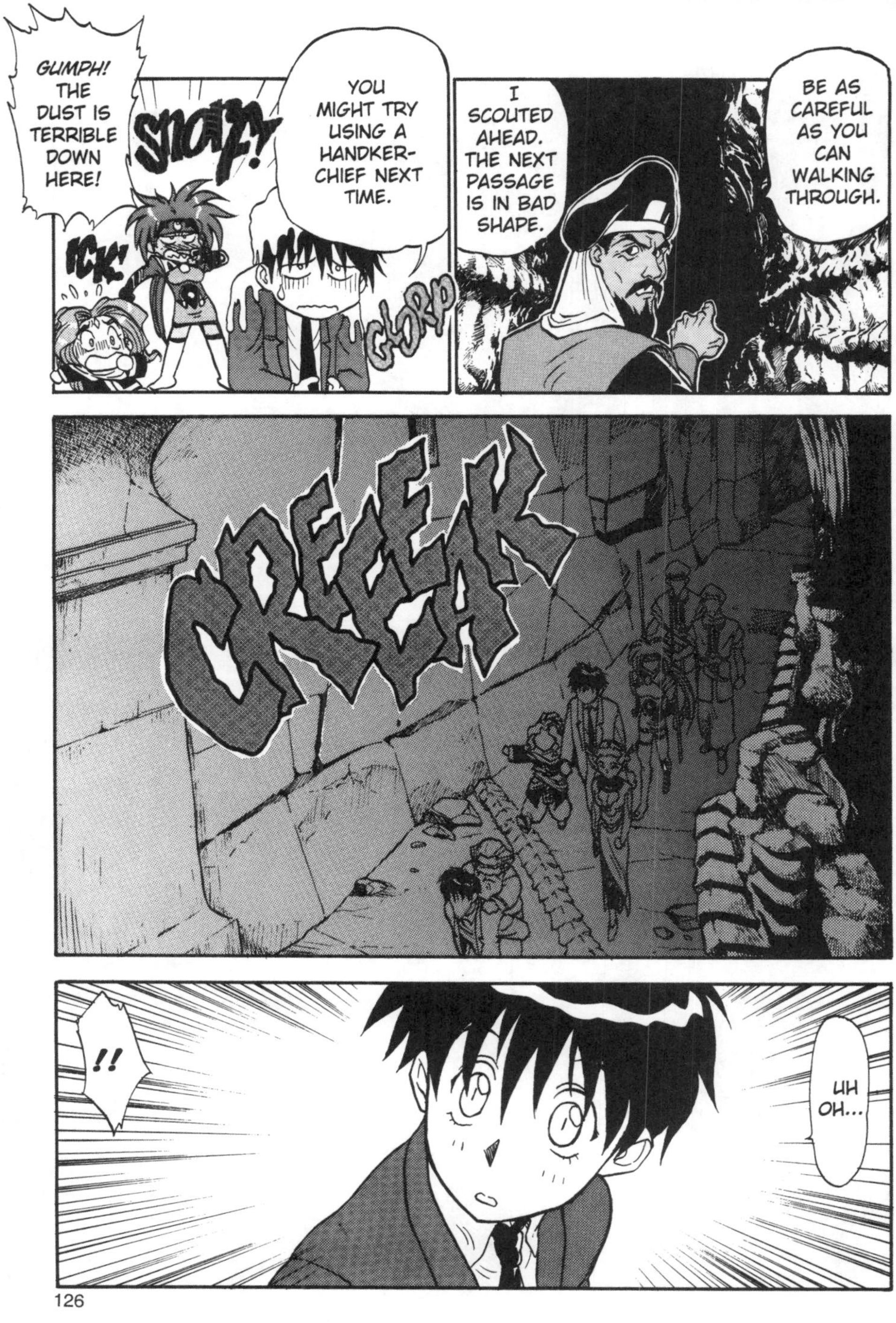
GUMPH! THE DUST IS TERRIBLE DOWN HERE!
ICK!
YOU MIGHT TRY USING A HANDKER-CHIEF NEXT TIME.
GLORP
I SCOUTED AHEAD. THE NEXT PASSAGE IS IN BAD SHAPE.
BE AS CAREFUL AS YOU CAN WALKING THROUGH.
CREEAK
!!
UH OH...

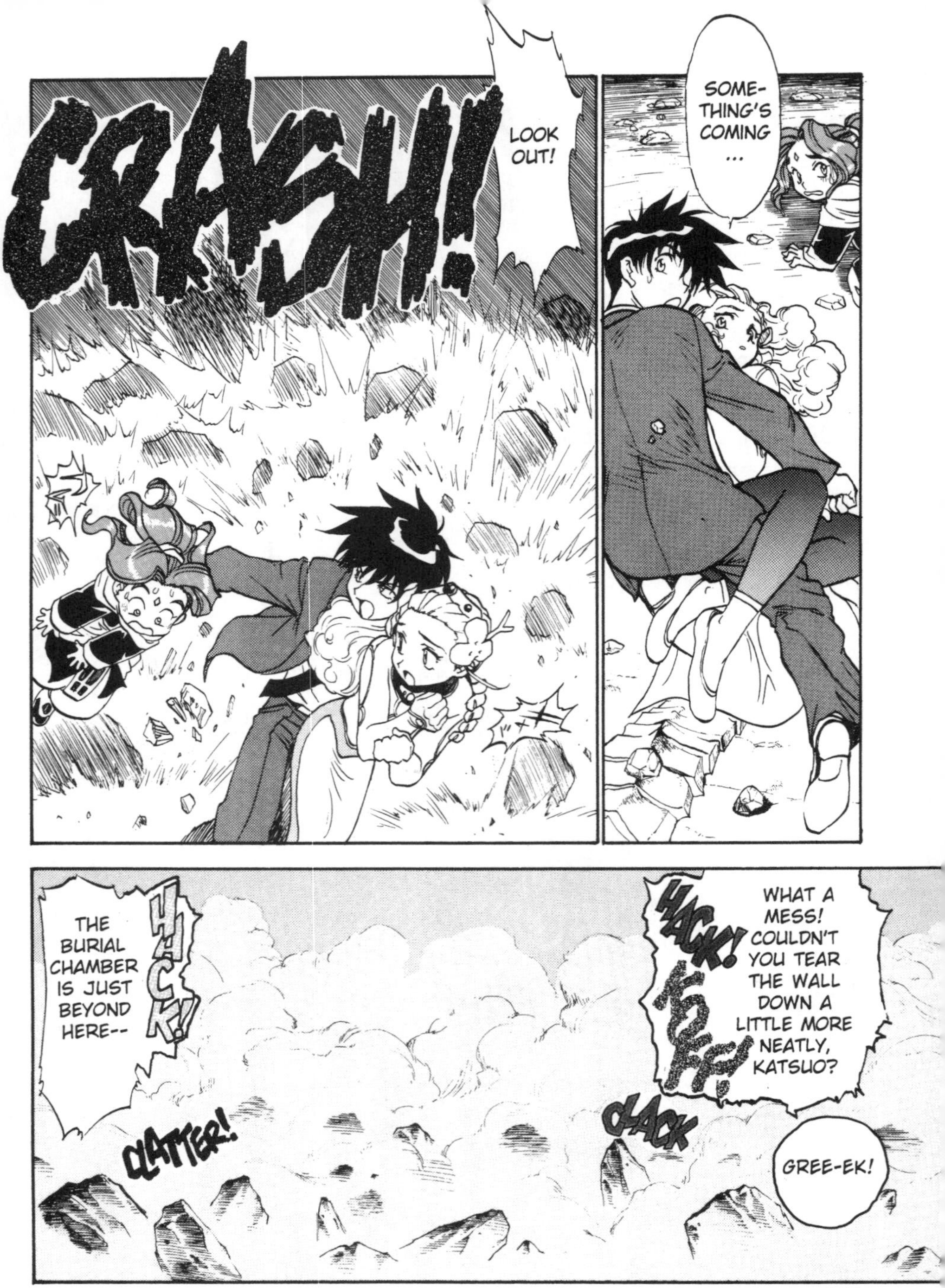
CRASH!
LOOK OUT!
SOME-THING'S COMING ...
THE BURIAL CHAMBER IS JUST BEYOND HERE--
HACK!
CLATTER!
HACK!
KOFF!
WHAT A MESS! COULDN'T YOU TEAR THE WALL DOWN A LITTLE MORE NEATLY, KATSUO?
CLACK
GREE-EK!

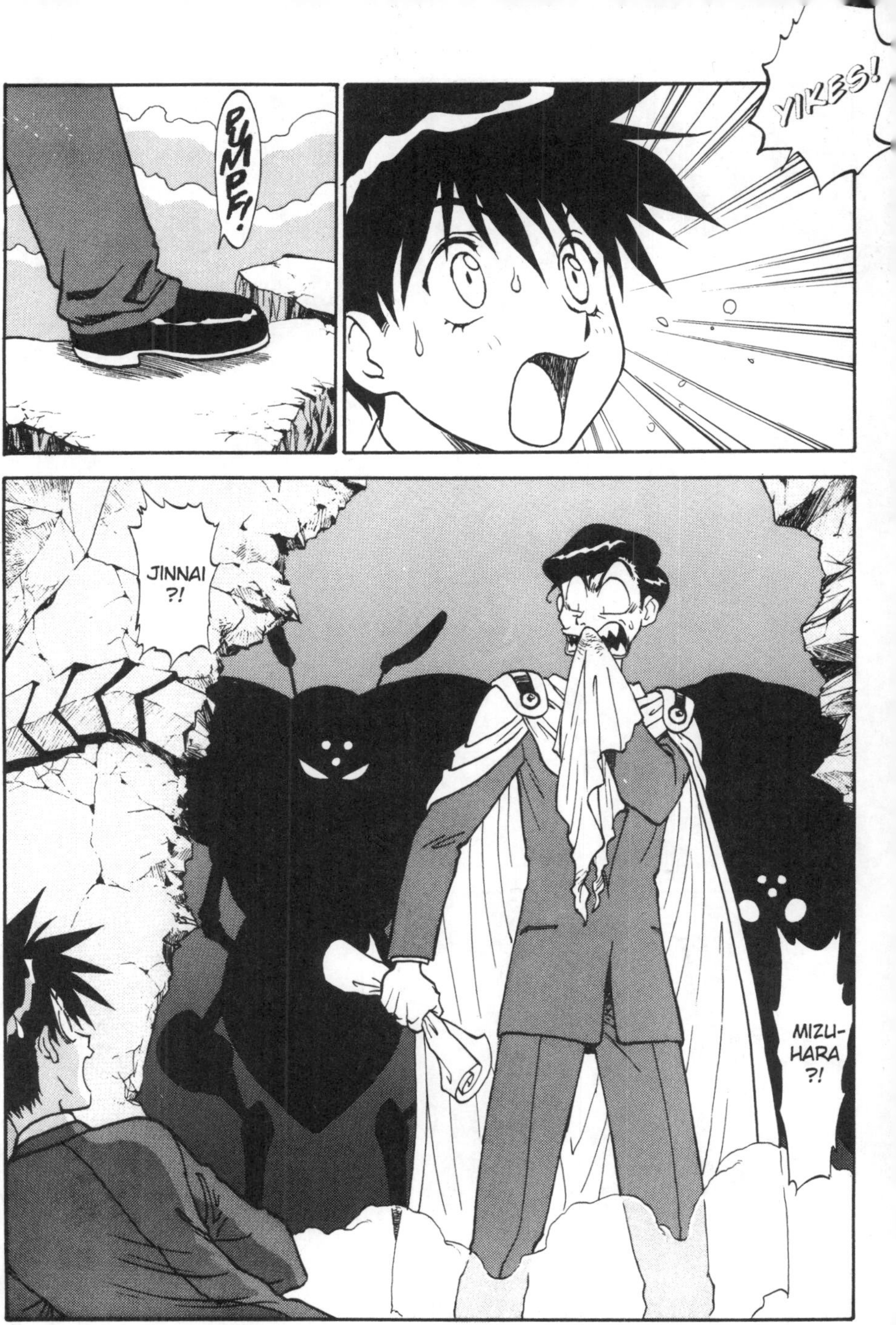
PUMPF!
YIKES!
JINNAI ?!
MIZU-HARA ?!

END OF EPISODE 4

EL-HAZARD THE MAGNIFICENT WORLD

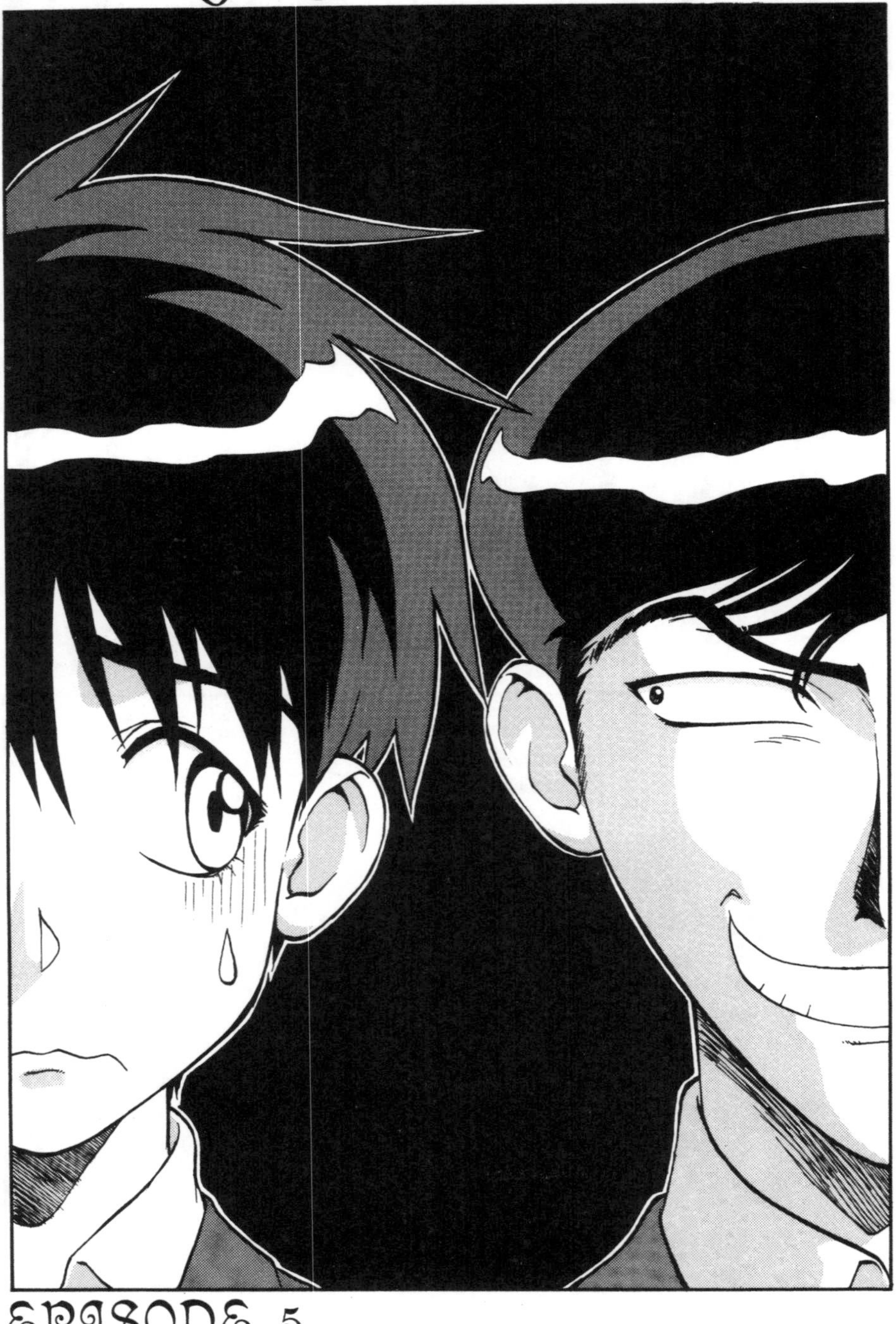

EPISODE 5

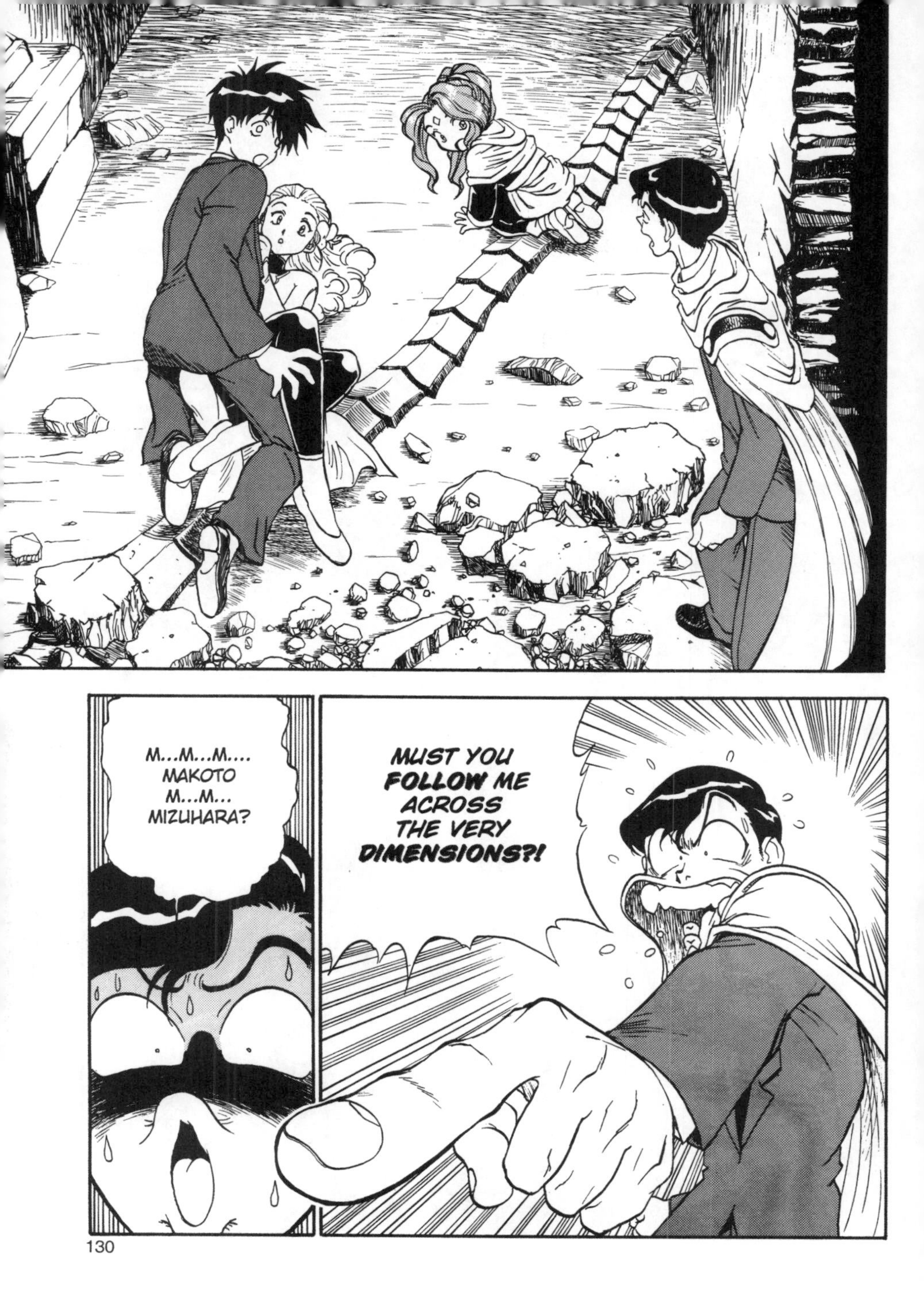
M...M...M....
MAKOTO
M...M...
MIZUHARA?
MUST YOU FOLLOW ME ACROSS THE VERY DIMENSIONS?!

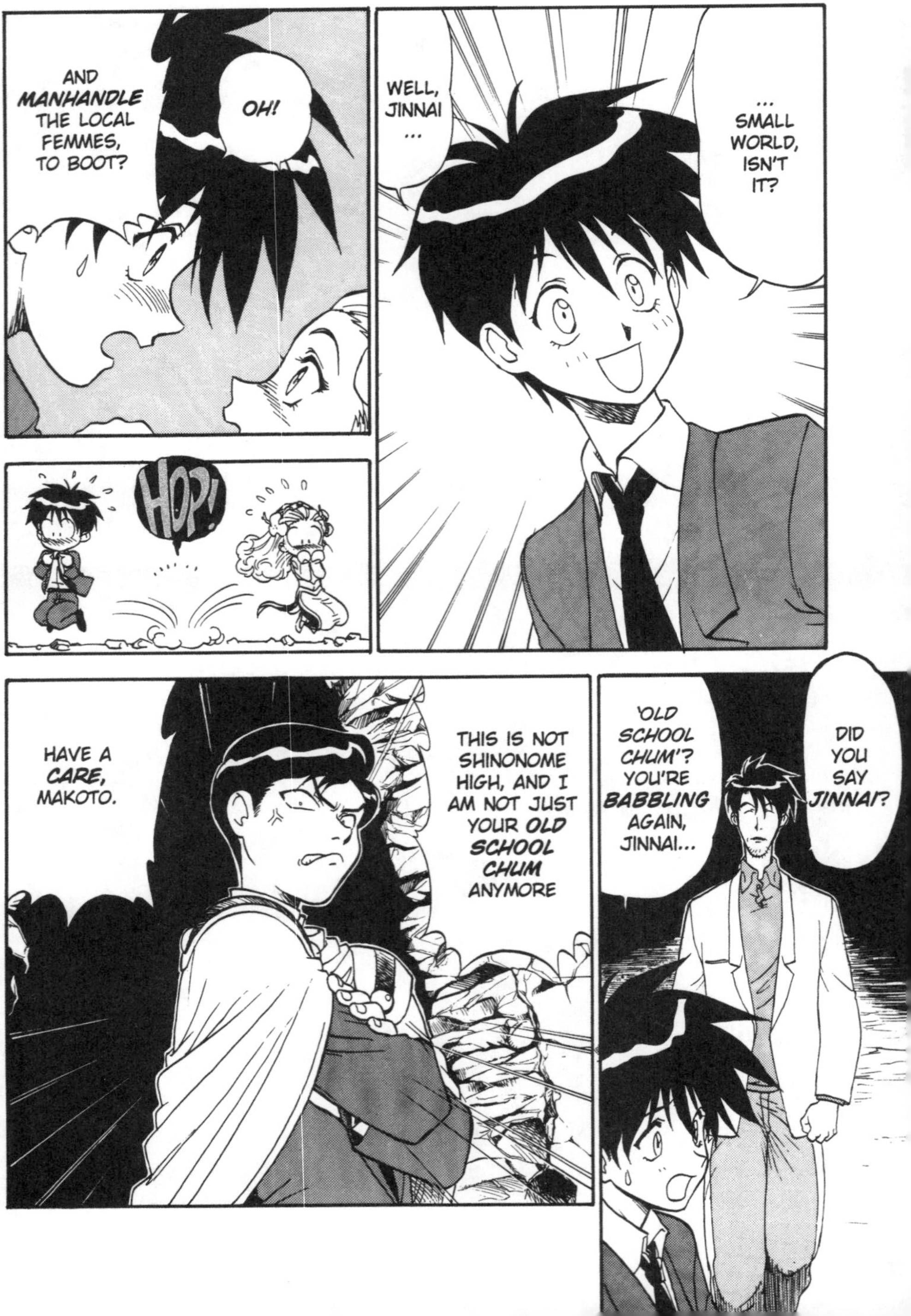
AND MANHANDLE THE LOCAL FEMMES, TO BOOT?
OH!
HOP!
WELL, JINNAI ...
... SMALL WORLD, ISN'T IT?
HAVE A CARE, MAKOTO.
THIS IS NOT SHINONOME HIGH, AND I AM NOT JUST YOUR OLD SCHOOL CHUM ANYMORE
'OLD SCHOOL CHUM'? YOU'RE BABBLING AGAIN, JINNAI...
DID YOU SAY JINNAI?

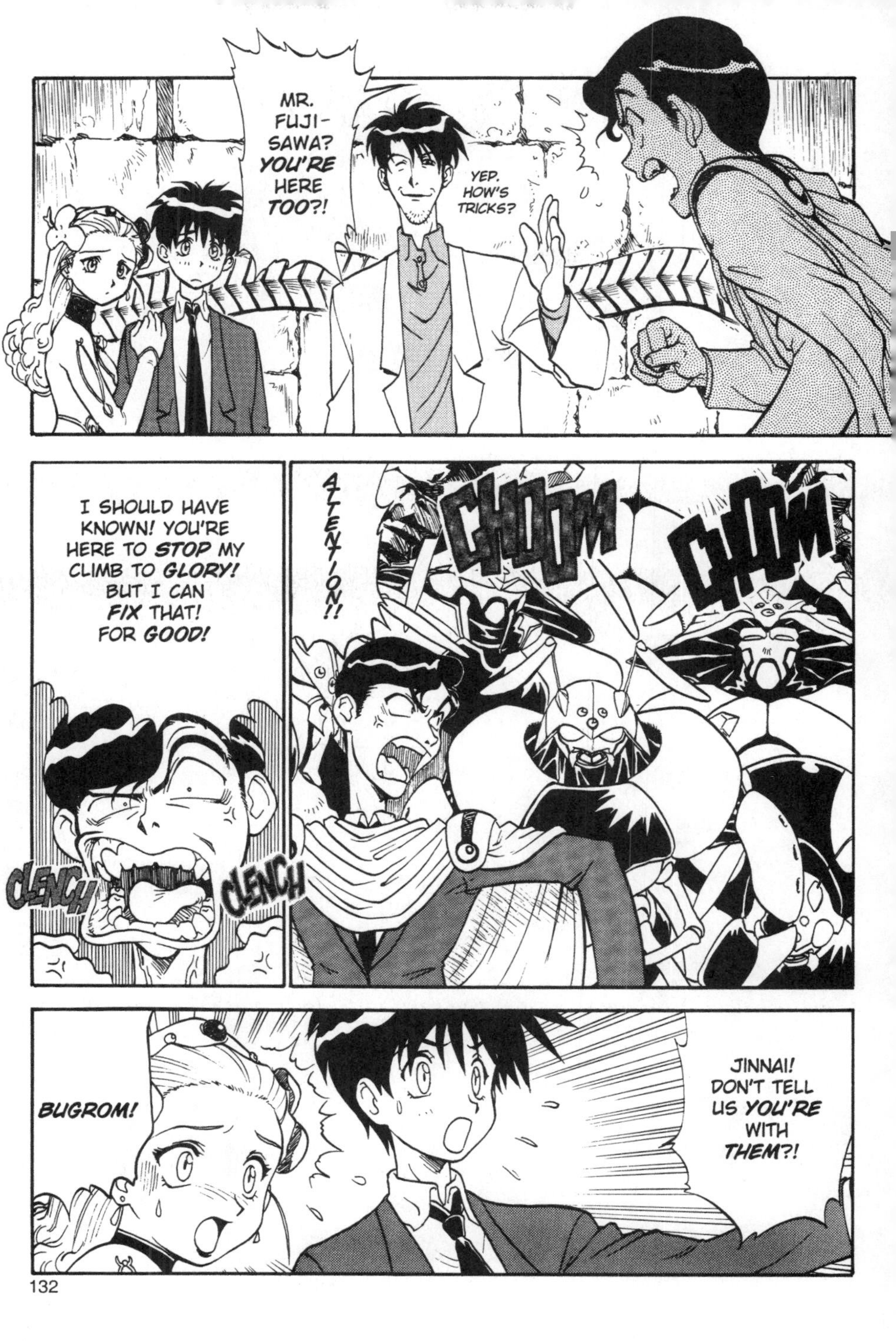

MR. FUJI-SAWA? YOU'RE HERE TOO?!
YEP. HOW'S TRICKS?
I SHOULD HAVE KNOWN! YOU'RE HERE TO STOP MY CLIMB TO GLORY! BUT I CAN FIX THAT! FOR GOOD!
CLENCH
CLENCH
ATTENTION!!
CHOOM
CHOOM
BUGROM!
JINNAI! DON'T TELL US YOU'RE WITH THEM?!

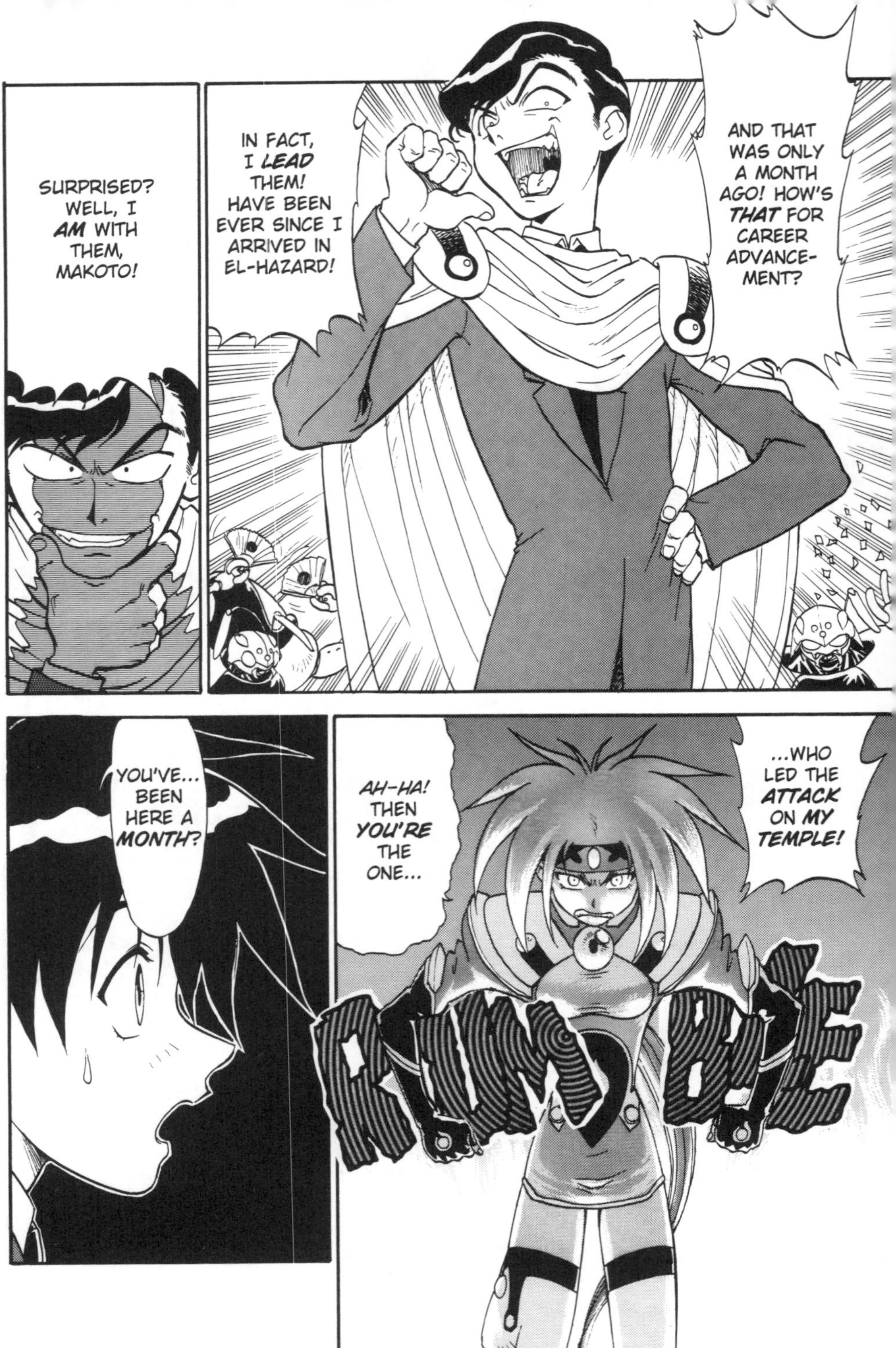
SURPRISED? WELL, I *AM* WITH THEM, MAKOTO!
IN FACT, I *LEAD* THEM! HAVE BEEN EVER SINCE I ARRIVED IN EL-HAZARD!
AND THAT WAS ONLY A MONTH AGO! HOW'S *THAT* FOR CAREER ADVANCE-MENT?
YOU'VE... BEEN HERE A *MONTH*?
AH-HA! THEN *YOU'RE* THE ONE...
...WHO LED THE *ATTACK* ON *MY TEMPLE!*

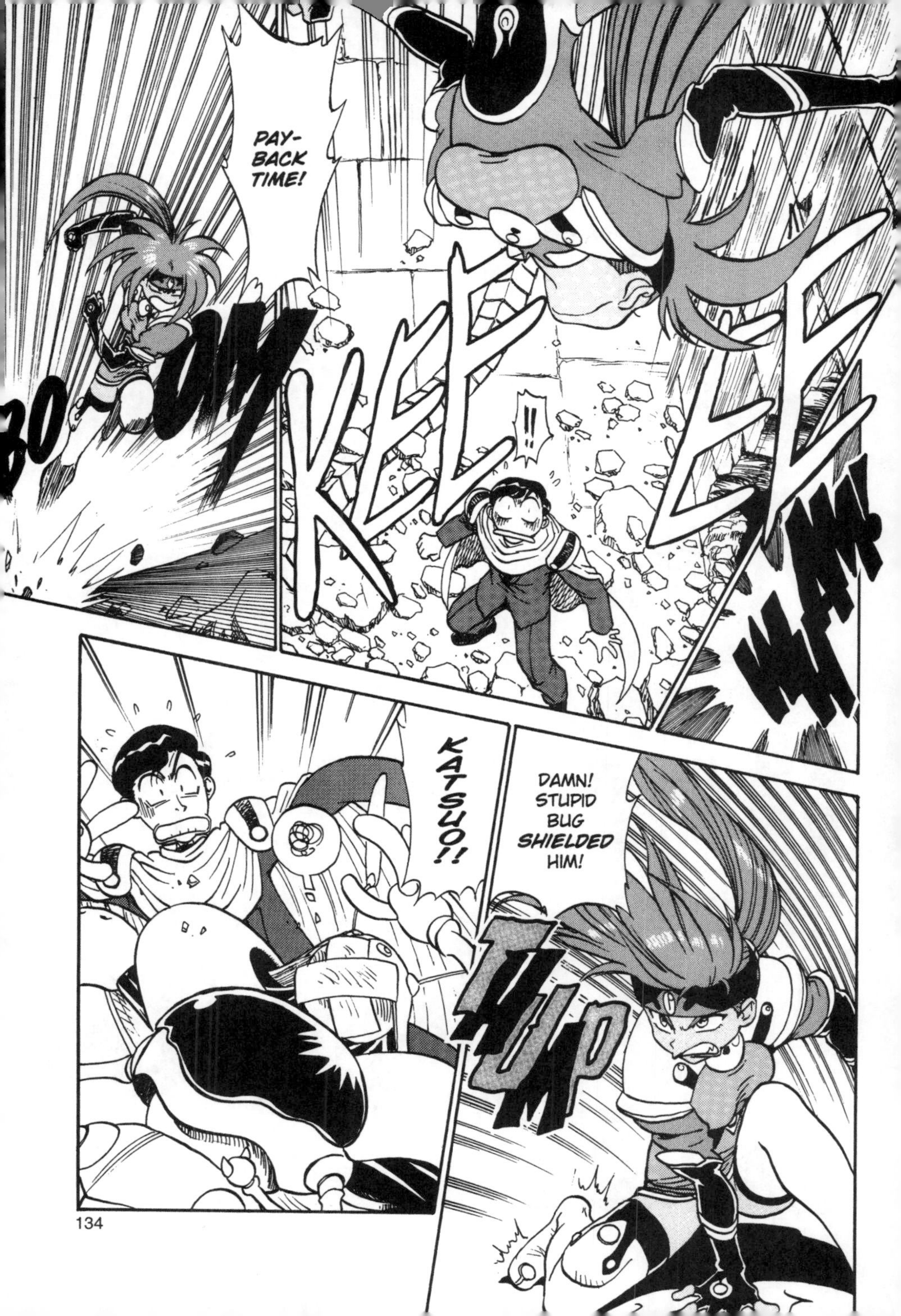
PAY-BACK TIME!
BOOM
KEEEE
!!
WHAM!
KATSUO!!
DAMN! STUPID BUG SHIELDED HIM!
THUMP

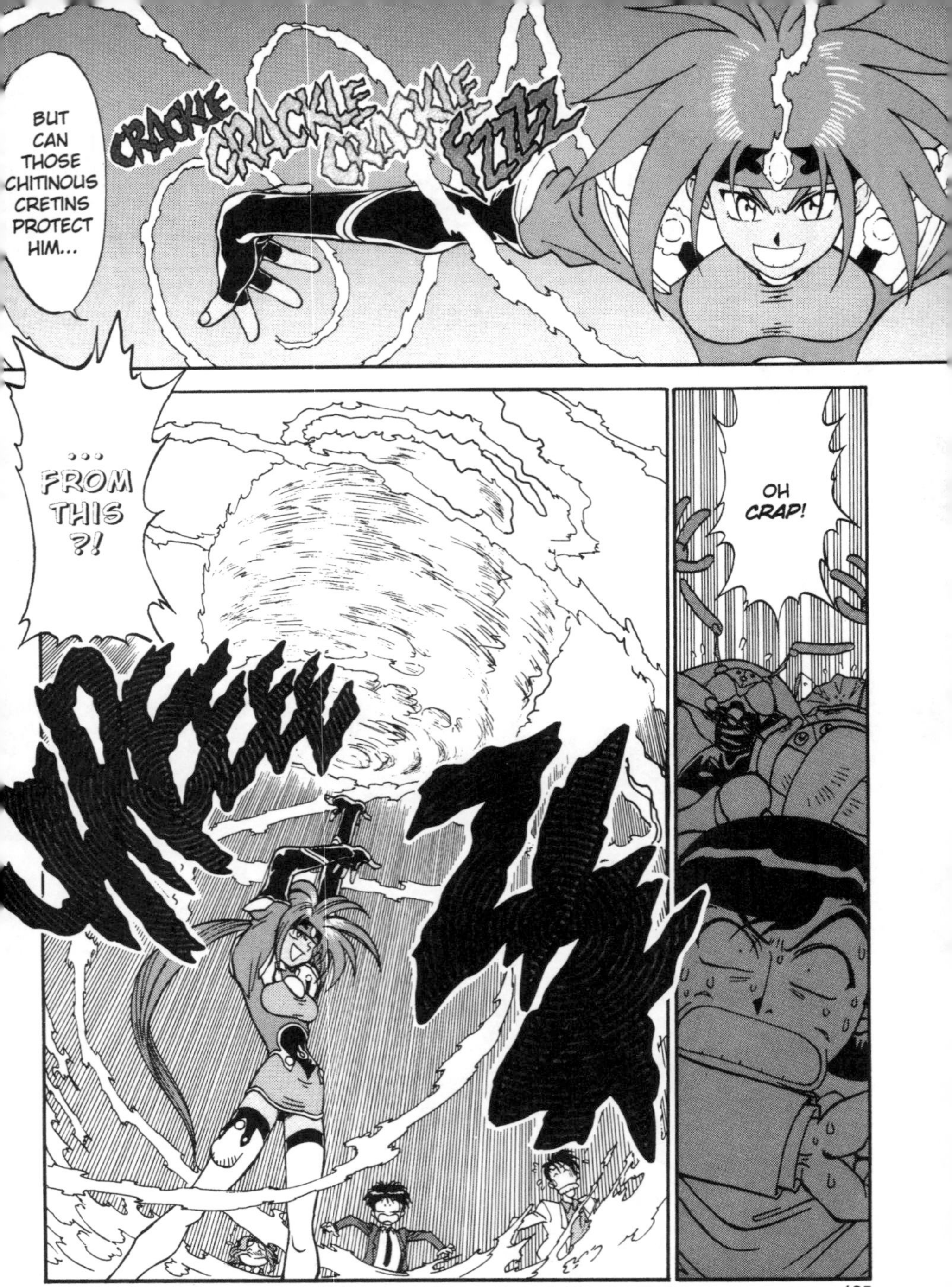
BUT CAN THOSE CHITINOUS CRETINS PROTECT HIM...
CRACKLE CRACKLE CRACKLE FZZZ
...FROM THIS?!
OH CRAP!

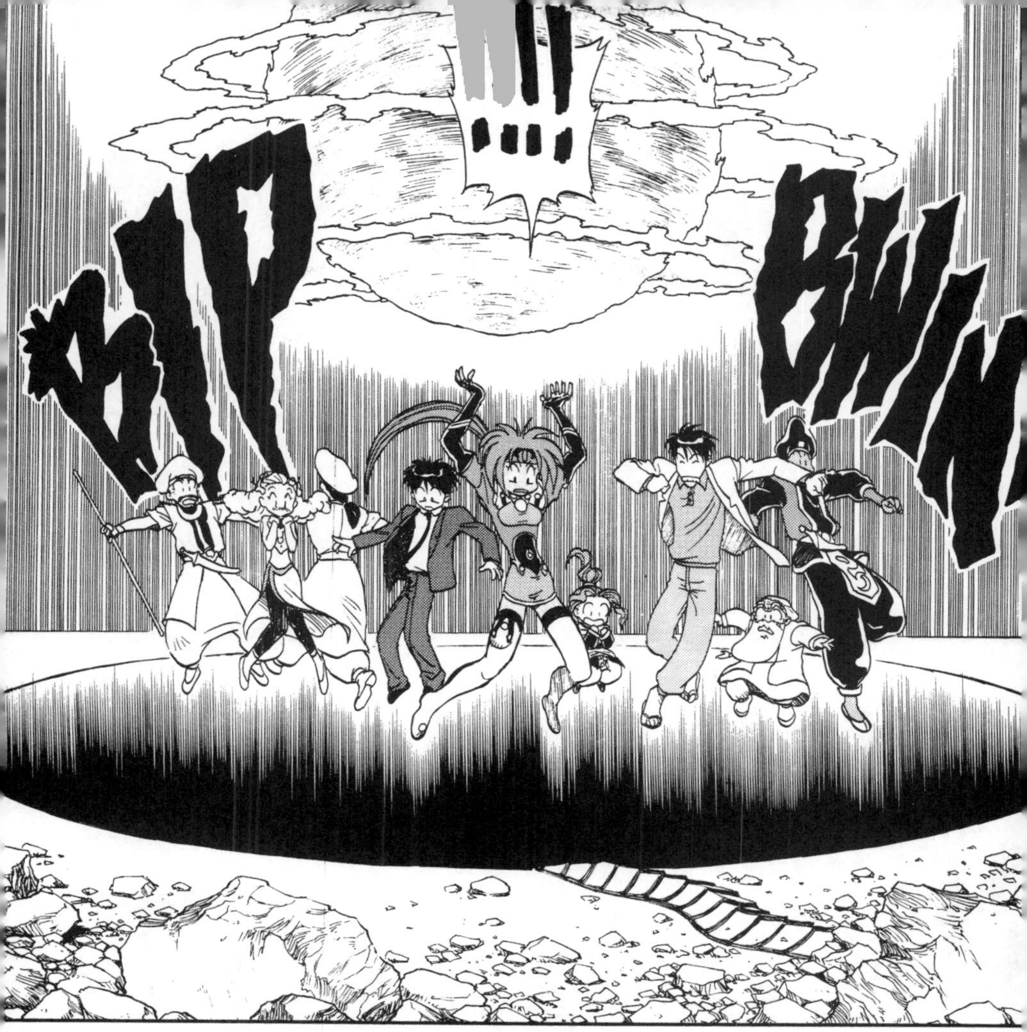

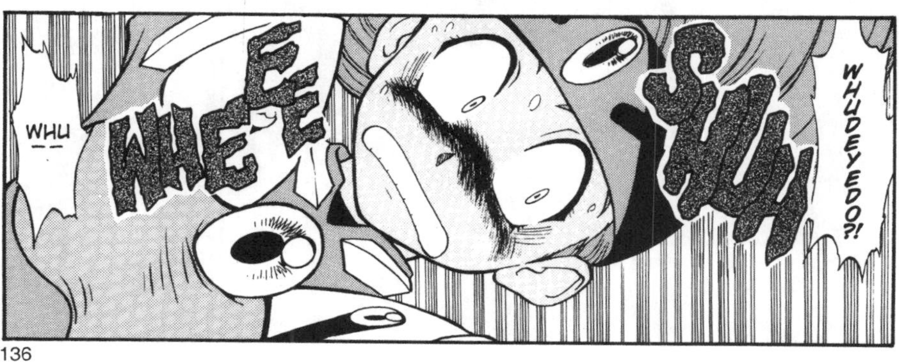
WHU --
WHEEE
WHUDEYEDO?!

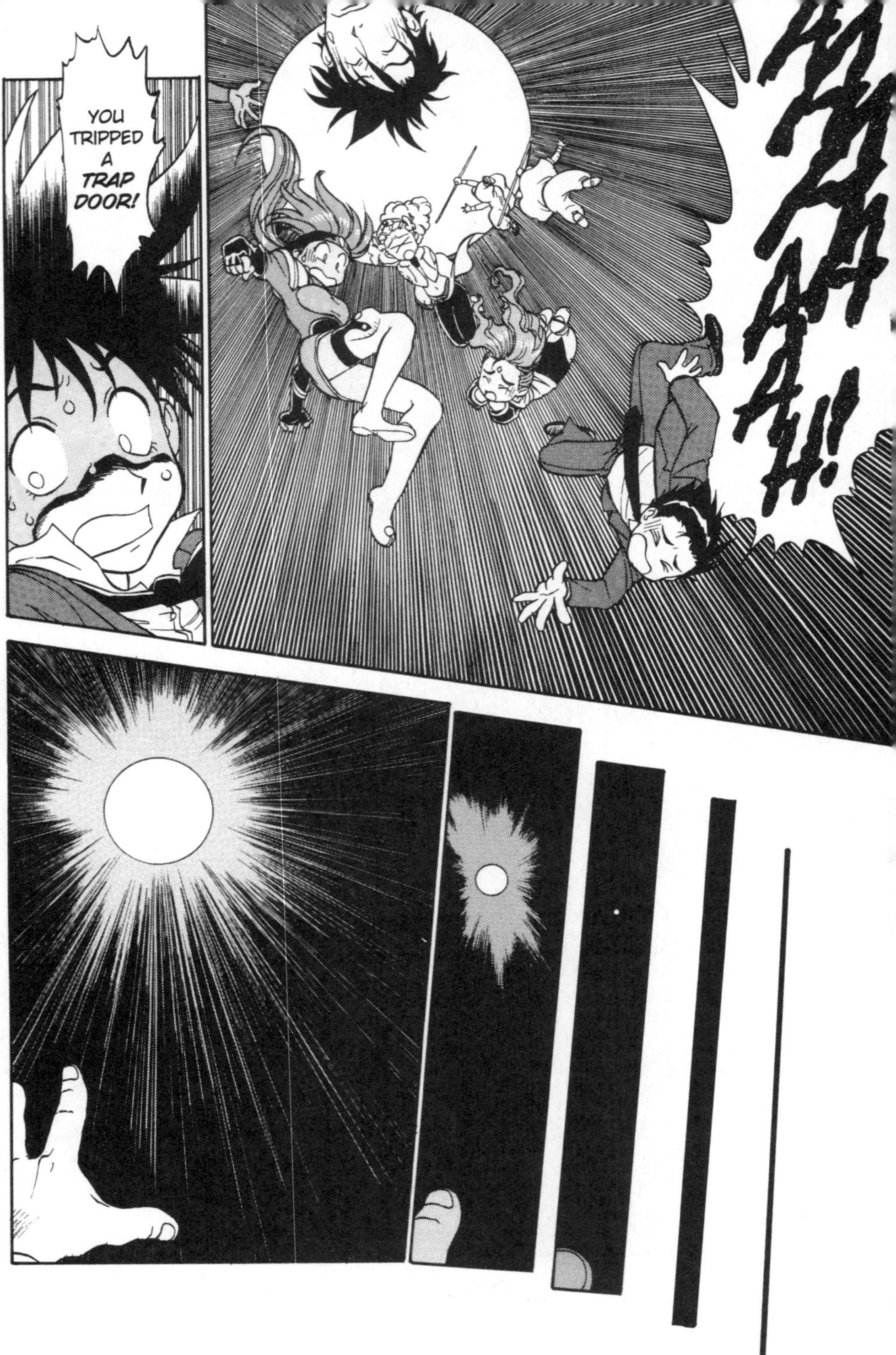
YOU TRIPPED A TRAP DOOR!
WAHHAAAAH!

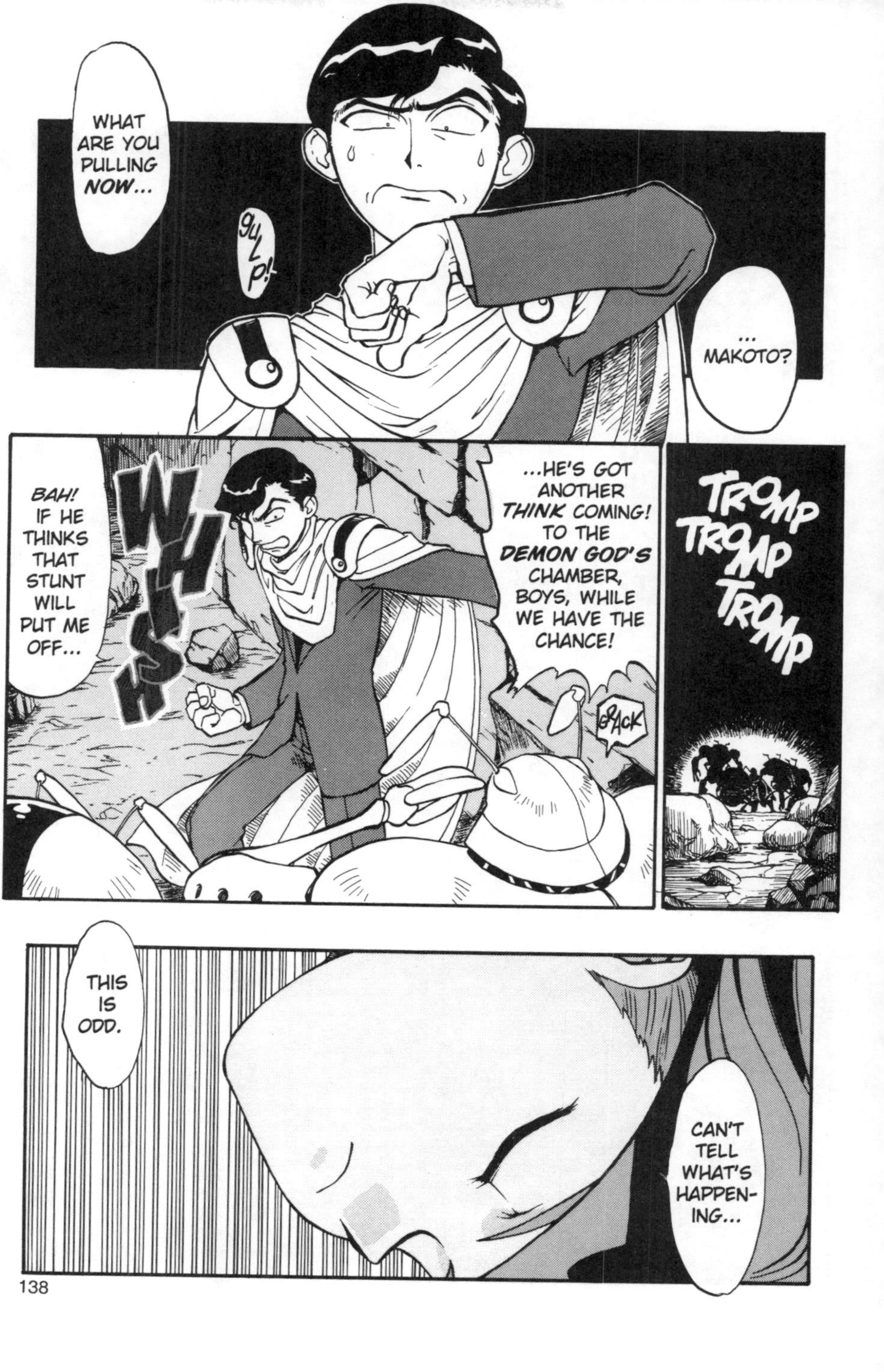
WHAT ARE YOU PULLING NOW...
GULP!
...MAKOTO?
BAH! IF HE THINKS THAT STUNT WILL PUT ME OFF...
WHISH
...HE'S GOT ANOTHER THINK COMING! TO THE DEMON GOD'S CHAMBER, BOYS, WHILE WE HAVE THE CHANCE!
CRACK
TROMP
TROMP
TROMP
THIS IS ODD.
CAN'T TELL WHAT'S HAPPEN-ING...

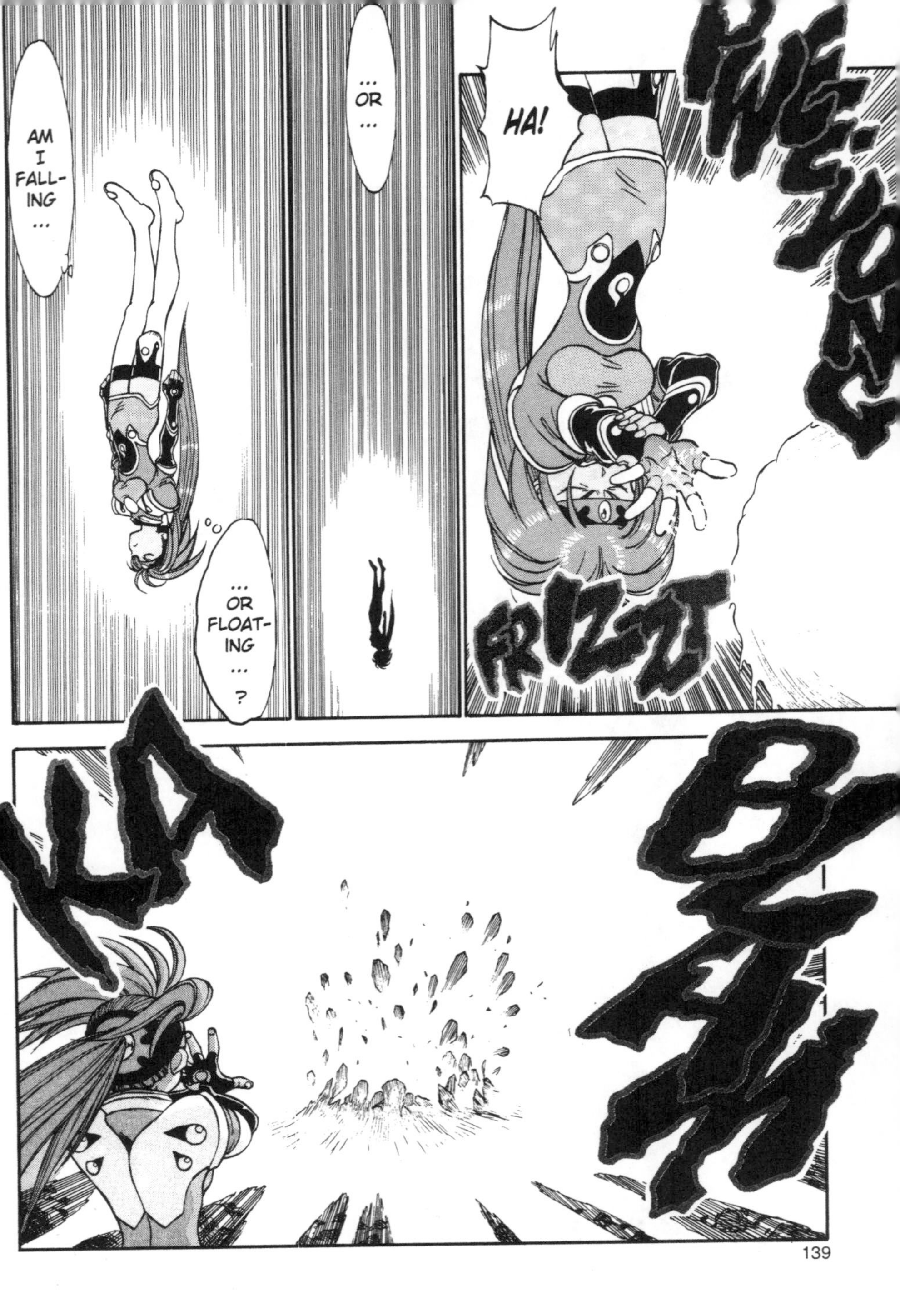
AM I FALLING-ING ...
... OR FLOAT-ING ... ?
... OR ...
HA!
FRIZZT
KA
BOOM

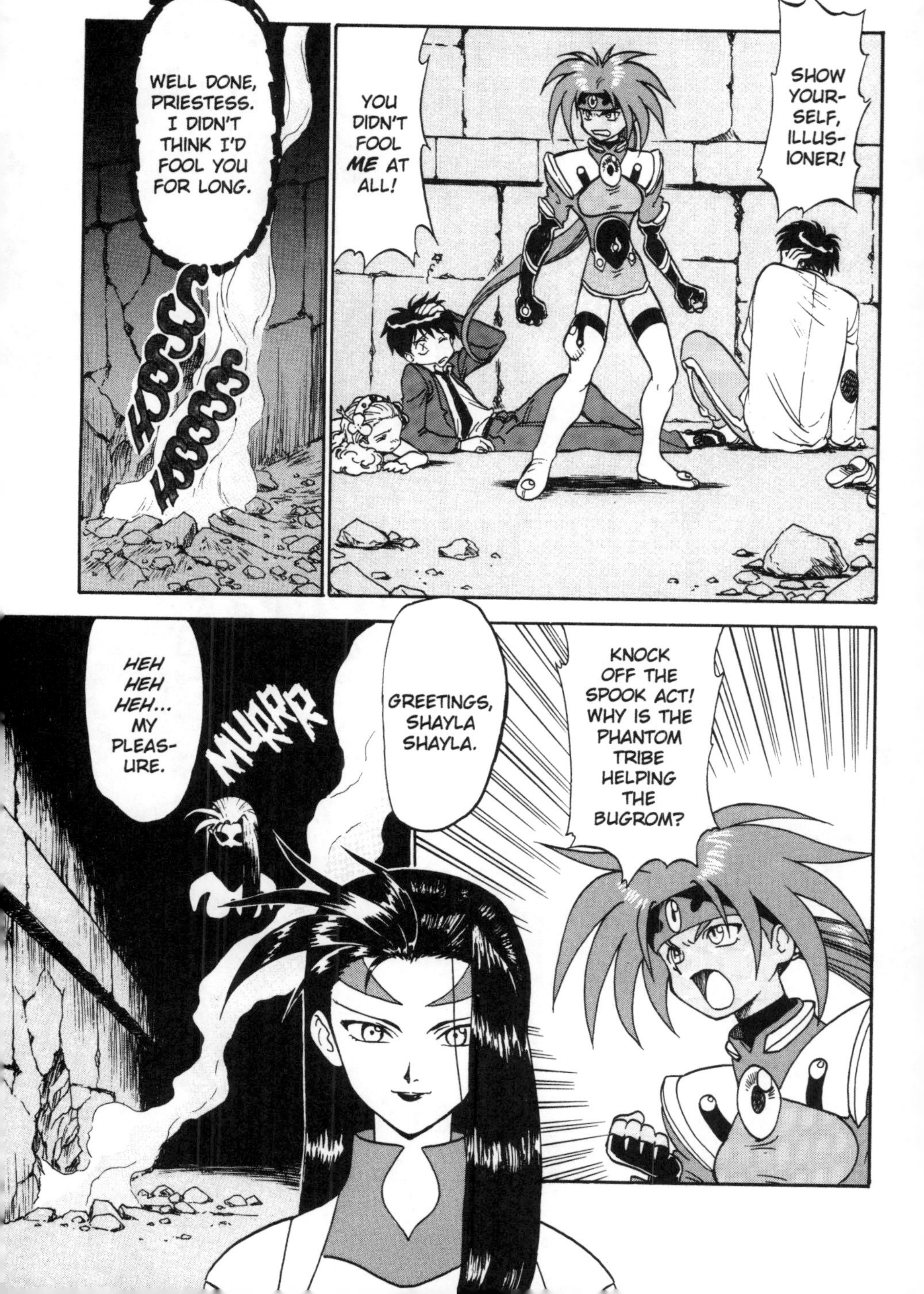
WELL DONE, PRIESTESS. I DIDN'T THINK I'D FOOL YOU FOR LONG.
HOSSS
HOSSSS
YOU DIDN'T FOOL *ME* AT ALL!
SHOW YOUR-SELF, ILLUS-IONER!
HEH HEH HEH... MY PLEAS-URE.
MURRR
GREETINGS, SHAYLA SHAYLA.
KNOCK OFF THE SPOOK ACT! WHY IS THE PHANTOM TRIBE HELPING THE BUGROM?

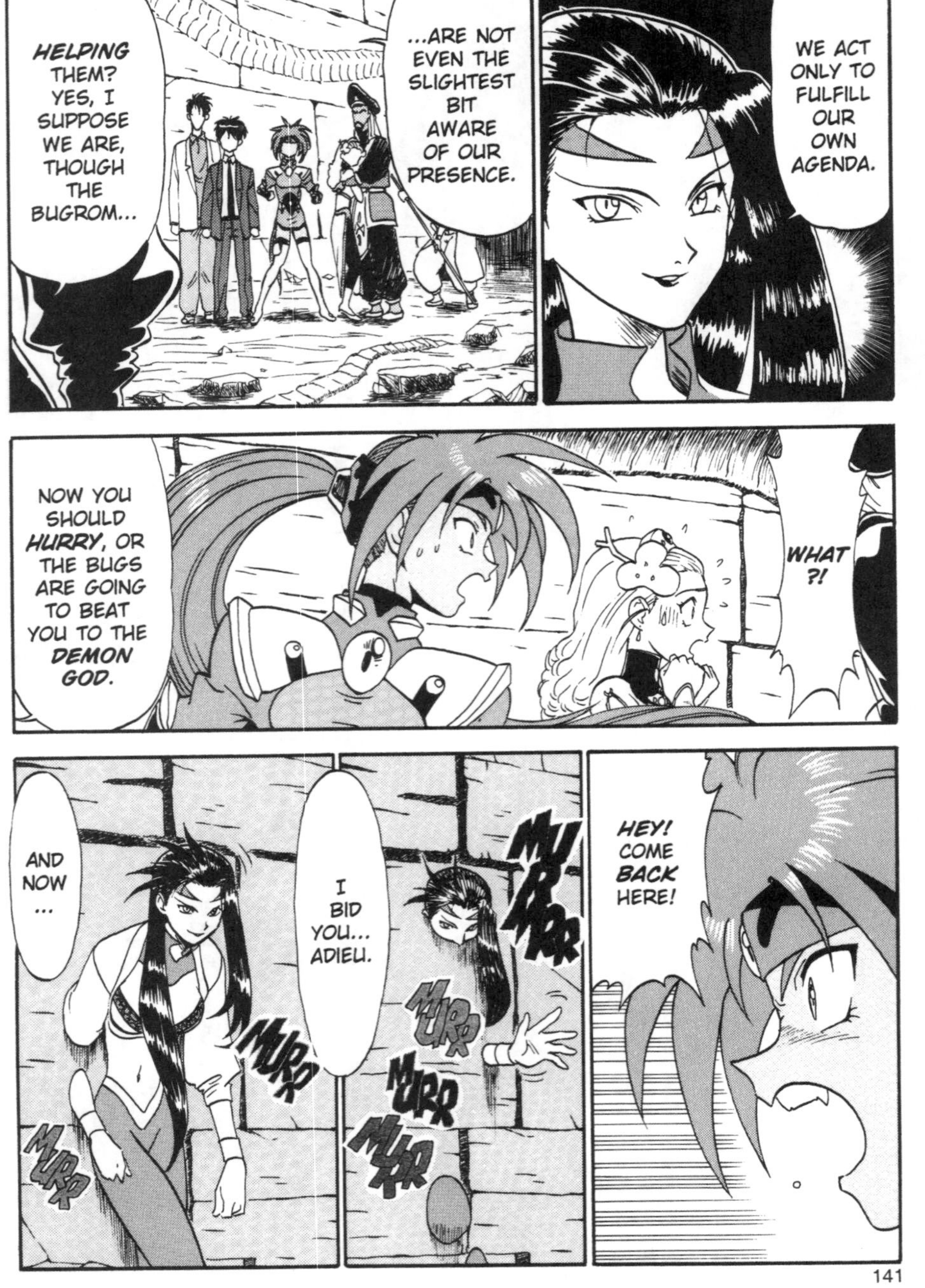
HELPING THEM? YES, I SUPPOSE WE ARE, THOUGH THE BUGROM...
...ARE NOT EVEN THE SLIGHTEST BIT AWARE OF OUR PRESENCE.
WE ACT ONLY TO FULFILL OUR OWN AGENDA.
NOW YOU SHOULD HURRY, OR THE BUGS ARE GOING TO BEAT YOU TO THE DEMON GOD.
WHAT ?!
AND NOW ...
I BID YOU... ADIEU.
MURR MURR
MURR
MURR
MURR
MURR
MURR
HEY! COME BACK HERE!

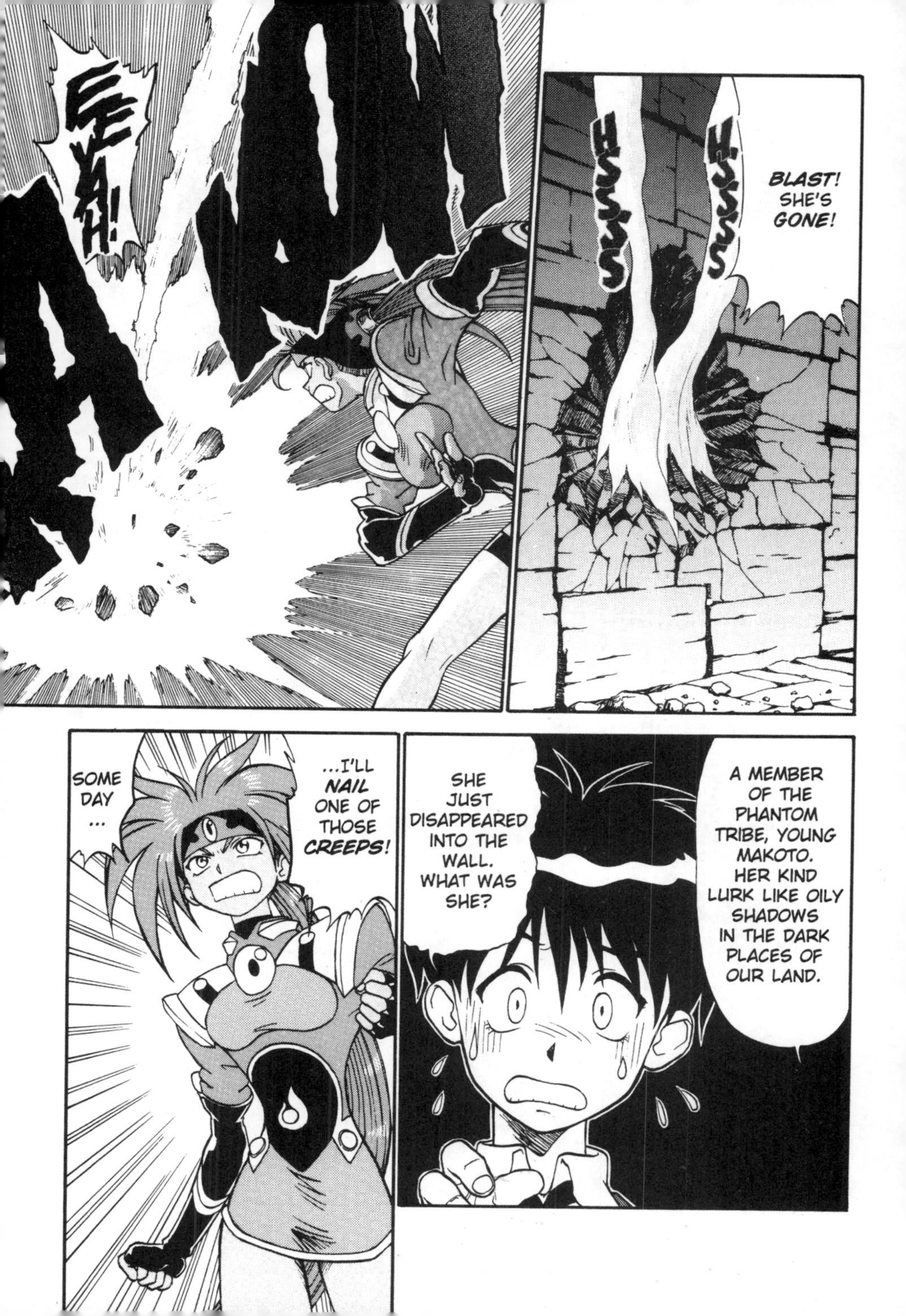
EEEYAH!
BLAST! SHE'S GONE!
HSSSSS
HSSSSS
SOME DAY ...
...I'LL NAIL ONE OF THOSE CREEPS!
SHE JUST DISAPPEARED INTO THE WALL. WHAT WAS SHE?
A MEMBER OF THE PHANTOM TRIBE, YOUNG MAKOTO. HER KIND LURK LIKE OILY SHADOWS IN THE DARK PLACES OF OUR LAND.

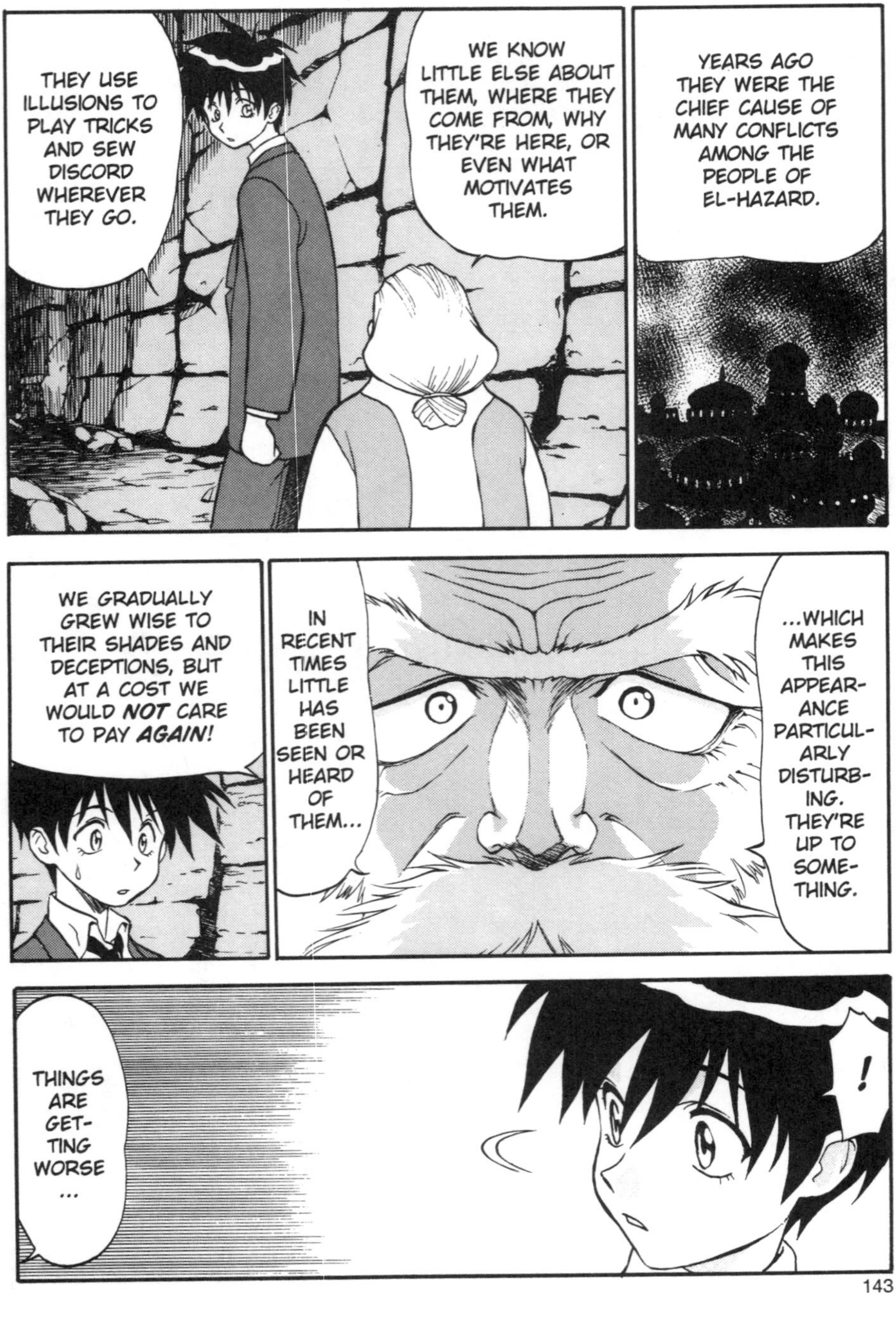

THEY USE ILLUSIONS TO PLAY TRICKS AND SEW DISCORD WHEREVER THEY GO.
WE KNOW LITTLE ELSE ABOUT THEM, WHERE THEY COME FROM, WHY THEY'RE HERE, OR EVEN WHAT MOTIVATES THEM.
YEARS AGO THEY WERE THE CHIEF CAUSE OF MANY CONFLICTS AMONG THE PEOPLE OF EL-HAZARD.
WE GRADUALLY GREW WISE TO THEIR SHADES AND DECEPTIONS, BUT AT A COST WE WOULD NOT CARE TO PAY AGAIN!
IN RECENT TIMES LITTLE HAS BEEN SEEN OR HEARD OF THEM...
...WHICH MAKES THIS APPEAR-ANCE PARTICUL-ARLY DISTURB-ING. THEY'RE UP TO SOME-THING.
THINGS ARE GET-TING WORSE ...
!

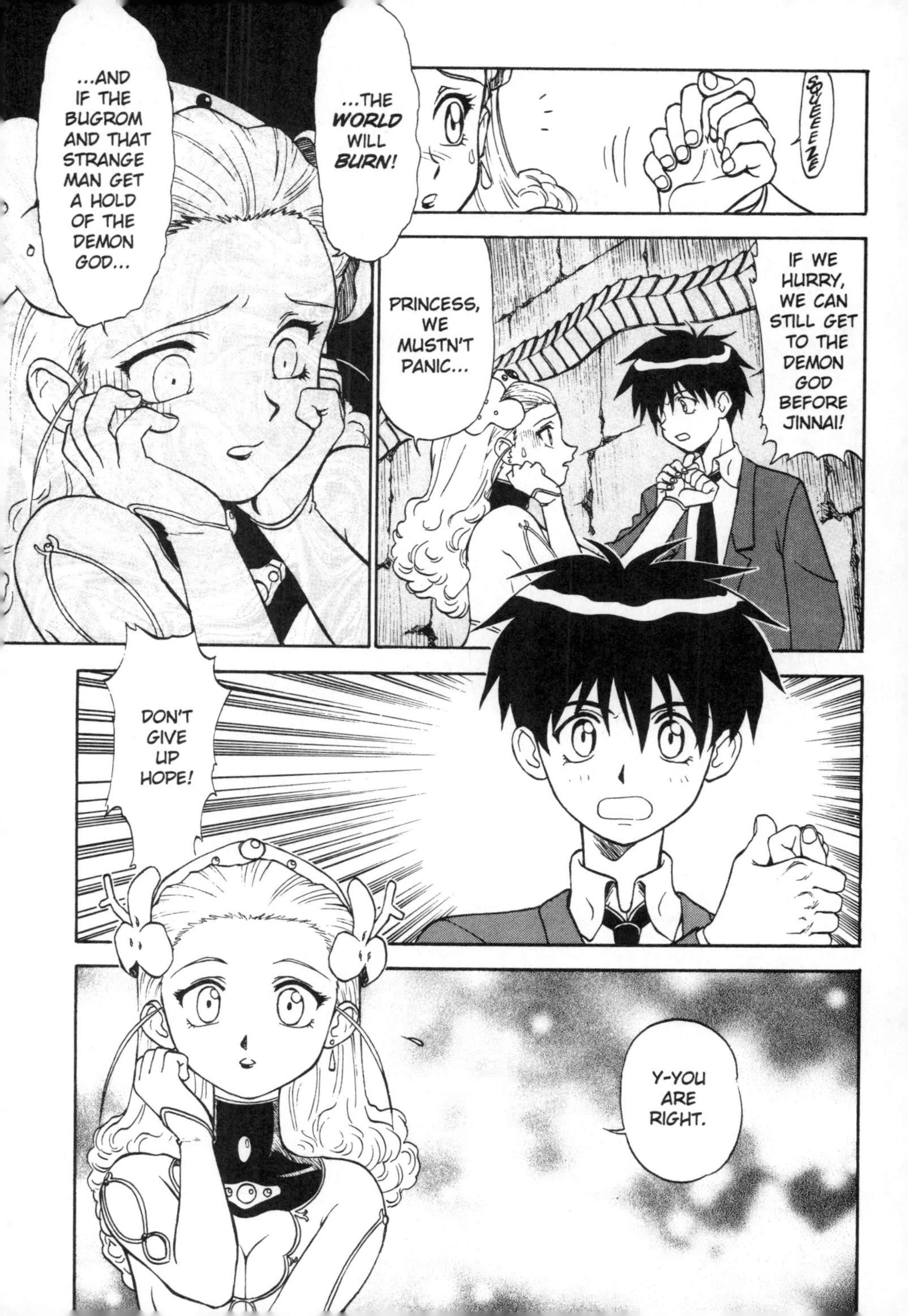
...AND IF THE BUGROM AND THAT STRANGE MAN GET A HOLD OF THE DEMON GOD...
...THE WORLD WILL BURN!
SQUEEEZE
PRINCESS, WE MUSTN'T PANIC...
IF WE HURRY, WE CAN STILL GET TO THE DEMON GOD BEFORE JINNAI!
DON'T GIVE UP HOPE!
Y-YOU ARE RIGHT.

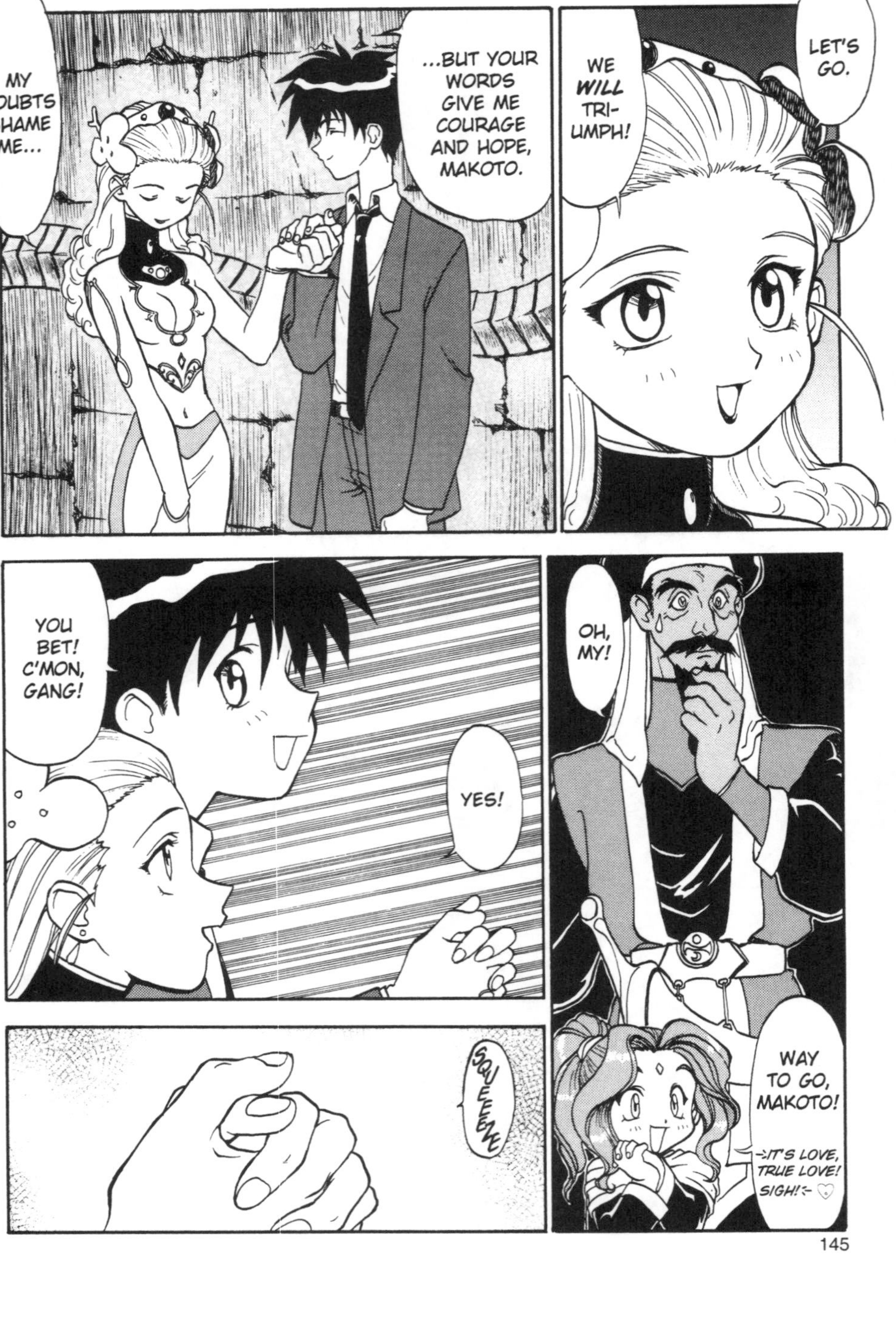
MY DOUBTS SHAME ME...
...BUT YOUR WORDS GIVE ME COURAGE AND HOPE, MAKOTO.
WE ***WILL*** TRI-UMPH!
LET'S GO.
YOU BET! C'MON, GANG!
YES!
SQUEEEZE
OH, MY!
WAY TO GO, MAKOTO!
IT'S LOVE, TRUE LOVE! SIGH! ♡

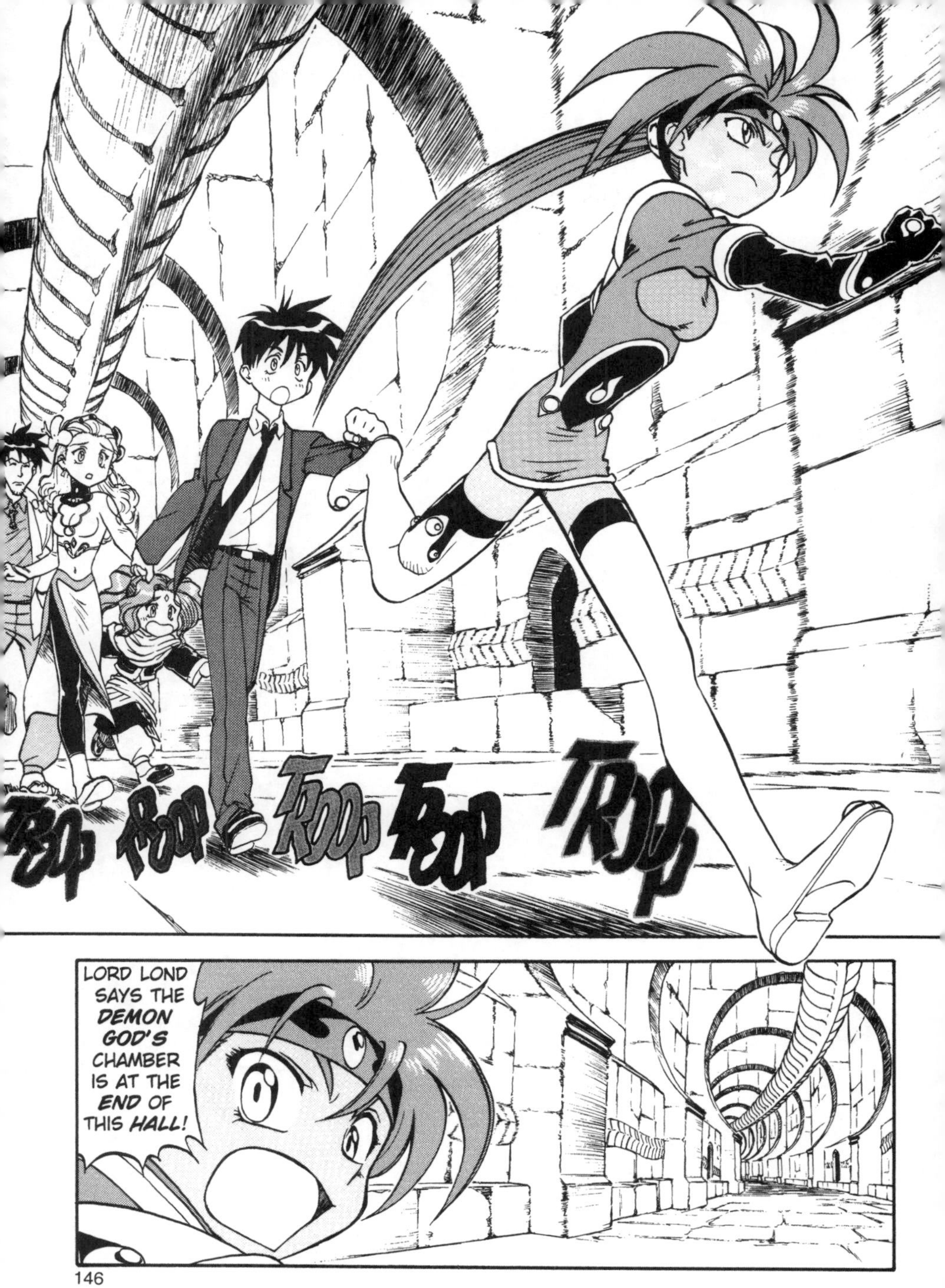
TROOP TROOP TROOP TROOP TROOP
LORD LOND SAYS THE DEMON GOD'S CHAMBER IS AT THE END OF THIS HALL!

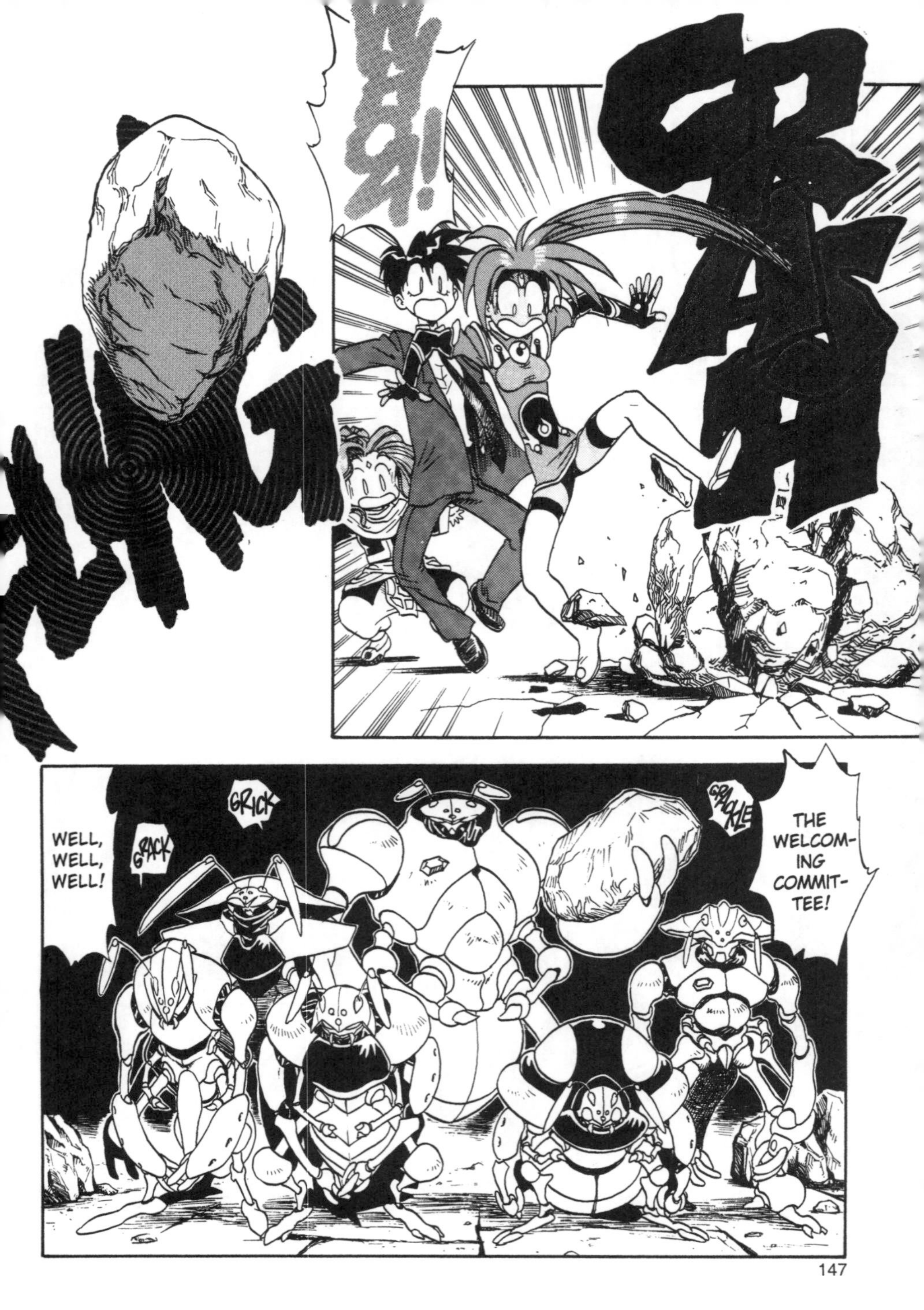
WELL, WELL, WELL!
GRACK
GRICK
GRACKLE
THE WELCOM-ING COMMIT-TEE!

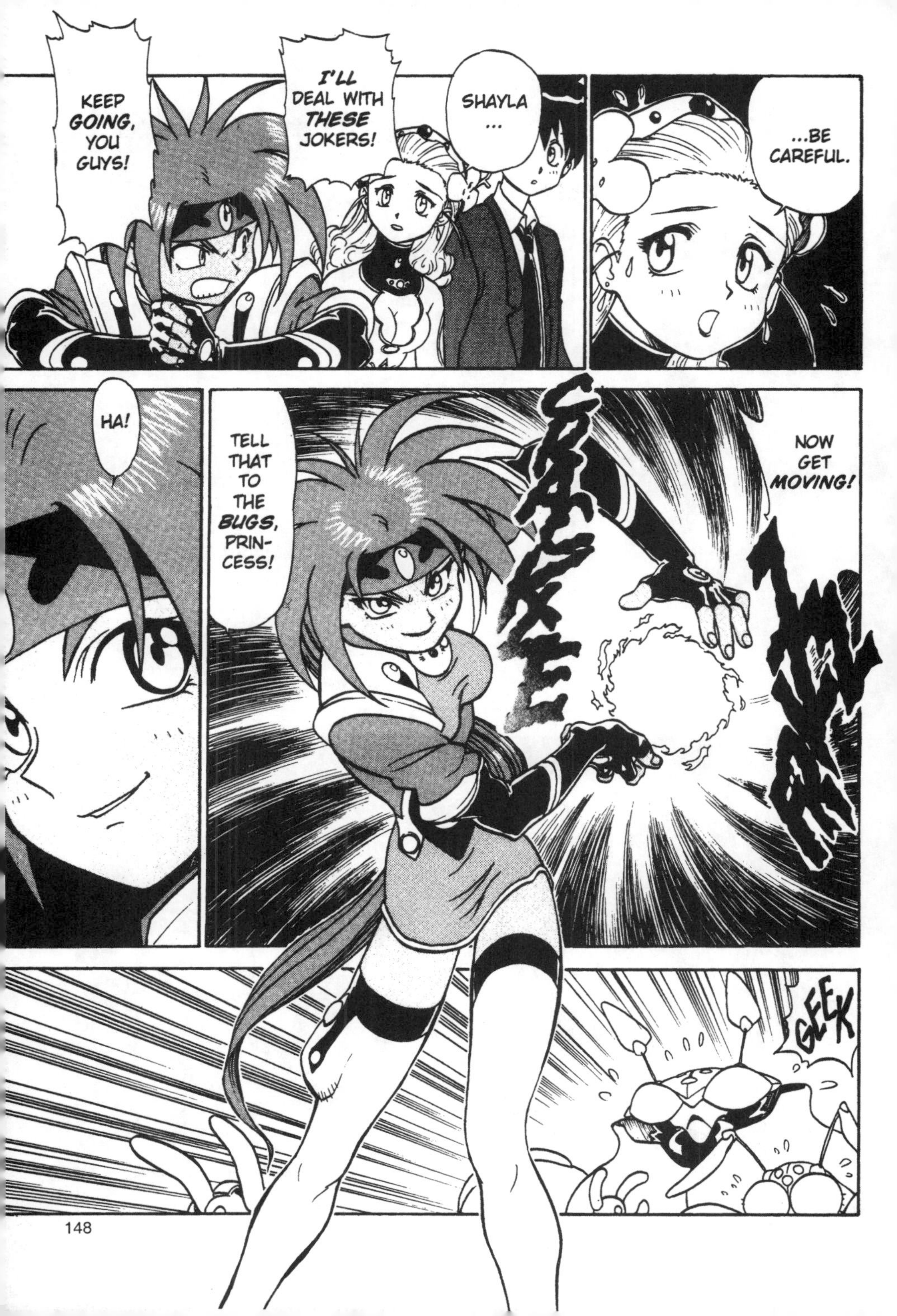

KEEP GOING, YOU GUYS!
I'LL DEAL WITH THESE JOKERS!
SHAYLA ...
...BE CAREFUL.
HA!
TELL THAT TO THE BUGS, PRIN-CESS!
NOW GET MOVING!
GEEK

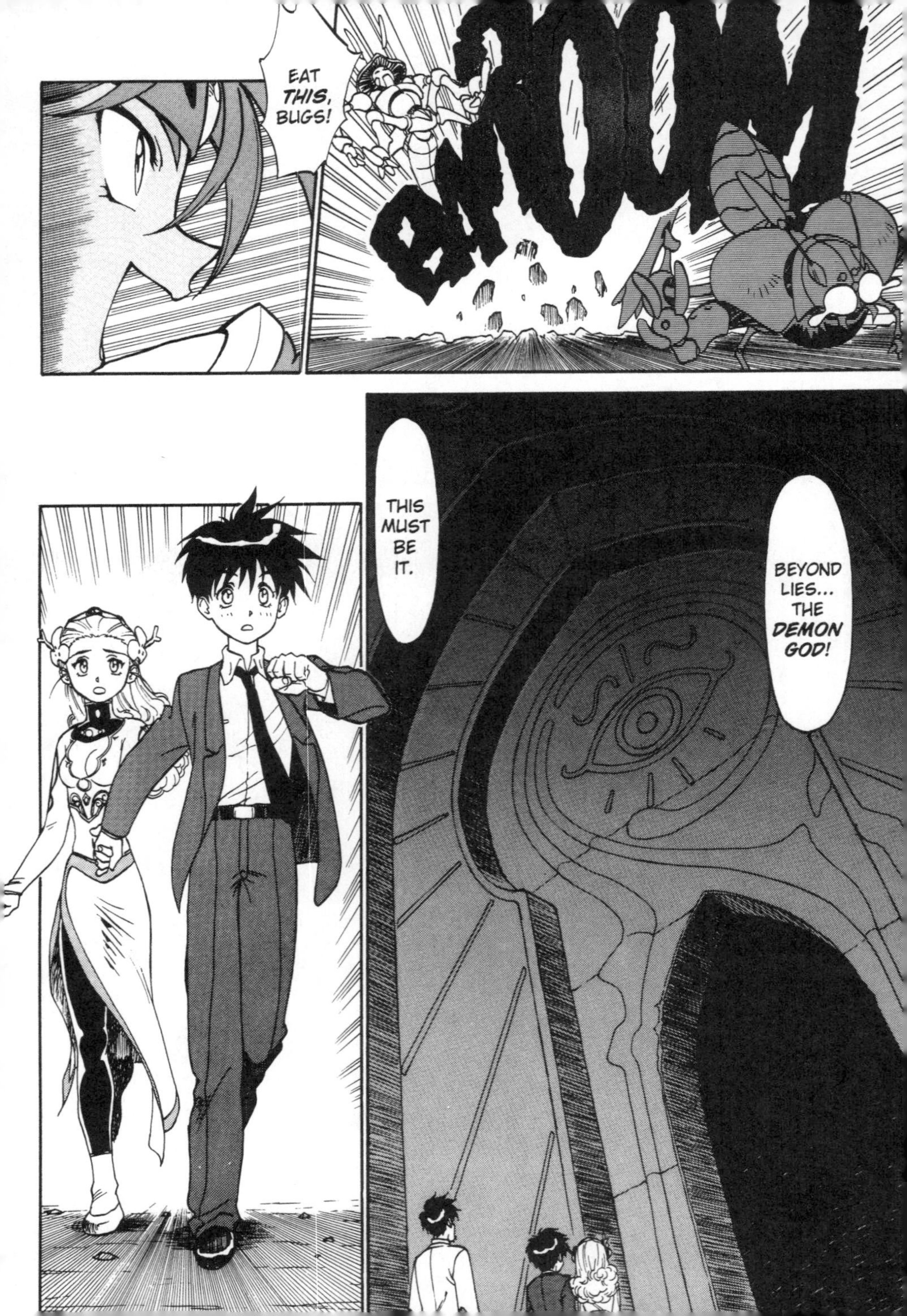
EAT *THIS*, BUGS!
THIS MUST BE IT.
BEYOND LIES... THE *DEMON GOD*!

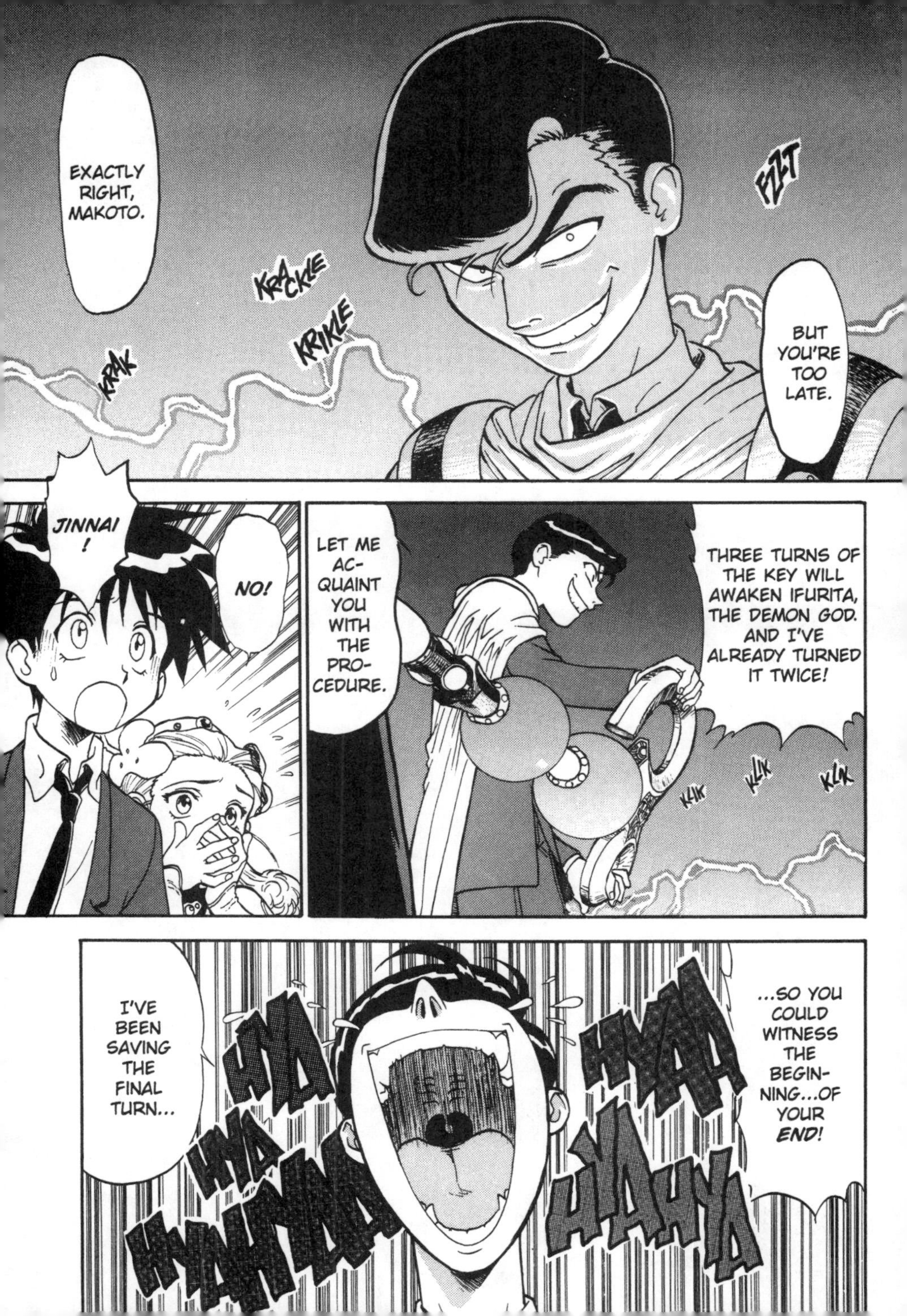
EXACTLY RIGHT, MAKOTO.
KRACKLE
KRIKLE
KRAK
FZZT
BUT YOU'RE TOO LATE.
JINNAI!
NO!
LET ME AC-QUAINT YOU WITH THE PRO-CEDURE.
THREE TURNS OF THE KEY WILL AWAKEN IFURITA, THE DEMON GOD. AND I'VE ALREADY TURNED IT TWICE!
KLIK
KLIK
KLIK
I'VE BEEN SAVING THE FINAL TURN...
HYA
HYA HYA
HYAHYAHYA
HYAA
HYAHYAHYA
...SO YOU COULD WITNESS THE BEGIN-NING...OF YOUR *END*!

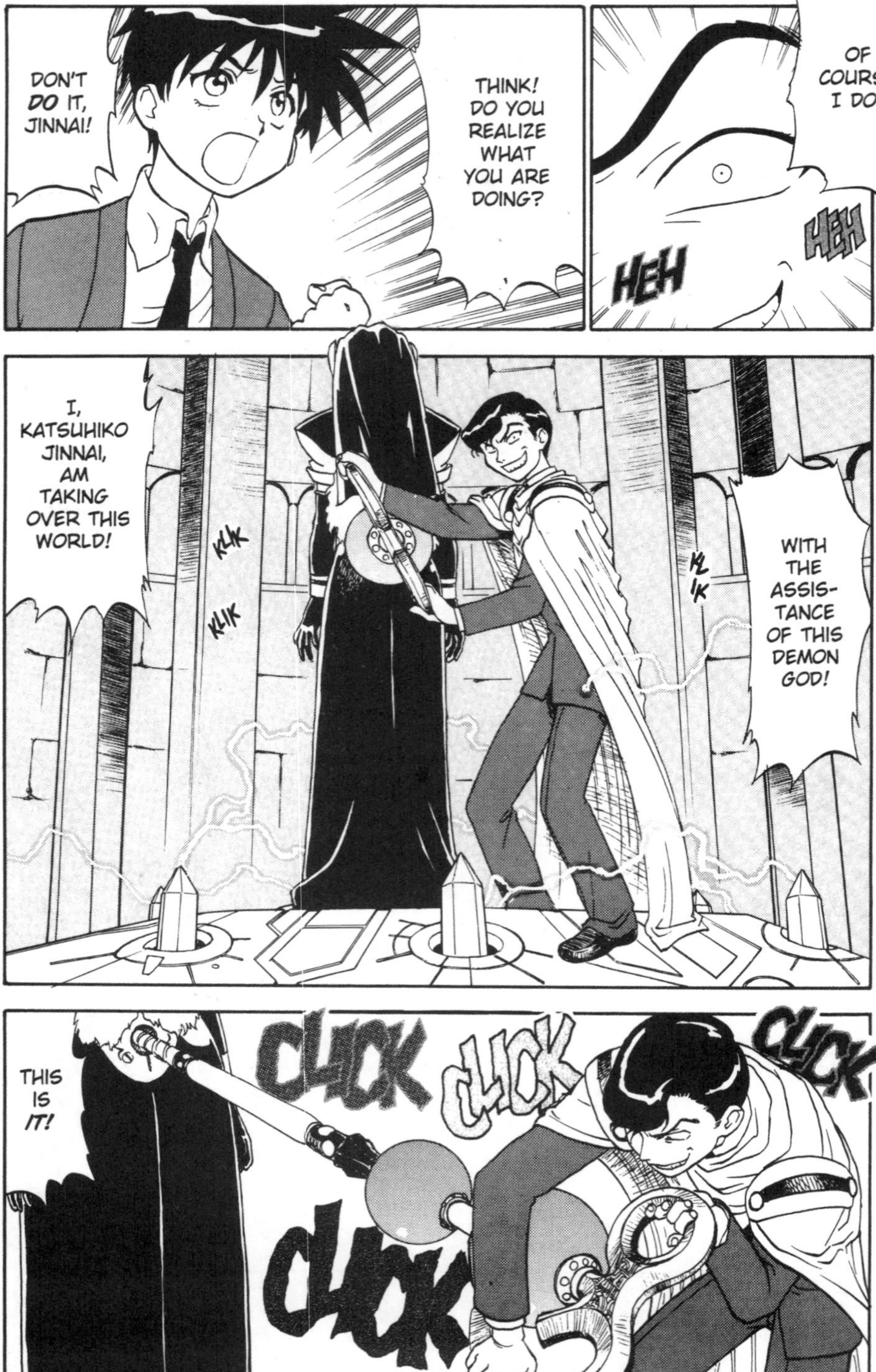
DON'T *DO* IT, JINNAI!
THINK! DO YOU REALIZE WHAT YOU ARE DOING?
OF COURSE I DO!
HEH
HEH
I, KATSUHIKO JINNAI, AM TAKING OVER THIS WORLD!
KLIK
KLIK
KLIK
WITH THE ASSISTANCE OF THIS DEMON GOD!
THIS IS *IT!*
CLICK
CLICK
CLICK
CLICK

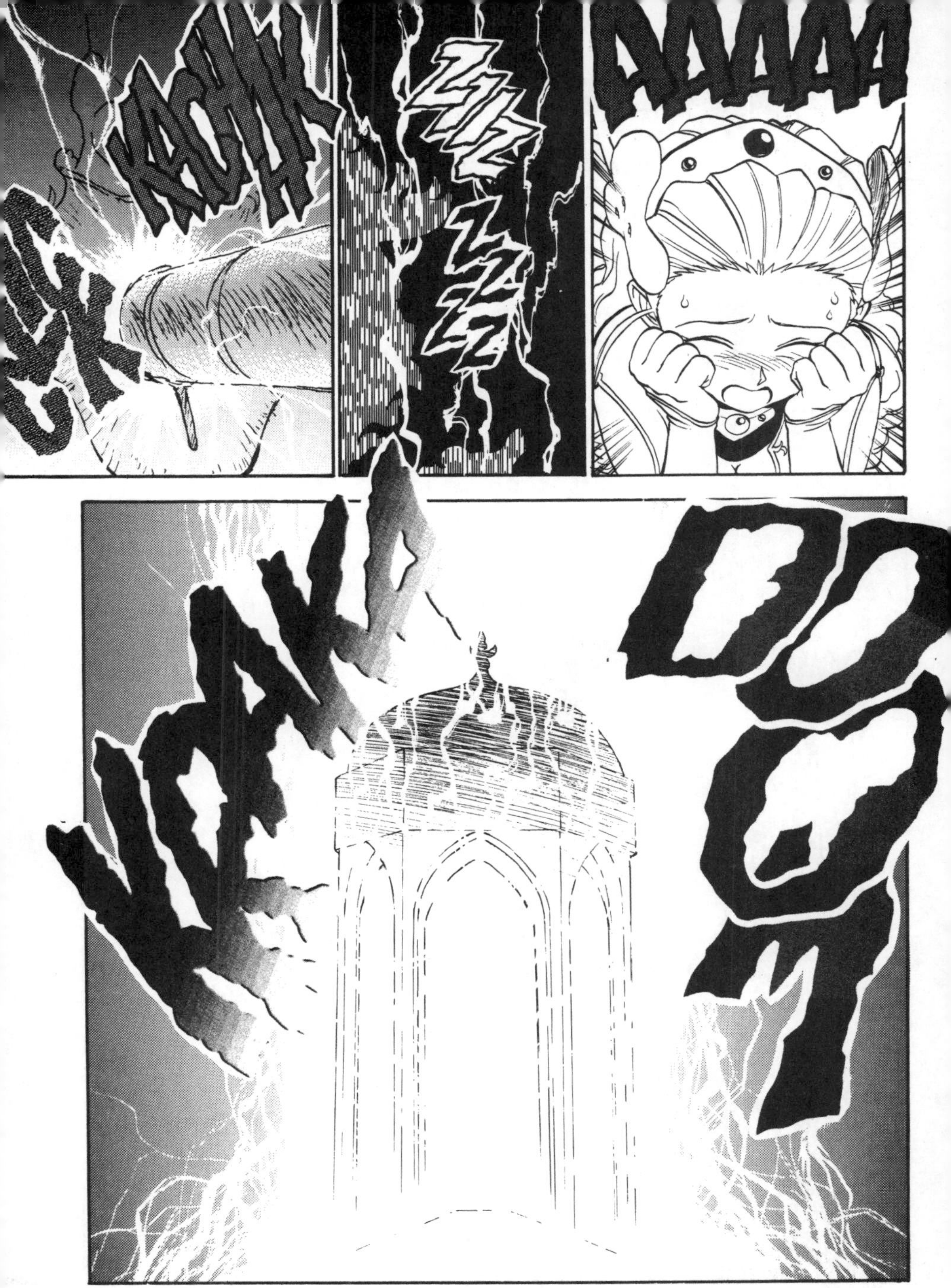
CK
KACHIK
ZZZZ
ZZZZZ
AAAAA
KRAKA
DOOM

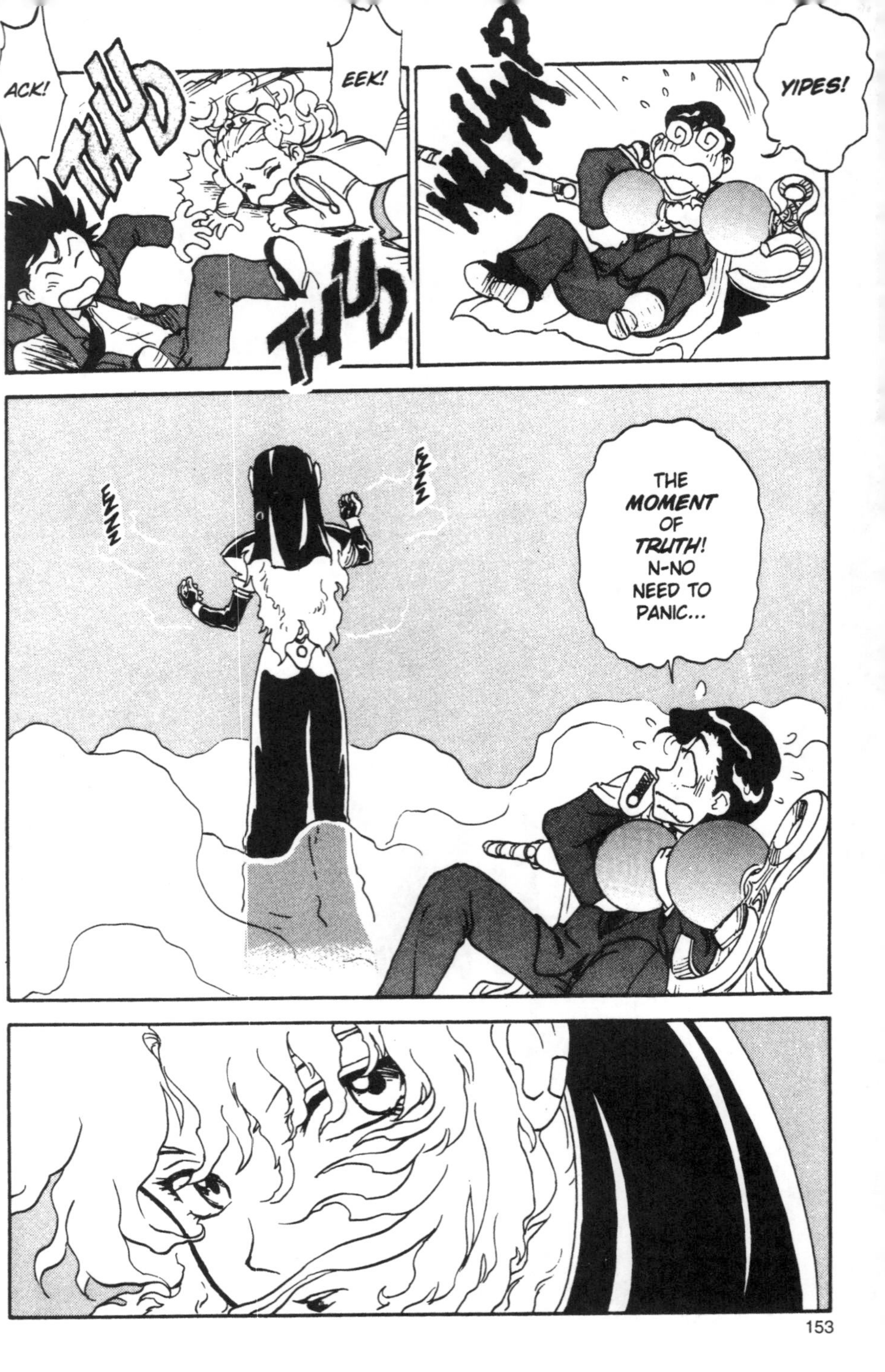
ACK!
THUD
EEK!
THUD
WHUMP
YIPES!
ZZZ
ZZZ
THE MOMENT OF TRUTH! N-NO NEED TO PANIC...

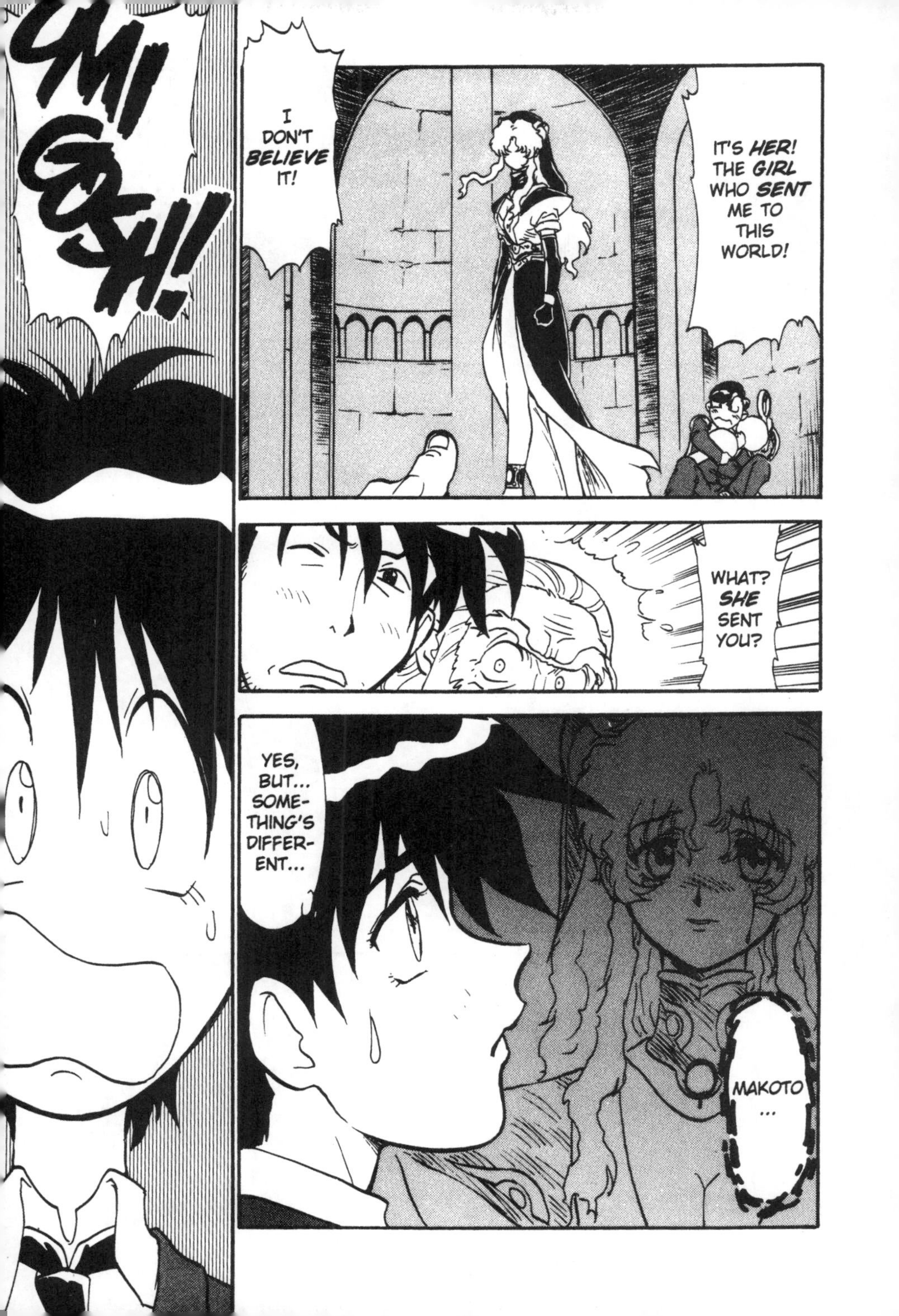
MI GOSH!!
I DON'T BELIEVE IT!
IT'S HER! THE GIRL WHO SENT ME TO THIS WORLD!
WHAT? SHE SENT YOU?
YES, BUT... SOME-THING'S DIFFER-ENT...
MAKOTO ...

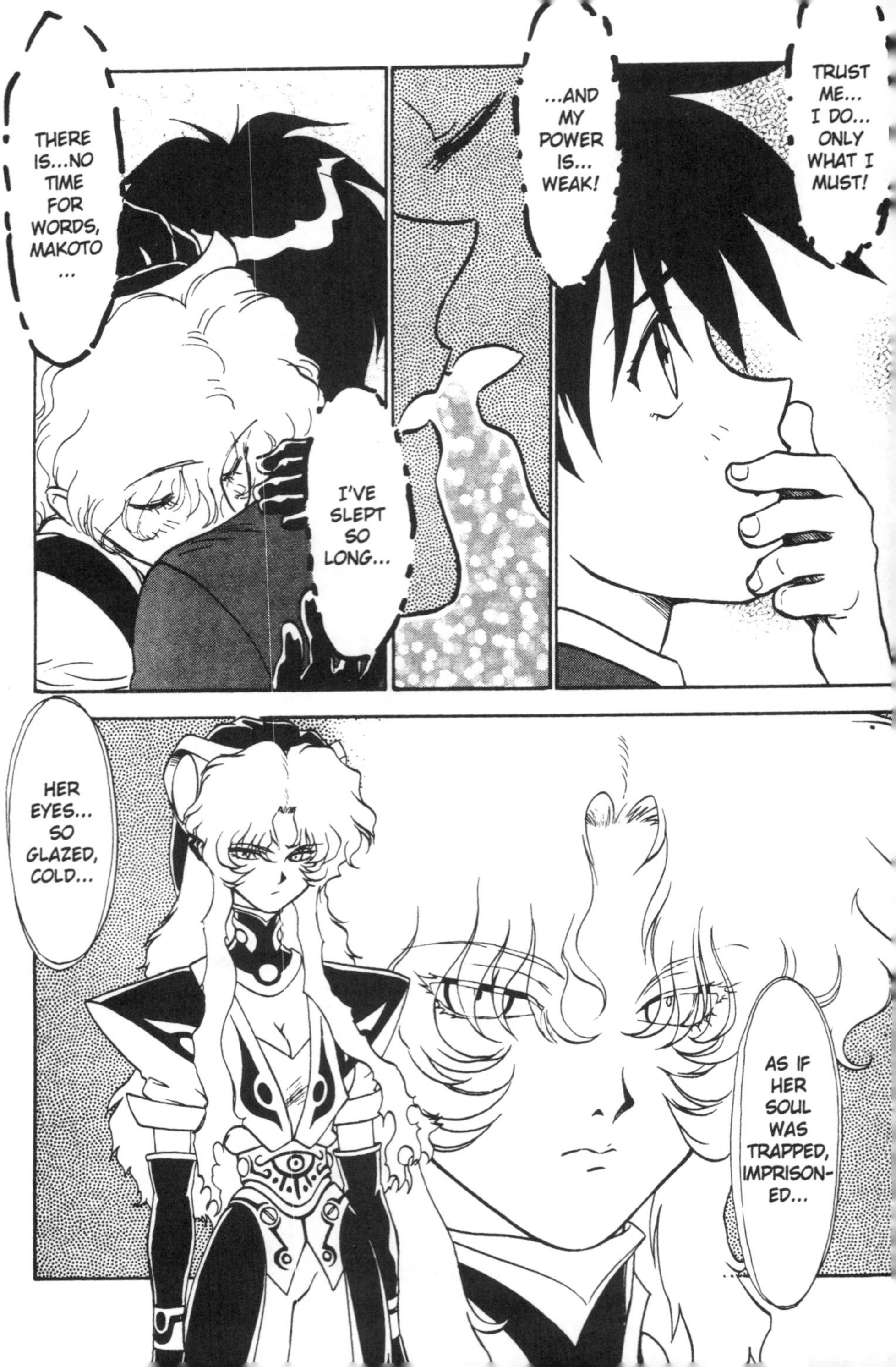
THERE IS...NO TIME FOR WORDS, MAKOTO ...
I'VE SLEPT SO LONG...
...AND MY POWER IS... WEAK!
TRUST ME... I DO... ONLY WHAT I MUST!
HER EYES... SO GLAZED, COLD...
AS IF HER SOUL WAS TRAPPED, IMPRISON-ED...

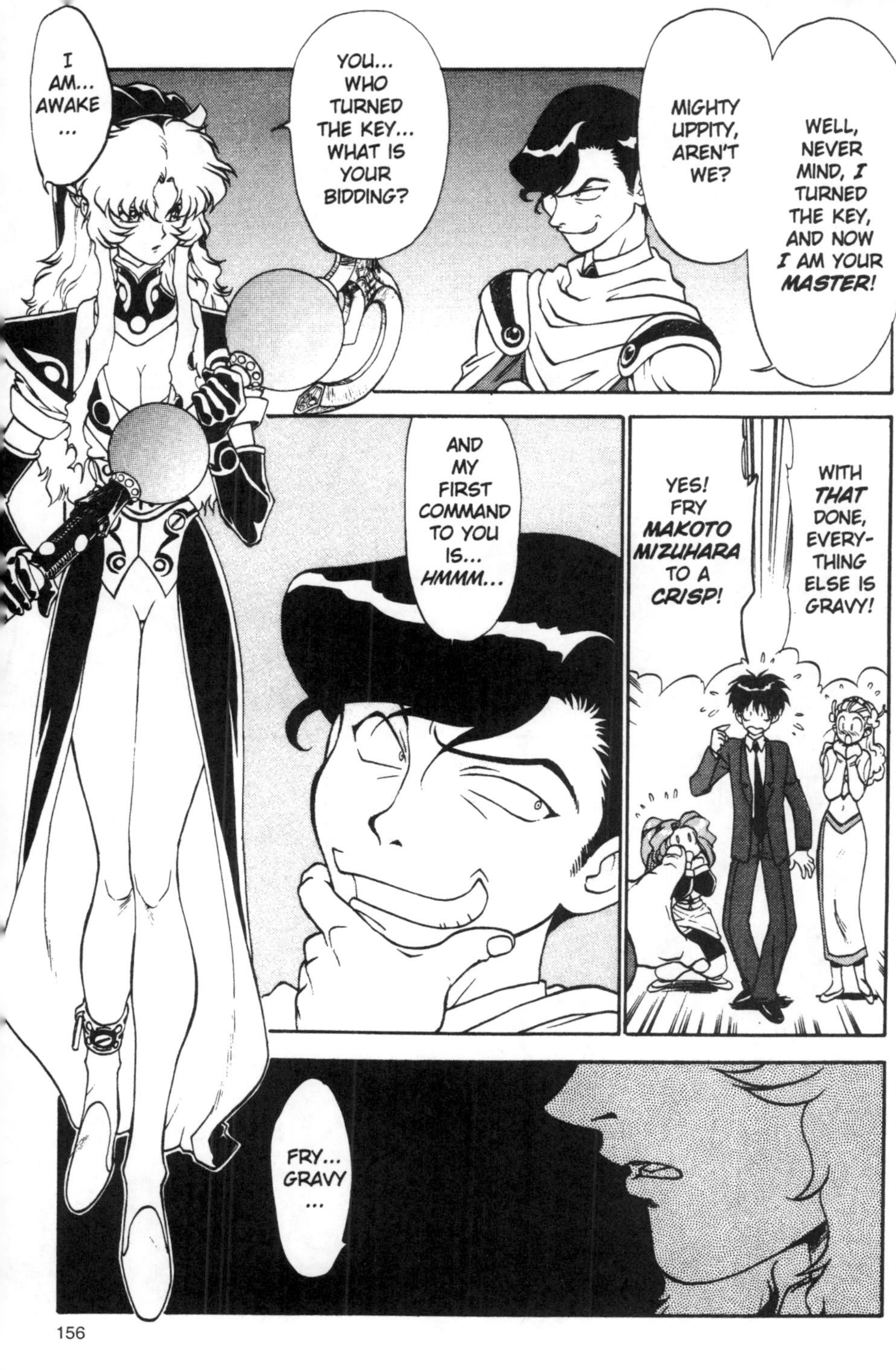
I AM... AWAKE ...
YOU... WHO TURNED THE KEY... WHAT IS YOUR BIDDING?
MIGHTY UPPITY, AREN'T WE?
WELL, NEVER MIND, I TURNED THE KEY, AND NOW I AM YOUR MASTER!
AND MY FIRST COMMAND TO YOU IS... HMMM...
YES! FRY MAKOTO MIZUHARA TO A CRISP!
WITH THAT DONE, EVERY-THING ELSE IS GRAVY!
FRY... GRAVY ...

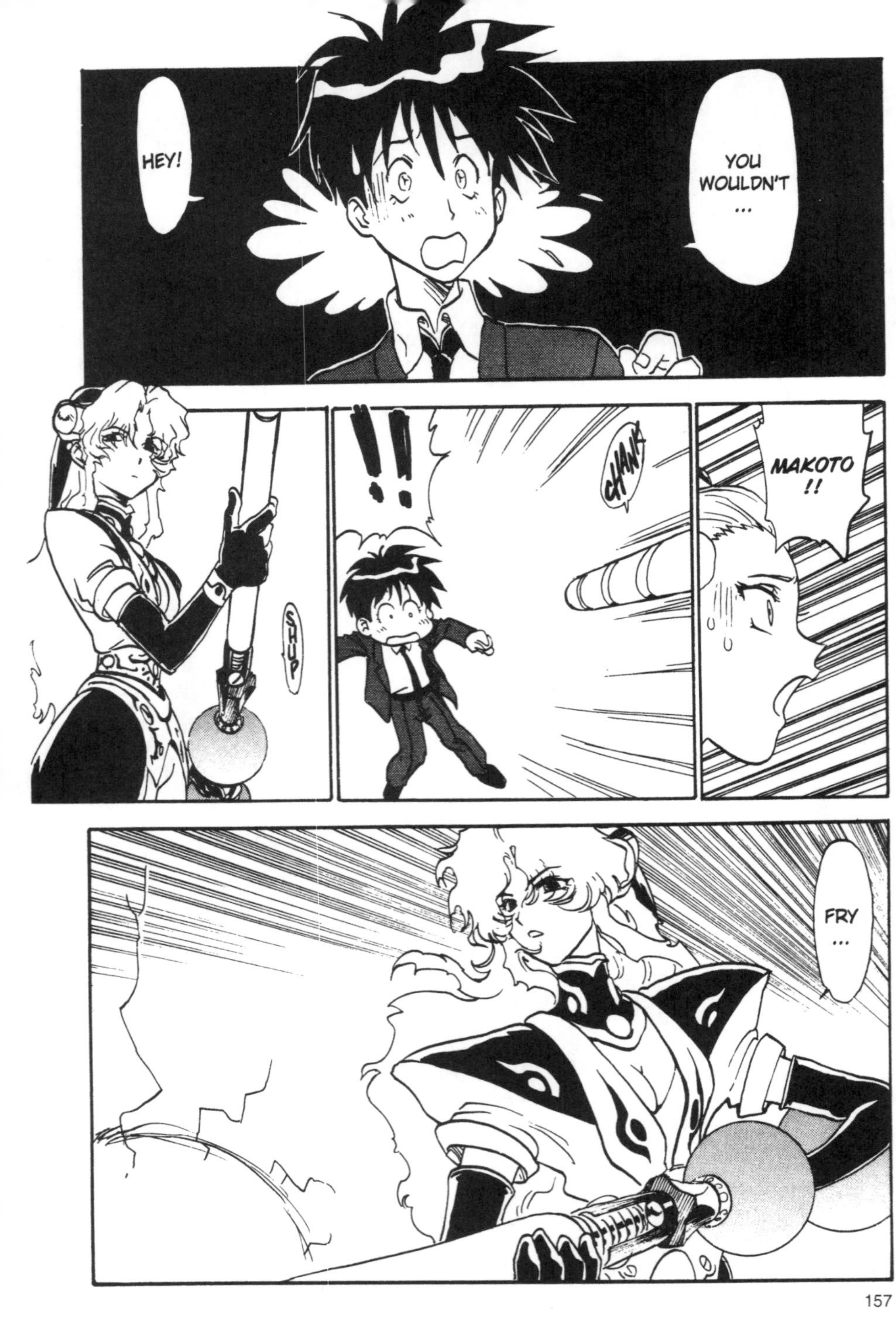
HEY!
YOU WOULDN'T ...
SHUP
!!
CHANK
MAKOTO !!
FRY ...

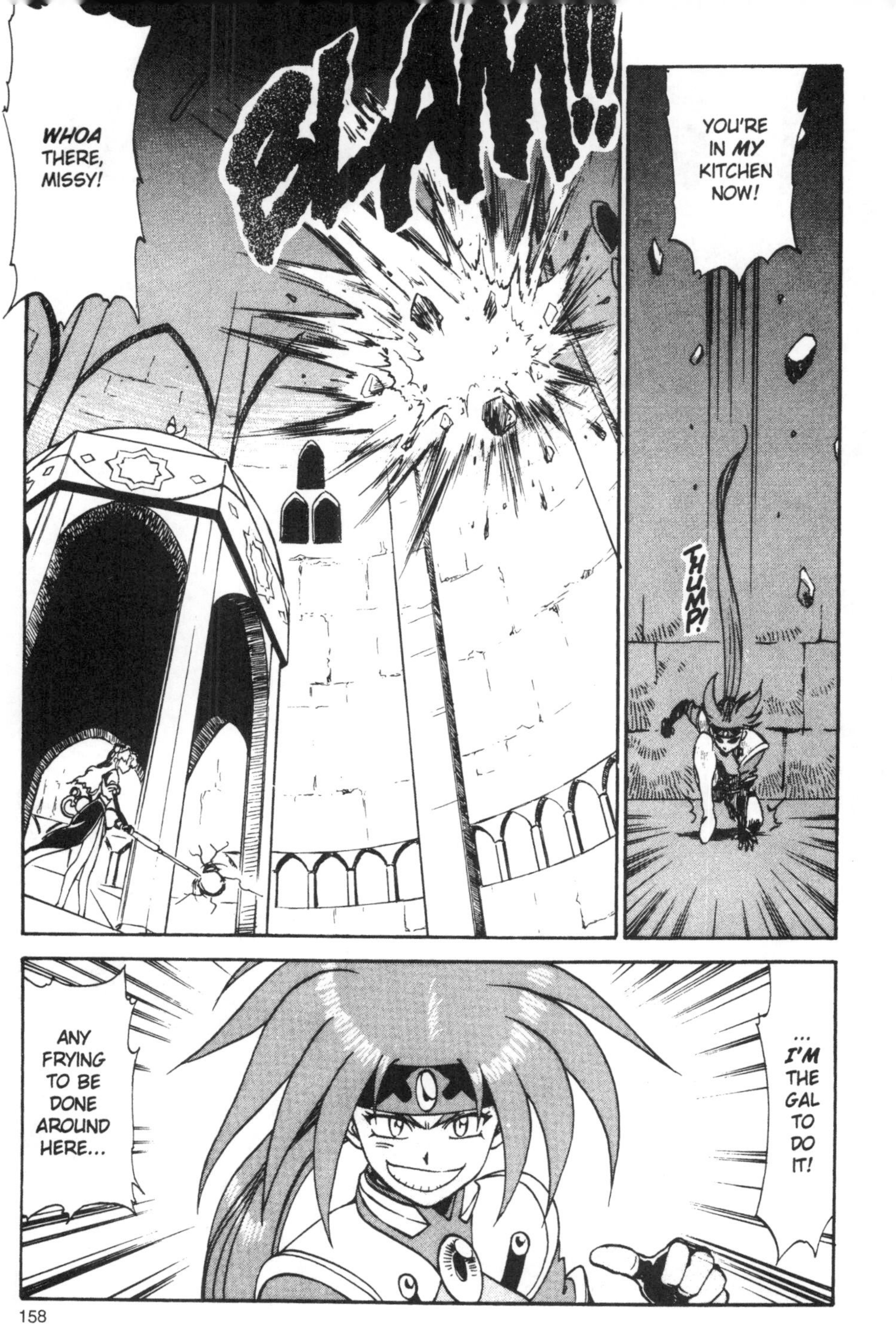
WHOA THERE, MISSY!
CLAM!!
YOU'RE IN MY KITCHEN NOW!
THUMP!
ANY FRYING TO BE DONE AROUND HERE...
...I'M THE GAL TO DO IT!

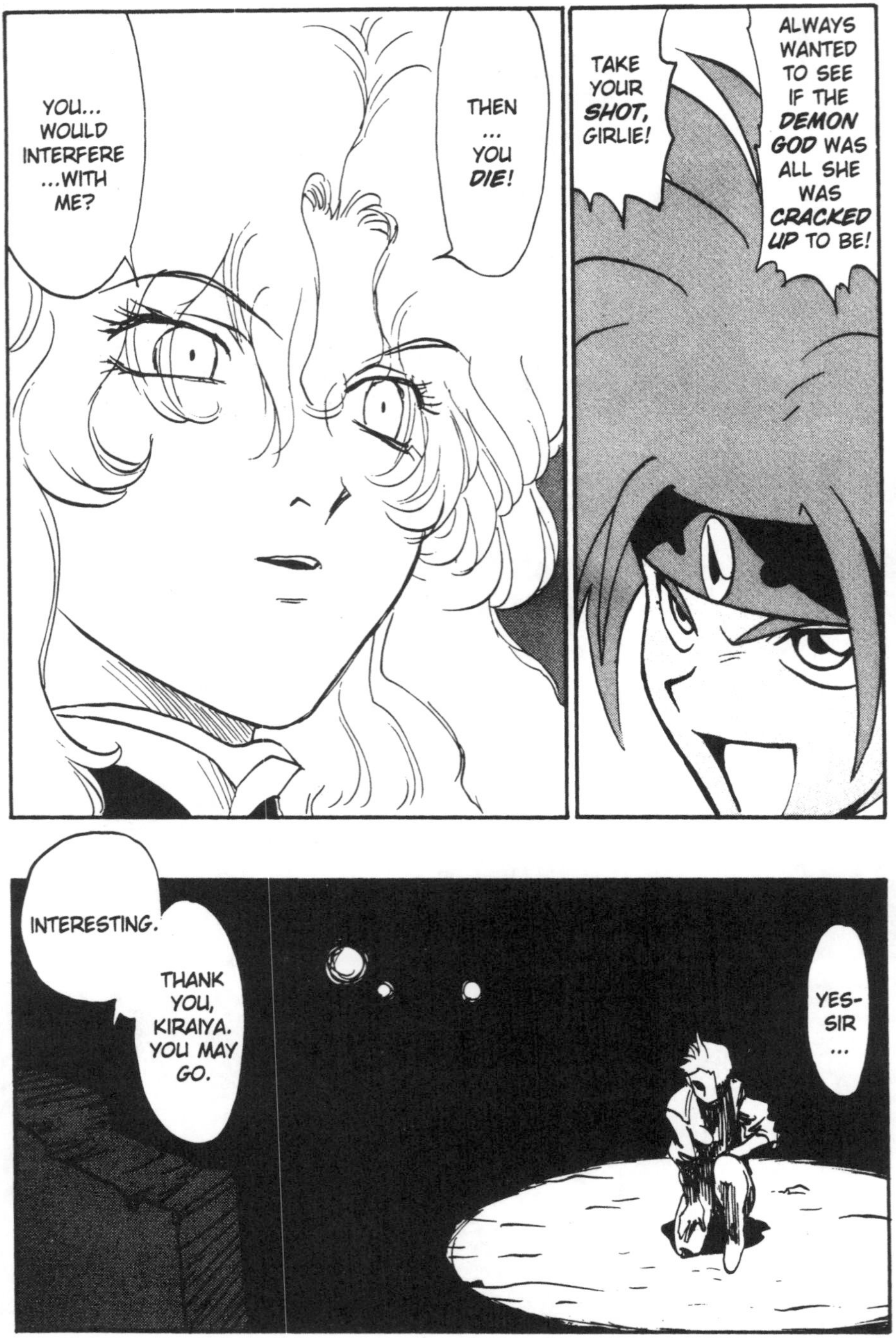

YOU... WOULD INTERFERE ...WITH ME?
THEN ... YOU DIE!
TAKE YOUR SHOT, GIRLIE!
ALWAYS WANTED TO SEE IF THE DEMON GOD WAS ALL SHE WAS CRACKED UP TO BE!
INTERESTING.
THANK YOU, KIRAIYA. YOU MAY GO.
YES-SIR ...

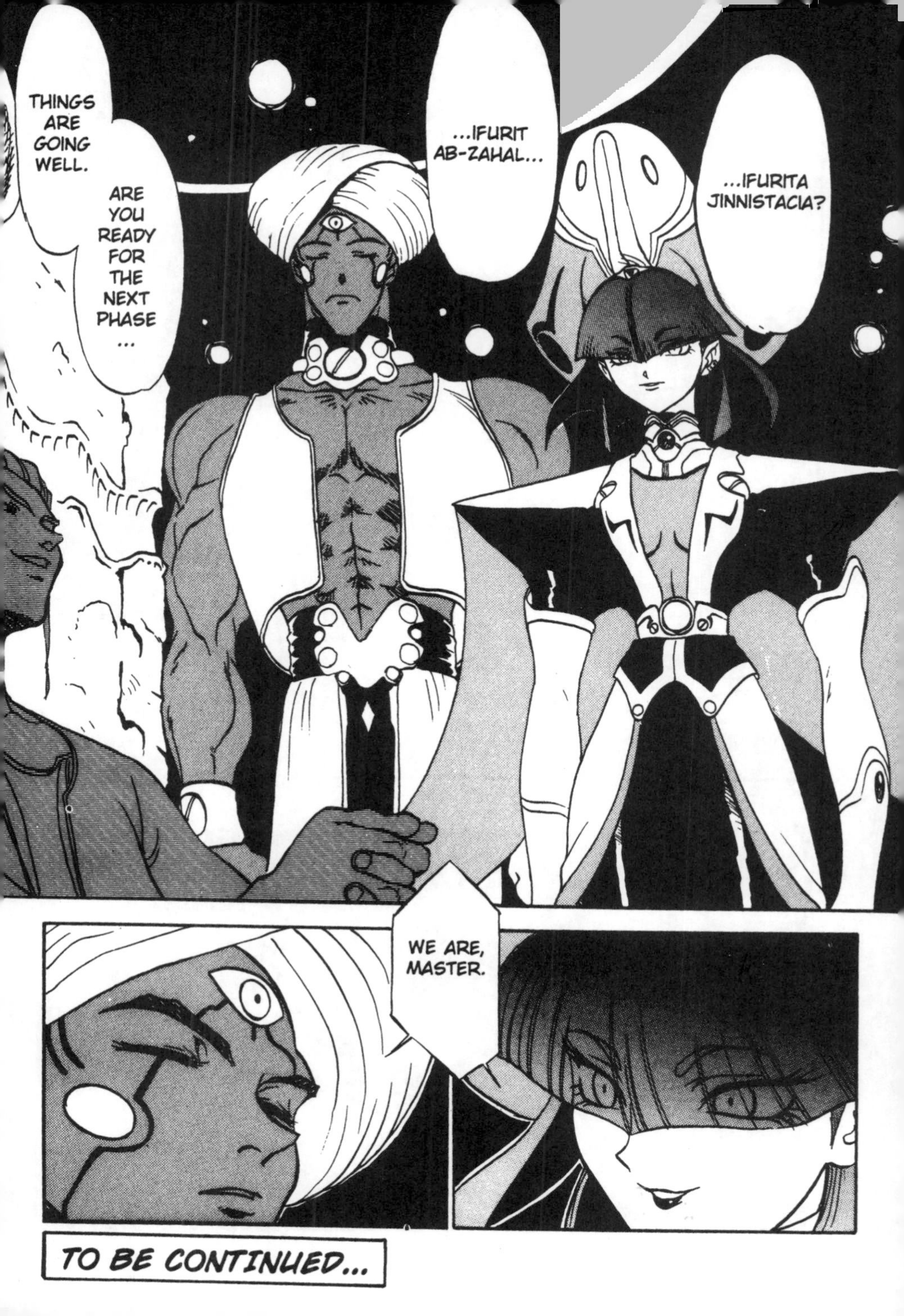
THINGS ARE GOING WELL.
ARE YOU READY FOR THE NEXT PHASE ...
...IFURIT AB-ZAHAL...
...IFURITA JINNISTACIA?
WE ARE, MASTER.
TO BE CONTINUED...

EL-HAZARD

The Magnificent Line Drawings

This and the following four pages show line drawings from the first OAV series: ***EL-HAZARD, The Magnificent World*** (distributed by Pioneer). Included with each character's sketches are descriptions of characteristics that distinguish them between the various anime series (the first OAV series, ***Thr Wanderers*** TV series, the second OAV series, the second ***Alternative World*** TV series) and the manga.

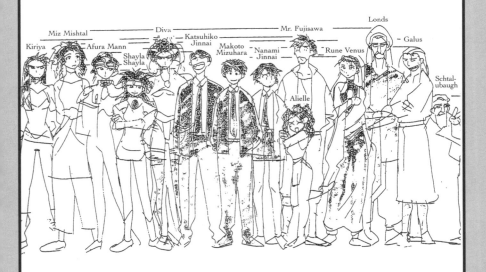

Londs
Miz Mishtal
Diva
Mr. Fujisawa
Galus
Katsuhiko Jinnai
Kiriya
Afura Mann
Makoto Mizuhara
Nanami Jinnai
Rune Venus
Shayla Shayla
Schtal-ubaugh
Alielle

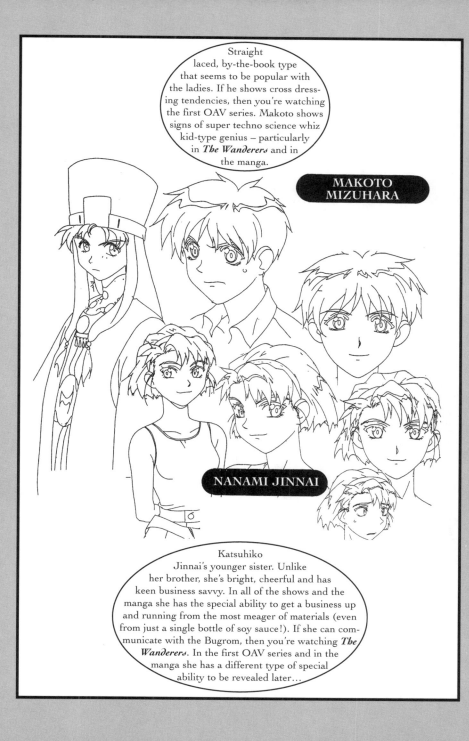

Straight laced, by-the-book type that seems to be popular with the ladies. If he shows cross dressing tendencies, then you're watching the first OAV series. Makoto shows signs of super techno science whiz kid-type genius – particularly in *The Wanderers* and in the manga.

MAKOTO MIZUHARA

NANAMI JINNAI

Katsuhiko Jinnai's younger sister. Unlike her brother, she's bright, cheerful and has keen business savvy. In all of the shows and the manga she has the special ability to get a business up and running from the most meager of materials (even from just a single bottle of soy sauce!). If she can communicate with the Bugrom, then you're watching *The Wanderers*. In the first OAV series and in the manga she has a different type of special ability to be revealed later…

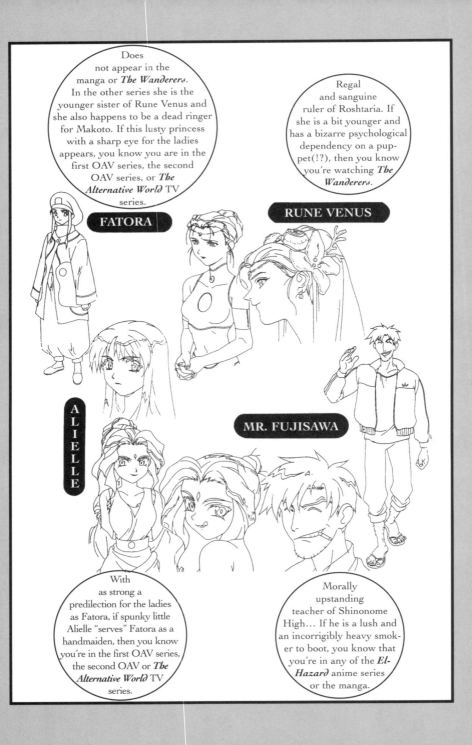

Does not appear in the manga or *The Wanderers*. In the other series she is the younger sister of Rune Venus and she also happens to be a dead ringer for Makoto. If this lusty princess with a sharp eye for the ladies appears, you know you are in the first OAV series, the second OAV series, or *The Alternative World* TV series.

Regal and sanguine ruler of Roshtaria. If she is a bit younger and has a bizarre psychological dependency on a puppet(!?), then you know you're watching *The Wanderers*.

FATORA

RUNE VENUS

A L I E L L E

MR. FUJISAWA

With as strong a predilection for the ladies as Fatora, if spunky little Alielle "serves" Fatora as a handmaiden, then you know you're in the first OAV series, the second OAV or *The Alternative World* TV series.

Morally upstanding teacher of Shinonome High… If he is a lush and an incorrigibly heavy smoker to boot, you know that you're in any of the *El-Hazard* anime series or the manga.

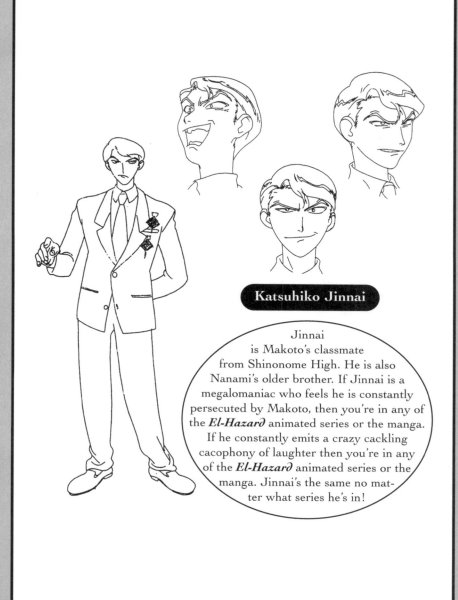

Katsuhiko Jinnai

Jinnai is Makoto's classmate from Shinonome High. He is also Nanami's older brother. If Jinnai is a megalomaniac who feels he is constantly persecuted by Makoto, then you're in any of the *El-Hazard* animated series or the manga. If he constantly emits a crazy cackling cacophony of laughter then you're in any of the *El-Hazard* animated series or the manga. Jinnai's the same no matter what series he's in!

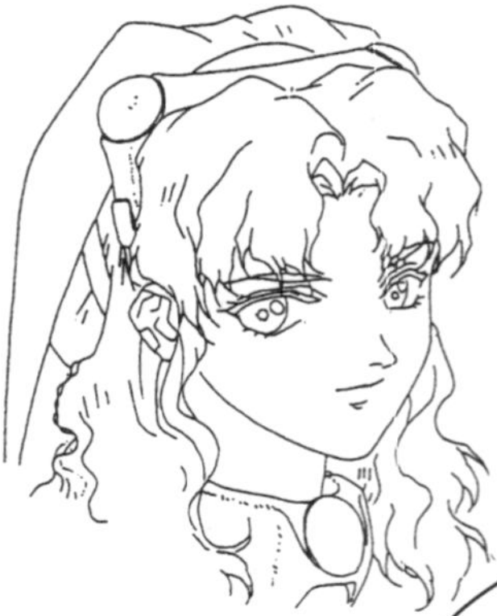

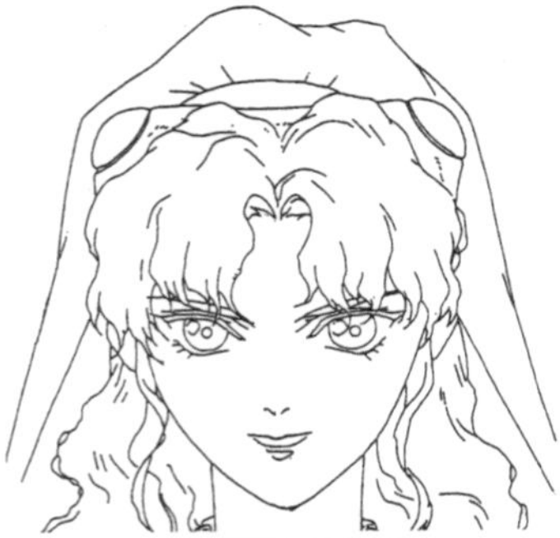

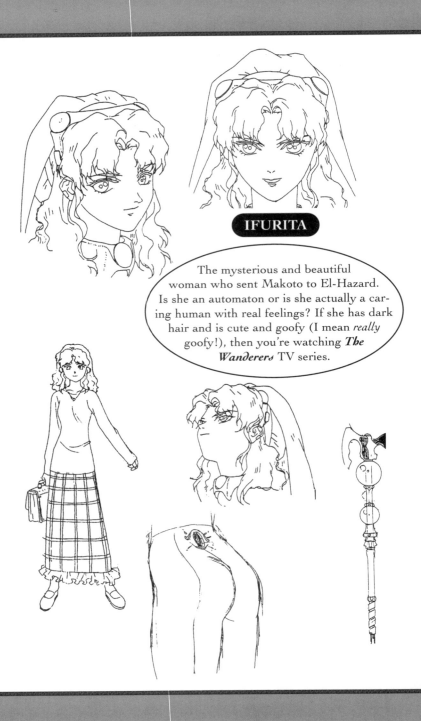

IFURITA

The mysterious and beautiful woman who sent Makoto to El-Hazard. Is she an automaton or is she actually a caring human with real feelings? If she has dark hair and is cute and goofy (I mean *really* goofy!), then you're watching ***The Wanderers*** TV series.

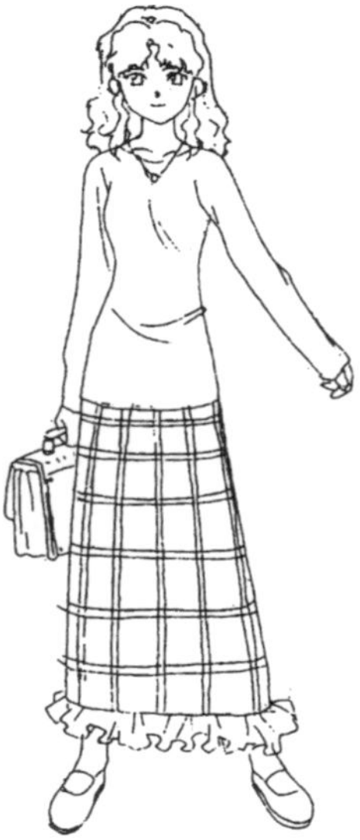

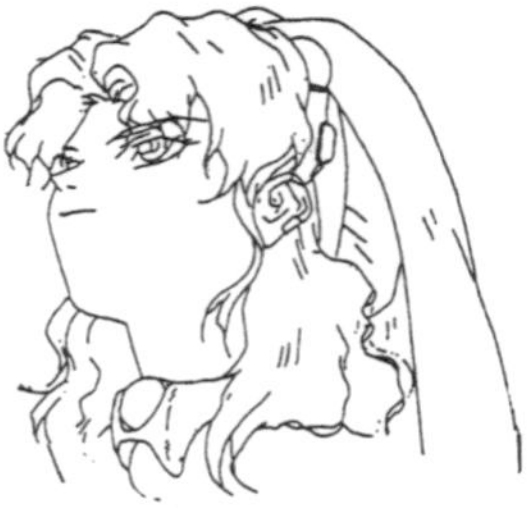

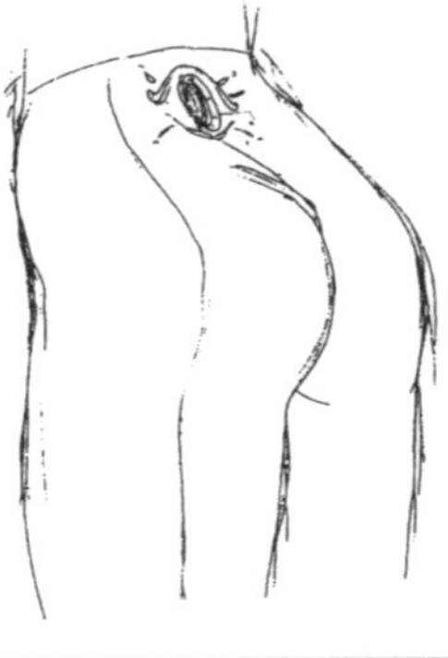

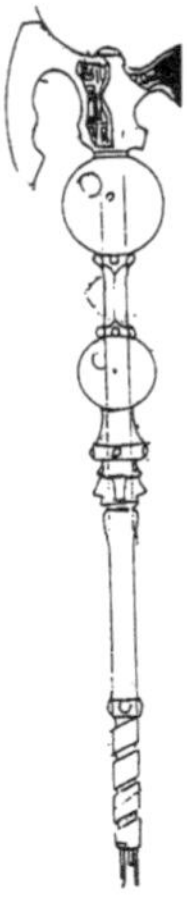

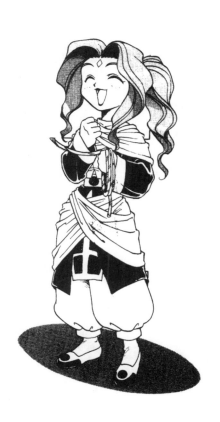

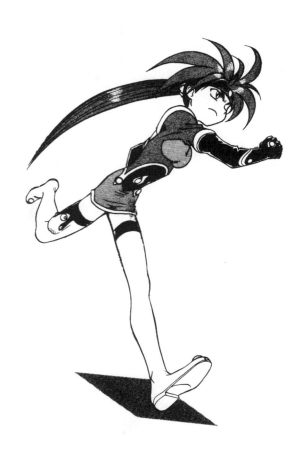

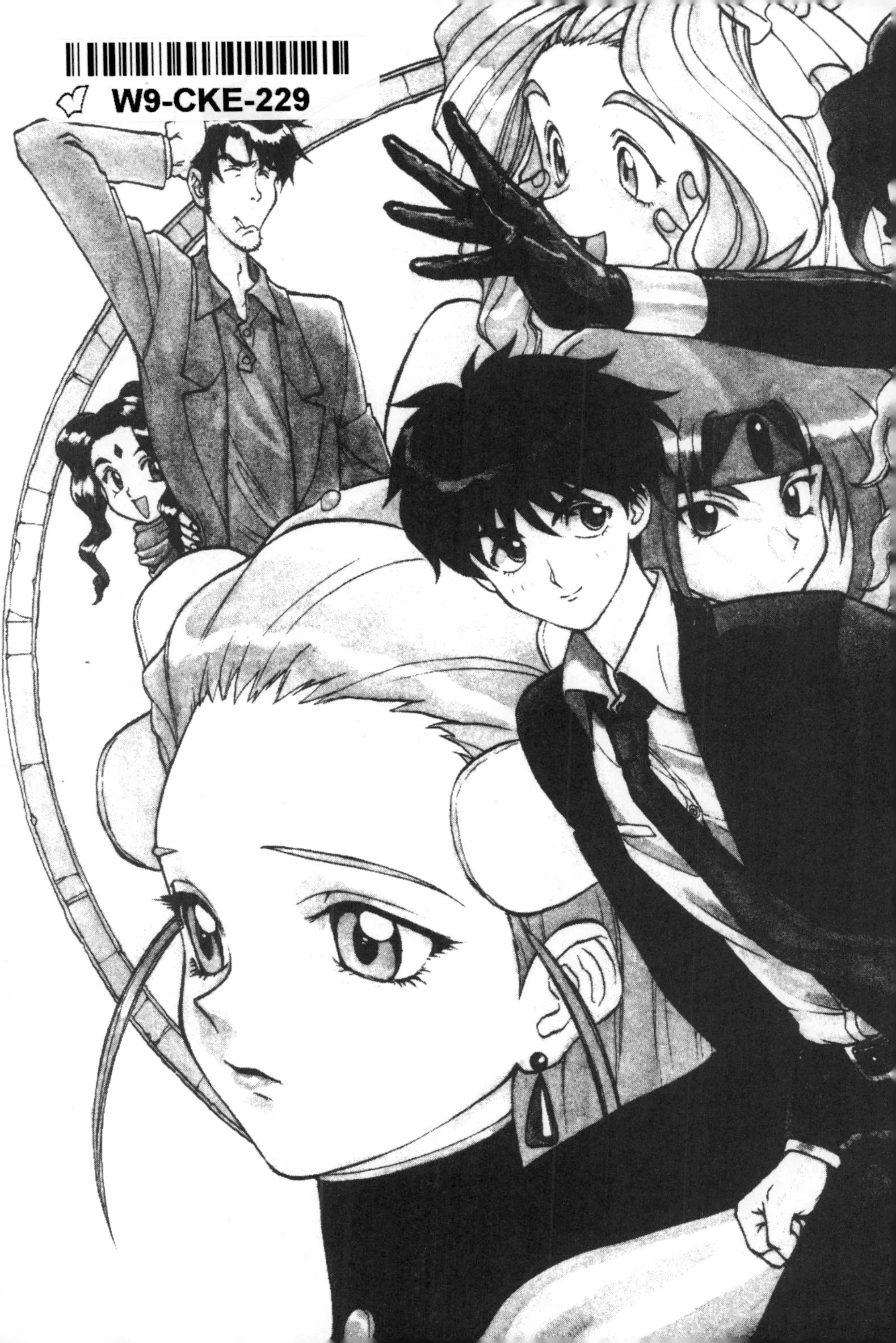